SHONEN JUMP MANGA

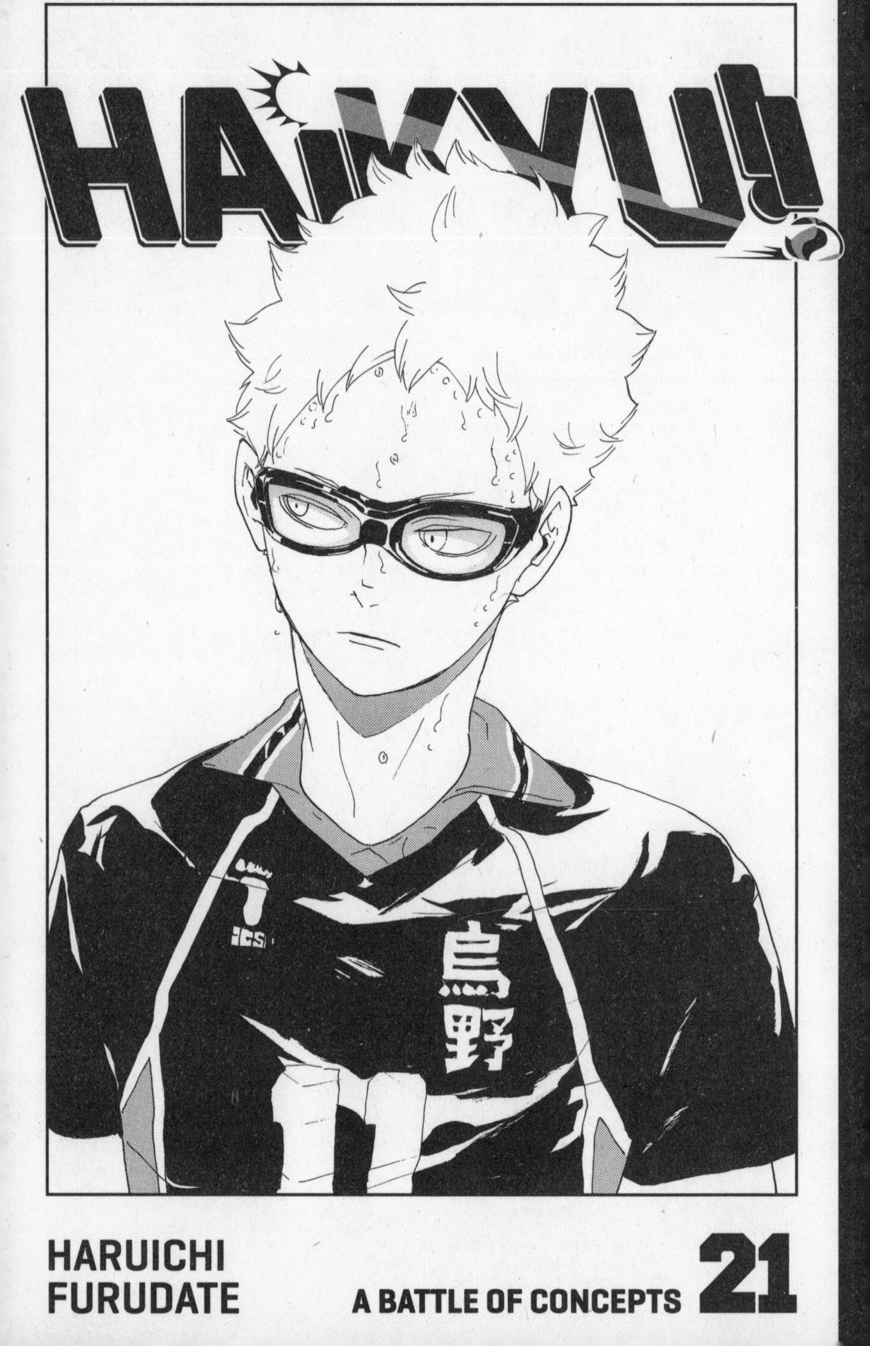
HAIKYU!!
烏野
11

HARUICHI
FURUDATE

A BATTLE OF CONCEPTS

21

Karasuno High School Volleyball Club

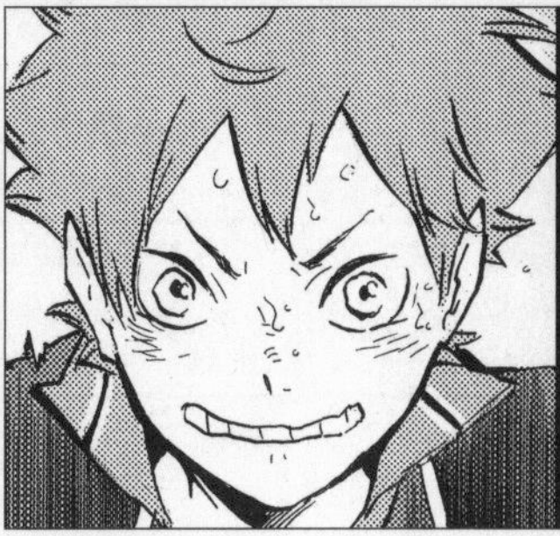

SHOYO HINATA

1ST YEAR / MIDDLE BLOCKER

Even though he doesn't have the best body type for volleyball, he is super athletic. Gets nervous easily.

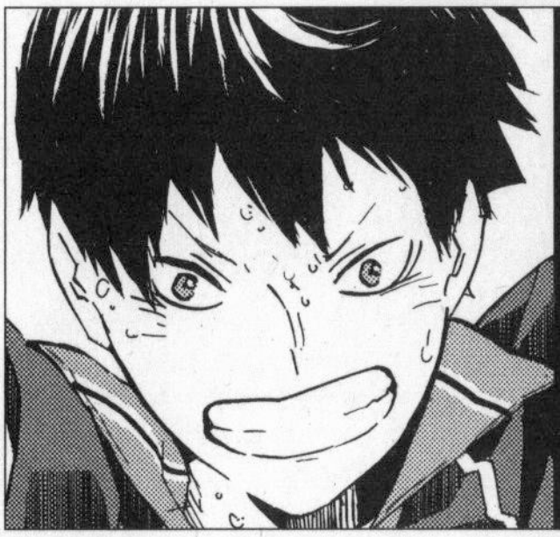

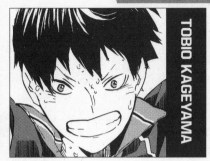

TOBIO KAGEYAMA

1ST YEAR / SETTER

His instincts and athletic talent are so good that he's like a "king" who rules the court. Demanding and egocentric.

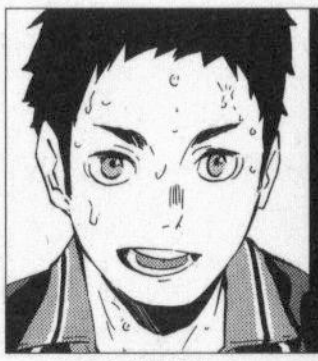

DAICHI SAWAMURA

3RD YEAR (CAPTAIN)
WING SPIKER

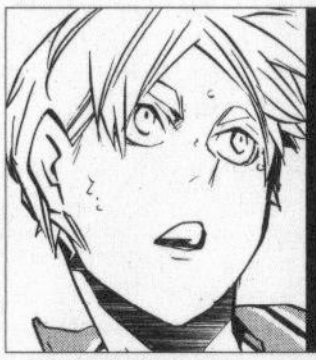

KOUSHI SUGAWARA

3RD YEAR (VICE CAPTAIN)
SETTER

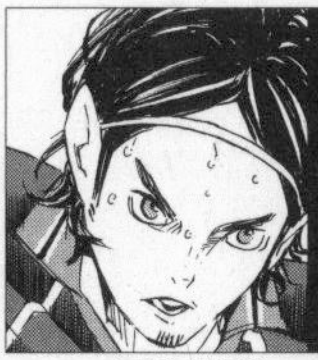

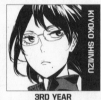

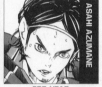

ASAHI AZUMANE

3RD YEAR
WING SPIKER

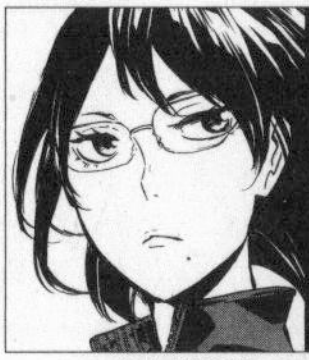

KIYOKO SHIMIZU

3RD YEAR
MANAGER

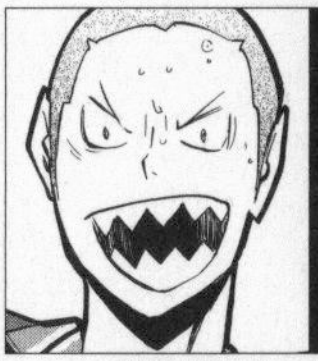

RYUNOSUKE TANAKA

2ND YEAR
WING SPIKER

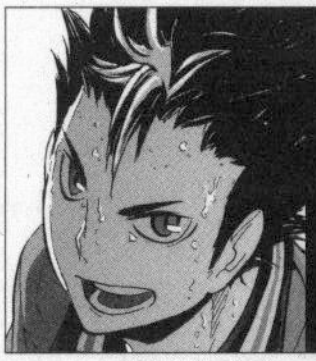

YU NISHINOYA

2ND YEAR
LIBERO

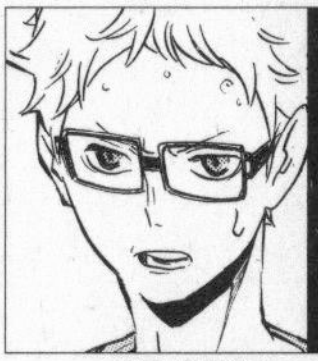

KEI TSUKISHIMA

1ST YEAR
MIDDLE BLOCKER

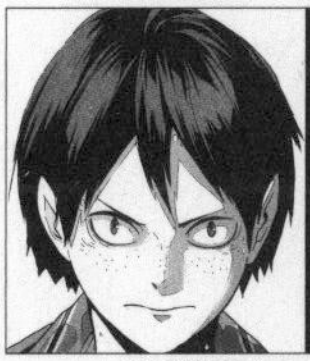

TADASHI YAMAGUCHI

1ST YEAR
MIDDLE BLOCKER

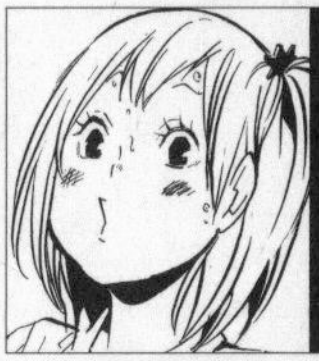

HITOKA YACHI

1ST YEAR
MANAGER

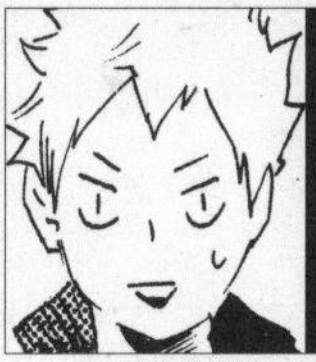

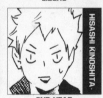

HISASHI KINOSHITA

2ND YEAR
WING SPIKER

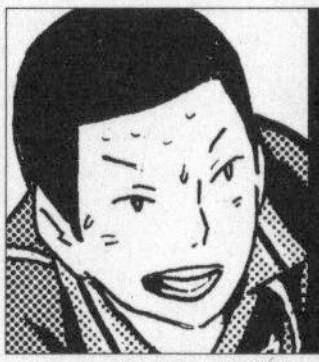

KAZUHITO NARITA

2ND YEAR
MIDDLE BLOCKER

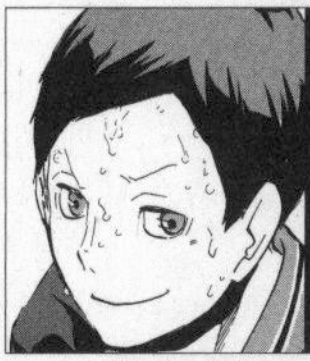

CHIKARA ENNOSHITA

2ND YEAR
WING SPIKER

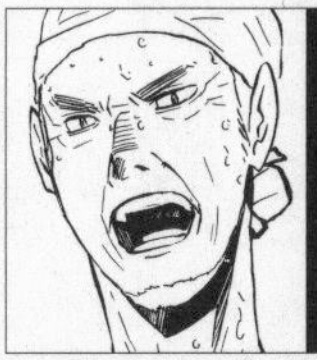

IKKEI UKAI

FORMER HEAD COACH

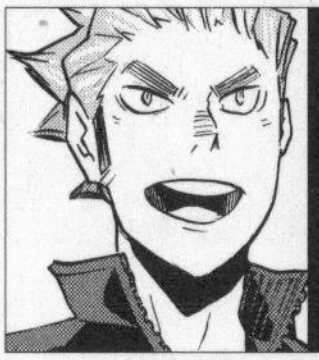

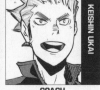

KEISHIN UKAI

COACH

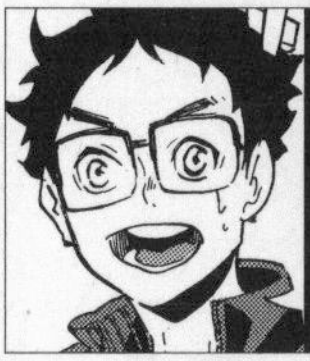

ITTETSU TAKEDA

ADVISER

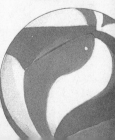

CHARACTERS

MIYAGI PREFECTURE SPRING TOURNAMENT QUALIFIER TOURNAMENT ARC

Shiratorizawa Team

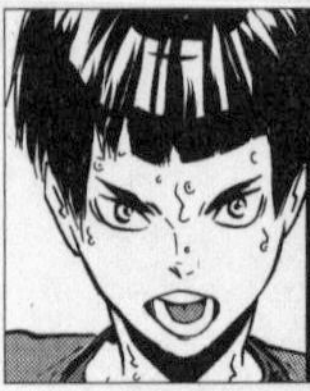
TSUTOMU GOSHIKI
1ST YEAR
WING SPIKER

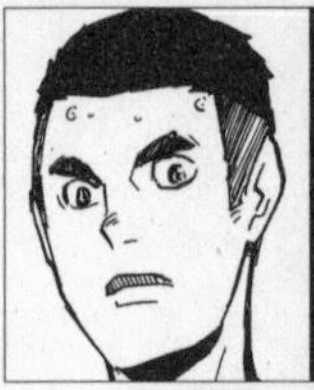
REON OHIRA
3RD YEAR
WING SPIKER

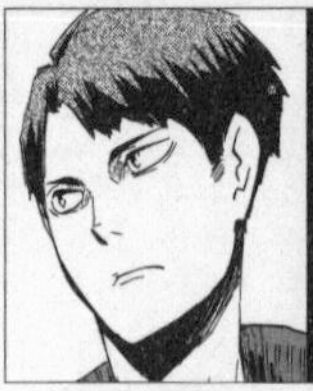
WAKATOSHI USHIJIMA
3RD YEAR (CAPTAIN)
WING SPIKER

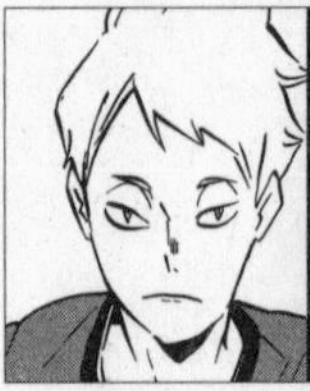
TAICHI KAWANISHI
2ND YEAR
MIDDLE BLOCKER

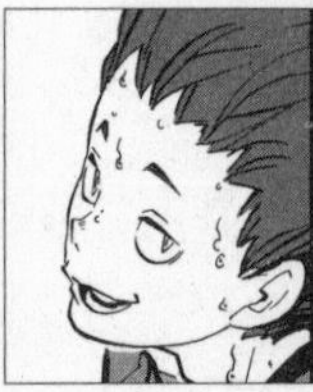
SATORI TENDO
3RD YEAR
MIDDLE BLOCKER

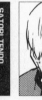

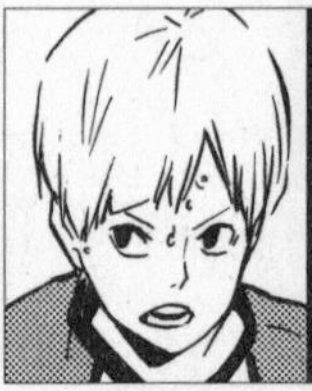
KENJIRO SHIRABU
2ND YEAR
SETTER

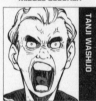

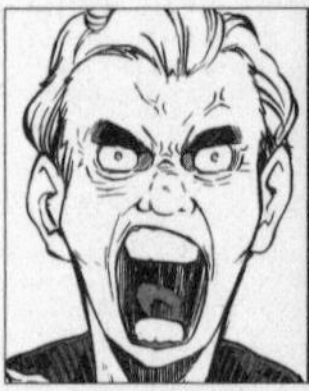
TANJI WASHIJO
HEAD COACH

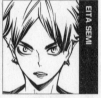

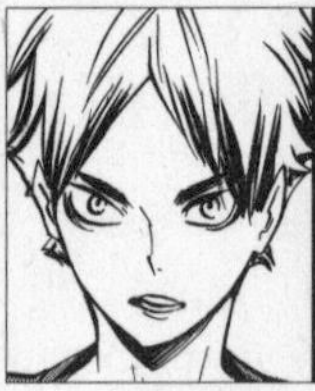
EITA SEMI
3RD YEAR
SETTER

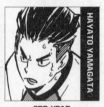

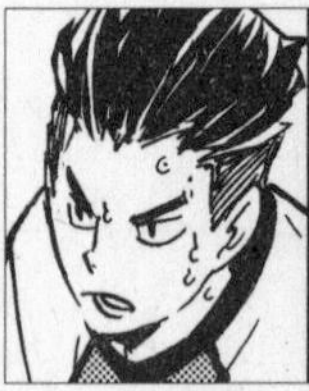
HAYATO YAMAGATA
3RD YEAR
LIBERO

Karasuno Cheer Squad

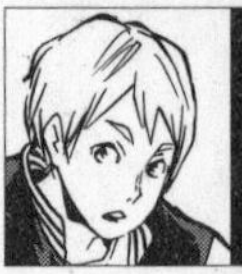
AKITERU TSUKISHIMA

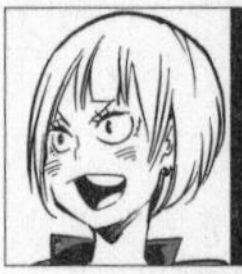
SAEKO TANAKA

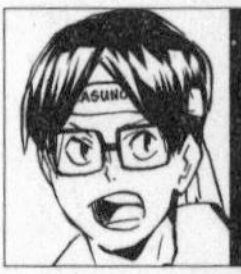
MAKOTO SHIMADA

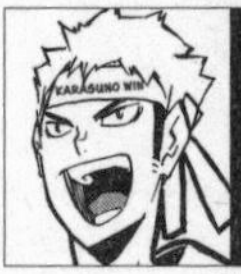
YUSUKE TAKINOUE

Ever since he saw the legendary player known as "the Little Giant" compete at the national volleyball finals, Shoyo Hinata has been aiming to be the best volleyball player ever! He decides to join the volleyball club at his middle school and gets to play in an official tournament during his third year. His team is crushed by a team led by volleyball prodigy Tobio Kageyama, also known as "the King of the Court." Swearing revenge on Kageyama, Hinata graduates middle school and enters Karasuno High School, the school where the Little Giant played. However, upon joining the club, he finds out that Kageyama is there too! The two of them bicker constantly, but they bring out the best in each other's talents and become a powerful combo. Having learned new skills from their summer training camp, the team heads into the spring tourney armed with new weapons. Karasuno has won its way to the finals of the Spring Tournament Qualifiers, where they face the perennial champions Shiratorizawa! At the end of the fourth set, Kageyama's exhaustion makes his setting erratic, but Hinata's quick reflexes save the day and Karasuno wins the set! With the set count even at two apiece, Karasuno goes into the fifth and final set with Sugawara as the starting setter. Even after Tsukishima leaves the game with an injury, Sugawara stays aggressive, going toe-to-toe with Shiratorizawa's Tendo. Halfway through the set, Kageyama finally comes back in, and the Freak Twins strike right away with a minus tempo attack!

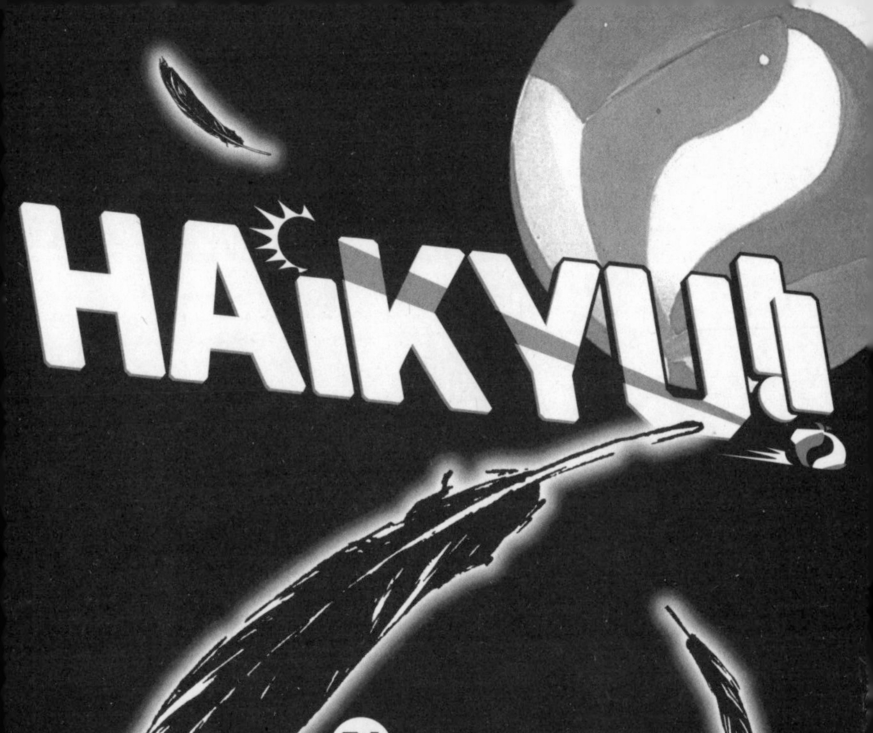
HAIKYU!!

21 A BATTLE OF CONCEPTS

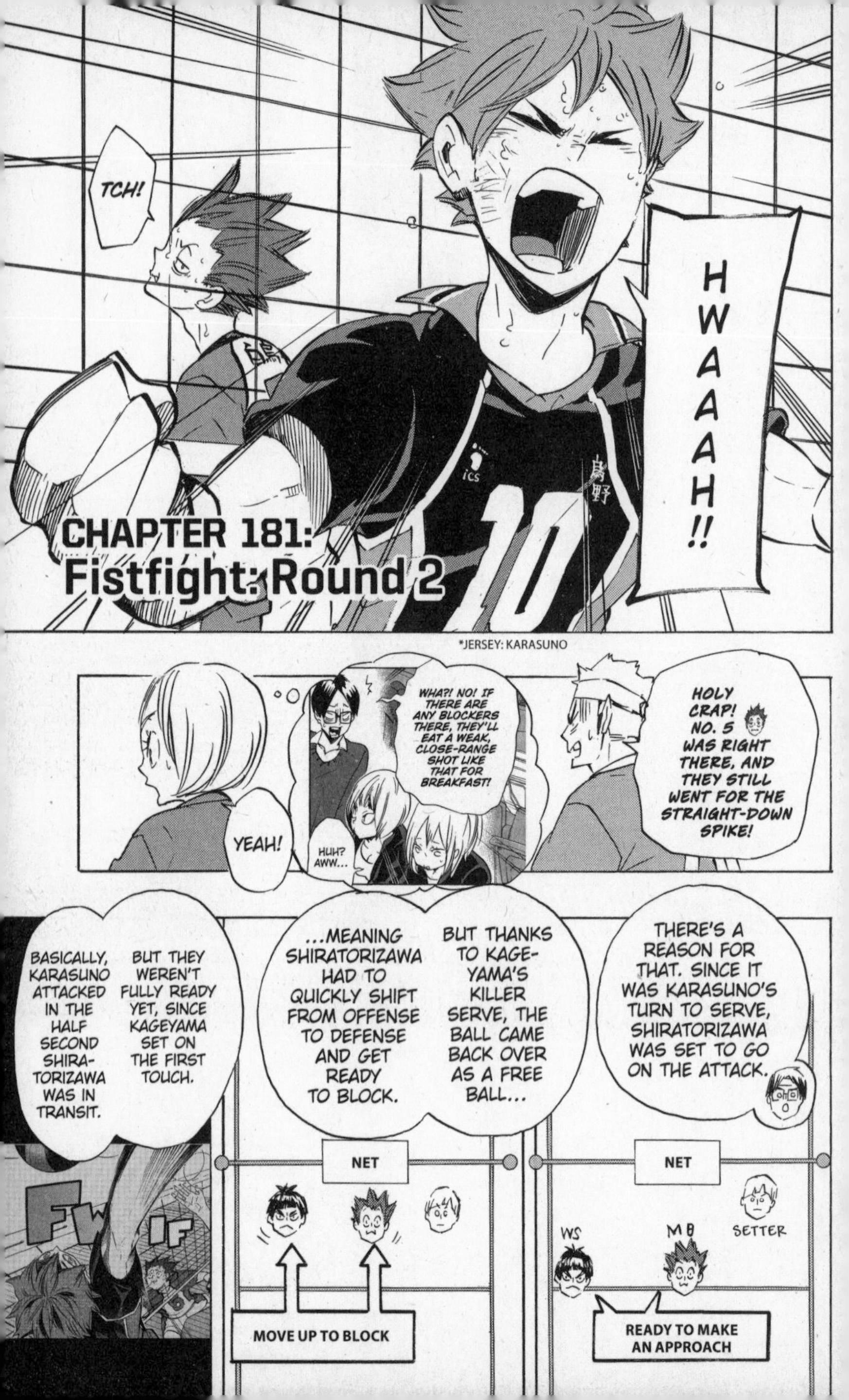
HWAAAAH!!
TCH!
CHAPTER 181:
Fistfight: Round 2
*JERSEY: KARASUNO
HOLY CRAP! NO. 5 WAS RIGHT THERE, AND THEY STILL WENT FOR THE STRAIGHT-DOWN SPIKE!
WHA?! NO! IF THERE ARE ANY BLOCKERS THERE, THEY'LL EAT A WEAK, CLOSE-RANGE SHOT LIKE THAT FOR BREAKFAST!
HUH? AWW...
YEAH!
THERE'S A REASON FOR THAT. SINCE IT WAS KARASUNO'S TURN TO SERVE, SHIRATORIZAWA WAS SET TO GO ON THE ATTACK.
NET
SETTER
MB
WS
READY TO MAKE AN APPROACH
BUT THANKS TO KAGE-YAMA'S KILLER SERVE, THE BALL CAME BACK OVER AS A FREE BALL...
...MEANING SHIRATORIZAWA HAD TO QUICKLY SHIFT FROM OFFENSE TO DEFENSE AND GET READY TO BLOCK.
NET
MOVE UP TO BLOCK
BUT THEY WEREN'T FULLY READY YET, SINCE KAGEYAMA SET ON THE FIRST TOUCH.
BASICALLY, KARASUNO ATTACKED IN THE HALF SECOND SHIRA-TORIZAWA WAS IN TRANSIT.
FWIF

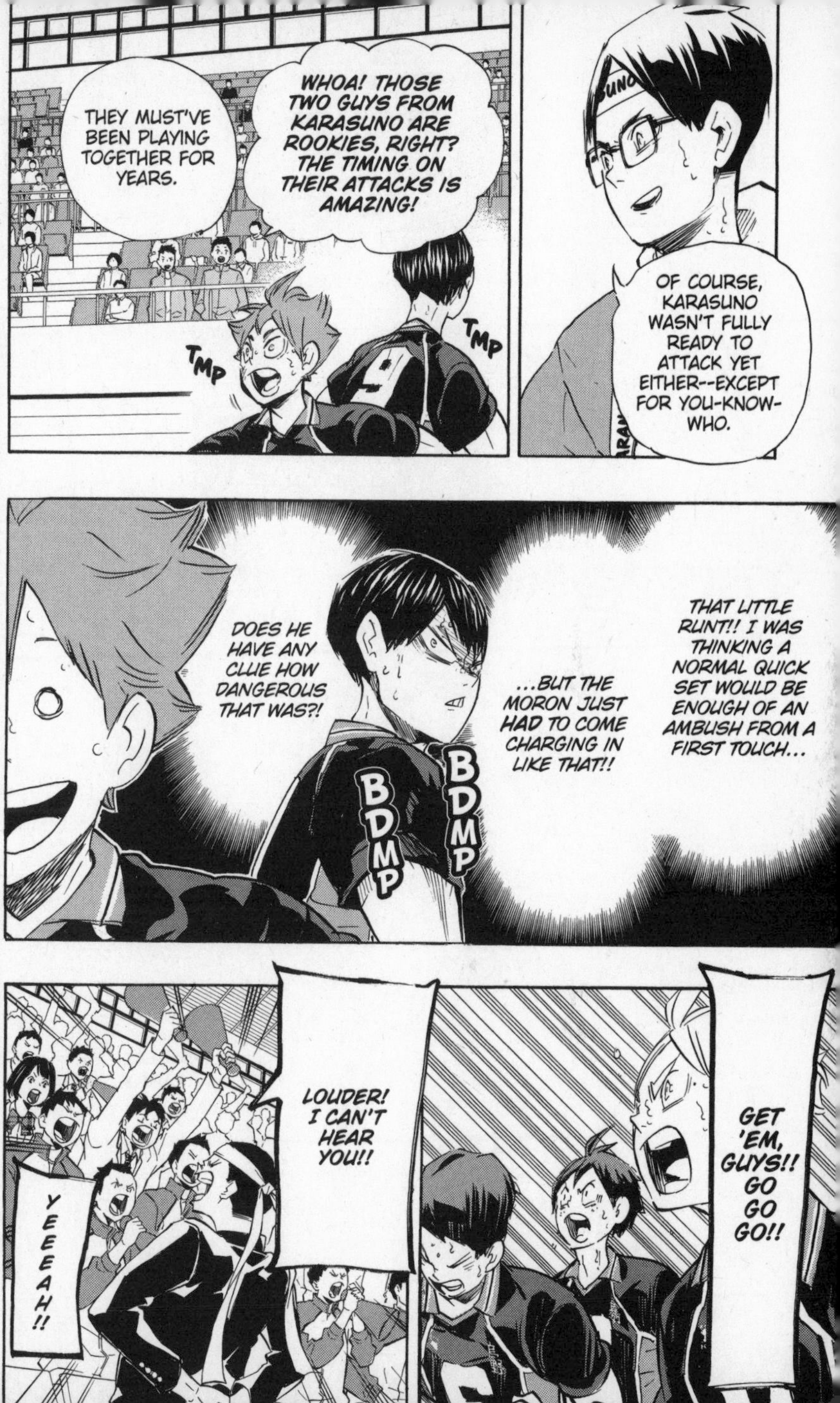
OF COURSE, KARASUNO WASN'T FULLY READY TO ATTACK YET EITHER--EXCEPT FOR YOU-KNOW-WHO.
WHOA! THOSE TWO GUYS FROM KARASUNO ARE ROOKIES, RIGHT? THE TIMING ON THEIR ATTACKS IS AMAZING!
THEY MUST'VE BEEN PLAYING TOGETHER FOR YEARS.
TMP
TMP
THAT LITTLE RUNT!! I WAS THINKING A NORMAL QUICK SET WOULD BE ENOUGH OF AN AMBUSH FROM A FIRST TOUCH...
...BUT THE MORON JUST HAD TO COME CHARGING IN LIKE THAT!!
BDMP
BDMP
DOES HE HAVE ANY CLUE HOW DANGEROUS THAT WAS?!
GET 'EM, GUYS!! GO GO GO!!
LOUDER! I CAN'T HEAR YOU!!
YEEEAH!!

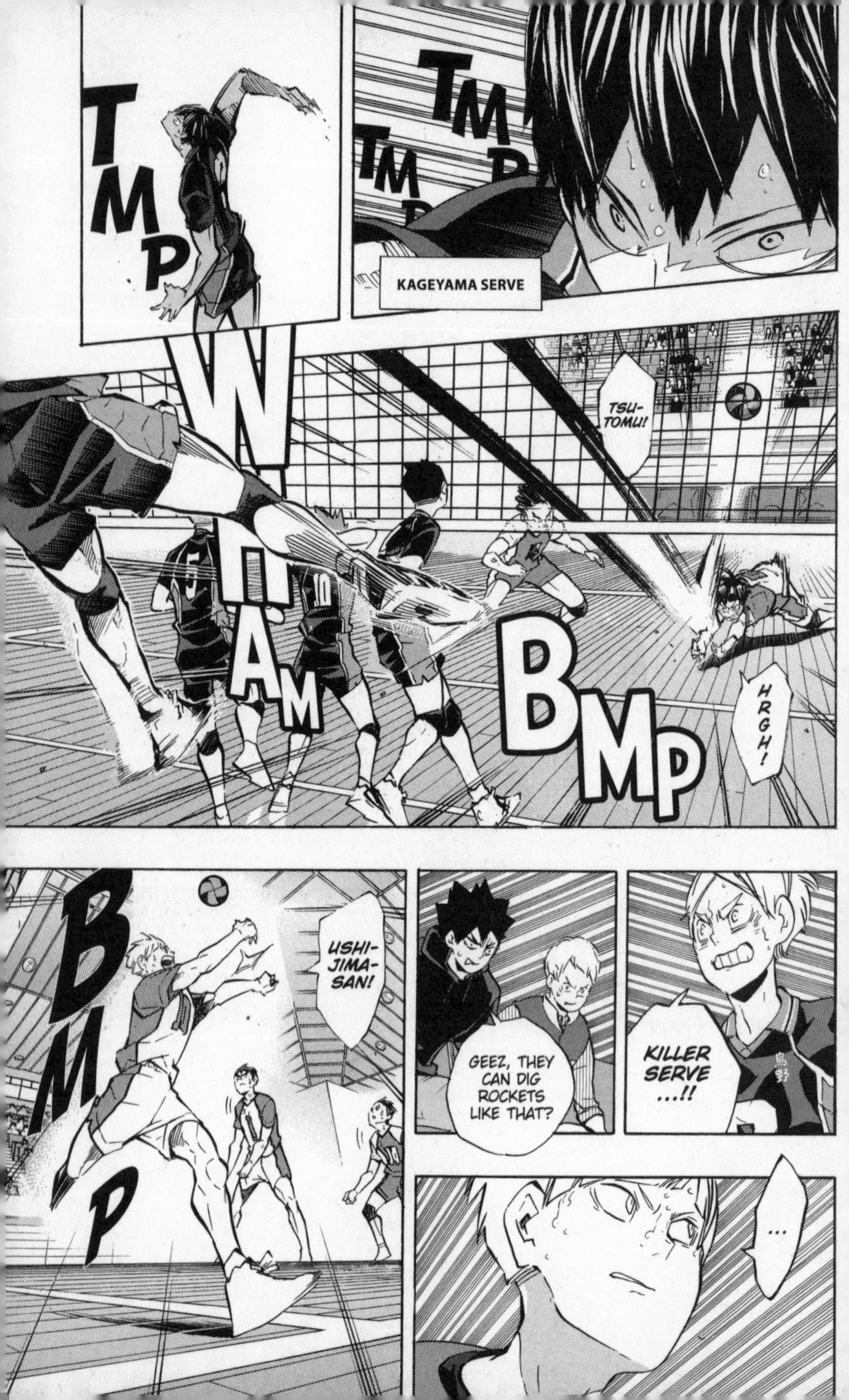
TMP TMP TMP
KAGEYAMA SERVE
TMP
TSU-TOMU!
HRGH!
BMP
WHAM
KILLER SERVE ...!!
GEEZ, THEY CAN DIG ROCKETS LIKE THAT?
...
USHI-JIMA-SAN!
BMP

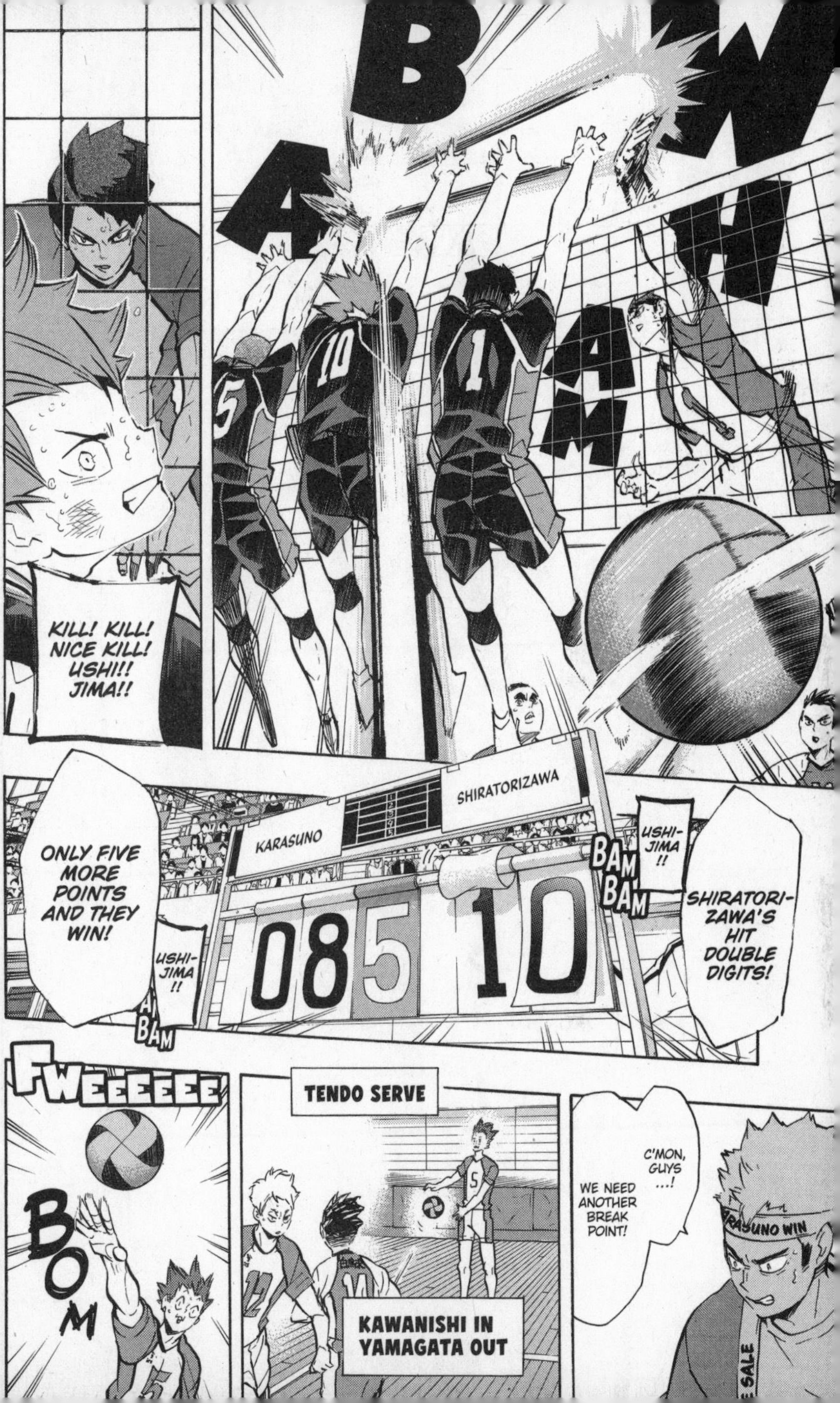
KILL! KILL! NICE KILL! USHI!! JIMA!!
SHIRATORI-ZAWA'S HIT DOUBLE DIGITS!
USHI-JIMA!!
BAM BAM
SHIRATORIZAWA
KARASUNO
08
5
10
ONLY FIVE MORE POINTS AND THEY WIN!
USHI-JIMA!!
BAM
C'MON, GUYS ...!
WE NEED ANOTHER BREAK POINT!
TENDO SERVE
KAWANISHI IN YAMAGATA OUT
FWEEEEEE
BOOM

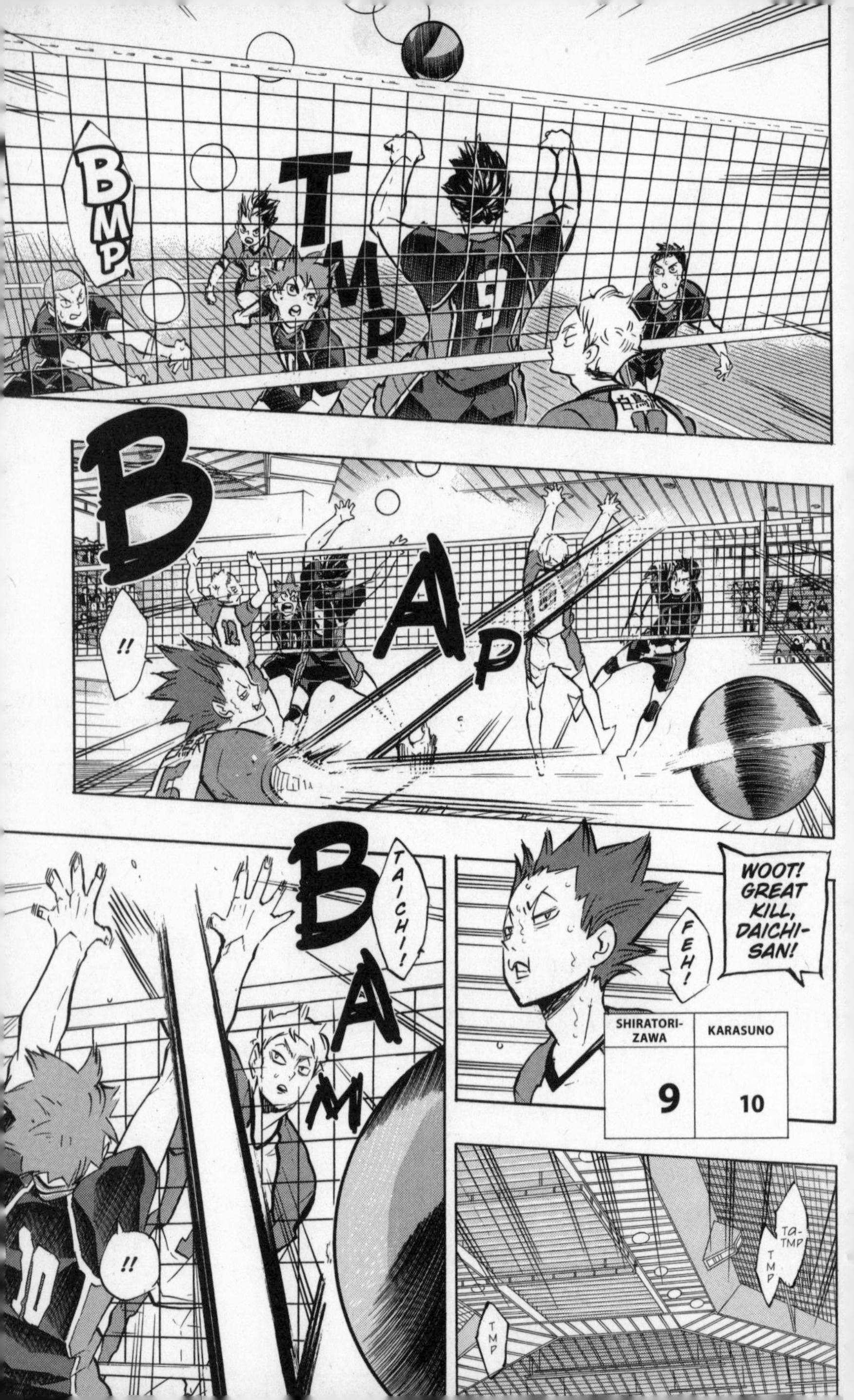
TMP
BMP
BAP
!!
WOOT! GREAT KILL, DAICHI-SAN!
FEH!
SHIRATORI-ZAWA 9
KARASUNO 10
Ta-TMP
TMP
TMP
TAICHI!
BAM
!!

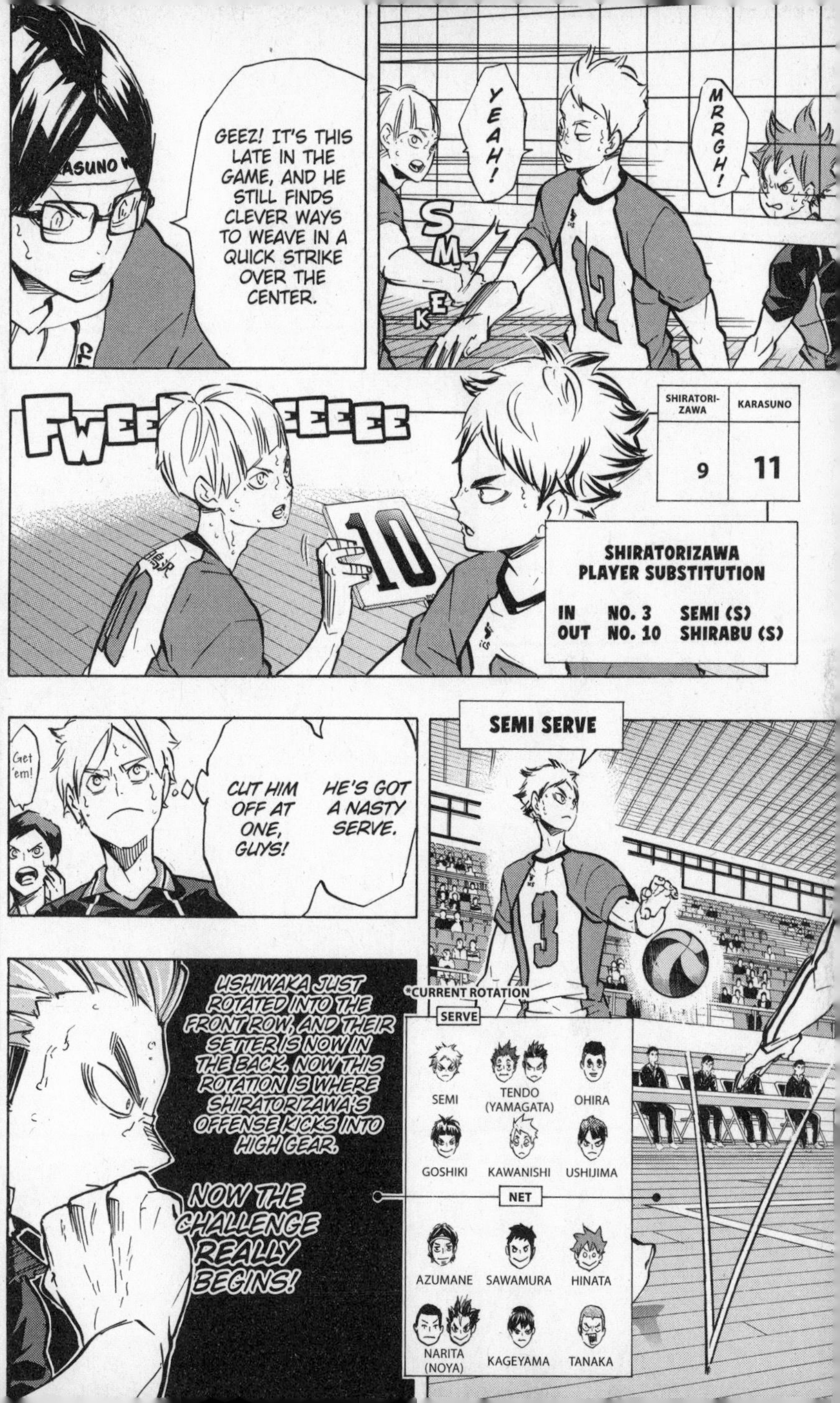
MRRGH!
YEAH!
SMEK
GEEZ! IT'S THIS LATE IN THE GAME, AND HE STILL FINDS CLEVER WAYS TO WEAVE IN A QUICK STRIKE OVER THE CENTER.
KARASUNO
SHIRATORIZAWA 9
KARASUNO 11
FWEE EEEEE
SHIRATORIZAWA PLAYER SUBSTITUTION
IN NO. 3 SEMI (S)
OUT NO. 10 SHIRABU (S)
SEMI SERVE
*CURRENT ROTATION
SERVE
SEMI
TENDO (YAMAGATA)
OHIRA
GOSHIKI
KAWANISHI
USHIJIMA
NET
AZUMANE
SAWAMURA
HINATA
NARITA (NOYA)
KAGEYAMA
TANAKA
HE'S GOT A NASTY SERVE.
CUT HIM OFF AT ONE, GUYS!
Get 'em!
USHIWAKA JUST ROTATED INTO THE FRONT ROW, AND THEIR SETTER IS NOW IN THE BACK. NOW THIS ROTATION IS WHERE SHIRATORIZAWA'S OFFENSE KICKS INTO HIGH GEAR.
NOW THE CHALLENGE REALLY BEGINS!

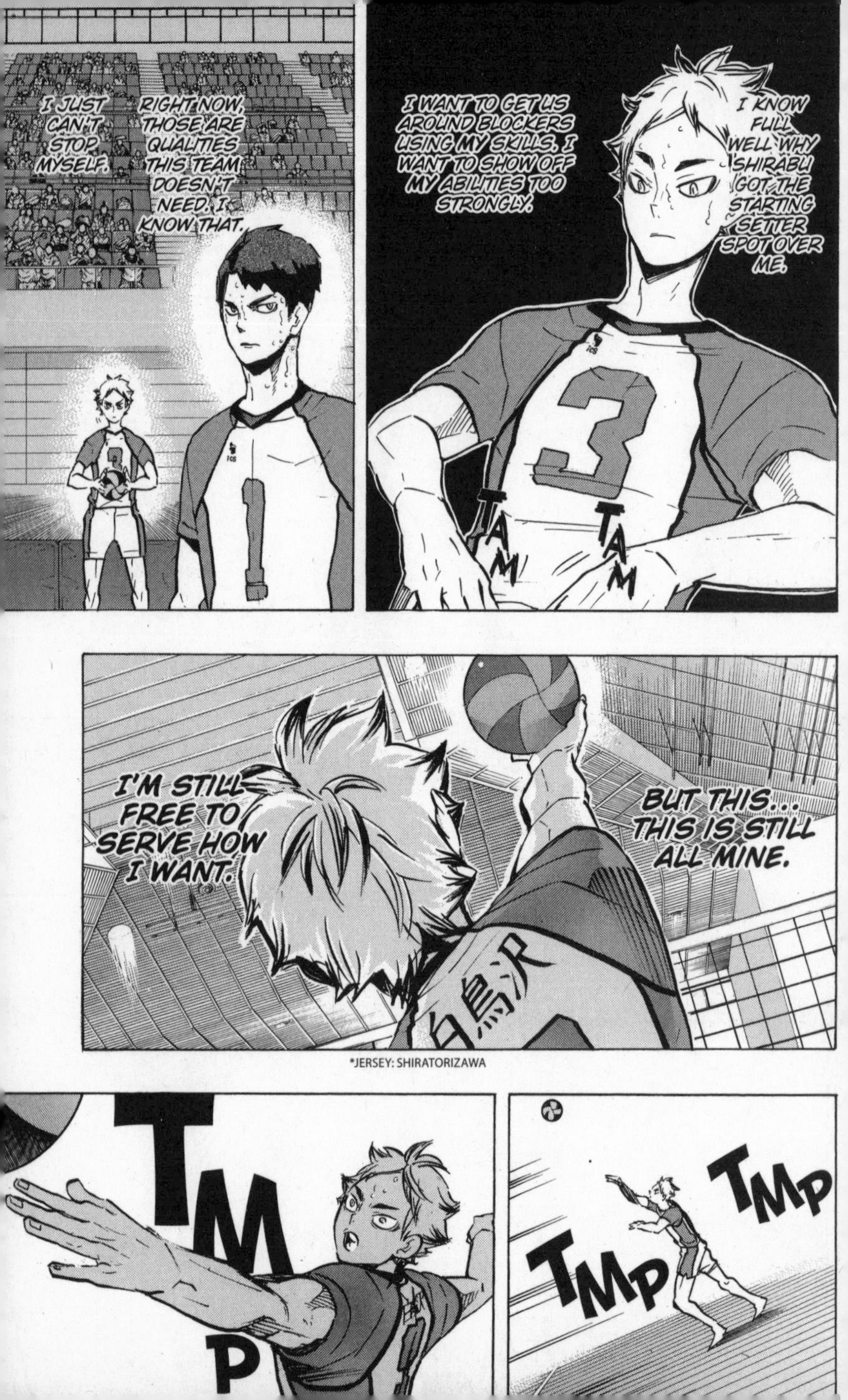
I KNOW FULL WELL WHY SHIRABU GOT THE STARTING SETTER SPOT OVER ME.
I WANT TO GET US AROUND BLOCKERS USING MY SKILLS. I WANT TO SHOW OFF MY ABILITIES TOO STRONGLY.
TAM
TAM
RIGHT NOW, THOSE ARE QUALITIES THIS TEAM DOESN'T NEED. I KNOW THAT.
I JUST CAN'T STOP MYSELF.
BUT THIS... THIS IS STILL ALL MINE.
I'M STILL FREE TO SERVE HOW I WANT.
TMP
TMP
TMP
*JERSEY: SHIRATORIZAWA

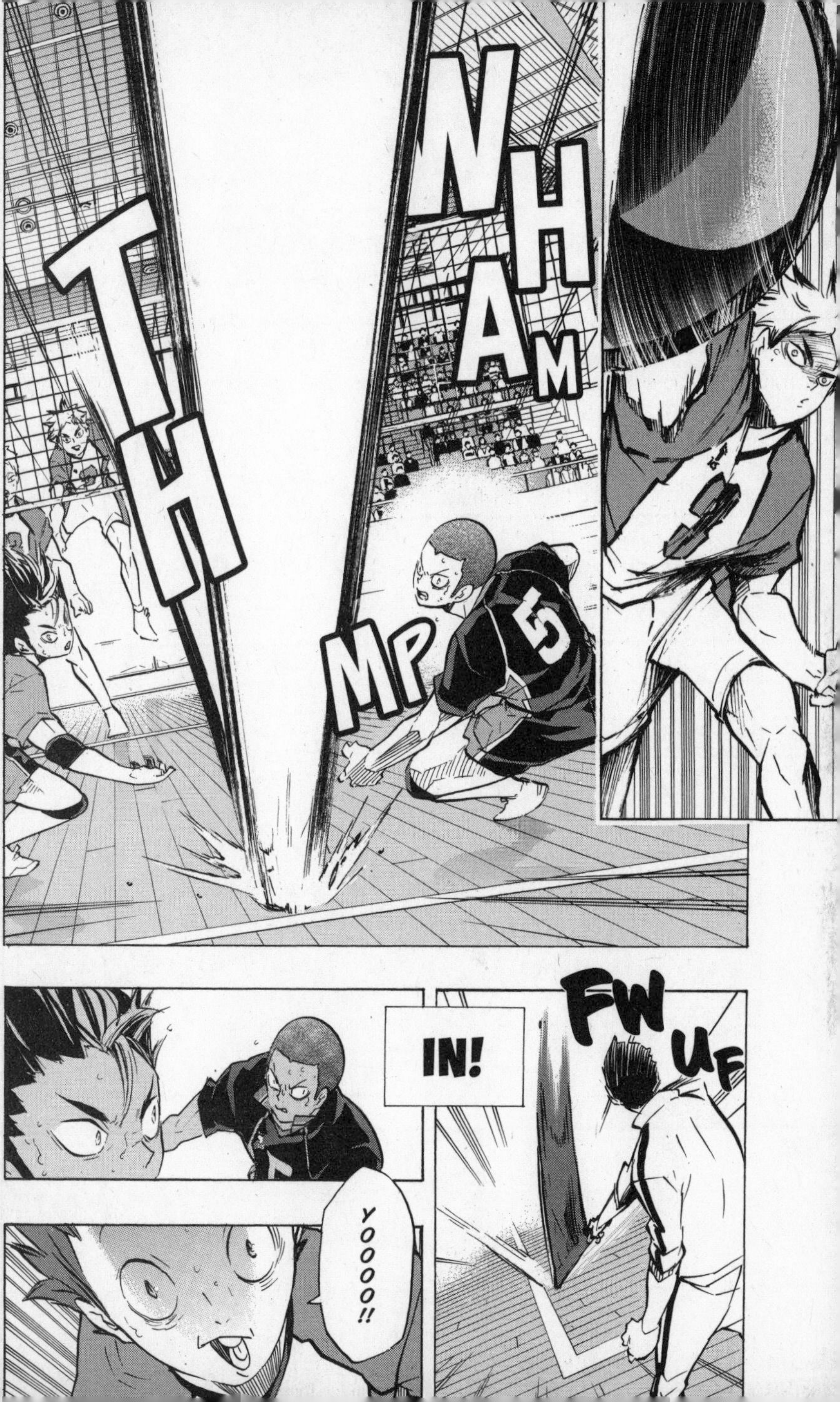

NHAM
THMP
IN!
FWUF
YOOOOO!!

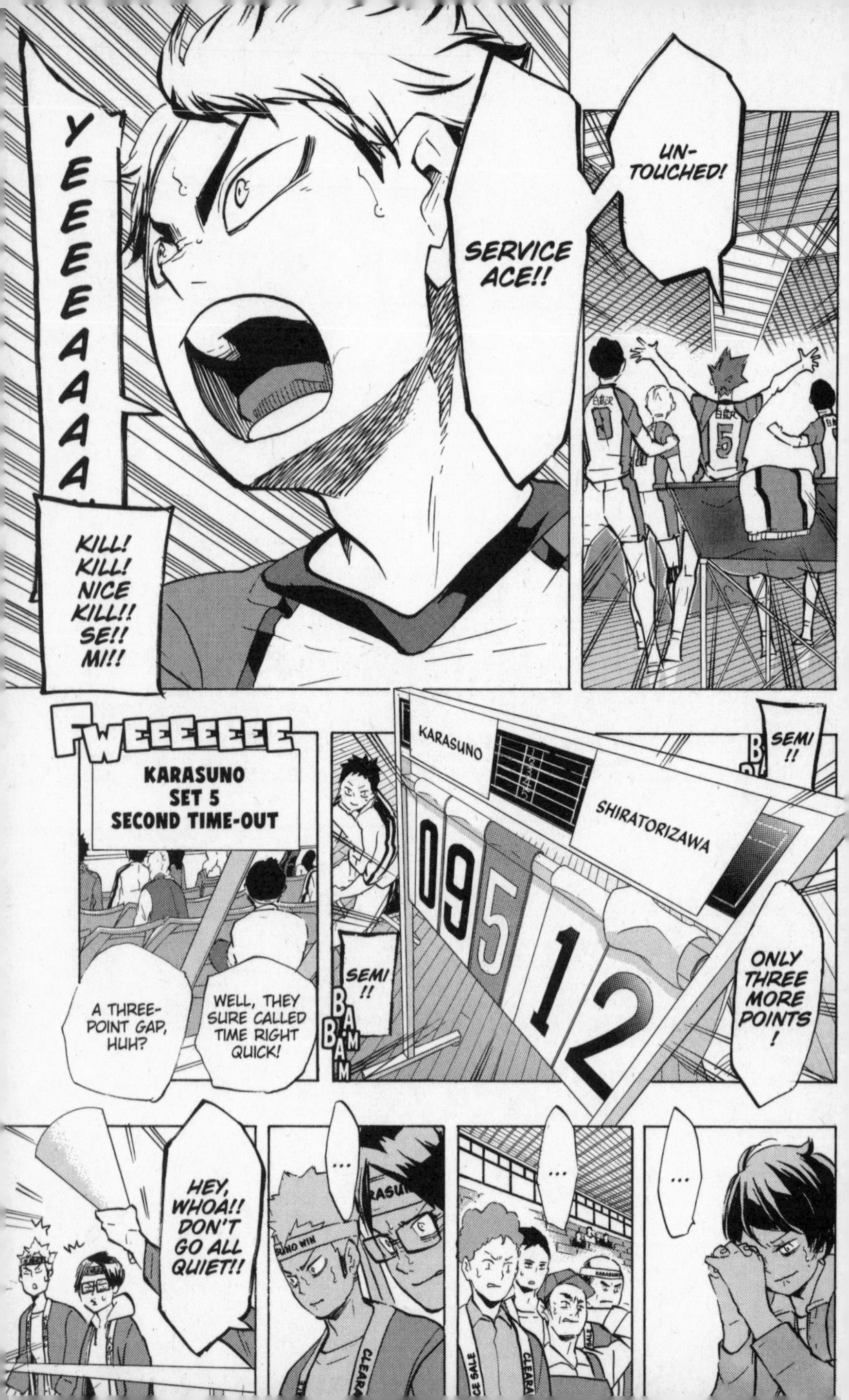
UN-TOUCHED!
SERVICE ACE!!
YEEEEAAAAA
KILL! KILL! NICE KILL!! SE!! MI!!
SEMI!!
ONLY THREE MORE POINTS!
KARASUNO
SHIRATORIZAWA
SEMI!!
BAM BAM
FWEEEEEEE
KARASUNO SET 5 SECOND TIME-OUT
WELL, THEY SURE CALLED TIME RIGHT QUICK!
A THREE-POINT GAP, HUH?
...
...
...
HEY, WHOA!! DON'T GO ALL QUIET!!

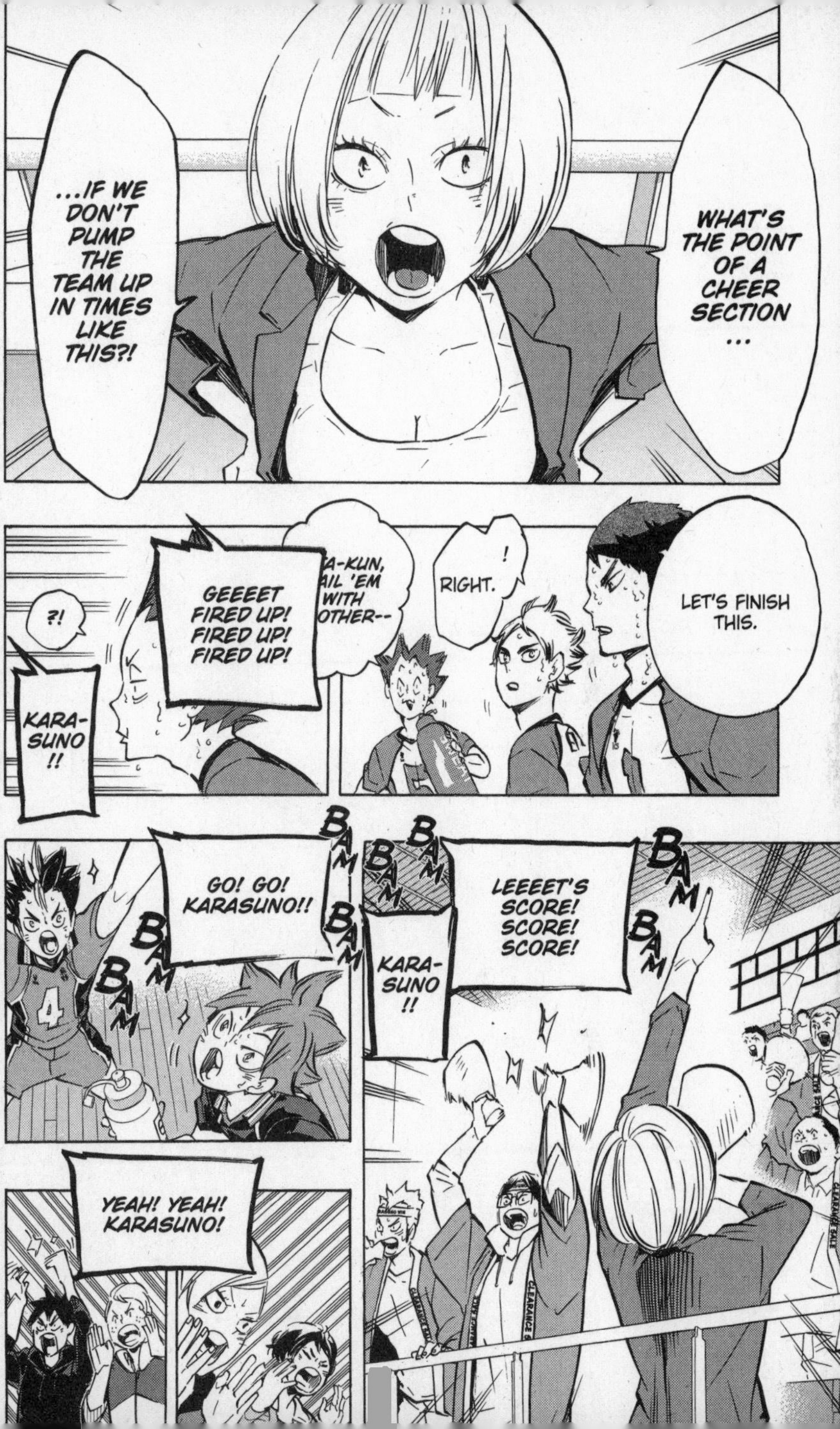
WHAT'S THE POINT OF A CHEER SECTION...
...IF WE DON'T PUMP THE TEAM UP IN TIMES LIKE THIS?!
LET'S FINISH THIS.
!
RIGHT.
A-KUN, AIL 'EM WITH OTHER--
GEEEET FIRED UP! FIRED UP! FIRED UP!
?!
KARA-SUNO!!
BAM BAM BAM BAM BAM BAM
LEEEET'S SCORE! SCORE! SCORE!
KARA-SUNO!!
CLEARANCE SALE
GO! GO! KARASUNO!!
BAM BAM
YEAH! YEAH! KARASUNO!

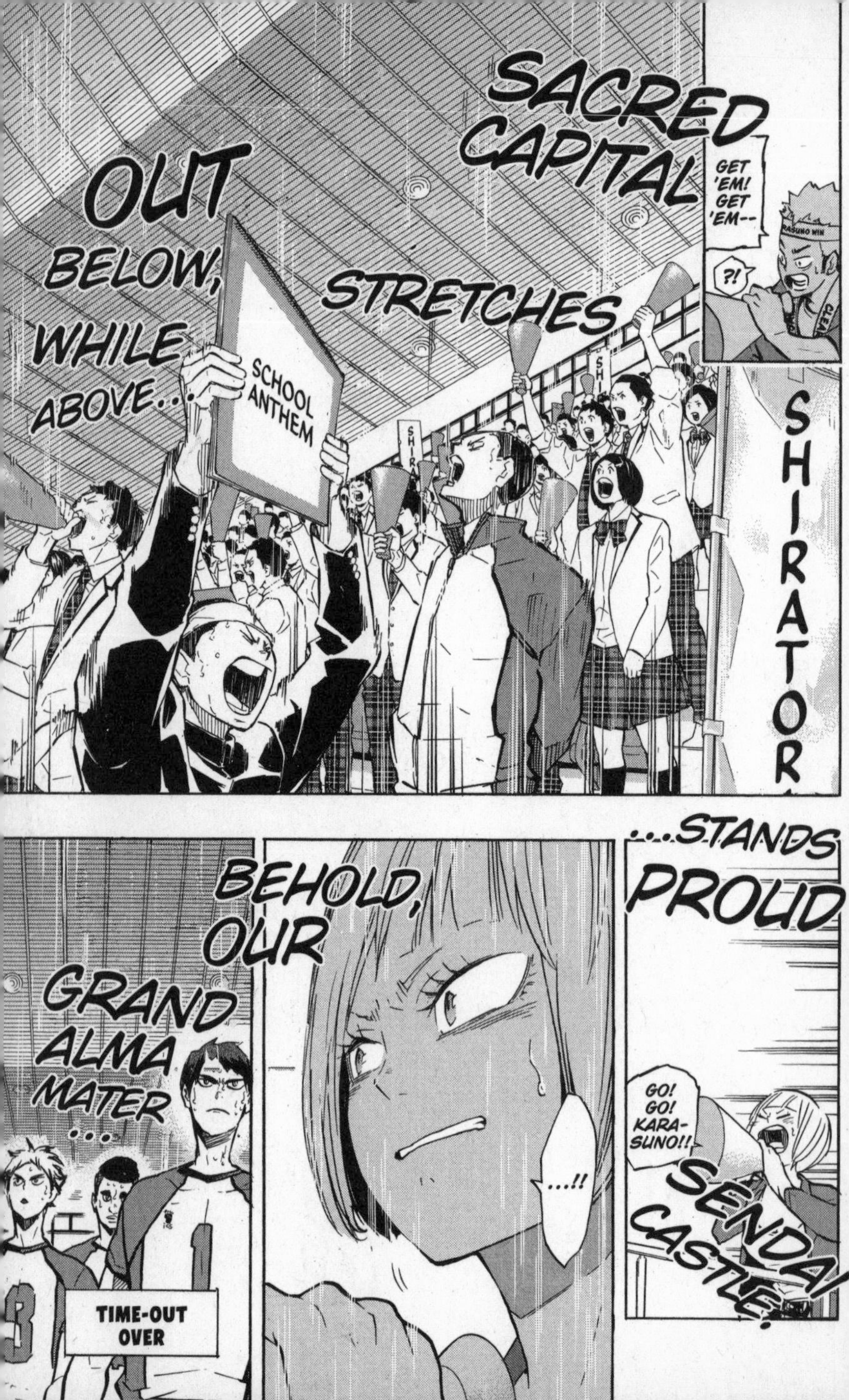
GET 'EM! GET 'EM--
RASUNO WIN
?!
SACRED CAPITAL
SHIRATORI
STRETCHES
OUT BELOW, WHILE ABOVE...
SCHOOL ANTHEM
...STANDS PROUD
GO! GO! KARA-SUNO!!
SENDAI CASTLE!
BEHOLD, OUR
...!!
GRAND ALMA MATER...
TIME-OUT OVER

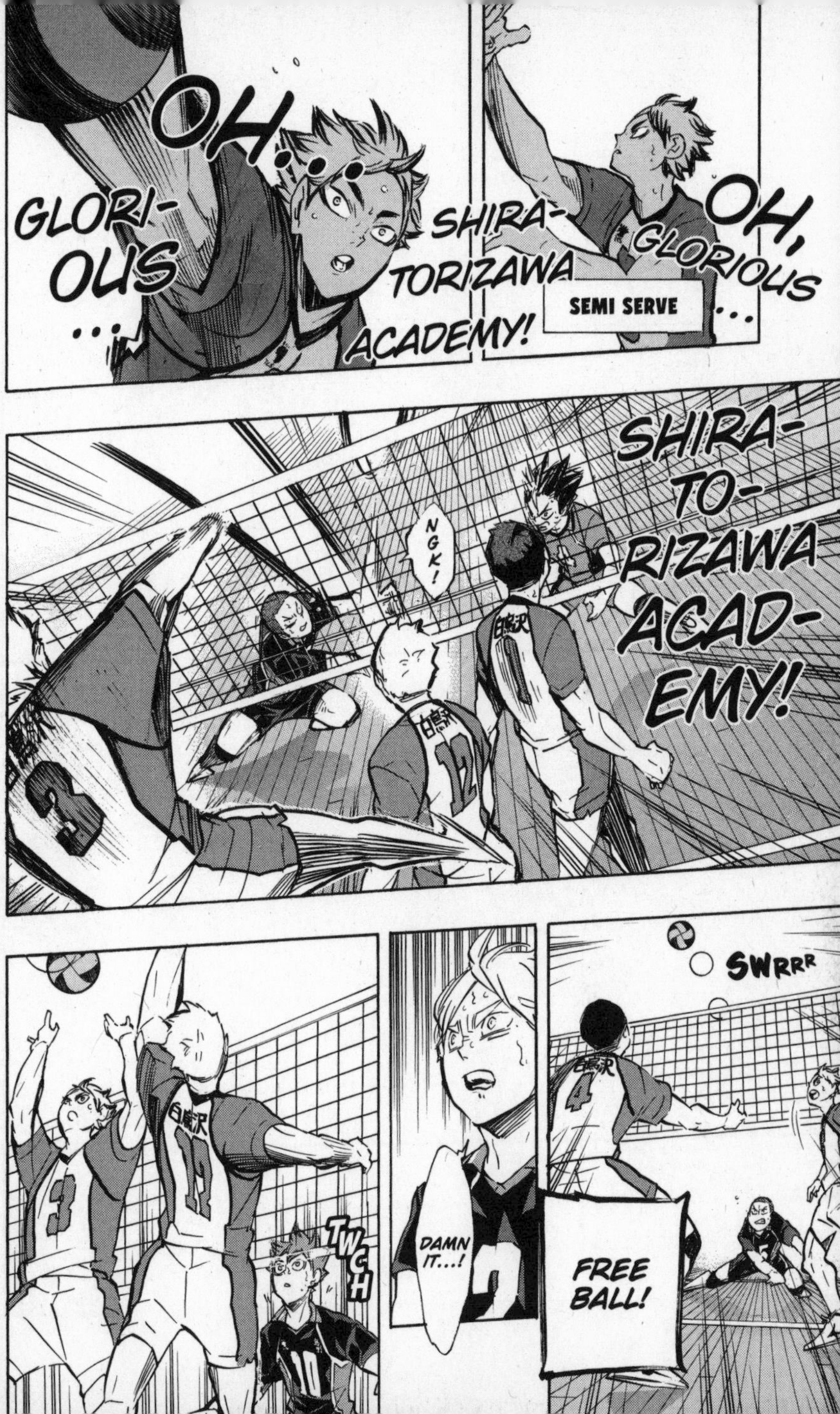

OH, GLORIOUS...
SEMI SERVE
OH...
GLORIOUS...
SHIRATORIZAWA ACADEMY!
SHIRA-TO-RIZAWA ACAD-EMY!
NGK!
SWRRR
FREE BALL!
DAMN IT...!
TWCH

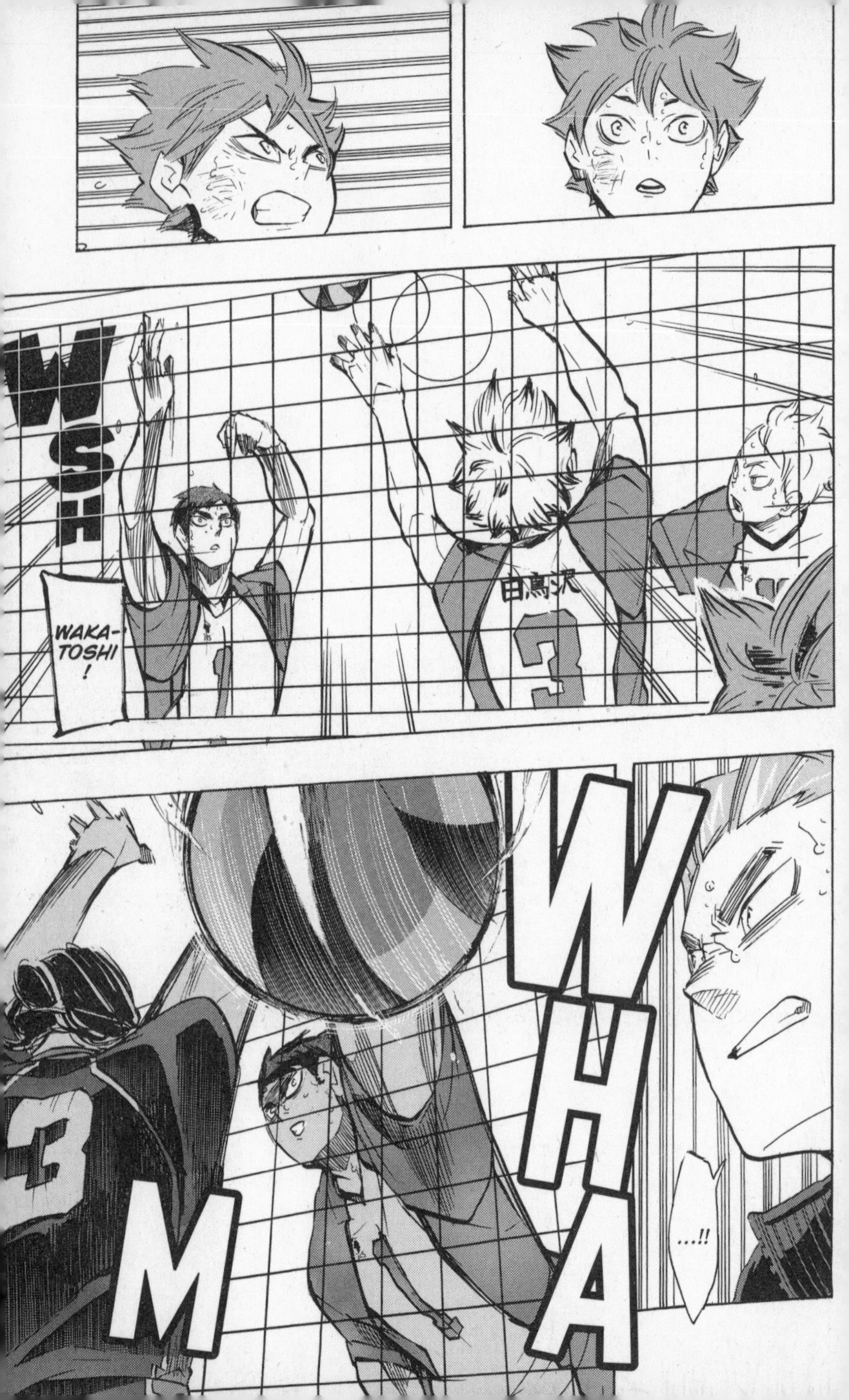
WSH
WAKA-
TOSHI
!
白鳥沢
...!!
WHAM

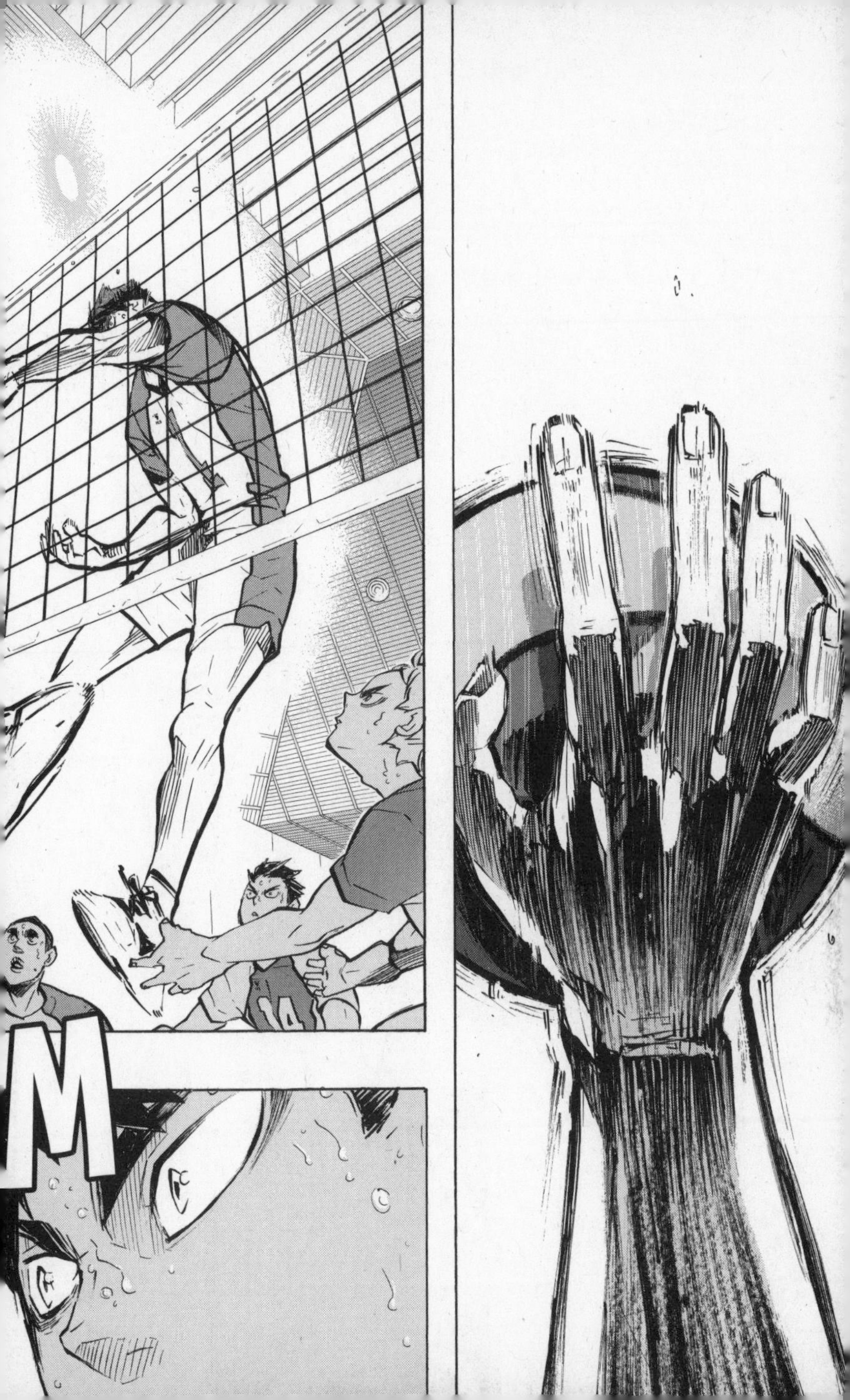
M

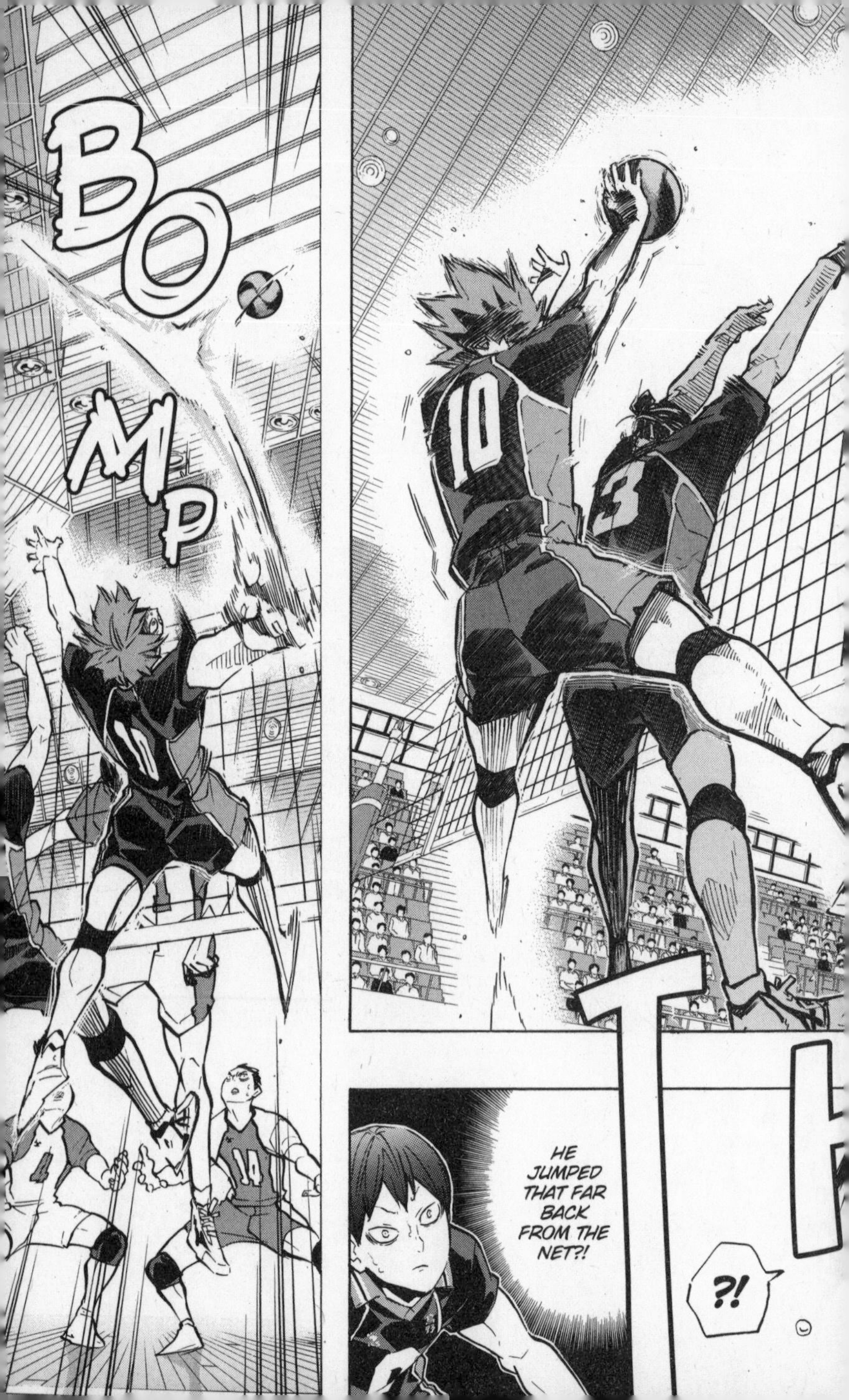
?!
HE JUMPED THAT FAR BACK FROM THE NET?!
BOOMP

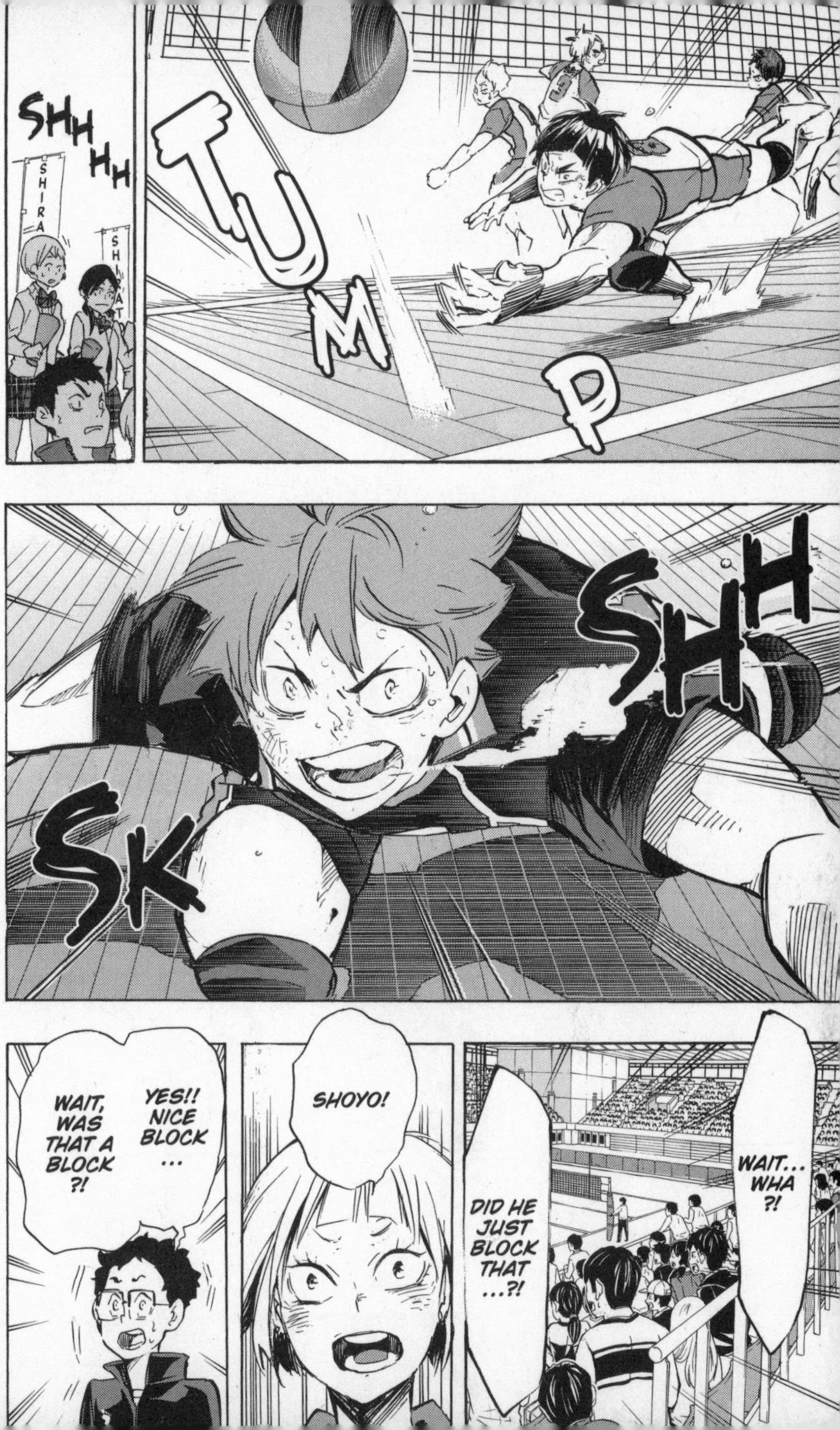
TUMP
SHHHH
SHIRA
SHIRAT
SHHH
SK
WAIT... WHA ?!
DID HE JUST BLOCK THAT ...?!
SHOYO!
YES!! NICE BLOCK ...
WAIT, WAS THAT A BLOCK ?!

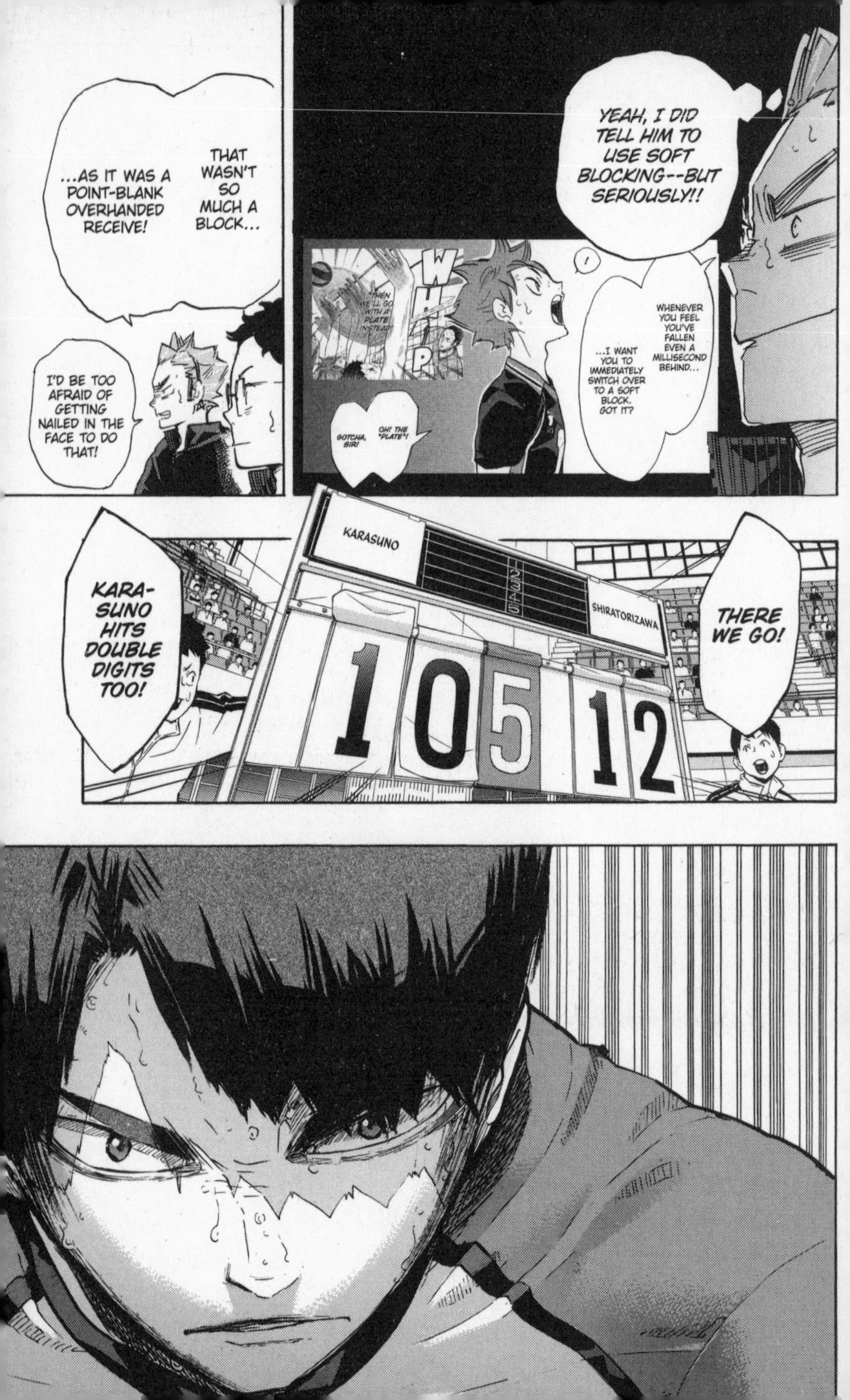
YEAH, I DID TELL HIM TO USE SOFT BLOCKING--BUT SERIOUSLY!!
WHENEVER YOU FEEL YOU'VE FALLEN EVEN A MILLISECOND BEHIND...
...I WANT YOU TO IMMEDIATELY SWITCH OVER TO A SOFT BLOCK. GOT IT?
!
OH! THE "PLATE"!
GOTCHA, SIR!
THEN WE'LL GO WITH A PLATE INSTEAD!
WHIP
THAT WASN'T SO MUCH A BLOCK...
...AS IT WAS A POINT-BLANK OVERHANDED RECEIVE!
I'D BE TOO AFRAID OF GETTING NAILED IN THE FACE TO DO THAT!
THERE WE GO!
KARASUNO
SHIRATORIZAWA
1 2 3 4 5
1 10 5 12
KARA-SUNO HITS DOUBLE DIGITS TOO!

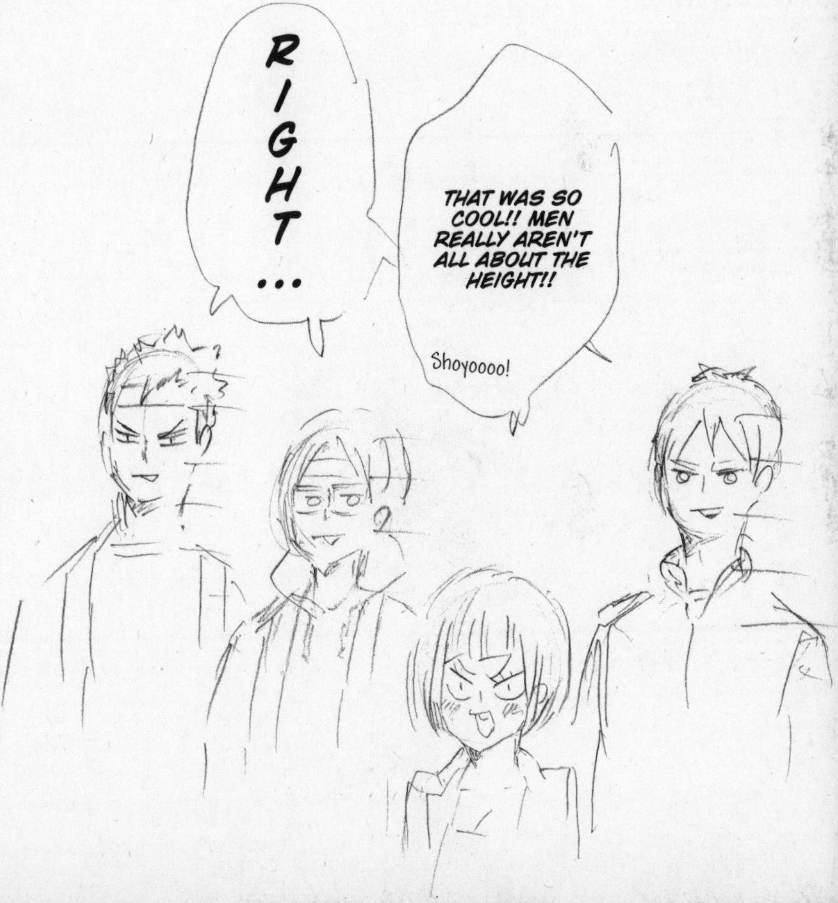
THAT WAS SO COOL!! MEN REALLY AREN'T ALL ABOUT THE HEIGHT!!
Shoyoooo!
RIGHT...

CHAPTER 182: Words from Me to You

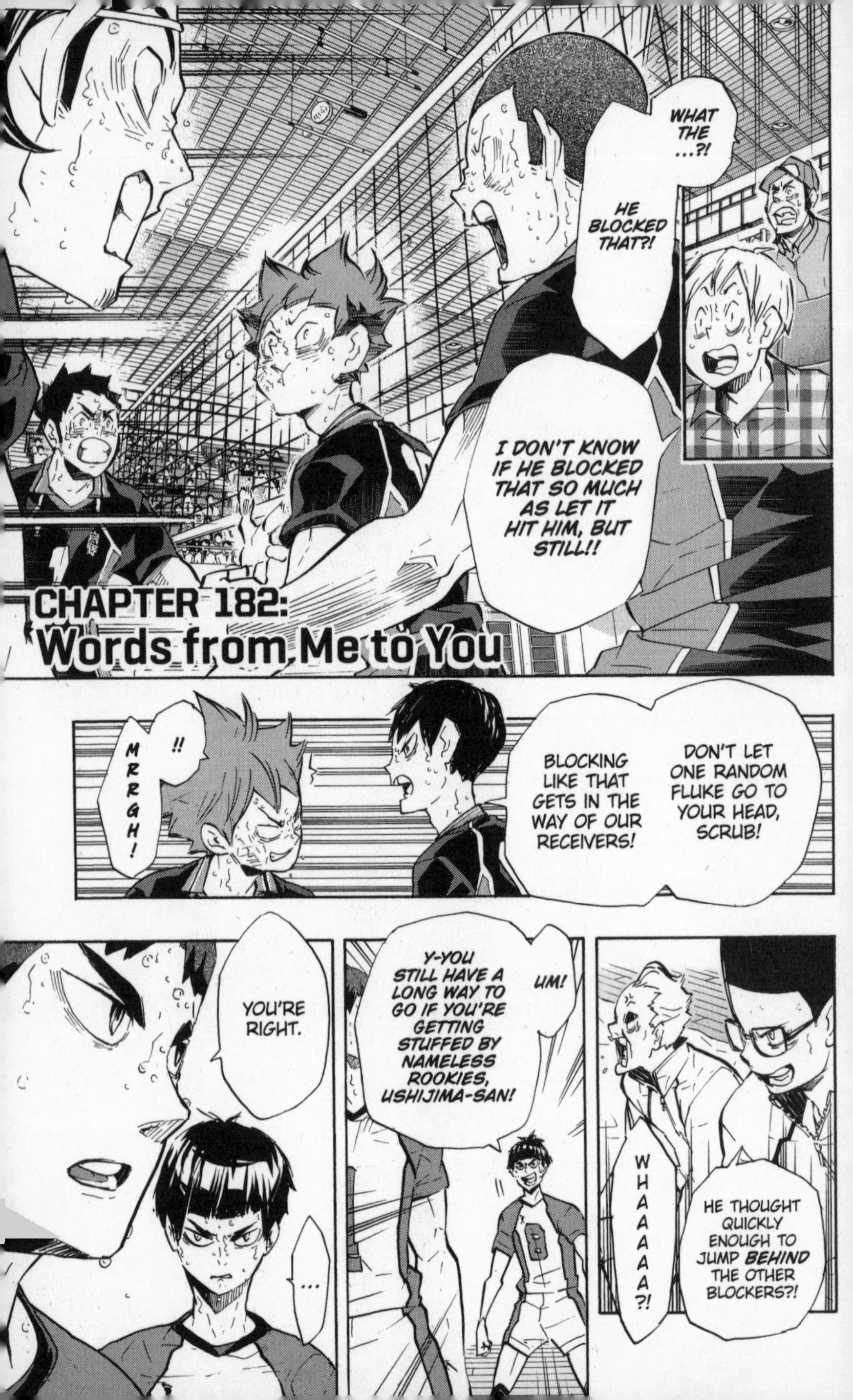
WHAT THE ...?!
HE BLOCKED THAT?!
I DON'T KNOW IF HE BLOCKED THAT SO MUCH AS LET IT HIT HIM, BUT STILL!!
DON'T LET ONE RANDOM FLUKE GO TO YOUR HEAD, SCRUB!
BLOCKING LIKE THAT GETS IN THE WAY OF OUR RECEIVERS!
!!
MRRGH!
HE THOUGHT QUICKLY ENOUGH TO JUMP BEHIND THE OTHER BLOCKERS?!
WHAAAAAAA?!
UM!
Y-YOU STILL HAVE A LONG WAY TO GO IF YOU'RE GETTING STUFFED BY NAMELESS ROOKIES, USHIJIMA-SAN!
YOU'RE RIGHT.
...

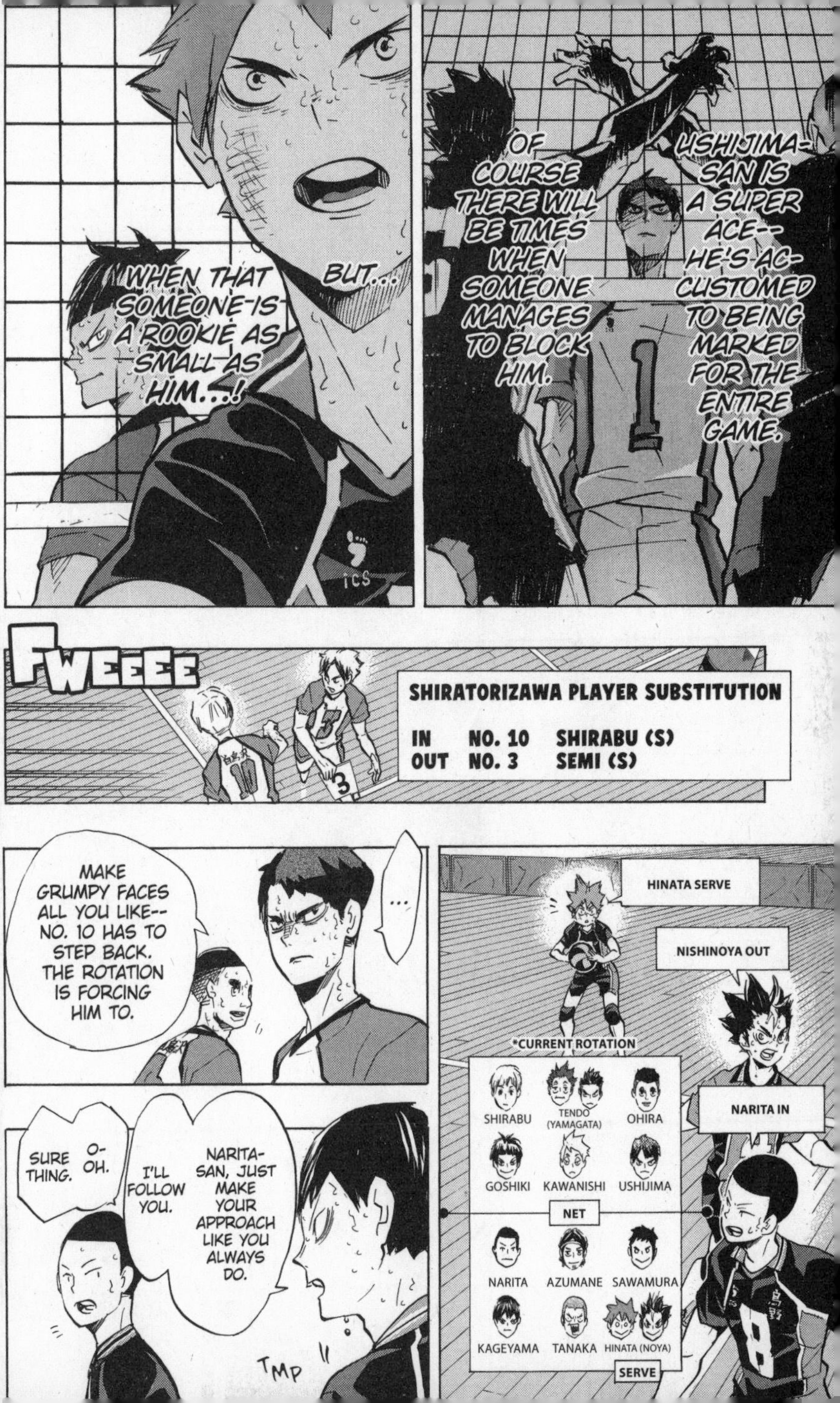
USHIJIMA-SAN IS A SUPER ACE-- HE'S ACCUSTOMED TO BEING MARKED FOR THE ENTIRE GAME.
OF COURSE THERE WILL BE TIMES WHEN SOMEONE MANAGES TO BLOCK HIM.
BUT...
WHEN THAT SOMEONE IS A ROOKIE AS SMALL AS HIM...!
FWEEEE
SHIRATORIZAWA PLAYER SUBSTITUTION
IN NO. 10 SHIRABU (S)
OUT NO. 3 SEMI (S)
HINATA SERVE
NISHINOYA OUT
NARITA IN
*CURRENT ROTATION
SHIRABU
TENDO (YAMAGATA)
OHIRA
GOSHIKI
KAWANISHI
USHIJIMA
NET
NARITA
AZUMANE
SAWAMURA
KAGEYAMA
TANAKA
HINATA (NOYA)
SERVE
...
MAKE GRUMPY FACES ALL YOU LIKE-- NO. 10 HAS TO STEP BACK. THE ROTATION IS FORCING HIM TO.
NARITA-SAN, JUST MAKE YOUR APPROACH LIKE YOU ALWAYS DO.
I'LL FOLLOW YOU.
O-OH.
SURE THING.
TMP

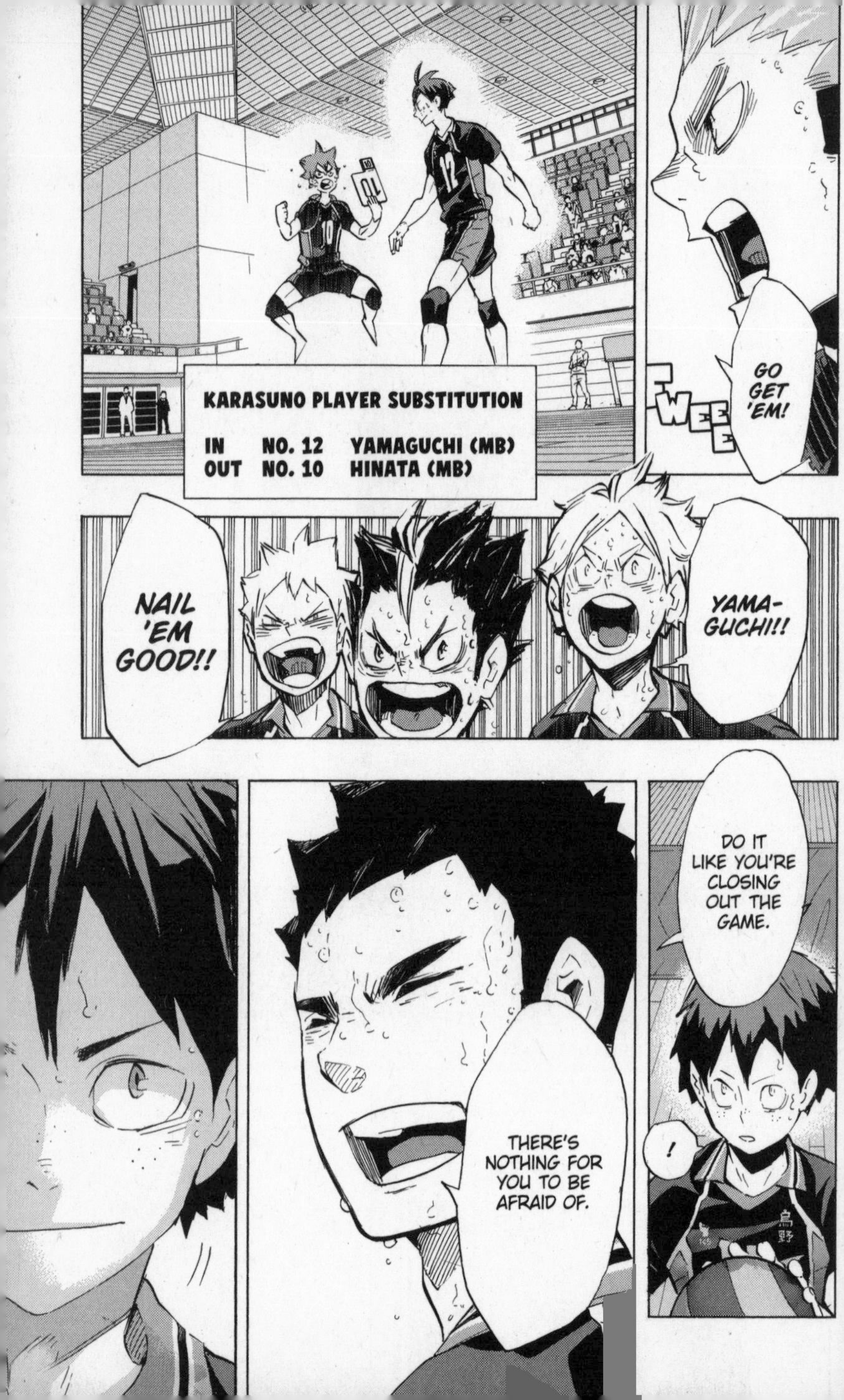
FWEEE
GO GET 'EM!
KARASUNO PLAYER SUBSTITUTION
IN NO. 12 YAMAGUCHI (MB)
OUT NO. 10 HINATA (MB)
YAMA-GUCHI!!
NAIL 'EM GOOD!!
DO IT LIKE YOU'RE CLOSING OUT THE GAME.
!
THERE'S NOTHING FOR YOU TO BE AFRAID OF.

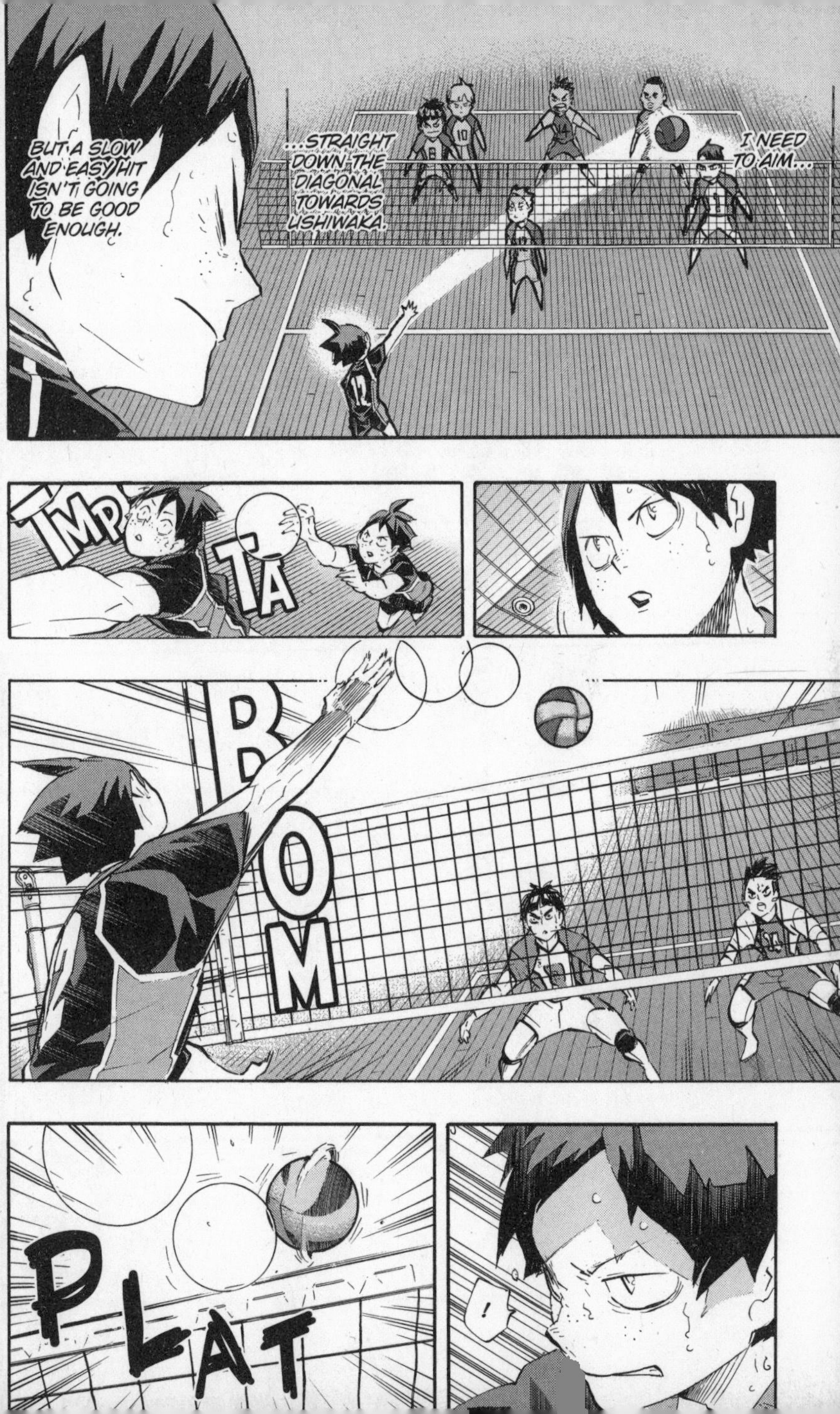
I NEED TO AIM...
...STRAIGHT DOWN THE DIAGONAL TOWARDS USHIWAKA.
BUT A SLOW AND EASY HIT ISN'T GOING TO BE GOOD ENOUGH.
TMP
TA
BOM
!
PLAT

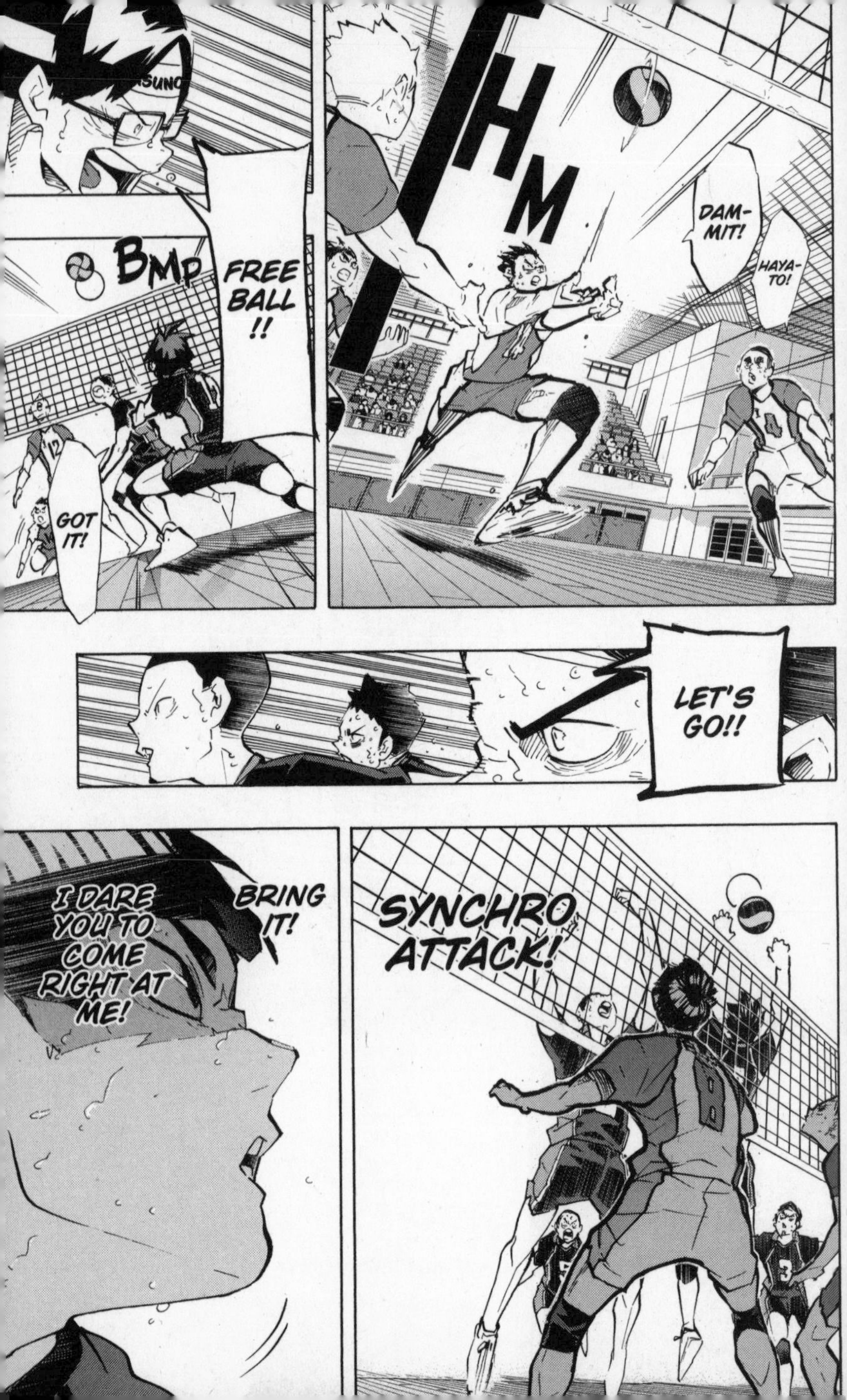
HM
DAM-MIT!
HAYA-TO!
BMP
FREE BALL!!
GOT IT!
LET'S GO!!
SYNCHRO ATTACK!
BRING IT!
I DARE YOU TO COME RIGHT AT ME!

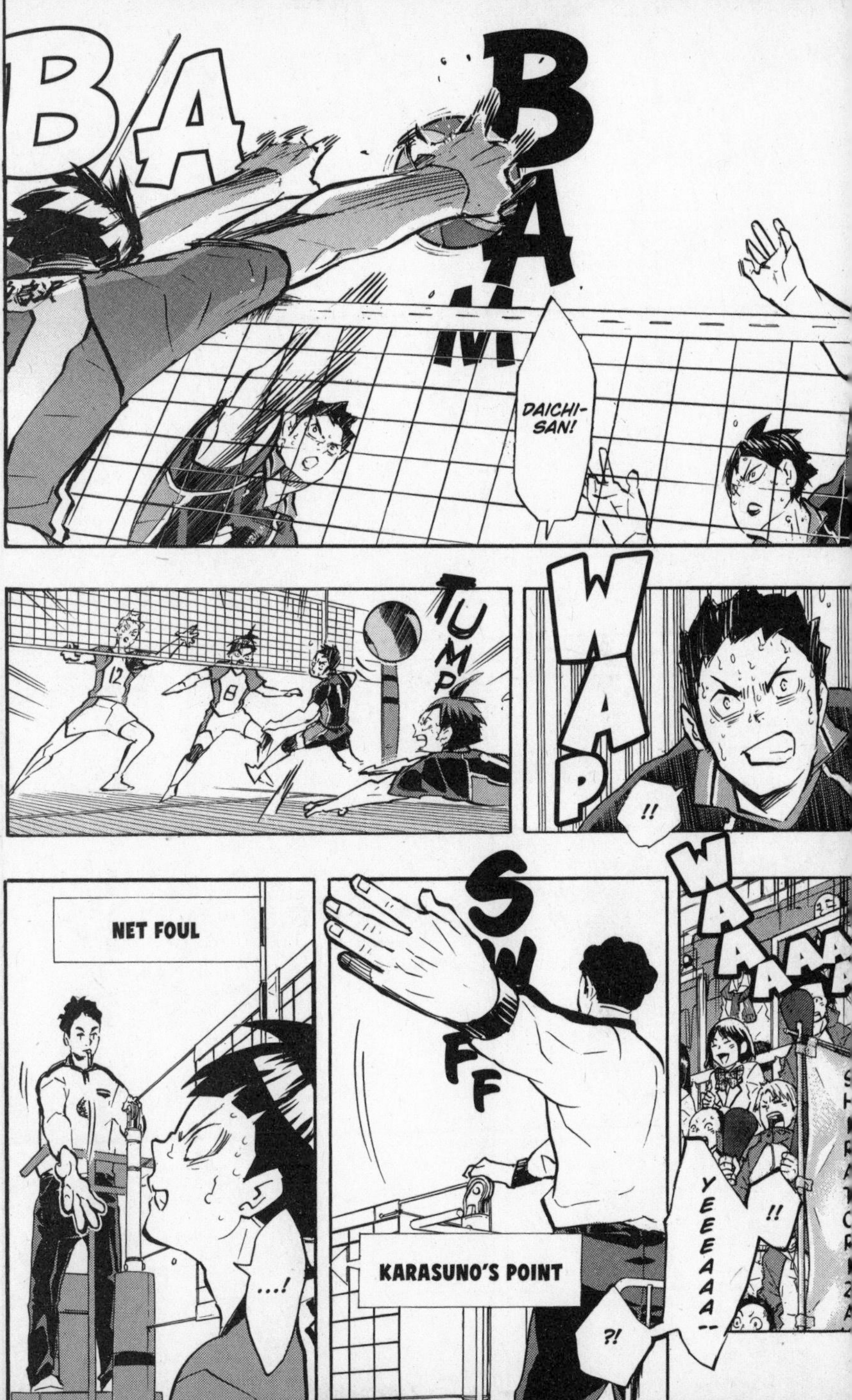
BA
BAM
DAICHI-SAN!
WAP
!!
TUMP
WAAAAAAA
YEEEAAA--
!!
?!
SWFF
KARASUNO'S POINT
NET FOUL
...!

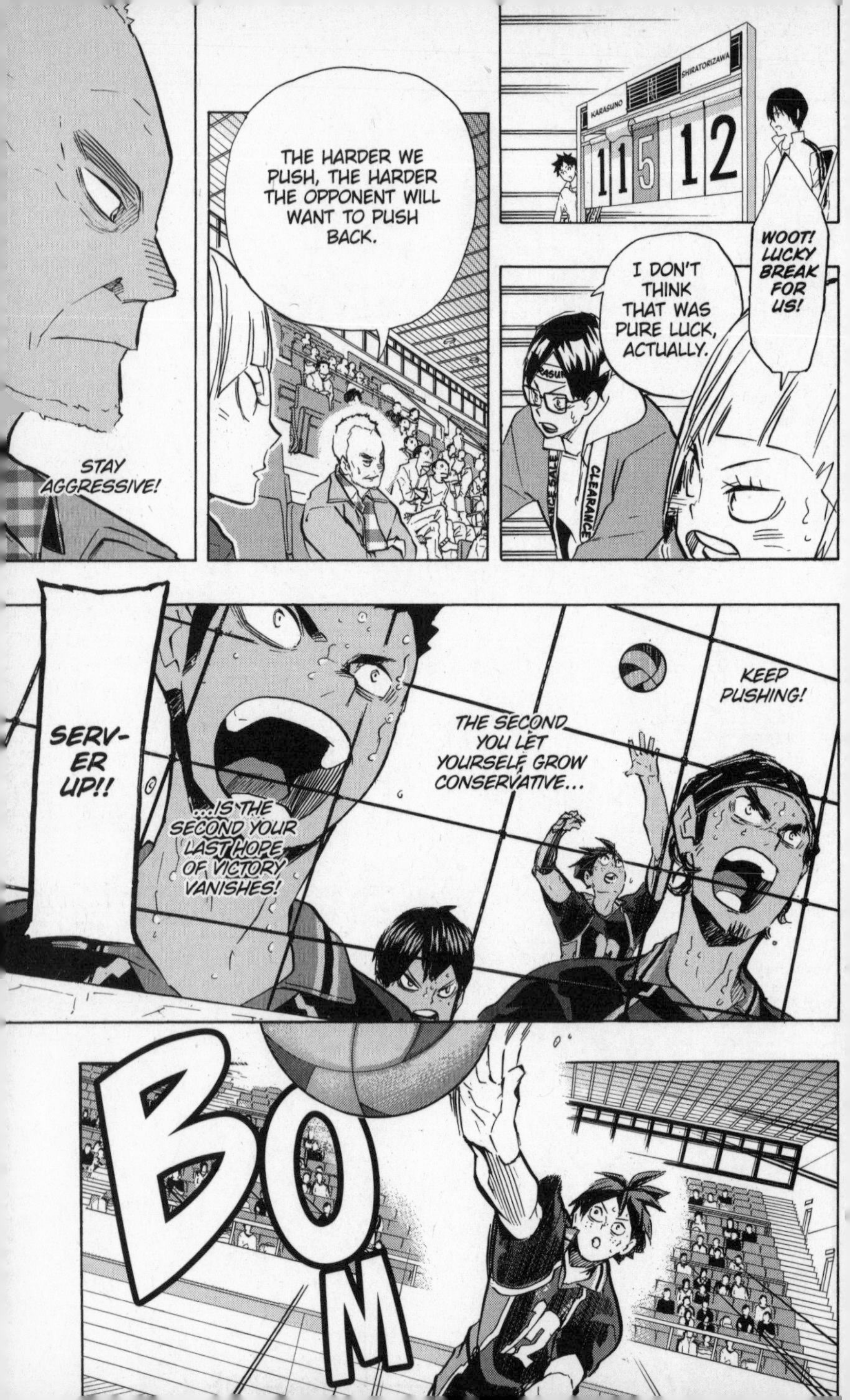
KARASUNO
SHIRATORIZAWA
WOOT! LUCKY BREAK FOR US!
I DON'T THINK THAT WAS PURE LUCK, ACTUALLY.
CLEARANCE
THE HARDER WE PUSH, THE HARDER THE OPPONENT WILL WANT TO PUSH BACK.
STAY AGGRESSIVE!
KEEP PUSHING!
THE SECOND YOU LET YOURSELF GROW CONSERVATIVE...
...IS THE SECOND YOUR LAST HOPE OF VICTORY VANISHES!
SERV-ER UP!!
BOOM

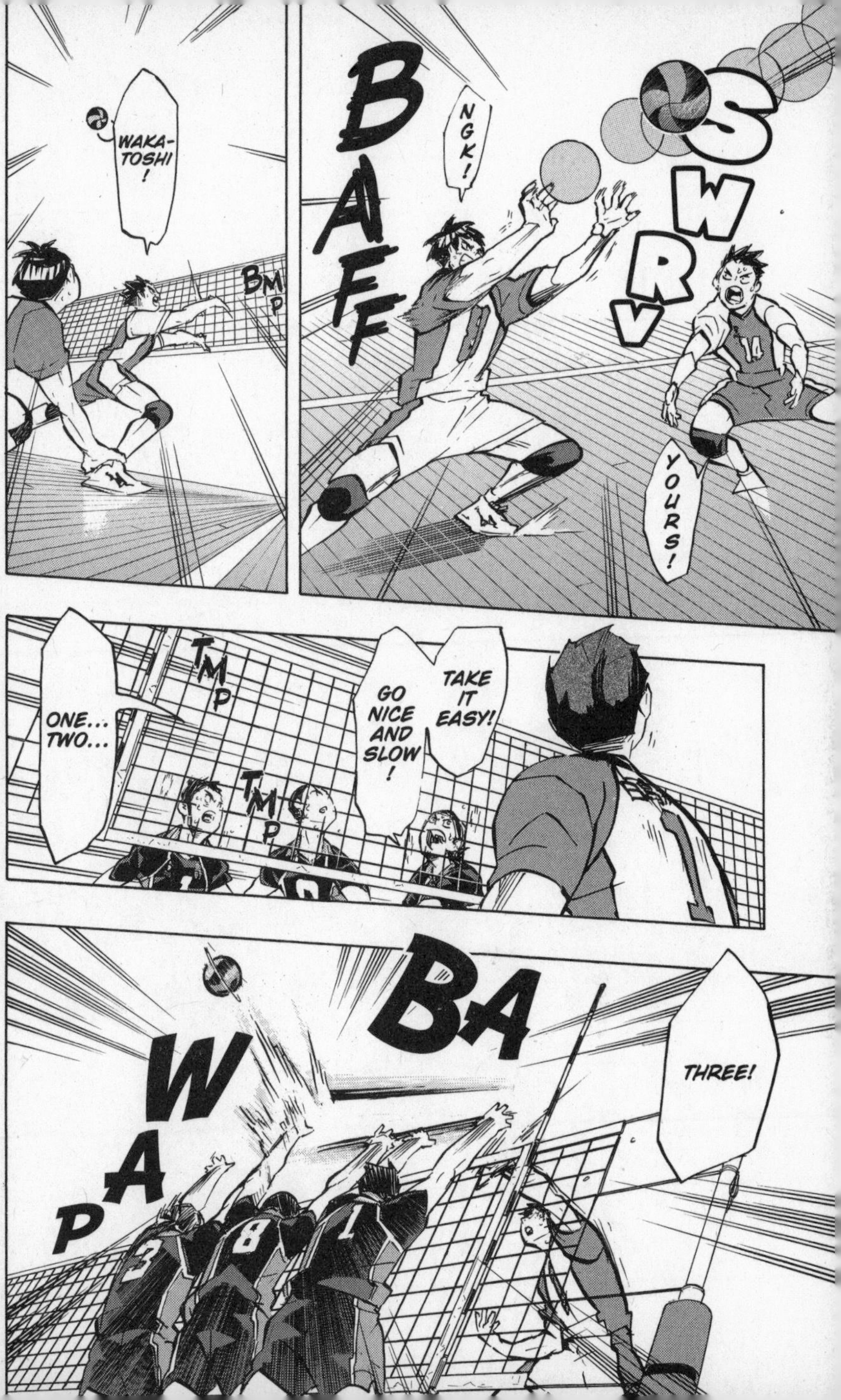
SWRV
NGK!
BAFF
YOURS!
WAKA-TOSHI!
BMP
TAKE IT EASY!
GO NICE AND SLOW!
TMP
TMP
ONE... TWO...
THREE!
BA
WAP

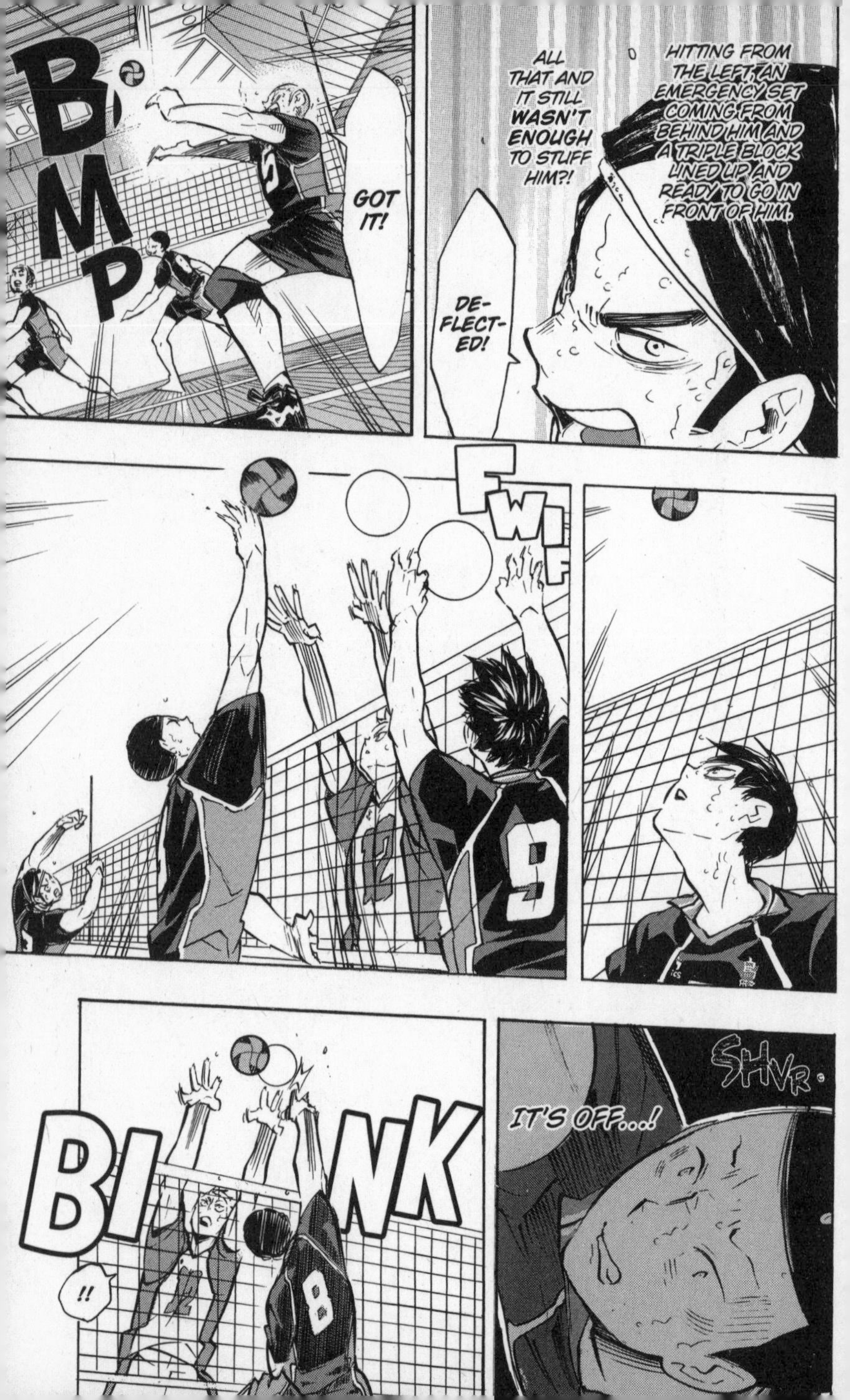
HITTING FROM THE LEFT, AN EMERGENCY SET COMING FROM BEHIND HIM AND A TRIPLE BLOCK LINED UP AND READY TO GO IN FRONT OF HIM.
ALL THAT AND IT STILL WASN'T ENOUGH TO STUFF HIM?!
DE-FLECT-ED!
GOT IT!
BMP
FWIF
SHVR
IT'S OFF...!
BI NK
!!

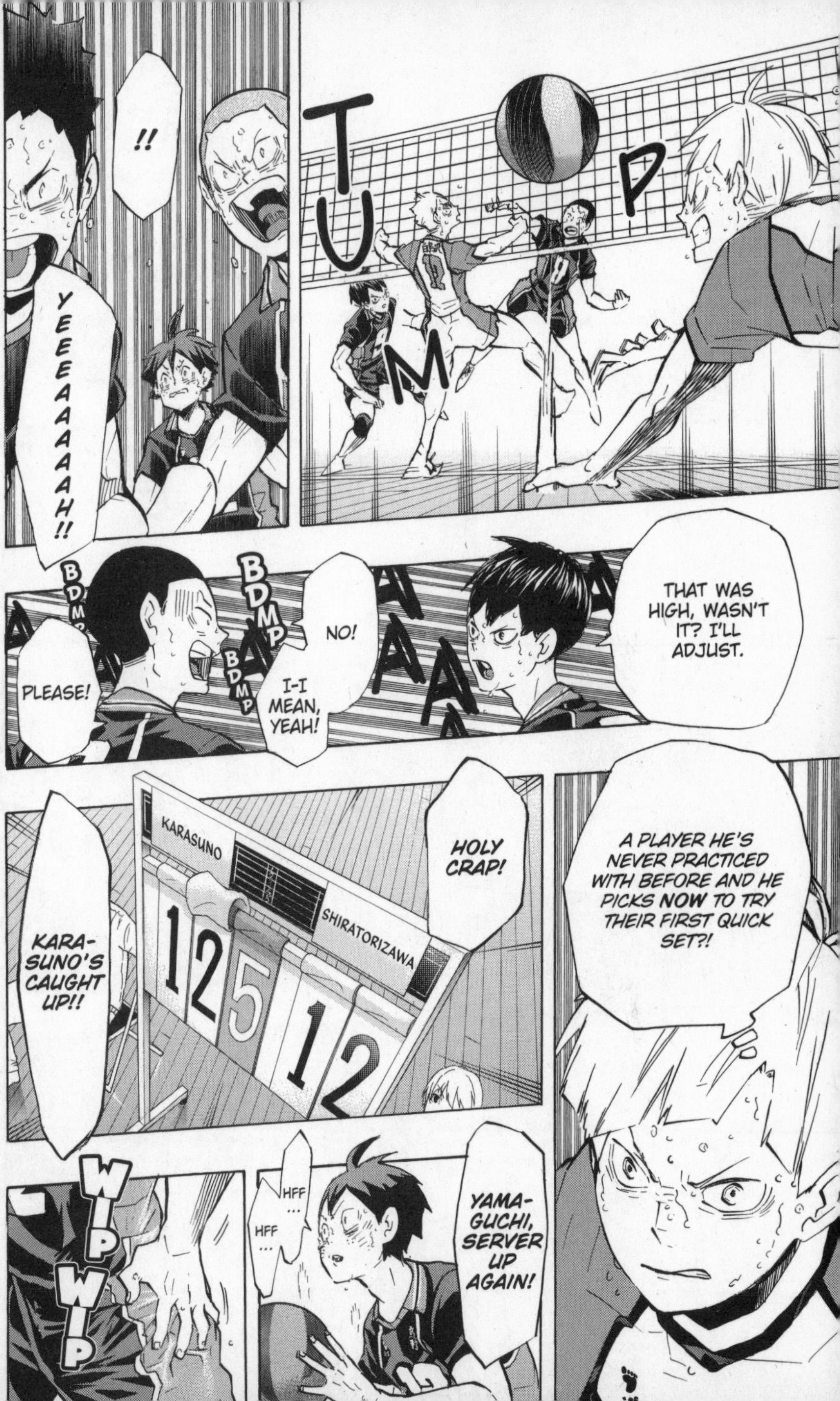
TUMP
!!
YEEEAAAAAAAH!!
THAT WAS HIGH, WASN'T IT? I'LL ADJUST.
AAAAA
NO!
I-I MEAN, YEAH!
BDMP
BDMP
BDMP
PLEASE!
A PLAYER HE'S NEVER PRACTICED WITH BEFORE AND HE PICKS NOW TO TRY THEIR FIRST QUICK SET?!
HOLY CRAP!
KARASUNO
SHIRATORIZAWA
12 5 12
KARA-SUNO'S CAUGHT UP!!
YAMA-GUCHI, SERVER UP AGAIN!
HFF...
HFF...
WIP WIP

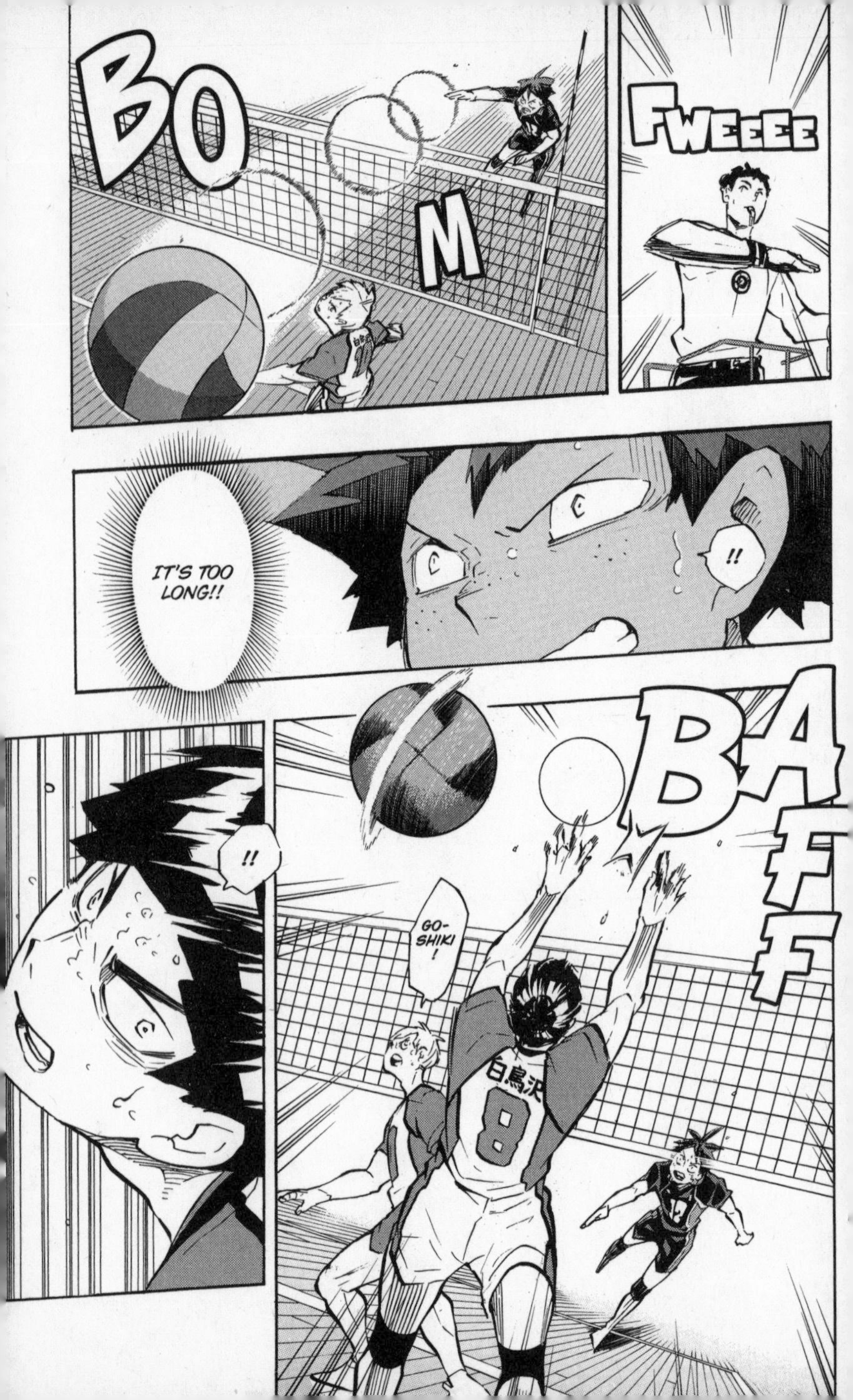
FWEEEE
BO
M
!!
IT'S TOO LONG!!
BAFF
GO-SHIKI!
白鳥沢
!!

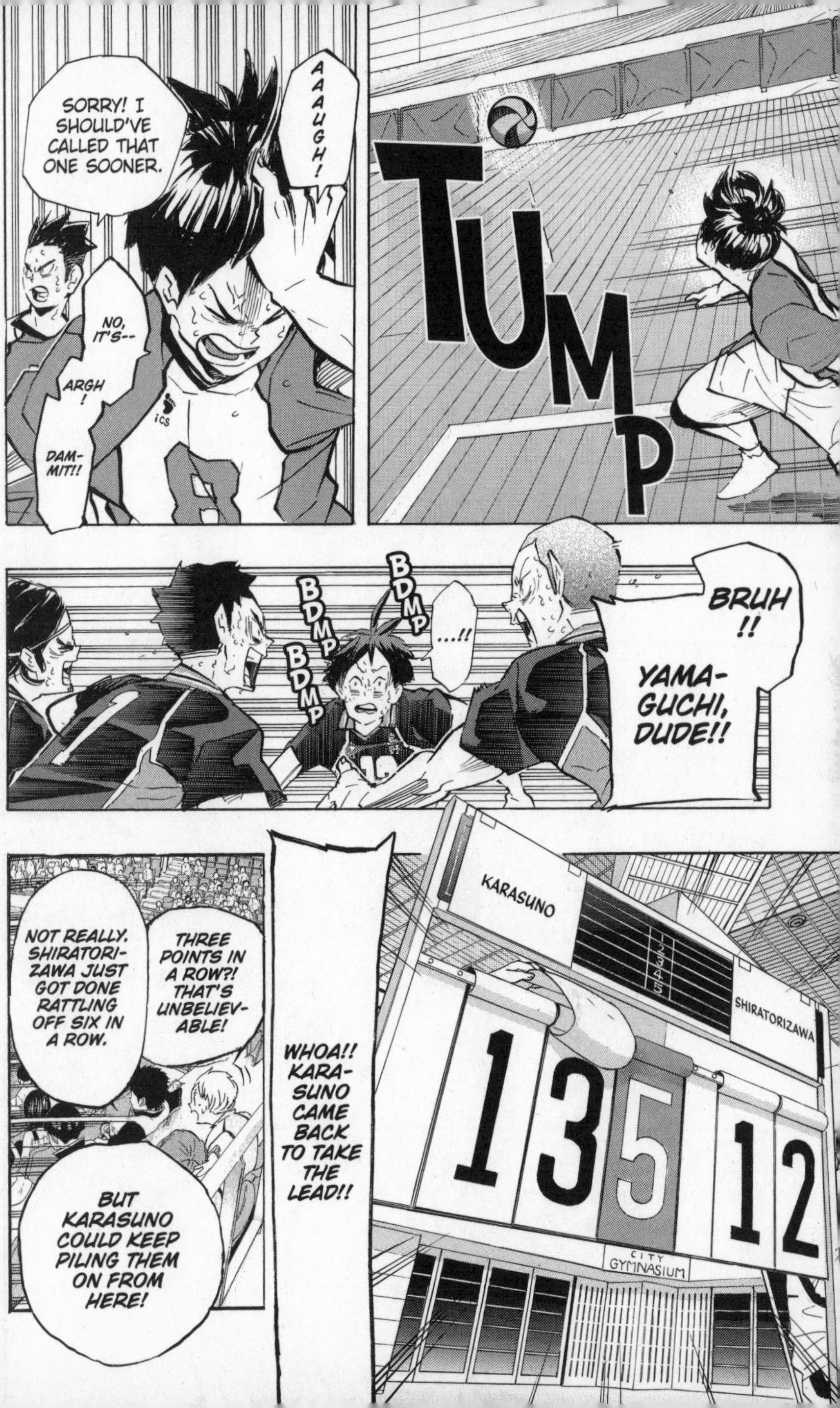
TUMP
AAAAUGH!
SORRY! I SHOULD'VE CALLED THAT ONE SOONER.
NO, IT'S--
ARGH!
DAM-MIT!!
BRUH!!
YAMA-GUCHI, DUDE!!
...!!
BDMP
BDMP
BDMP
BDMP
KARASUNO
SHIRATORIZAWA
1 2 3 4 5
13 5 12
CITY GYMNASIUM
WHOA!! KARA-SUNO CAME BACK TO TAKE THE LEAD!!
THREE POINTS IN A ROW?! THAT'S UNBELIEV-ABLE!
NOT REALLY. SHIRATORI-ZAWA JUST GOT DONE RATTLING OFF SIX IN A ROW.
BUT KARASUNO COULD KEEP PILING THEM ON FROM HERE!

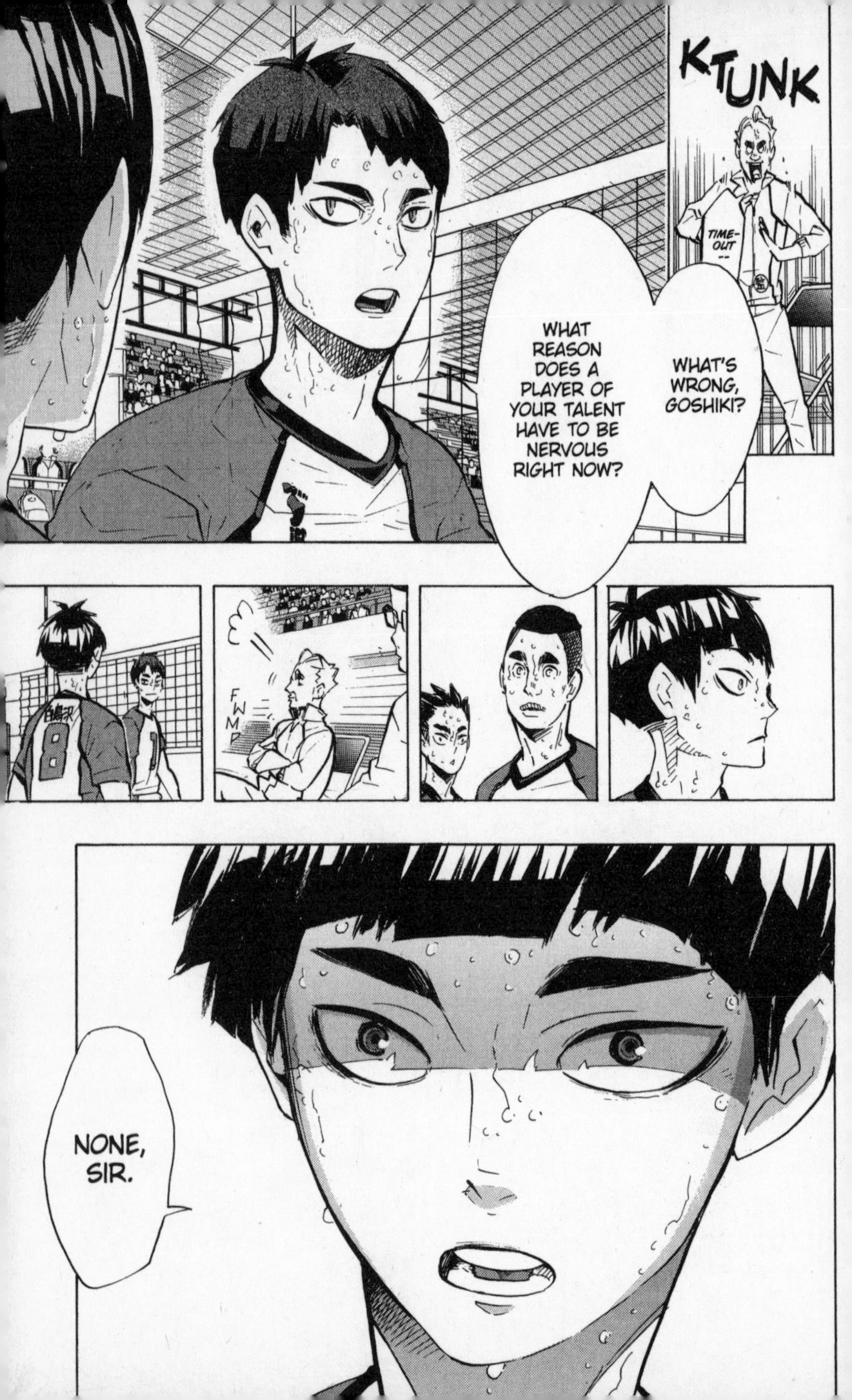
KTUNK
TIME-OUT
WHAT'S WRONG, GOSHIKI?
WHAT REASON DOES A PLAYER OF YOUR TALENT HAVE TO BE NERVOUS RIGHT NOW?
FWMP
NONE, SIR.

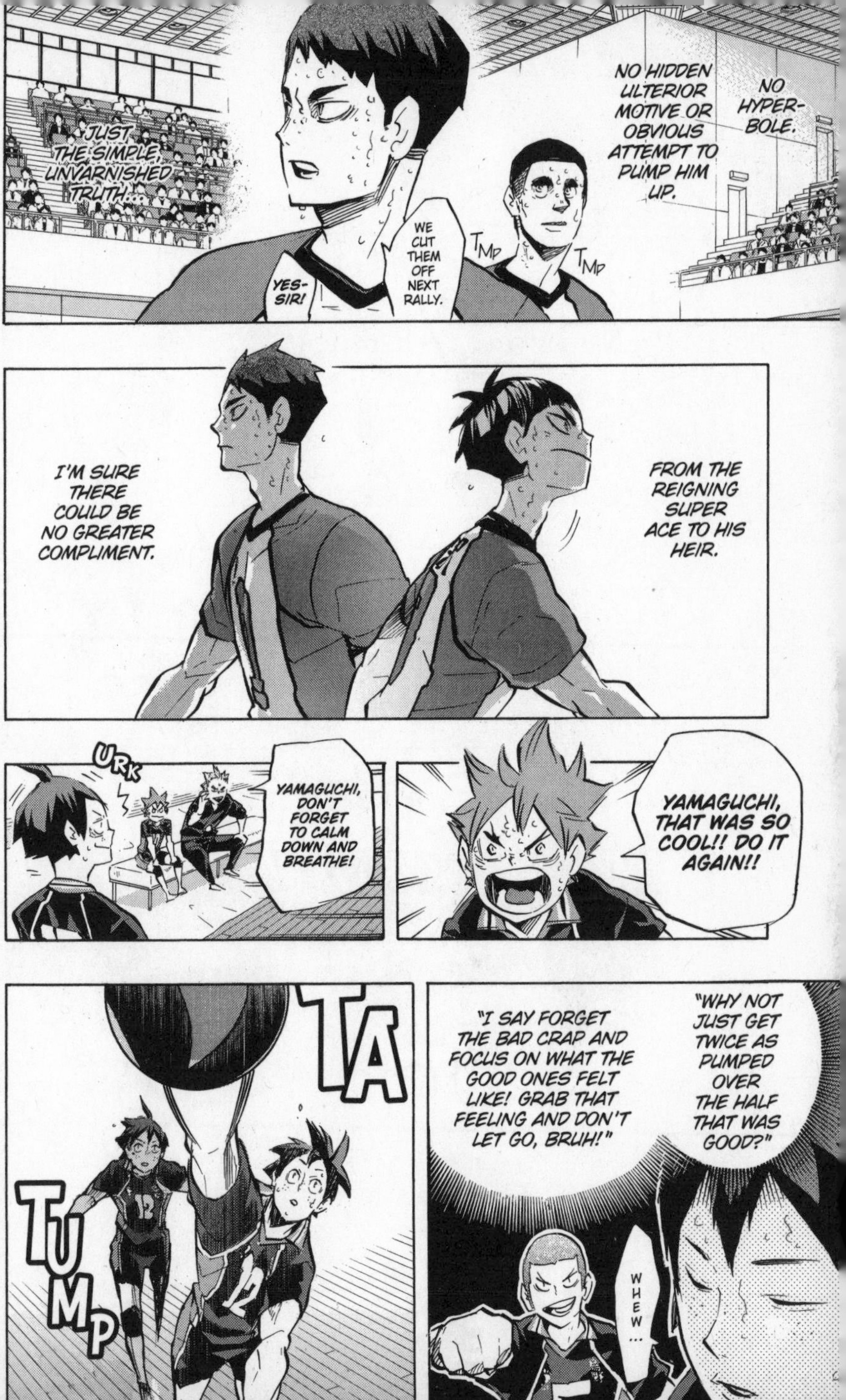
NO HYPER-BOLE.
NO HIDDEN ULTERIOR MOTIVE OR OBVIOUS ATTEMPT TO PUMP HIM UP.
JUST THE SIMPLE, UNVARNISHED TRUTH...
WE CUT THEM OFF NEXT RALLY.
TMP TMP
YES-SIR!
FROM THE REIGNING SUPER ACE TO HIS HEIR.
I'M SURE THERE COULD BE NO GREATER COMPLIMENT.
YAMAGUCHI, THAT WAS SO COOL!! DO IT AGAIN!!
YAMAGUCHI, DON'T FORGET TO CALM DOWN AND BREATHE!
URK
"WHY NOT JUST GET TWICE AS PUMPED OVER THE HALF THAT WAS GOOD?"
"I SAY FORGET THE BAD CRAP AND FOCUS ON WHAT THE GOOD ONES FELT LIKE! GRAB THAT FEELING AND DON'T LET GO, BRUH!"
WHEW...
TA
TUMP

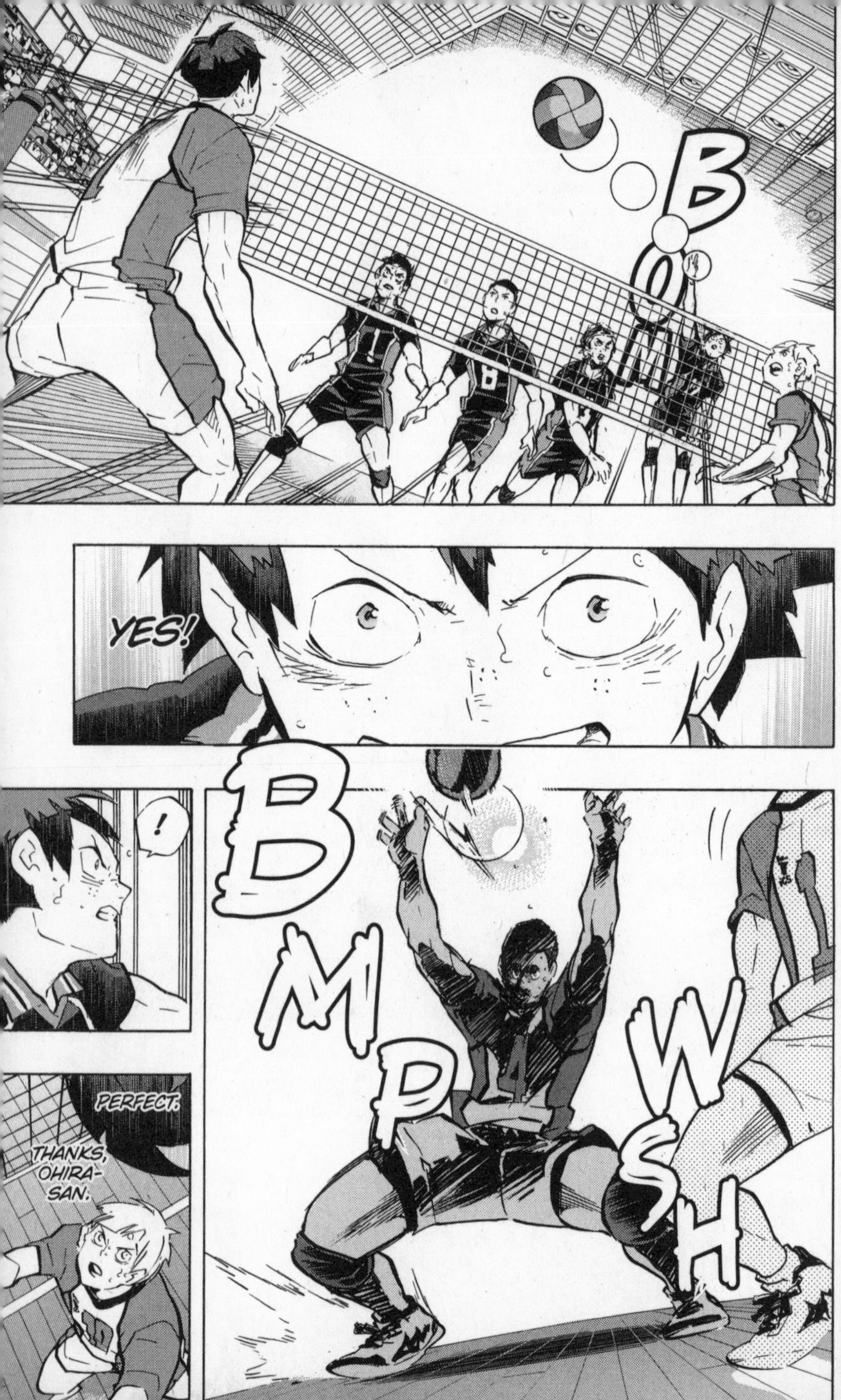
BOM
YES!
BMP
WSH
!
PERFECT.
THANKS, OHIRA-SAN.

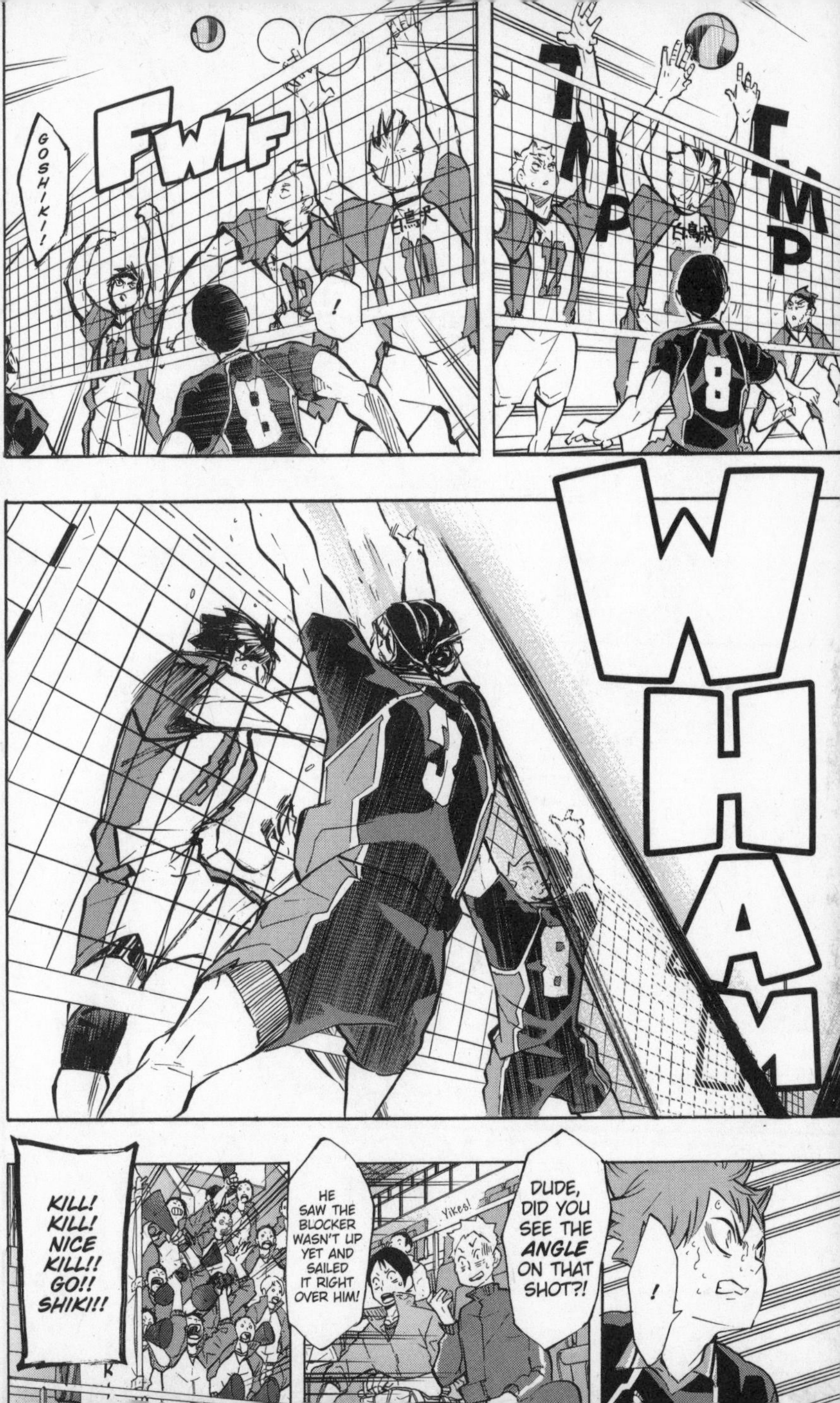
TMP
TMP
FWIF
GOSHIKI!!
!
WHAM
!
DUDE, DID YOU SEE THE *ANGLE* ON THAT SHOT?!
HE SAW THE BLOCKER WASN'T UP YET AND SAILED IT RIGHT OVER HIM!
Yikes!
KILL! KILL! NICE KILL!! GO!! SHIKI!!

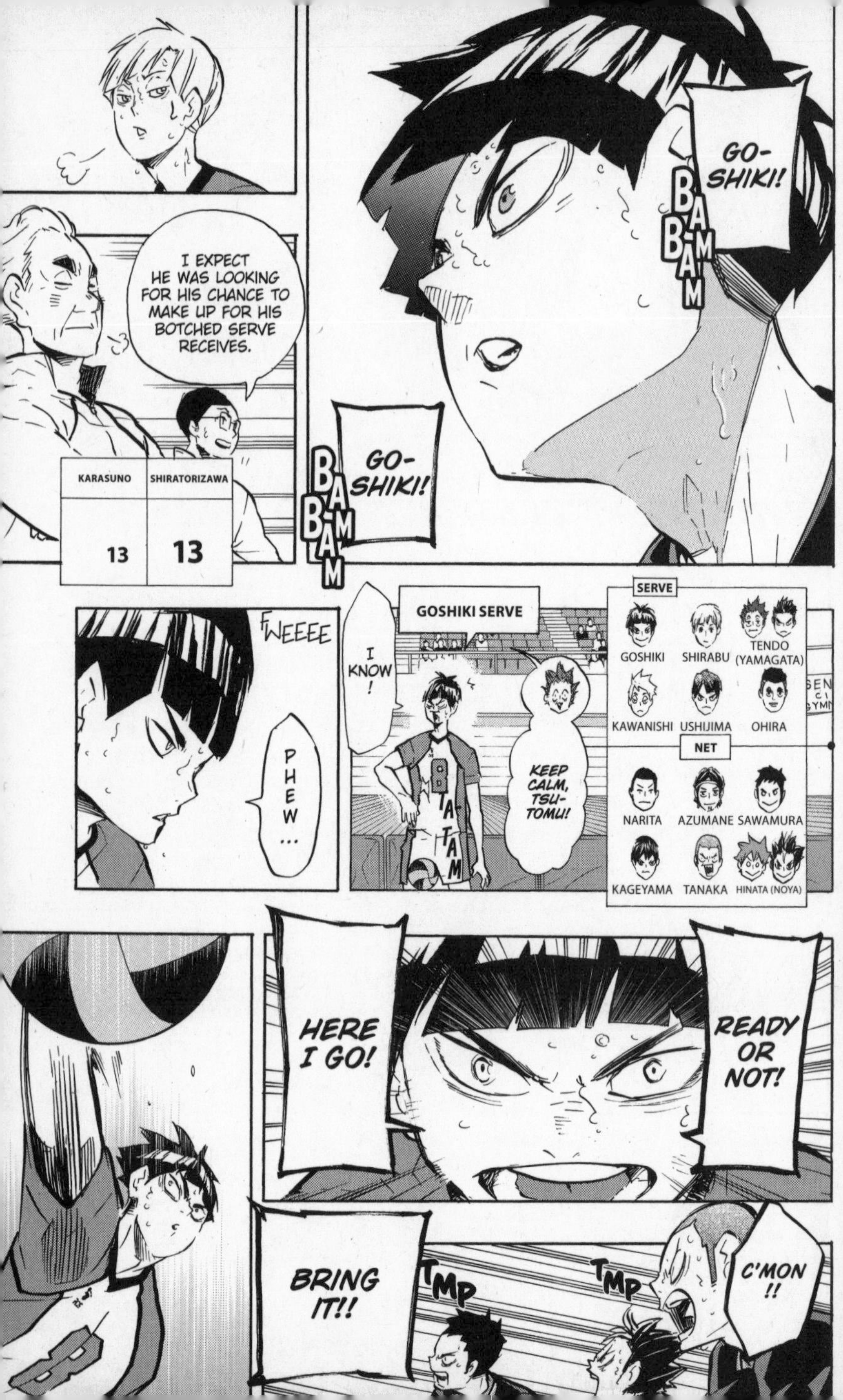

GO-SHIKI!
BABAM
GO-SHIKI!
BABAM
I EXPECT HE WAS LOOKING FOR HIS CHANCE TO MAKE UP FOR HIS BOTCHED SERVE RECEIVES.
KARASUNO 13
SHIRATORIZAWA 13
SERVE
GOSHIKI
SHIRABU
TENDO (YAMAGATA)
KAWANISHI
USHIJIMA
OHIRA
NET
NARITA
AZUMANE
SAWAMURA
KAGEYAMA
TANAKA
HINATA (NOYA)
GOSHIKI SERVE
I KNOW!
KEEP CALM, TSUTOMU!
TATAM
FWEEEE
PHEW...
READY OR NOT!
HERE I GO!
C'MON!!
TMP
TMP
BRING IT!!

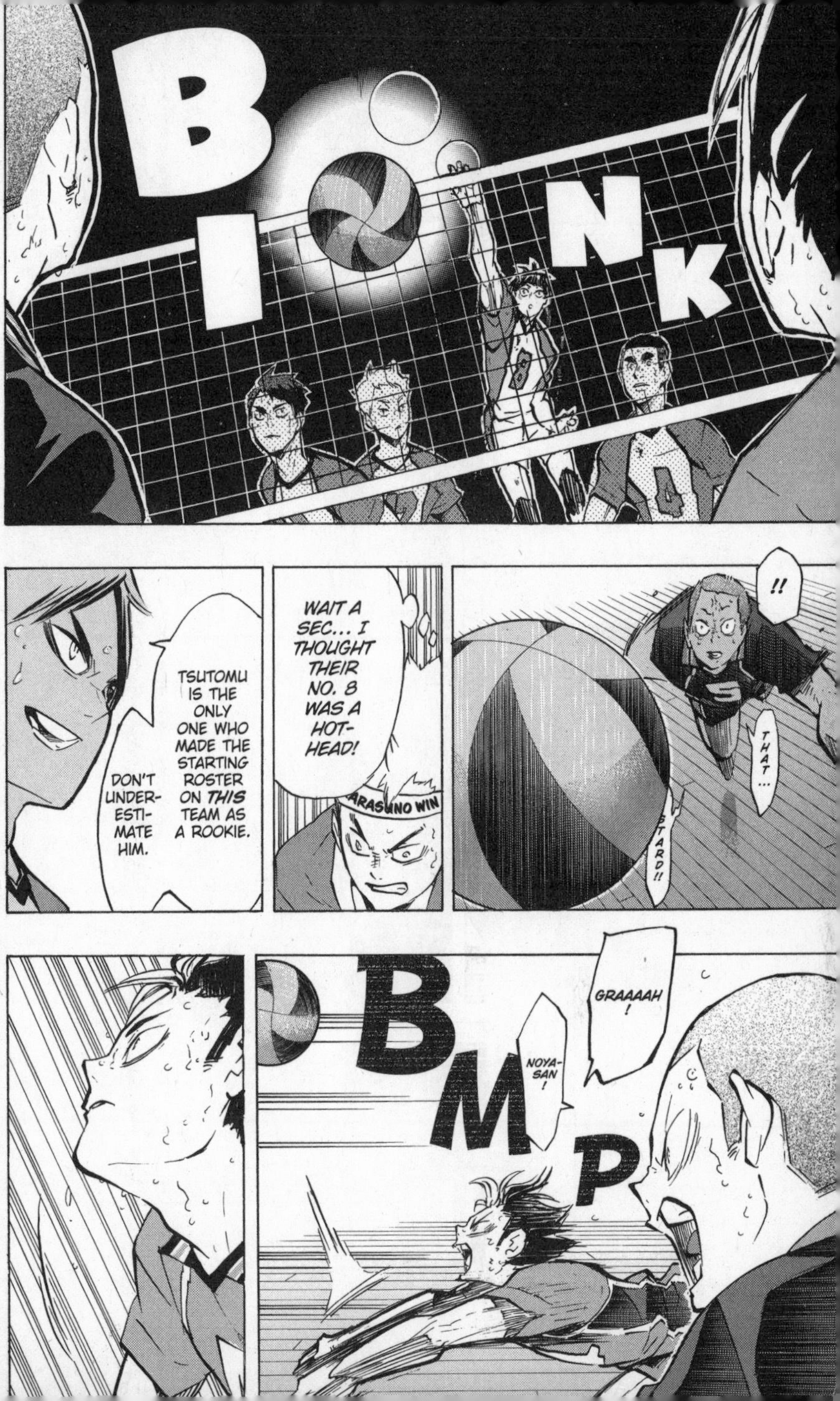
BONK
!!
THAT...
...STARD!!
WAIT A SEC... I THOUGHT THEIR NO. 8 WAS A HOT-HEAD!
ARASUNO WIN
TSUTOMU IS THE ONLY ONE WHO MADE THE STARTING ROSTER ON *THIS* TEAM AS A ROOKIE.
DON'T UNDER-ESTI-MATE HIM.
GRAAAAH!
NOYA-SAN!
BMP

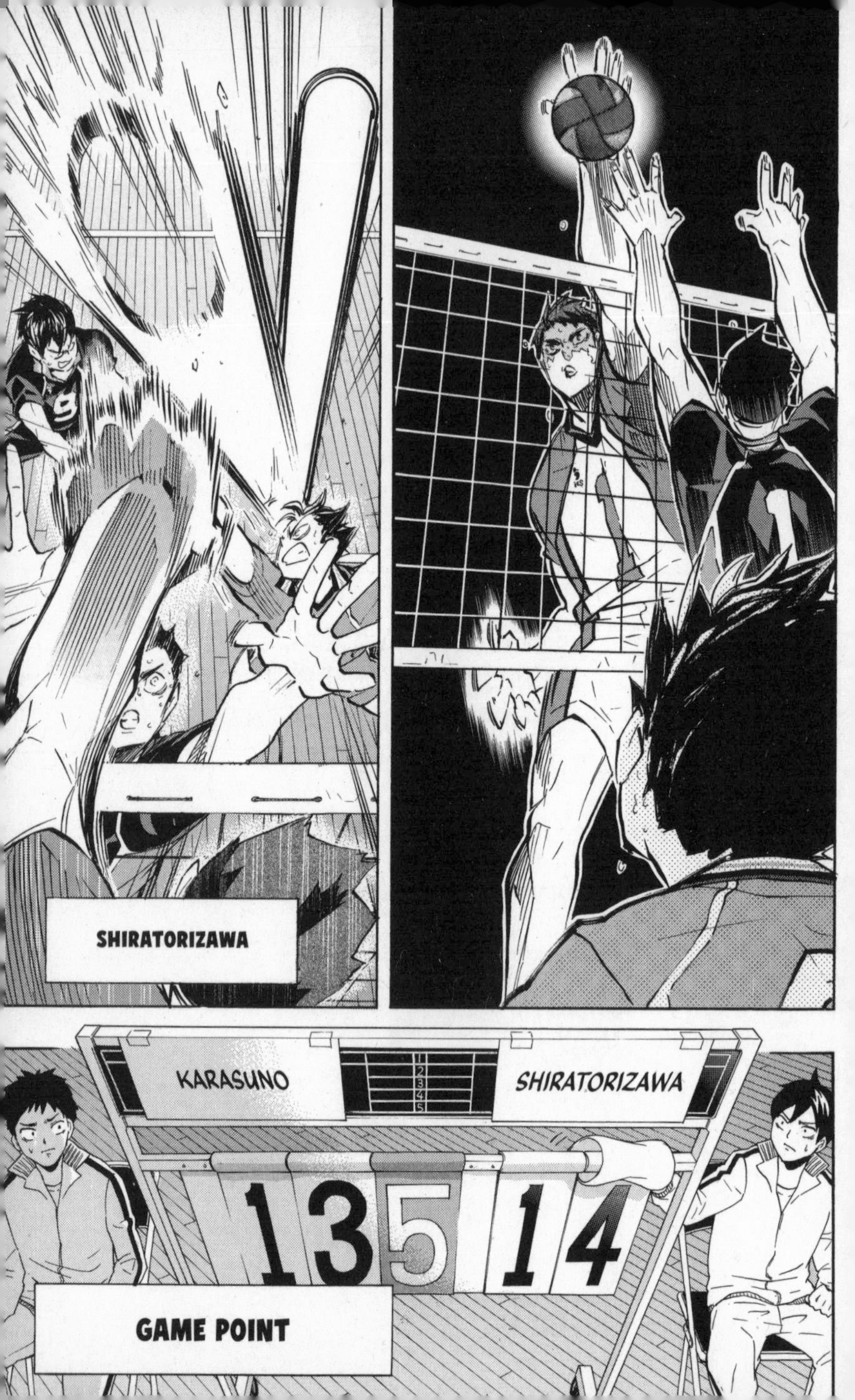
SHIRATORIZAWA
KARASUNO
SHIRATORIZAWA
13 5 14
GAME POINT

I HAVE A PROBLEM.
A PROBLEM WHERE I
DRAW TSUTOMU WITH
THE NO. 5 JERSEY…

CONSTANTLY

HEY!!
TSUTOMU,
THAT'S
MINE!

?

CHAPTER 183

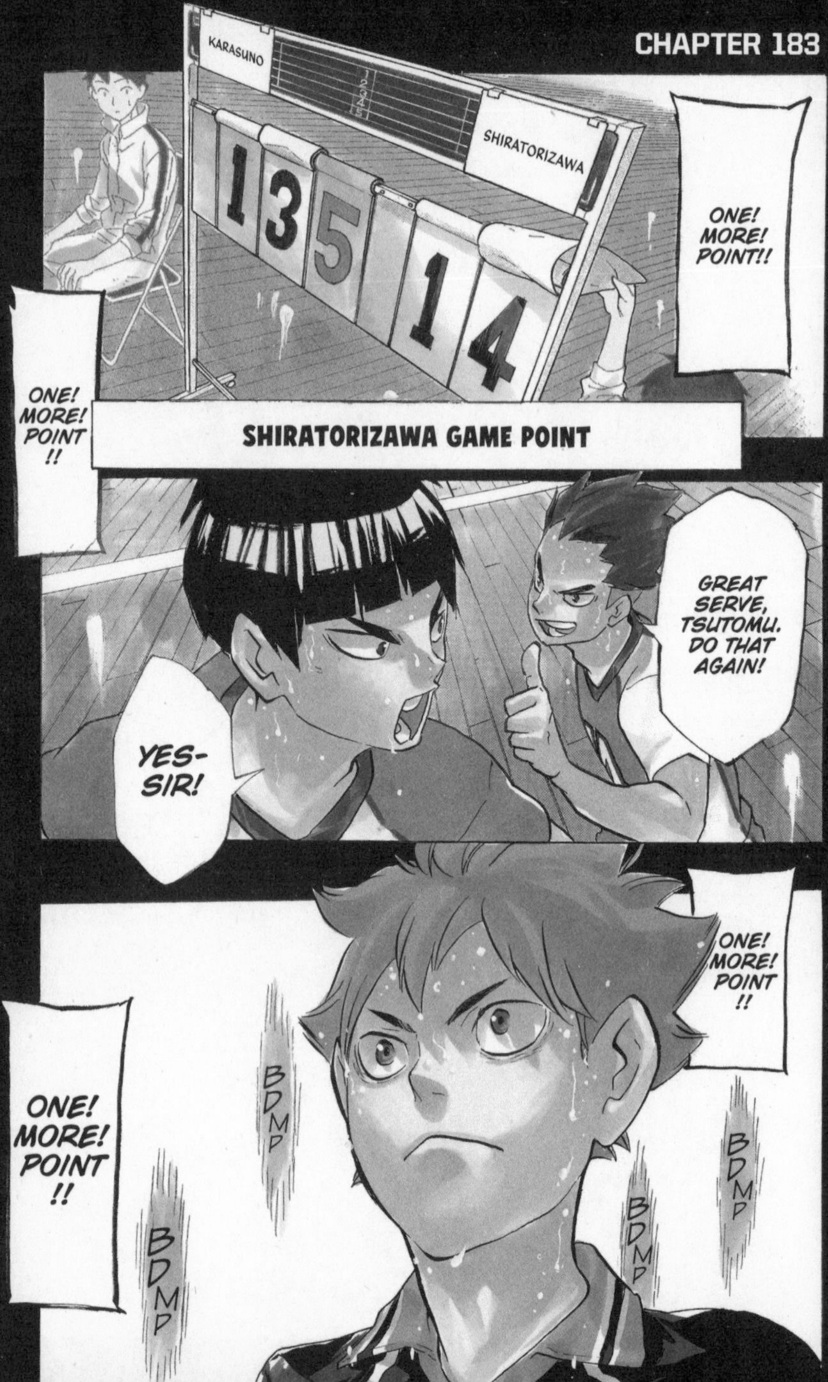
KARASUNO
SHIRATORIZAWA
13
5
14
ONE! MORE! POINT!!
SHIRATORIZAWA GAME POINT
ONE! MORE! POINT !!
GREAT SERVE, TSUTOMU. DO THAT AGAIN!
YES-SIR!
ONE! MORE! POINT !!
BDMP
BDMP
BDMP
BDMP
ONE! MORE! POINT !!

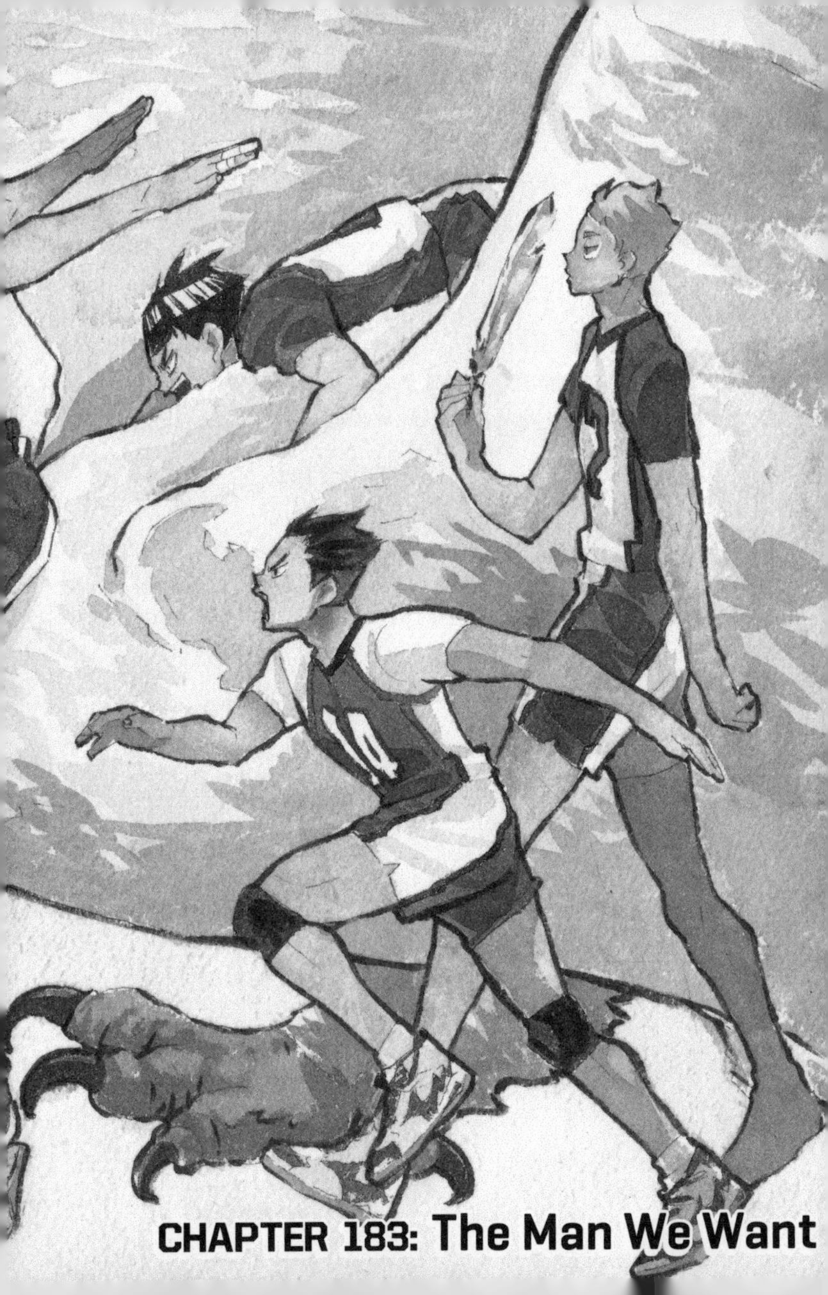

CHAPTER 183: The Man We Want

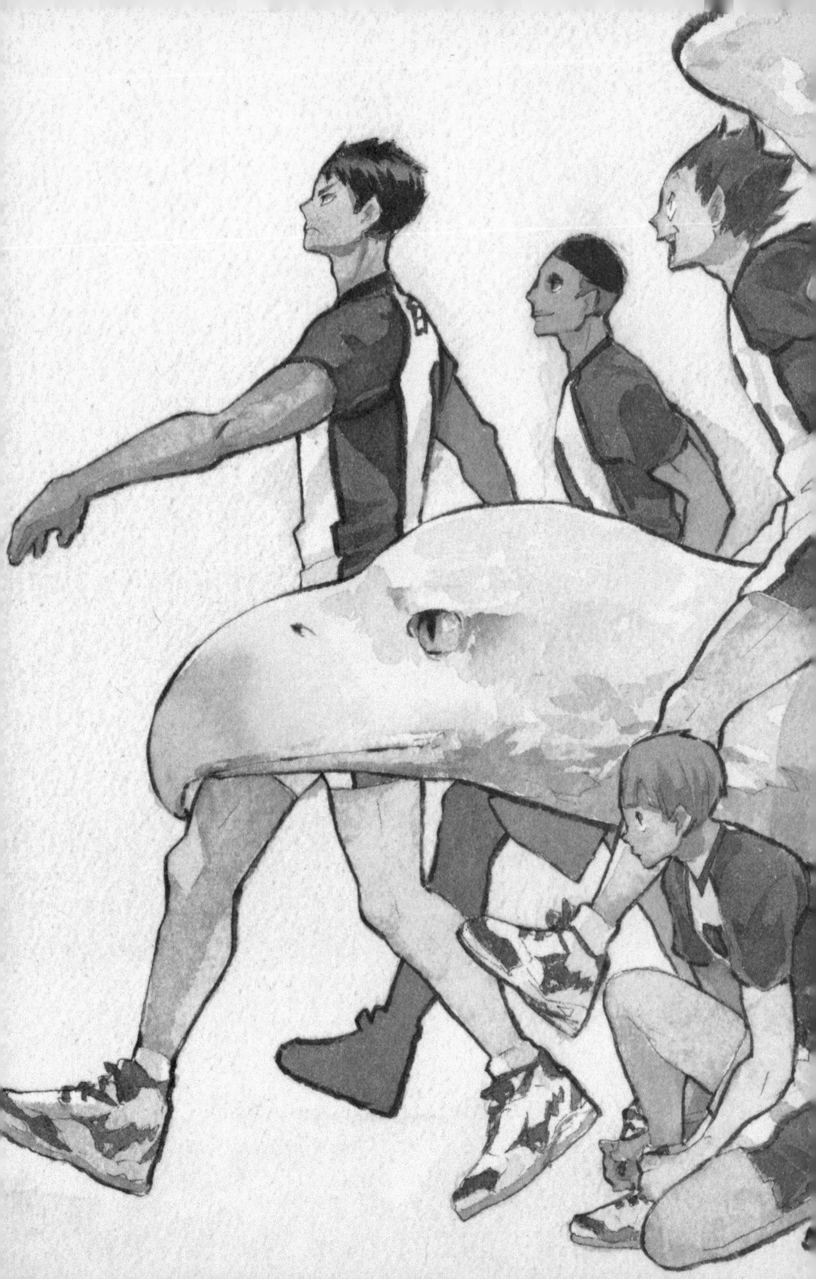

HAIKYU!!

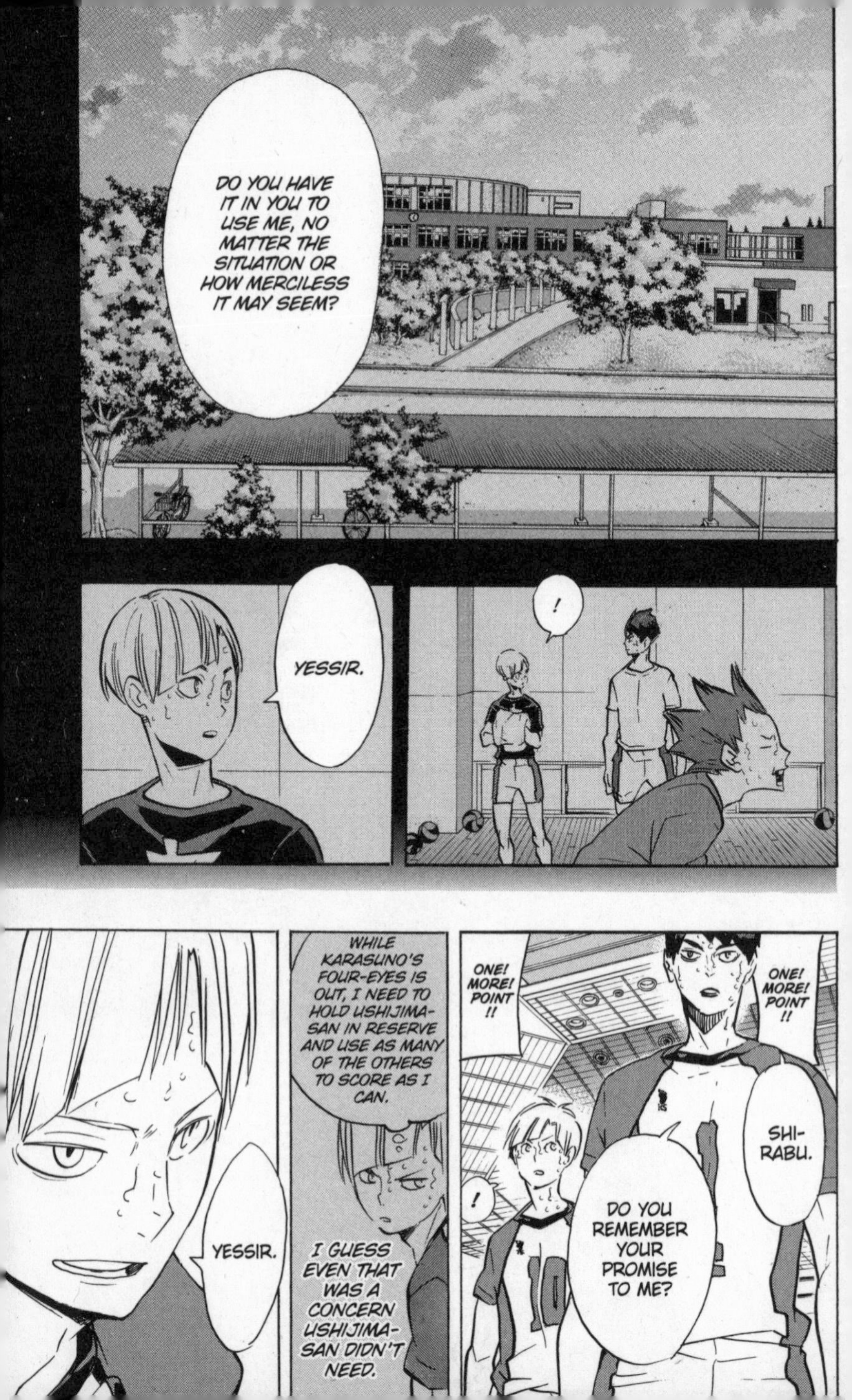
DO YOU HAVE IT IN YOU TO USE ME, NO MATTER THE SITUATION OR HOW MERCILESS IT MAY SEEM?
!
YESSIR.
ONE! MORE! POINT !!
ONE! MORE! POINT !!
SHI-RABU.
DO YOU REMEMBER YOUR PROMISE TO ME?
!
WHILE KARASUNO'S FOUR-EYES IS OUT, I NEED TO HOLD USHIJIMA-SAN IN RESERVE AND USE AS MANY OF THE OTHERS TO SCORE AS I CAN.
I GUESS EVEN THAT WAS A CONCERN USHIJIMA-SAN DIDN'T NEED.
YESSIR.

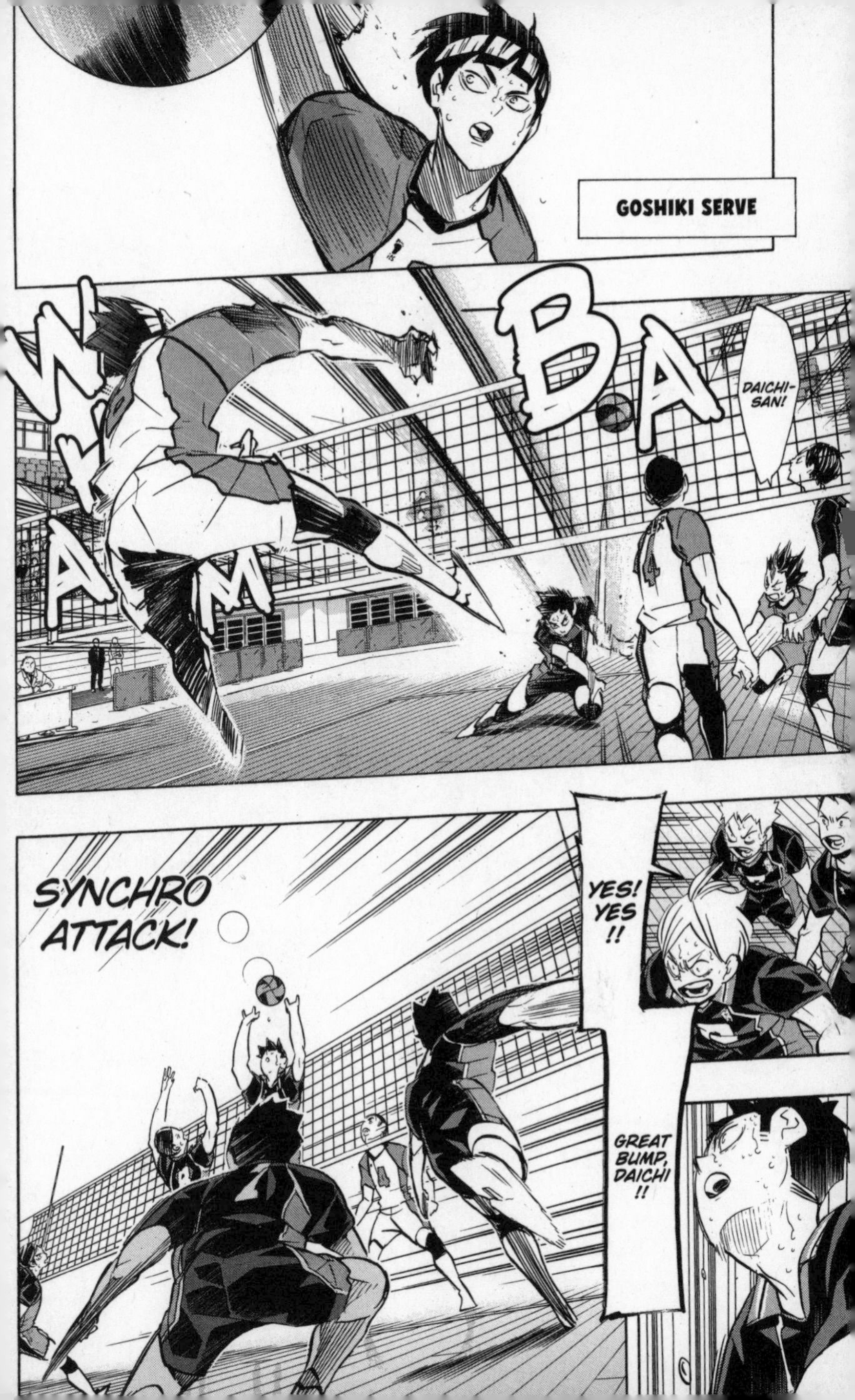
GOSHIKI SERVE
DAICHI-SAN!
BA
WHAM
YES! YES!!
SYNCHRO ATTACK!
GREAT BUMP, DAICHI!!

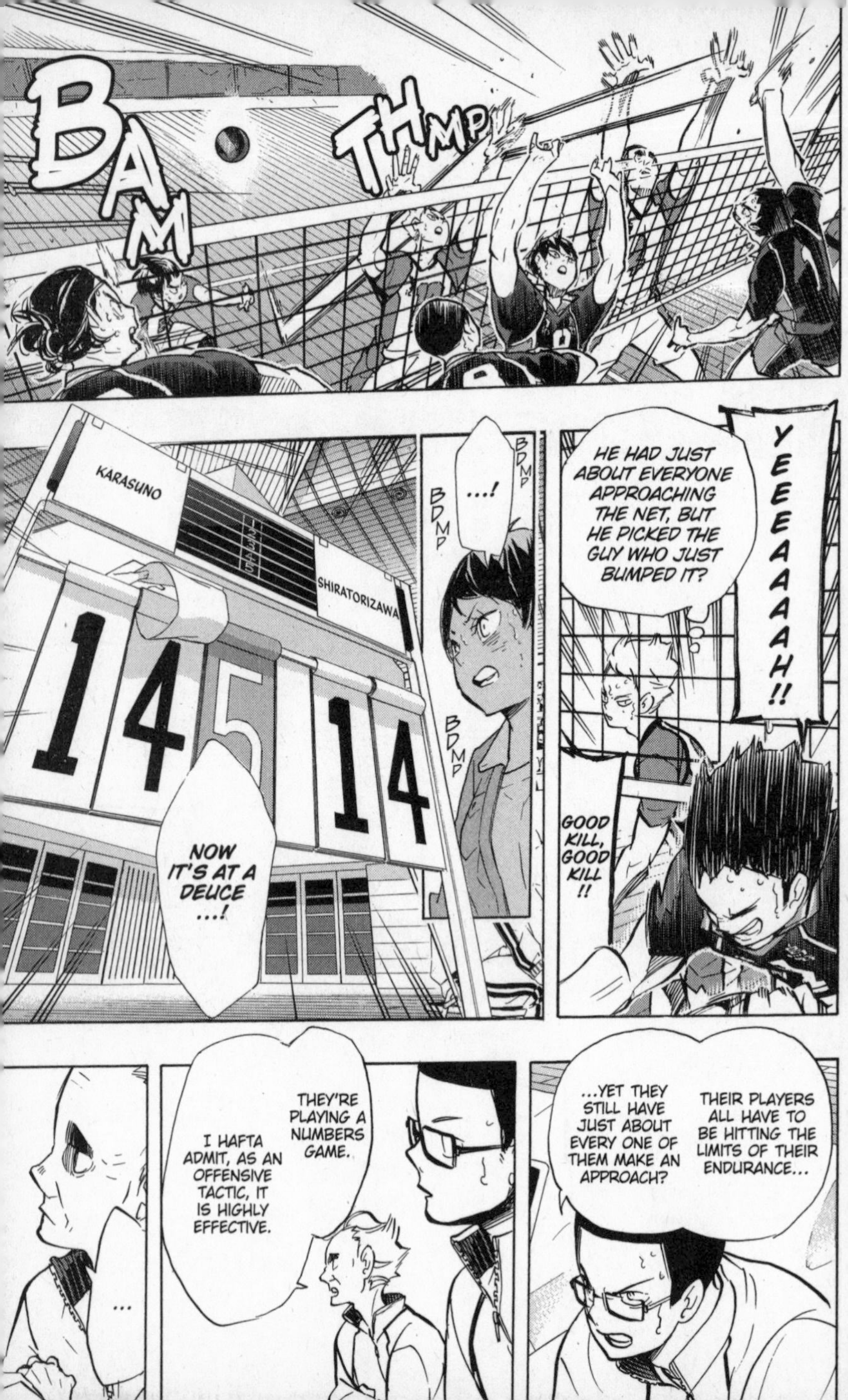
THMP
BAM
YEEEEAAAAAH!!
HE HAD JUST ABOUT EVERYONE APPROACHING THE NET, BUT HE PICKED THE GUY WHO JUST BUMPED IT?
GOOD KILL, GOOD KILL!!
BDMP
...!
BDMP
BDMP
KARASUNO
SHIRATORIZAWA
14
14
NOW IT'S AT A DEUCE...!
THEIR PLAYERS ALL HAVE TO BE HITTING THE LIMITS OF THEIR ENDURANCE...
...YET THEY STILL HAVE JUST ABOUT EVERY ONE OF THEM MAKE AN APPROACH?
THEY'RE PLAYING A NUMBERS GAME.
I HAFTA ADMIT, AS AN OFFENSIVE TACTIC, IT IS HIGHLY EFFECTIVE.
...

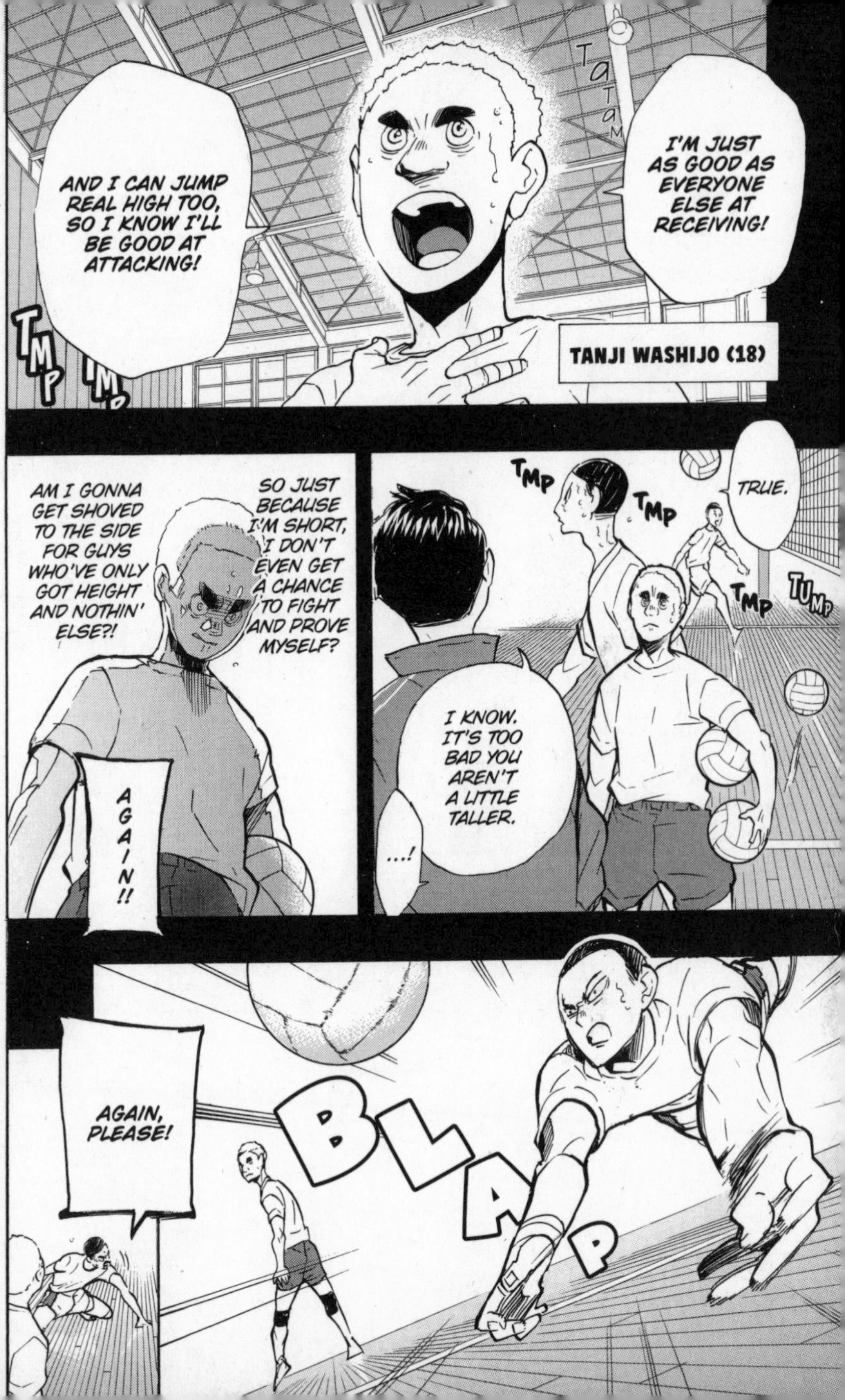
TaTaTaM
I'M JUST AS GOOD AS EVERYONE ELSE AT RECEIVING!
TANJI WASHIJO (18)
AND I CAN JUMP REAL HIGH TOO, SO I KNOW I'LL BE GOOD AT ATTACKING!
TMP
TRUE.
TMP
TMP
TMP
TUMP
I KNOW. IT'S TOO BAD YOU AREN'T A LITTLE TALLER.
...!
SO JUST BECAUSE I'M SHORT, I DON'T EVEN GET A CHANCE TO FIGHT AND PROVE MYSELF?
AM I GONNA GET SHOVED TO THE SIDE FOR GUYS WHO'VE ONLY GOT HEIGHT AND NOTHIN' ELSE?!
AGAIN!!
BLAP
AGAIN, PLEASE!

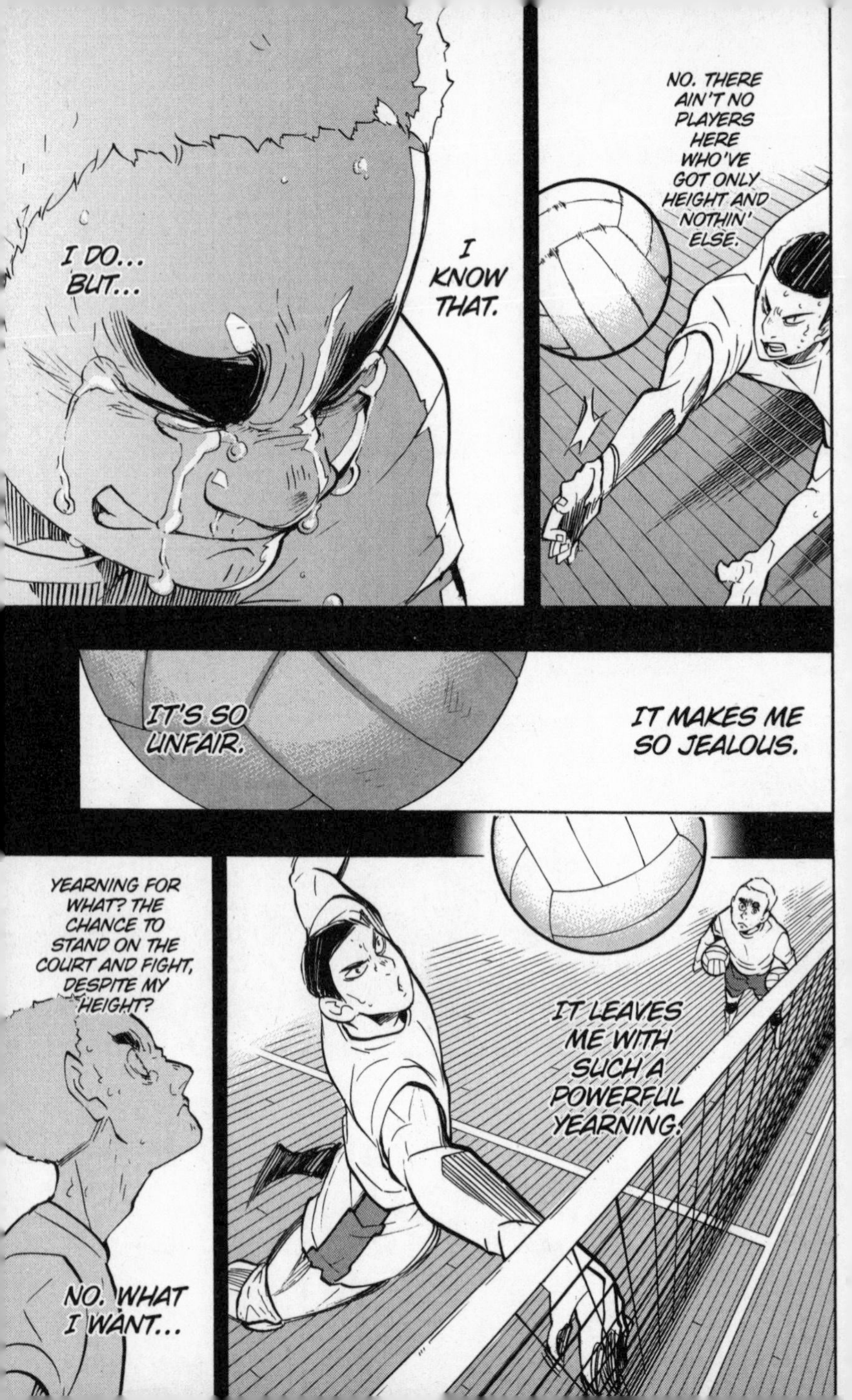
NO. THERE AIN'T NO PLAYERS HERE WHO'VE GOT ONLY HEIGHT AND NOTHIN' ELSE.
I KNOW THAT.
I DO... BUT...
IT MAKES ME SO JEALOUS.
IT'S SO UNFAIR.
IT LEAVES ME WITH SUCH A POWERFUL YEARNING.
YEARNING FOR WHAT? THE CHANCE TO STAND ON THE COURT AND FIGHT, DESPITE MY HEIGHT?
NO. WHAT I WANT...

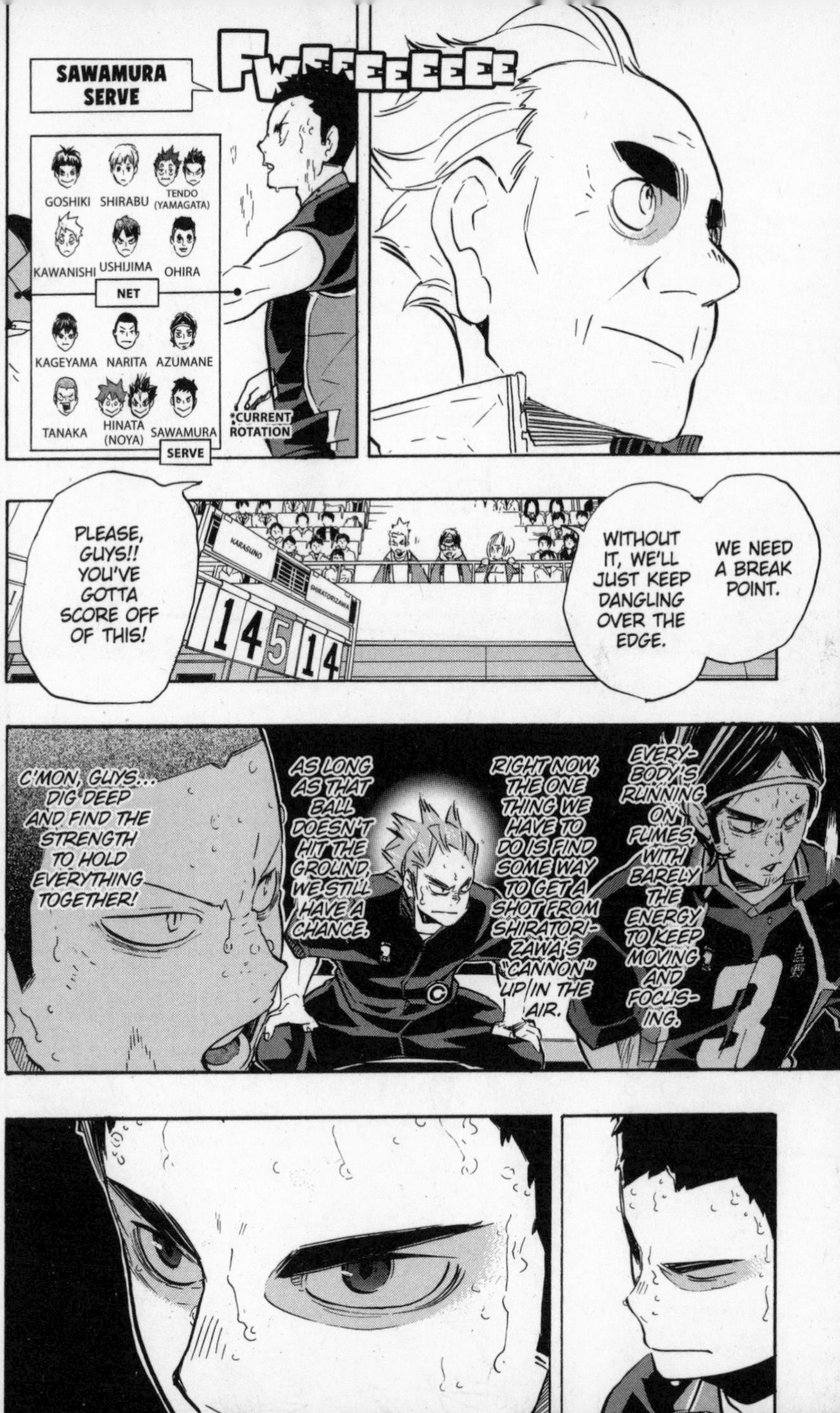
FWEEEEEEEE
SAWAMURA SERVE
GOSHIKI
SHIRABU
TENDO (YAMAGATA)
KAWANISHI
USHIJIMA
OHIRA
NET
KAGEYAMA
NARITA
AZUMANE
TANAKA
HINATA (NOYA)
SAWAMURA
SERVE
*CURRENT ROTATION
WE NEED A BREAK POINT.
WITHOUT IT, WE'LL JUST KEEP DANGLING OVER THE EDGE.
KARASUNO
SHIRATORIZAWA
14 5 14
PLEASE, GUYS!! YOU'VE GOTTA SCORE OFF OF THIS!
EVERYBODY'S RUNNING ON FUMES, WITH BARELY THE ENERGY TO KEEP MOVING AND FOCUSING.
RIGHT NOW, THE ONE THING WE HAVE TO DO IS FIND SOME WAY TO GET A SHOT FROM SHIRATORIZAWA'S "CANNON" UP IN THE AIR.
AS LONG AS THAT BALL DOESN'T HIT THE GROUND, WE STILL HAVE A CHANCE.
C'MON, GUYS... DIG DEEP AND FIND THE STRENGTH TO HOLD EVERYTHING TOGETHER!

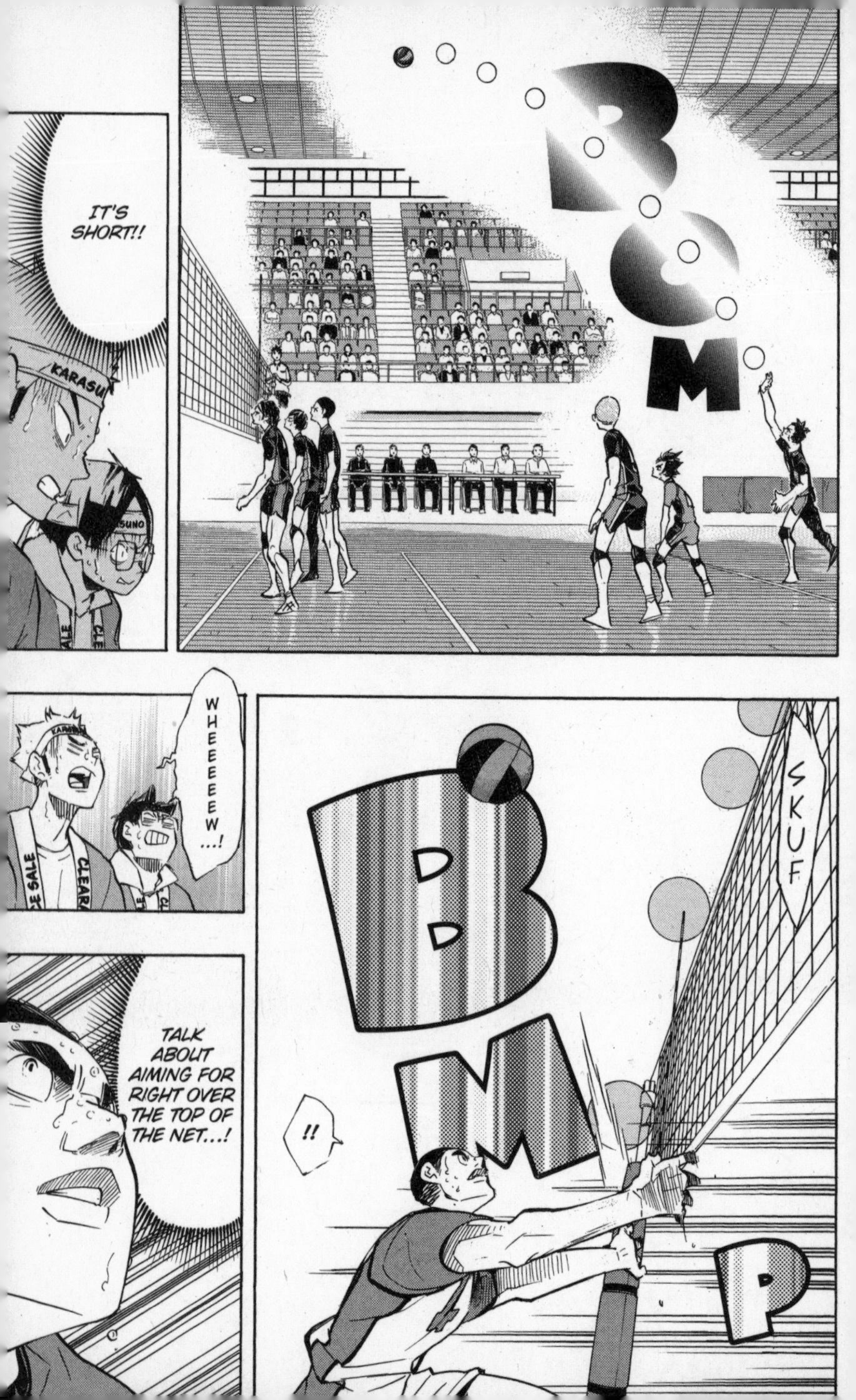
BOOM
IT'S SHORT!!
SKUF
BOMP
!!
WHEEEEEW...!
TALK ABOUT AIMING FOR RIGHT OVER THE TOP OF THE NET...!

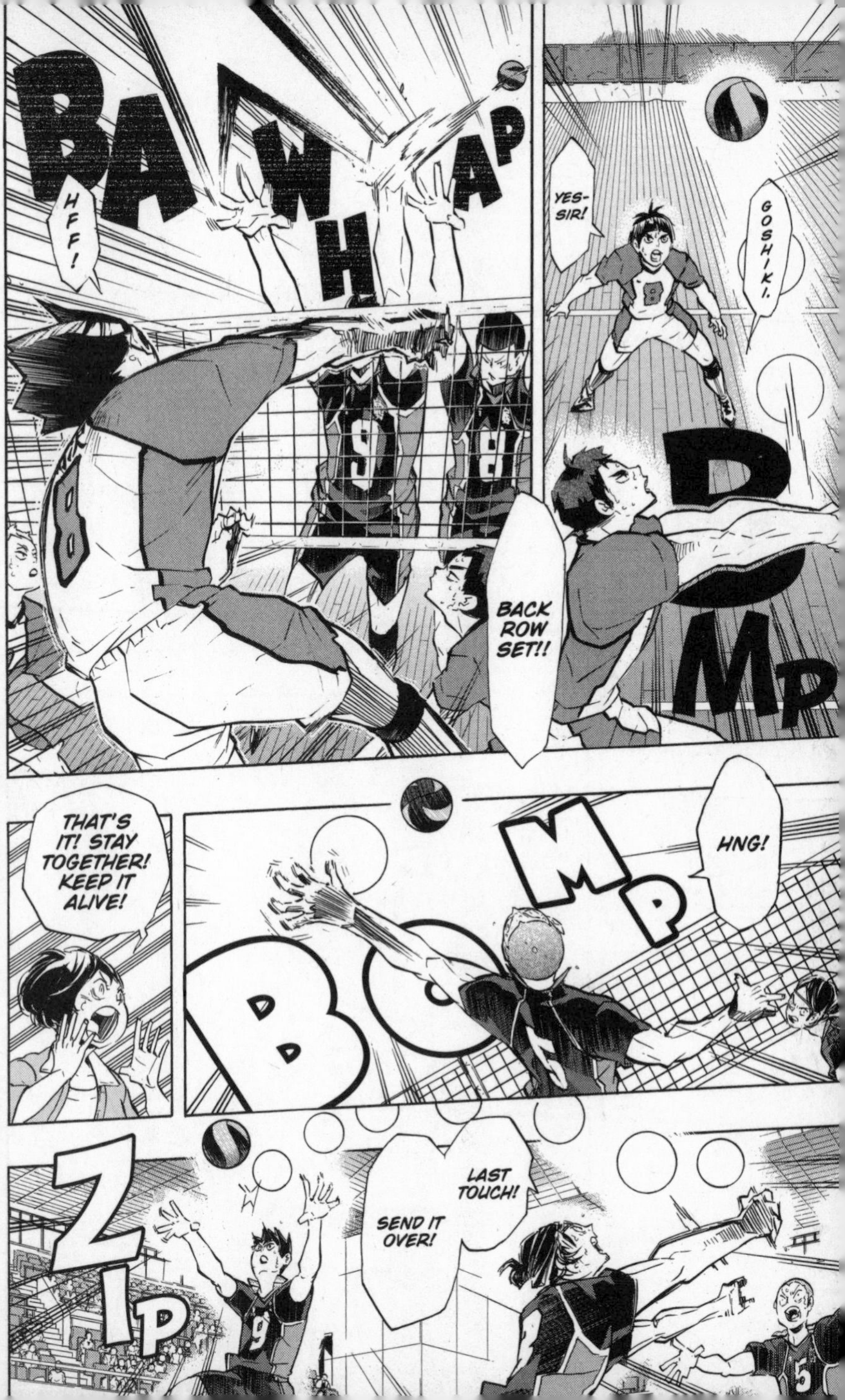
GOSHIKI!
YES-SIR!
DMP
BACK ROW SET!!
BAWHAP
HFF!
HNG!
BOMP
THAT'S IT! STAY TOGETHER! KEEP IT ALIVE!
LAST TOUCH!
SEND IT OVER!
ZIP

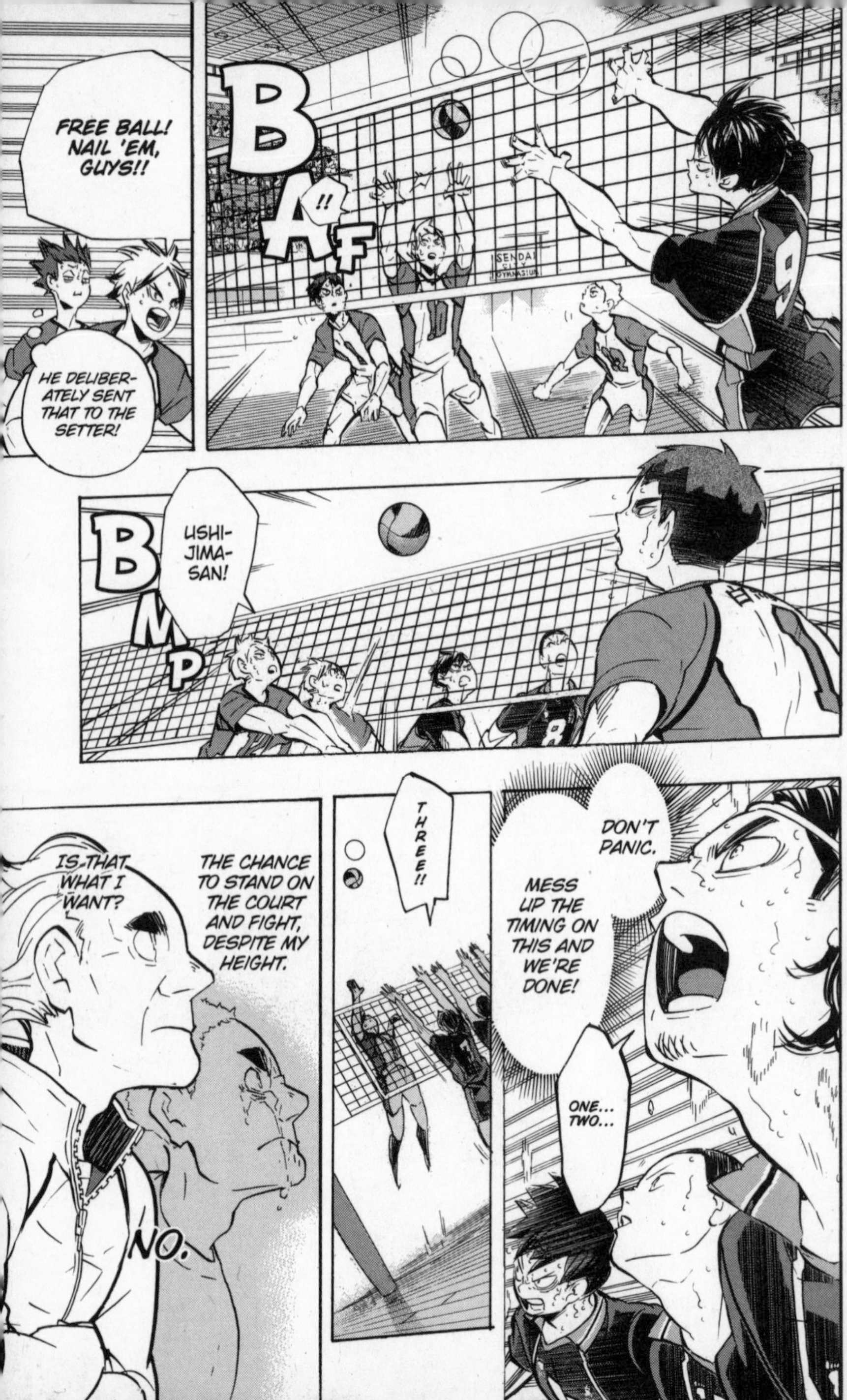
BAF
!!
FREE BALL! NAIL 'EM, GUYS!!
HE DELIBERATELY SENT THAT TO THE SETTER!
SENDAI CITY GYMNASIUM
BUMP
USHIJIMA-SAN!
DON'T PANIC.
MESS UP THE TIMING ON THIS AND WE'RE DONE!
ONE... TWO...
THREE!!
THE CHANCE TO STAND ON THE COURT AND FIGHT, DESPITE MY HEIGHT.
IS THAT WHAT I WANT?
NO.

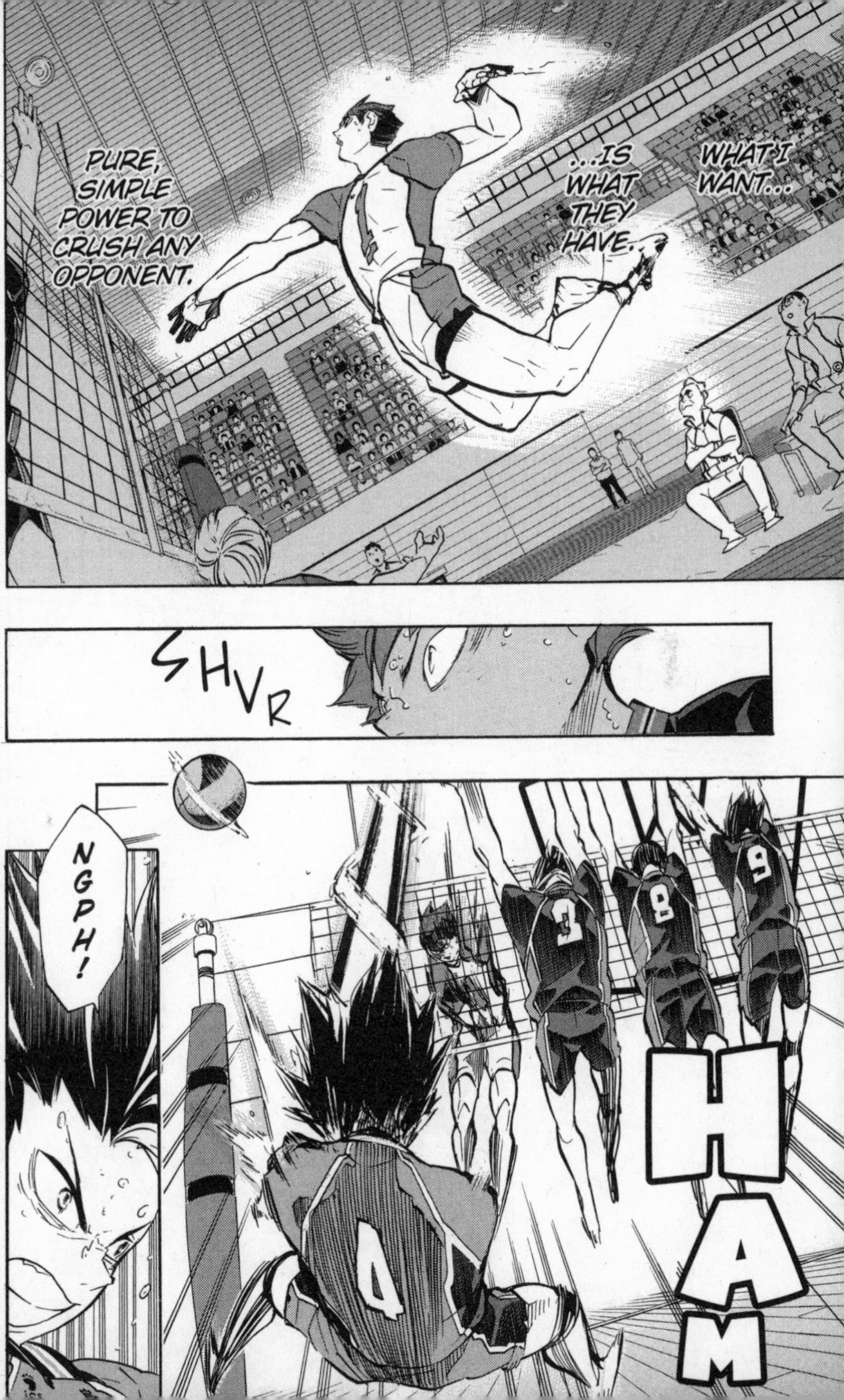
WHAT I WANT...
...IS WHAT THEY HAVE.
PURE, SIMPLE POWER TO CRUSH ANY OPPONENT.
SHVR
HAM
NGPH!

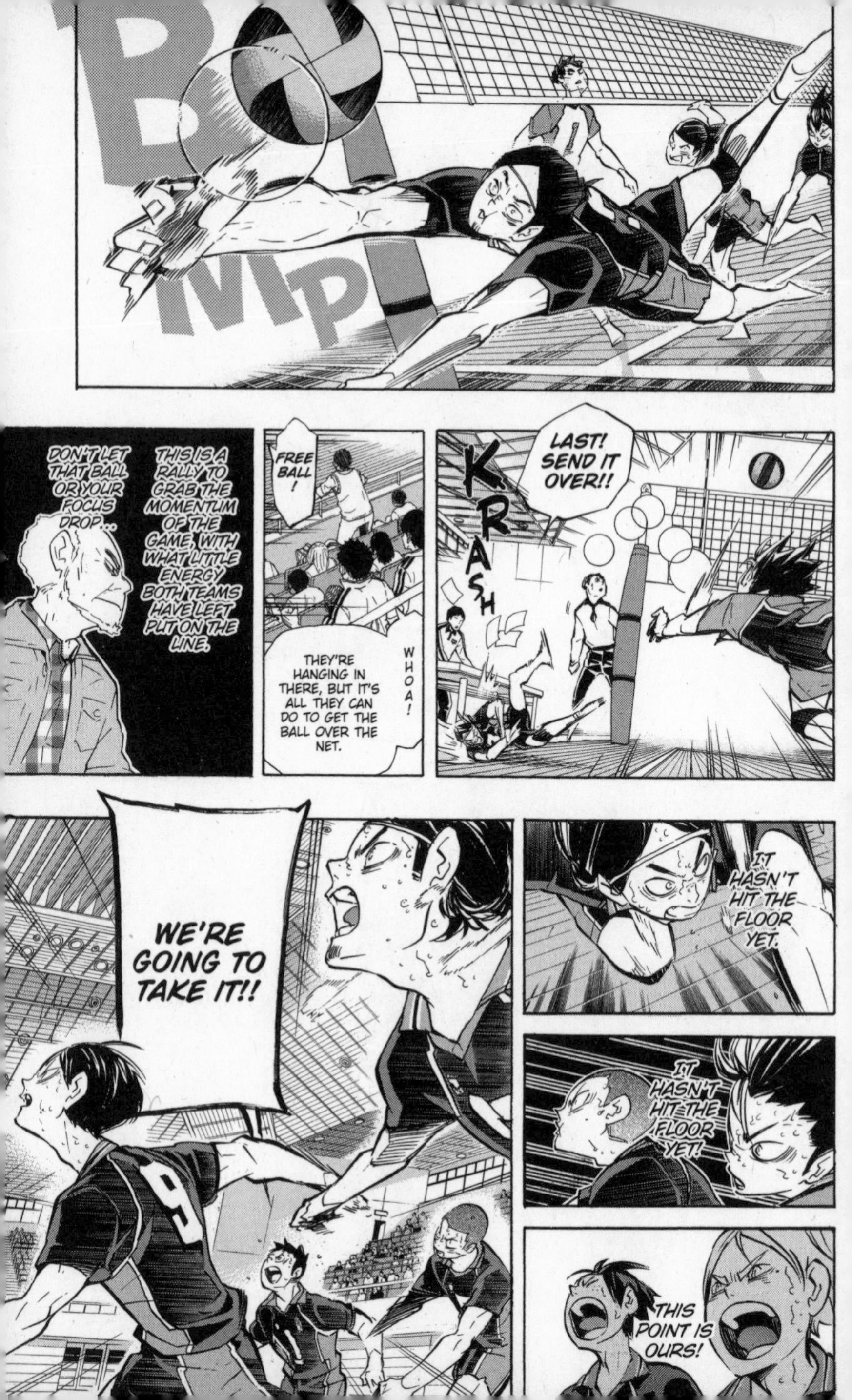
BOMP
LAST! SEND IT OVER!!
KRASH
FREE BALL!
WHOA!
THEY'RE HANGING IN THERE, BUT IT'S ALL THEY CAN DO TO GET THE BALL OVER THE NET.
THIS IS A RALLY TO GRAB THE MOMENTUM OF THE GAME, WITH WHAT LITTLE ENERGY BOTH TEAMS HAVE LEFT PUT ON THE LINE.
DON'T LET THAT BALL OR YOUR FOCUS DROP...
IT HASN'T HIT THE FLOOR YET.
IT HASN'T HIT THE FLOOR YET!
THIS POINT IS OURS!
WE'RE GOING TO TAKE IT!!

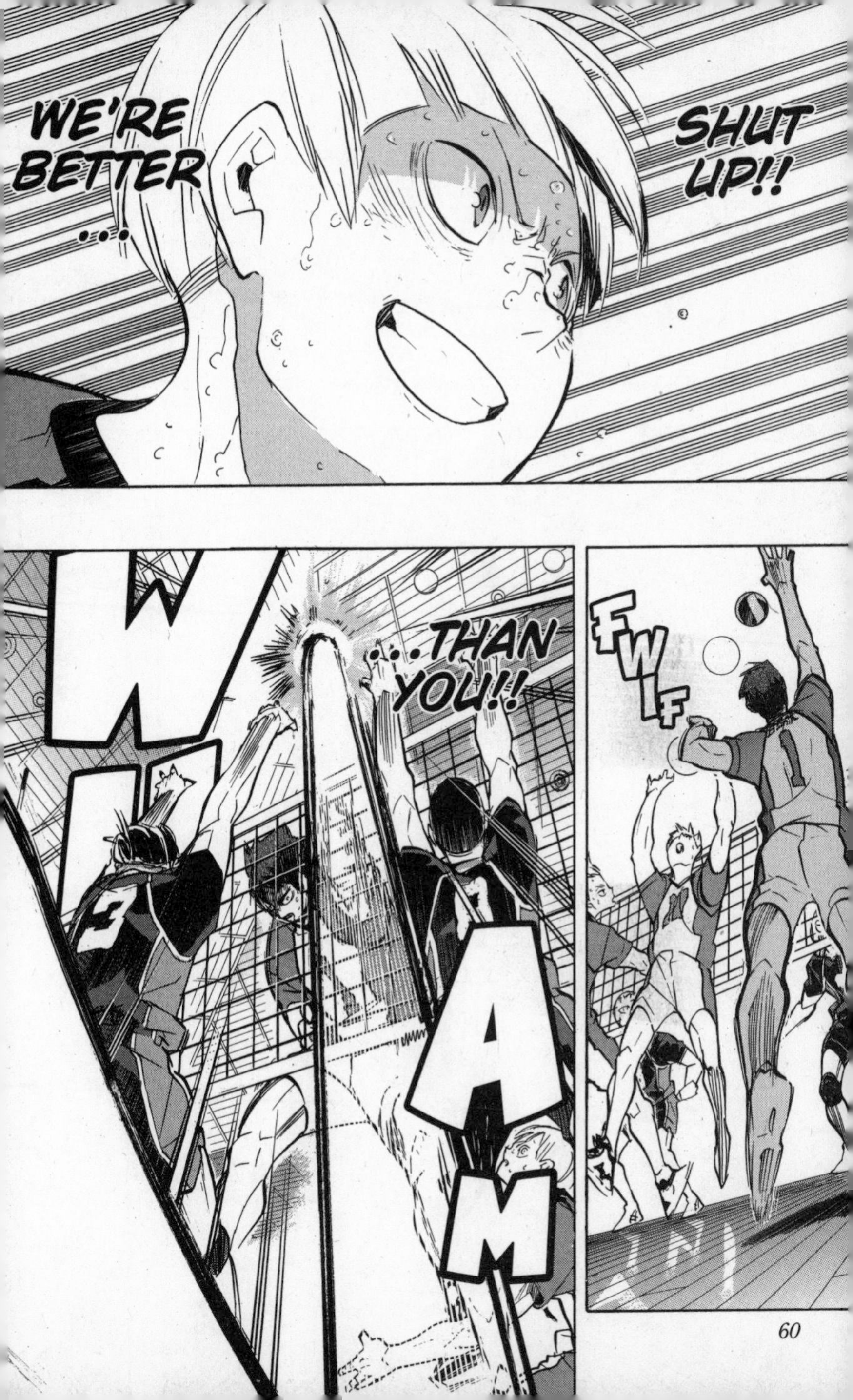
SHUT UP!!
WE'RE BETTER ...
FWIF
...THAN YOU!!
WHAM

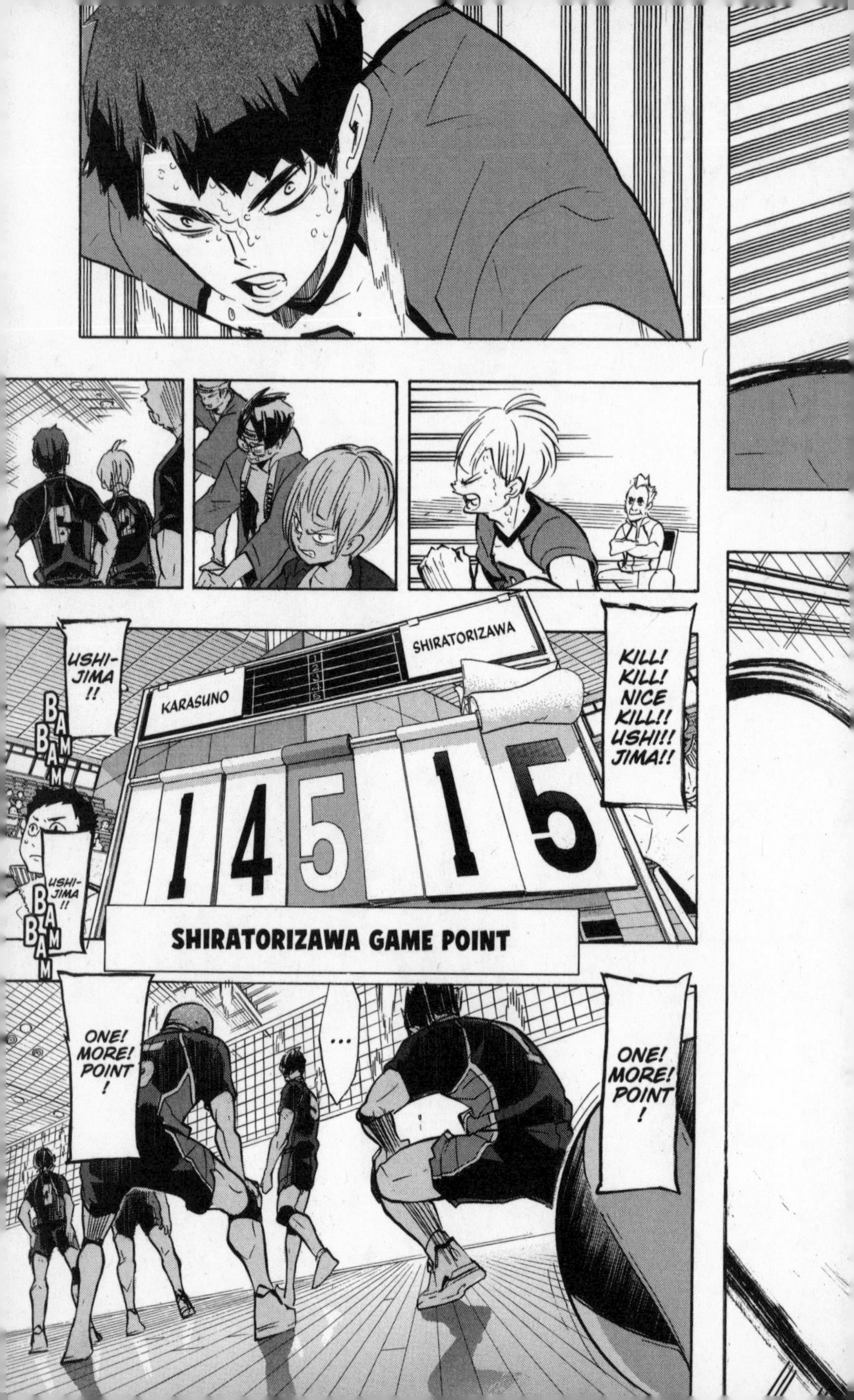
KILL! KILL! NICE KILL!! USHI!!! JIMA!!
SHIRATORIZAWA
KARASUNO
1
2
3
4
5
14 5 1 5
USHI-JIMA!!
BAM BAM
USHI-JIMA!!
BAM BAM
SHIRATORIZAWA GAME POINT
ONE! MORE! POINT!
...
ONE! MORE! POINT!

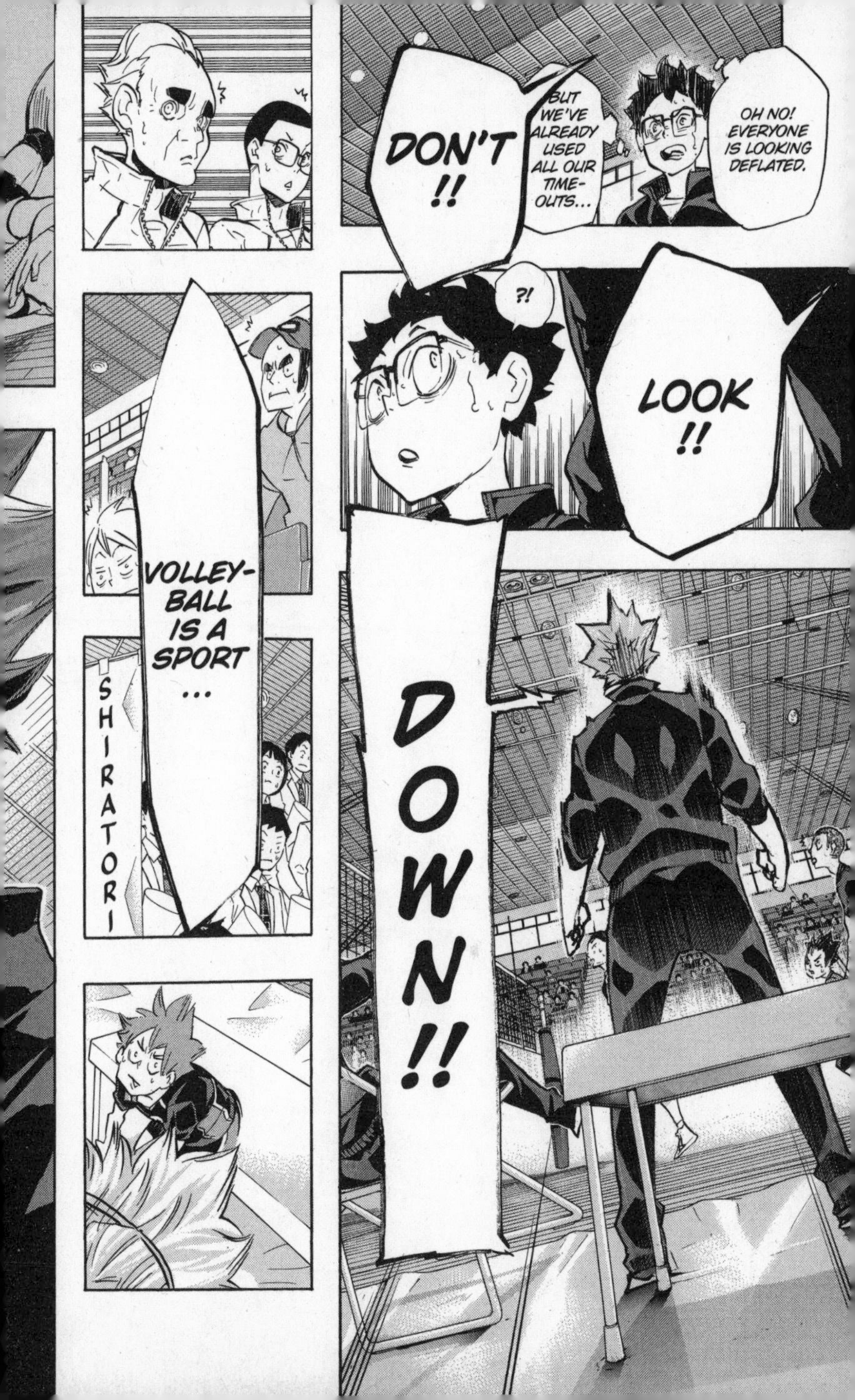
OH NO! EVERYONE IS LOOKING DEFLATED.
BUT WE'VE ALREADY USED ALL OUR TIME-OUTS...
DON'T !!
LOOK !!
?!
DOWN!!
VOLLEY-BALL IS A SPORT ...
SHIRATORI

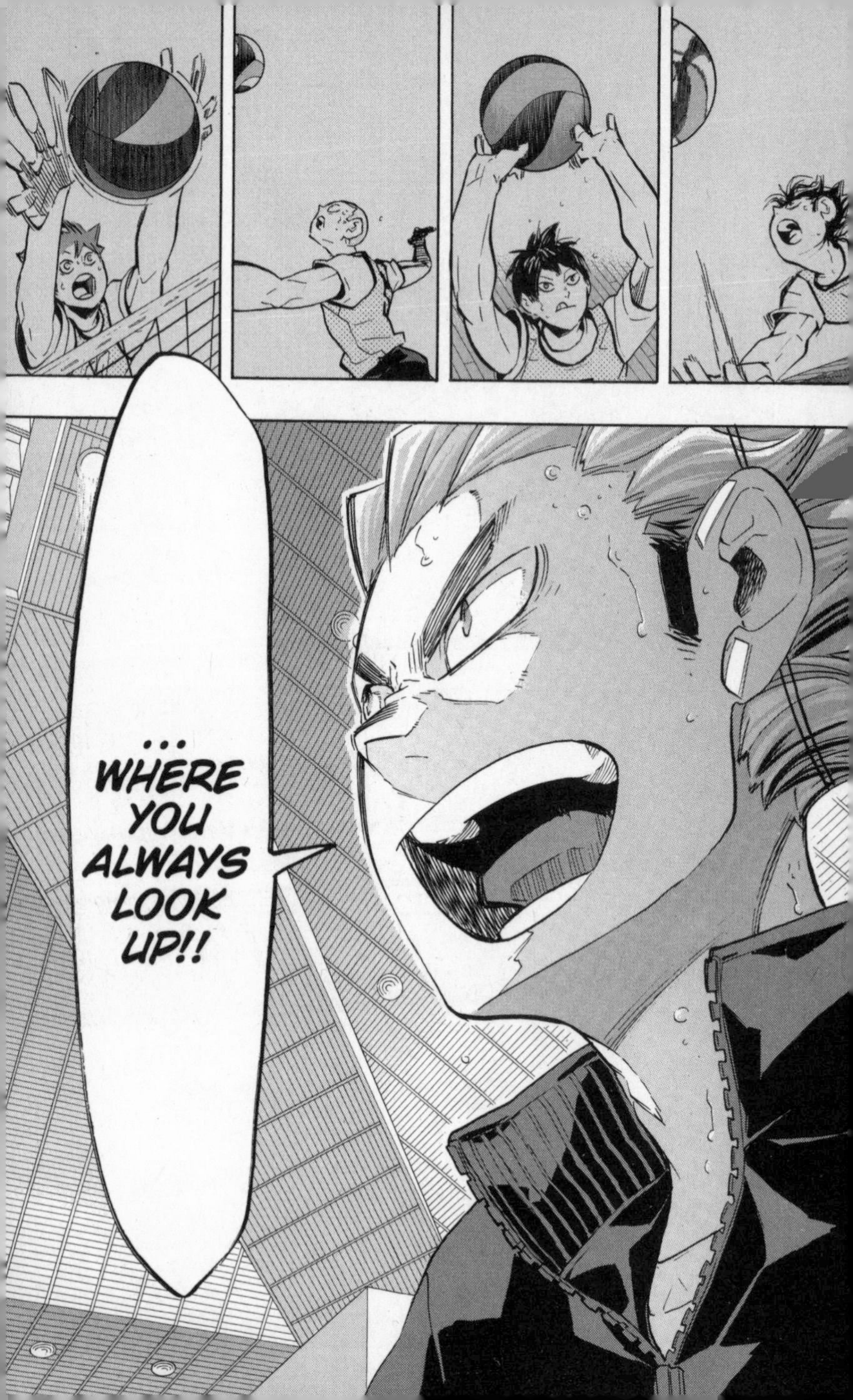
...WHERE YOU ALWAYS LOOK UP!!

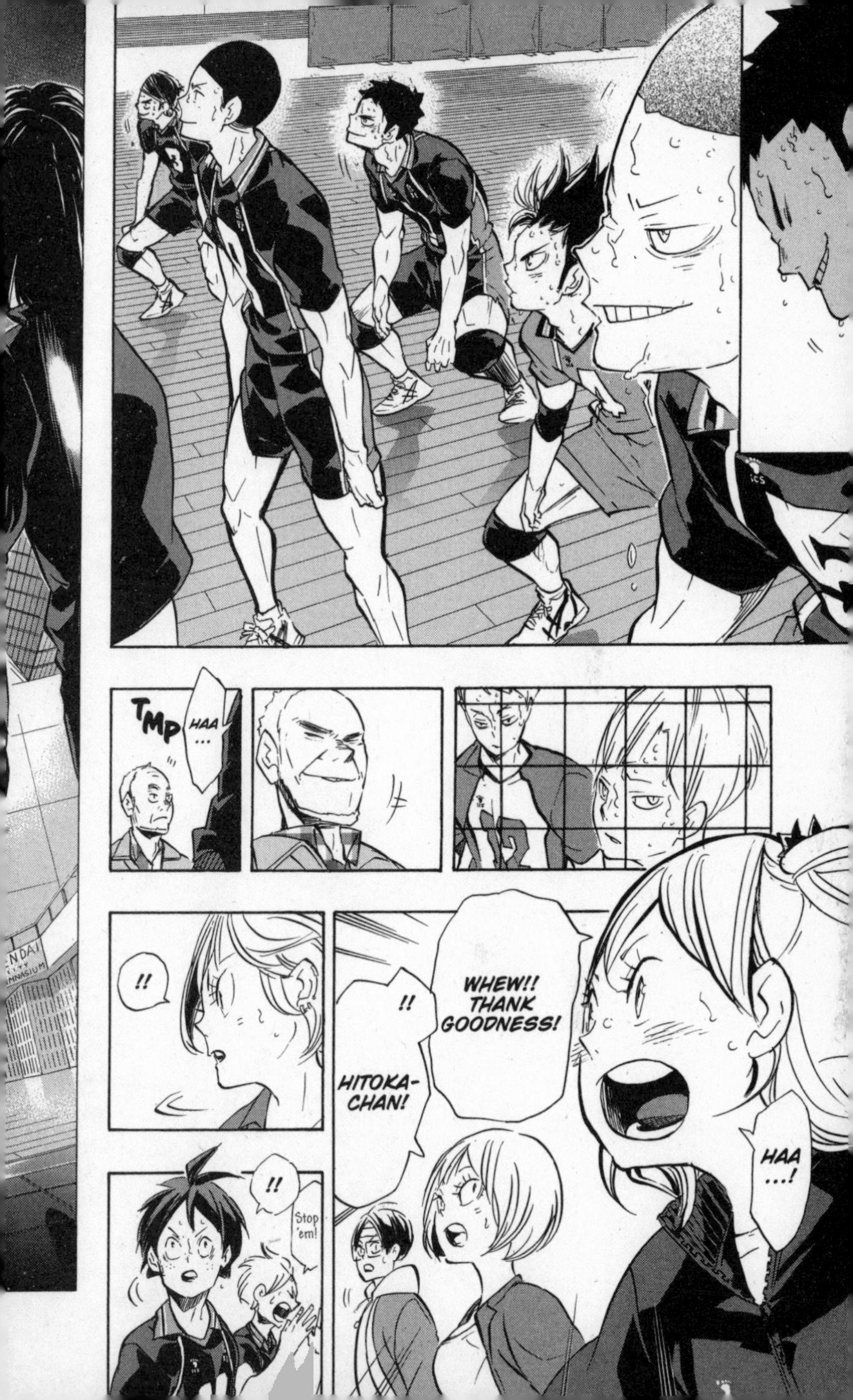
TMP
HAA...
WHEW!! THANK GOODNESS!
HAA...!
!!
HITOKA-CHAN!
!!
!!
Stop 'em!

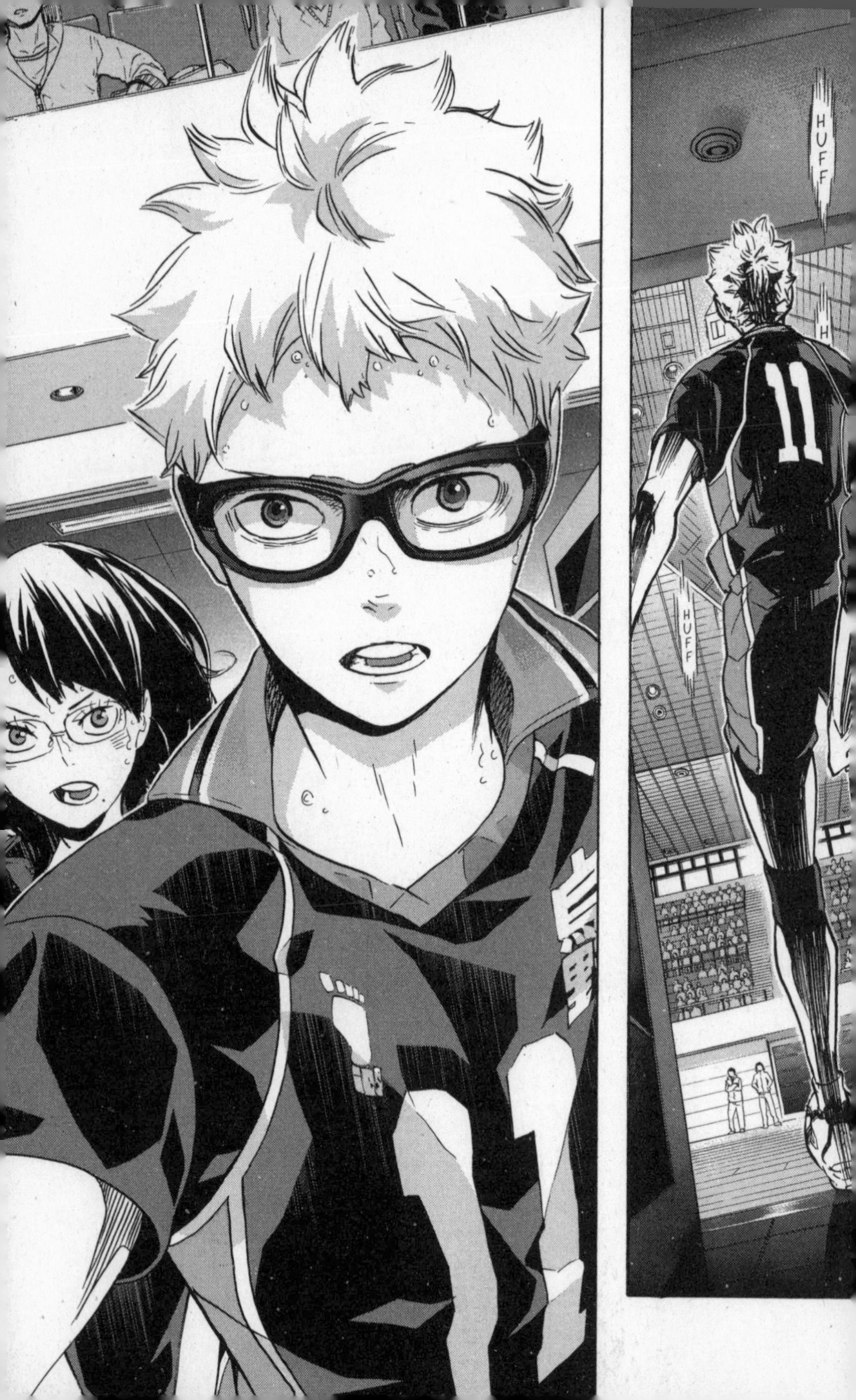
HUFF
HUFF

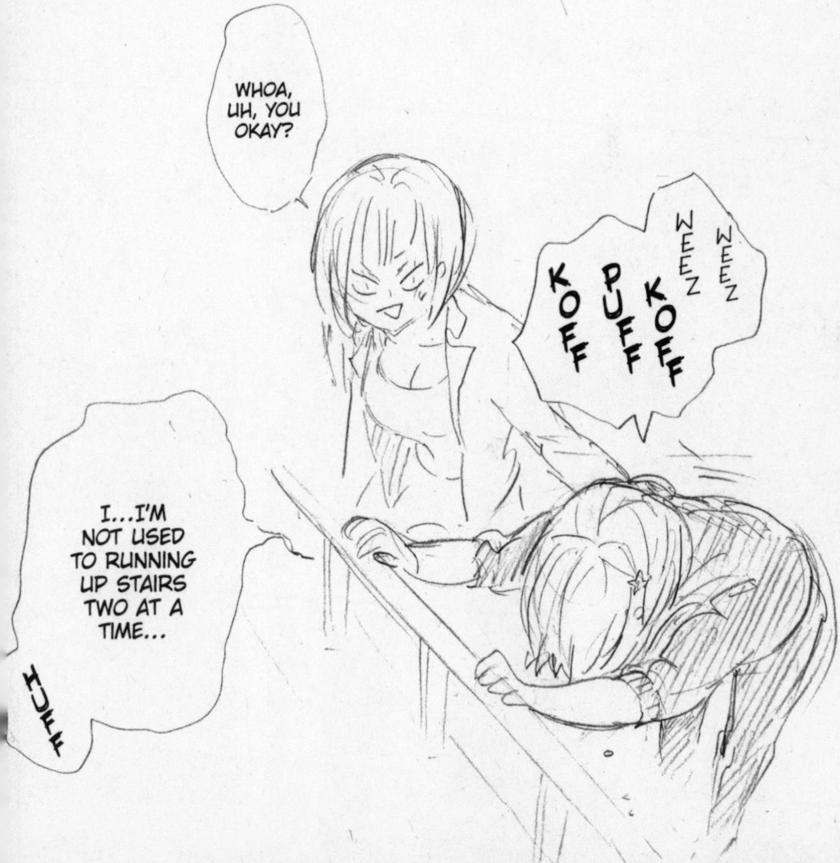
WHOA, UH, YOU OKAY?
KOFF PUFF KOFF WEEZ WEEZ
I...I'M NOT USED TO RUNNING UP STAIRS TWO AT A TIME...
HUFF

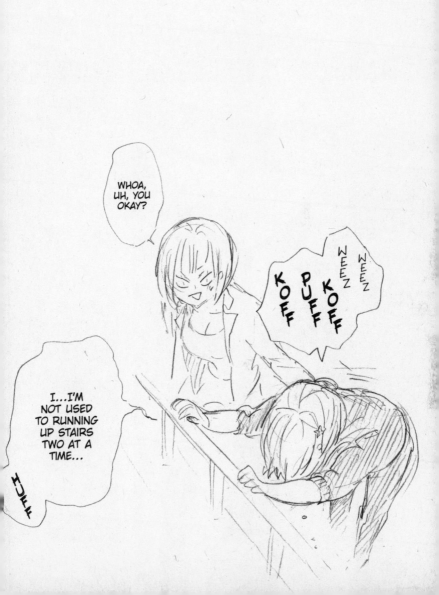

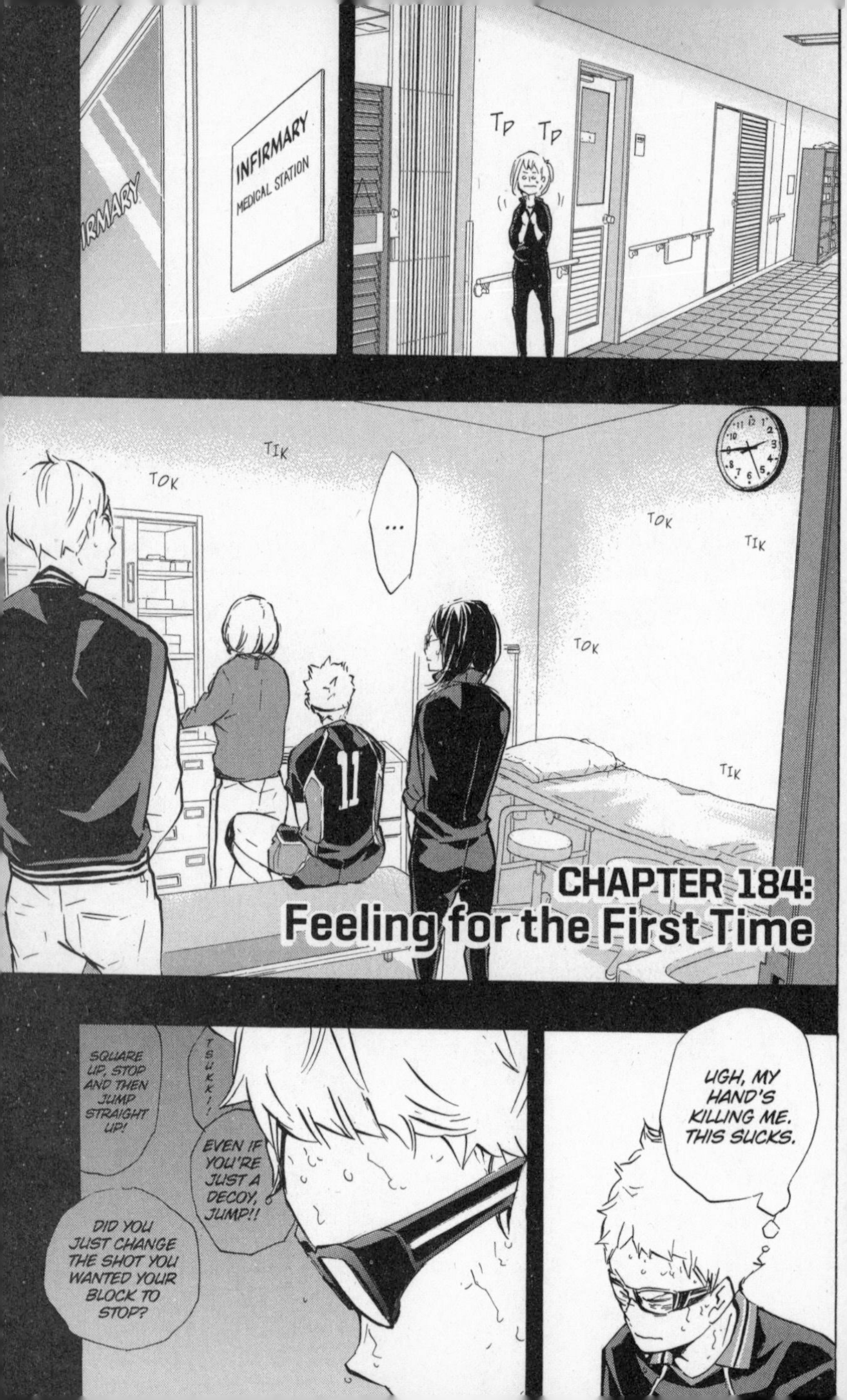
TP TP
INFIRMARY
MEDICAL STATION
IRMARY
TIK
TOK
...
TOK
TIK
TOK
TIK
CHAPTER 184:
Feeling for the First Time
UGH, MY HAND'S KILLING ME. THIS SUCKS.
TSUKKI!
SQUARE UP, STOP AND THEN JUMP STRAIGHT UP!
EVEN IF YOU'RE JUST A DECOY, JUMP!!
DID YOU JUST CHANGE THE SHOT YOU WANTED YOUR BLOCK TO STOP?

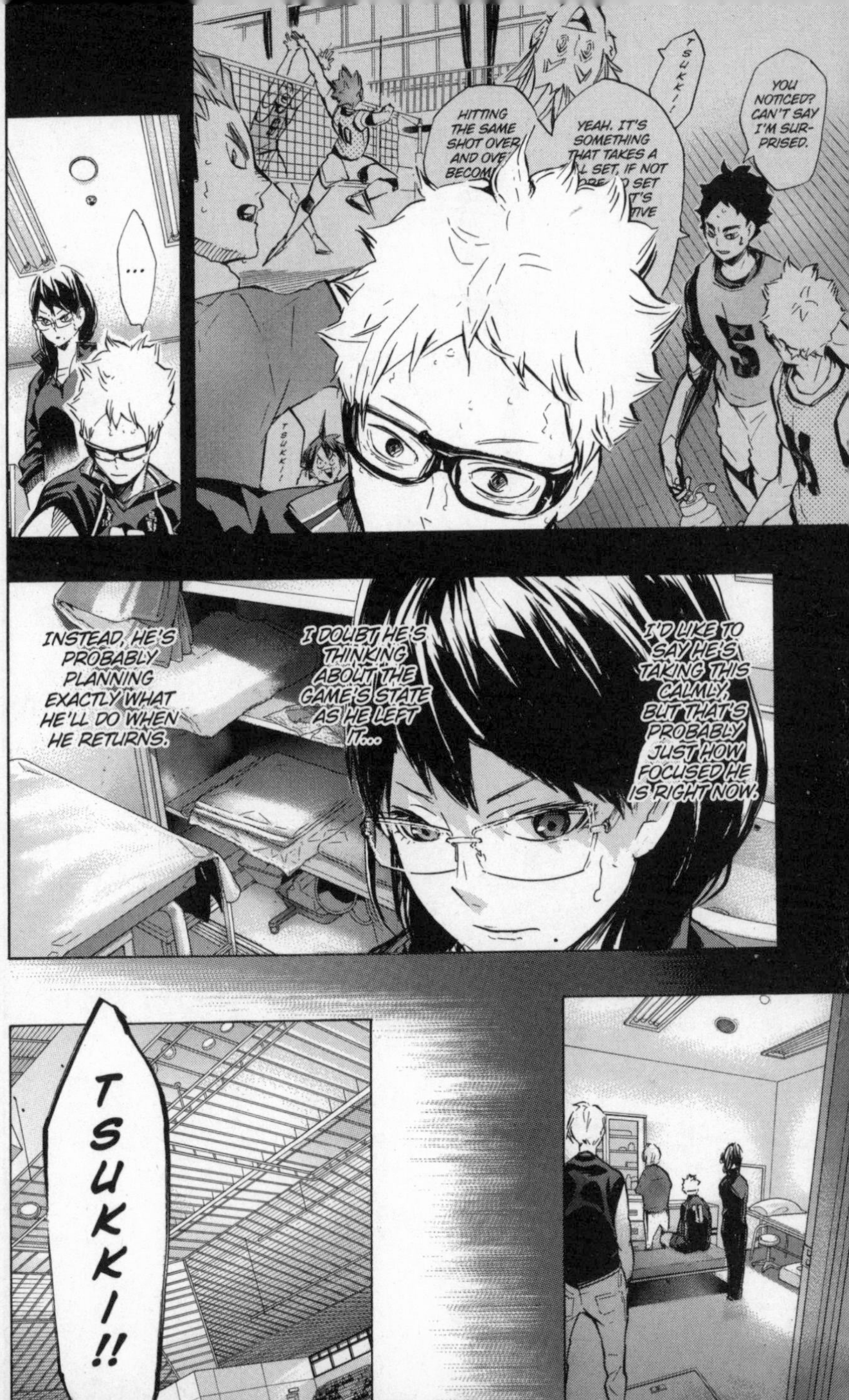
YOU NOTICED? CAN'T SAY I'M SURPRISED.
TSUKKI!!
YEAH. IT'S SOMETHING THAT TAKES A
SET, IF NOT
SET
TIVE
HITTING THE SAME SHOT OVER AND OVE
BECOM
TSUKKI!
...
I'D LIKE TO SAY HE'S TAKING THIS CALMLY, BUT THAT'S PROBABLY JUST HOW FOCUSED HE IS RIGHT NOW.
I DOUBT HE'S THINKING ABOUT THE GAME'S STATE AS HE LEFT IT...
INSTEAD, HE'S PROBABLY PLANNING EXACTLY WHAT HE'LL DO WHEN HE RETURNS.
TSUKKI!!

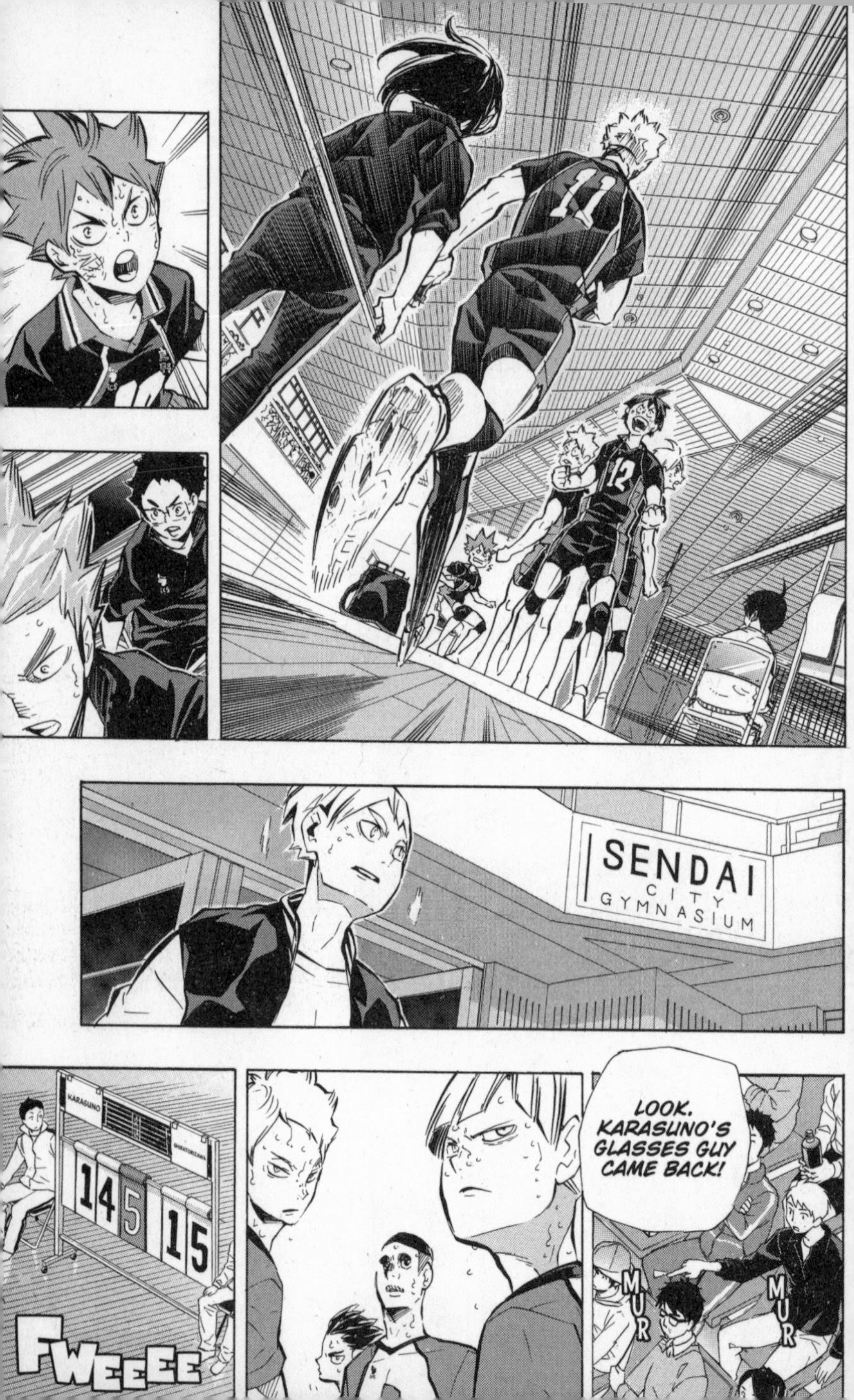
SENDAI CITY GYMNASIUM
LOOK. KARASUNO'S GLASSES GUY CAME BACK!
MUR
MUR
KARASUNO
14
5
15
FWEEEE

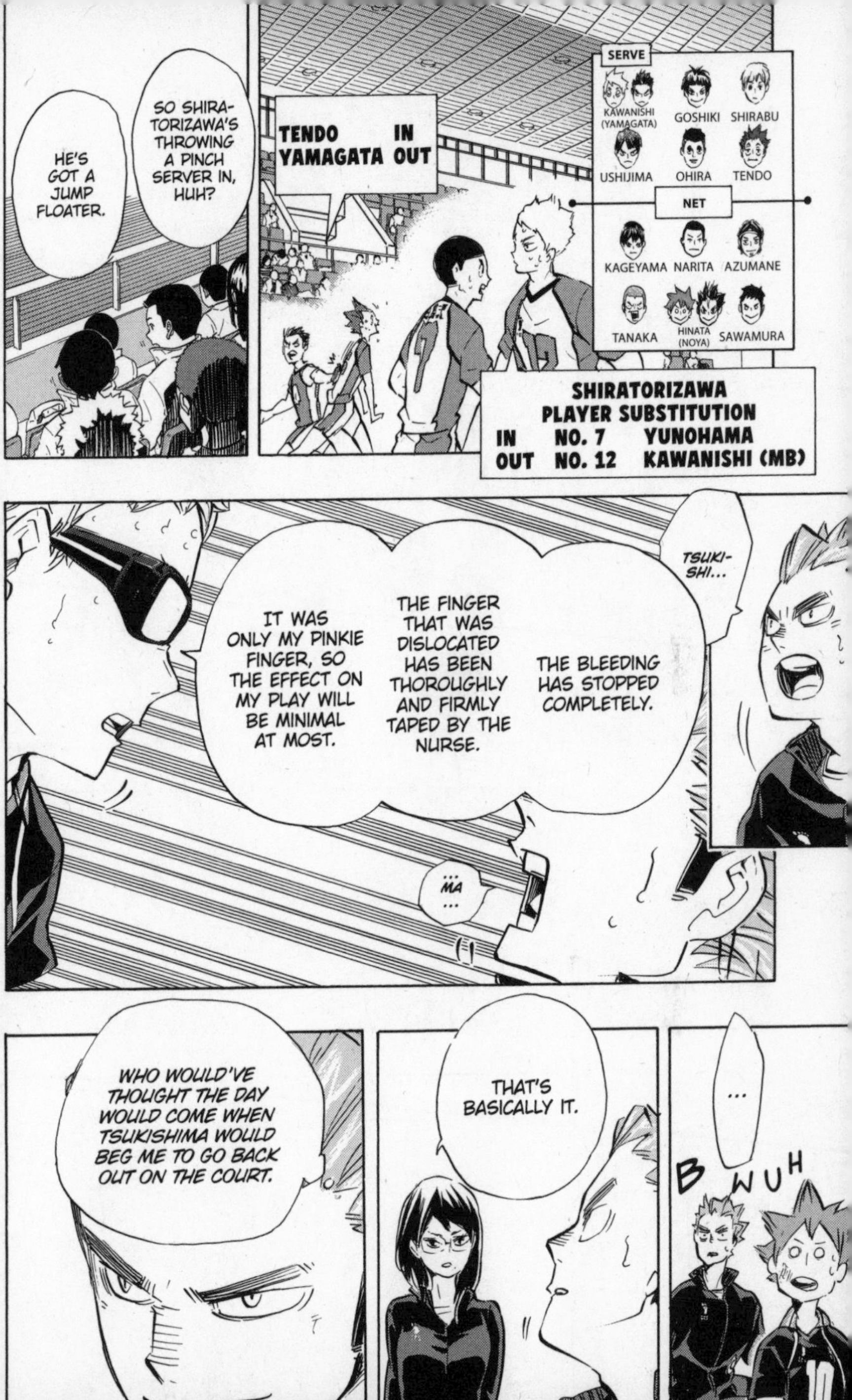
TENDO IN
YAMAGATA OUT
SERVE
KAWANISHI (YAMAGATA)
GOSHIKI
SHIRABU
USHIJIMA
OHIRA
TENDO
NET
KAGEYAMA
NARITA
AZUMANE
TANAKA
HINATA (NOYA)
SAWAMURA
SHIRATORIZAWA PLAYER SUBSTITUTION
IN NO. 7 YUNOHAMA
OUT NO. 12 KAWANISHI (MB)
SO SHIRATORIZAWA'S THROWING A PINCH SERVER IN, HUH?
HE'S GOT A JUMP FLOATER.
TSUKISHI...
THE BLEEDING HAS STOPPED COMPLETELY.
THE FINGER THAT WAS DISLOCATED HAS BEEN THOROUGHLY AND FIRMLY TAPED BY THE NURSE.
IT WAS ONLY MY PINKIE FINGER, SO THE EFFECT ON MY PLAY WILL BE MINIMAL AT MOST.
...MA...
...
BWUH
THAT'S BASICALLY IT.
WHO WOULD'VE THOUGHT THE DAY WOULD COME WHEN TSUKISHIMA WOULD BEG ME TO GO BACK OUT ON THE COURT.

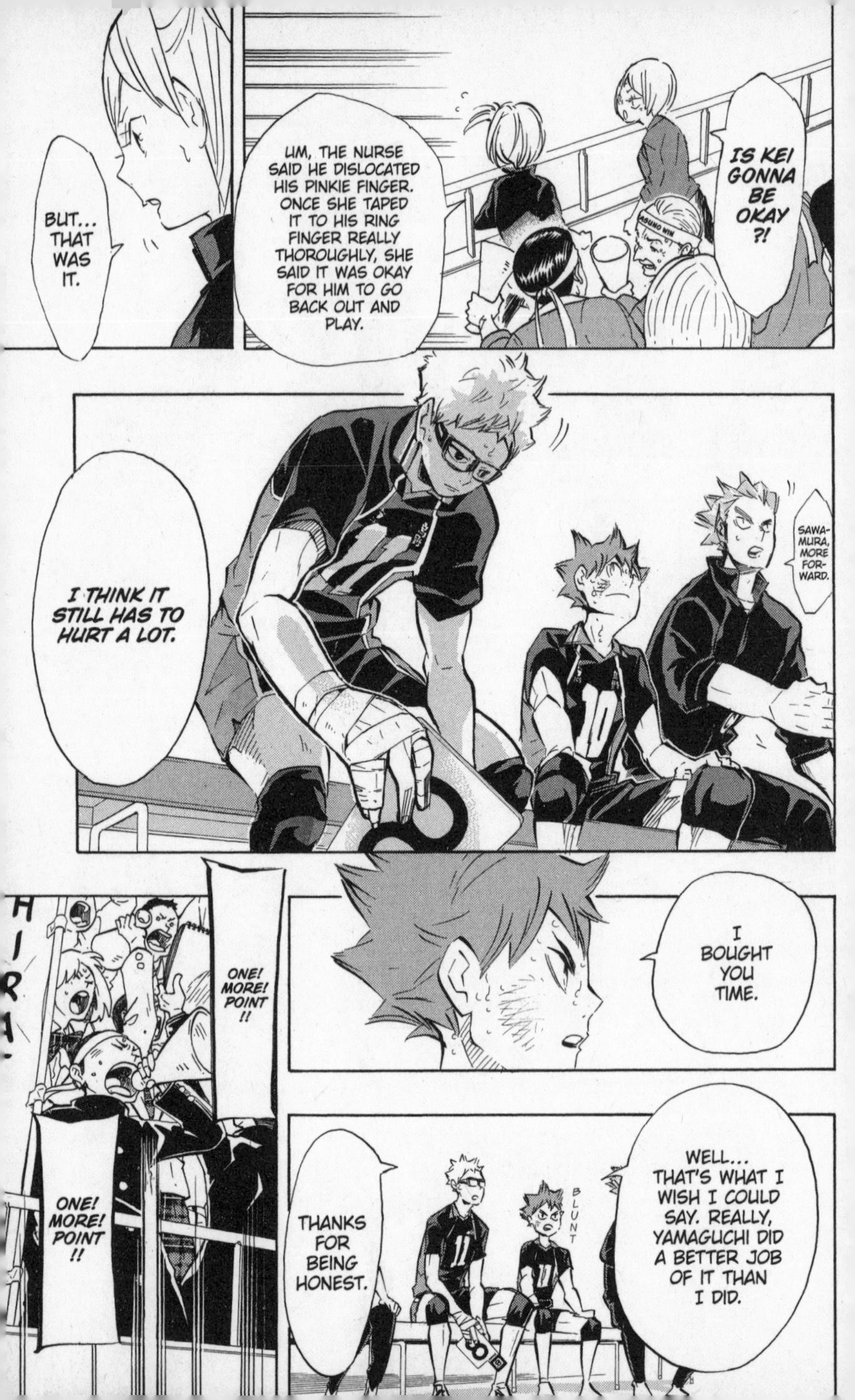
IS KEI GONNA BE OKAY?!
UM, THE NURSE SAID HE DISLOCATED HIS PINKIE FINGER. ONCE SHE TAPED IT TO HIS RING FINGER REALLY THOROUGHLY, SHE SAID IT WAS OKAY FOR HIM TO GO BACK OUT AND PLAY.
BUT... THAT WAS IT.
SAWAMURA, MORE FORWARD.
I THINK IT STILL HAS TO HURT A LOT.
I BOUGHT YOU TIME.
WELL... THAT'S WHAT I WISH I COULD SAY. REALLY, YAMAGUCHI DID A BETTER JOB OF IT THAN I DID.
BLUNT
THANKS FOR BEING HONEST.
ONE! MORE! POINT!!
ONE! MORE! POINT!!

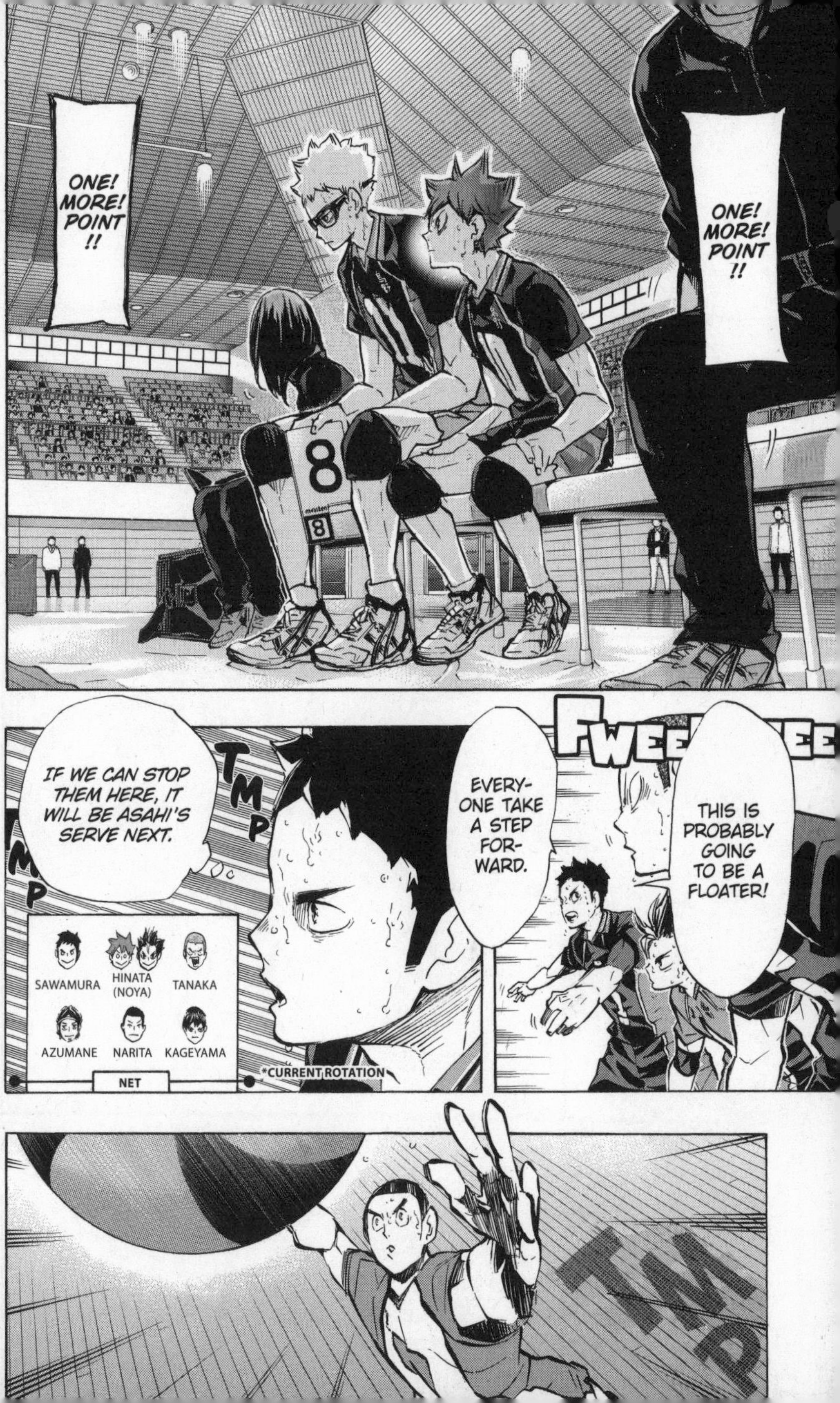
ONE! MORE! POINT!!
ONE! MORE! POINT!!
FWEE
EE
THIS IS PROBABLY GOING TO BE A FLOATER!
EVERY-ONE TAKE A STEP FOR-WARD.
TMP
IF WE CAN STOP THEM HERE, IT WILL BE ASAHI'S SERVE NEXT.
TMP
SAWAMURA
HINATA (NOYA)
TANAKA
AZUMANE
NARITA
KAGEYAMA
NET
*CURRENT ROTATION
TMP

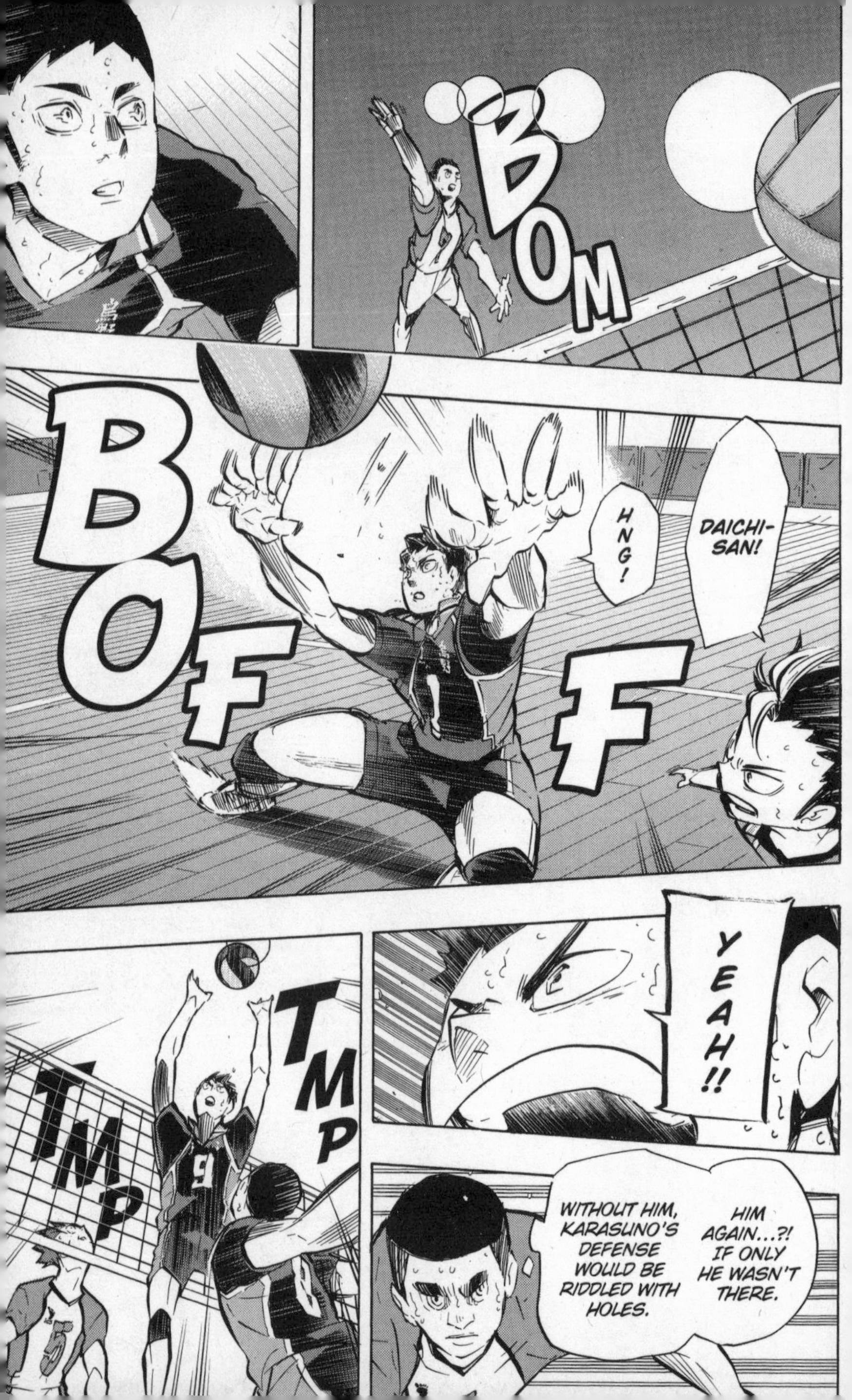
BOM
DAICHI-SAN!
HNG!
BOFF
YEAH!!
HIM AGAIN...?! IF ONLY HE WASN'T THERE.
WITHOUT HIM, KARASUNO'S DEFENSE WOULD BE RIDDLED WITH HOLES.
TMP
TMP

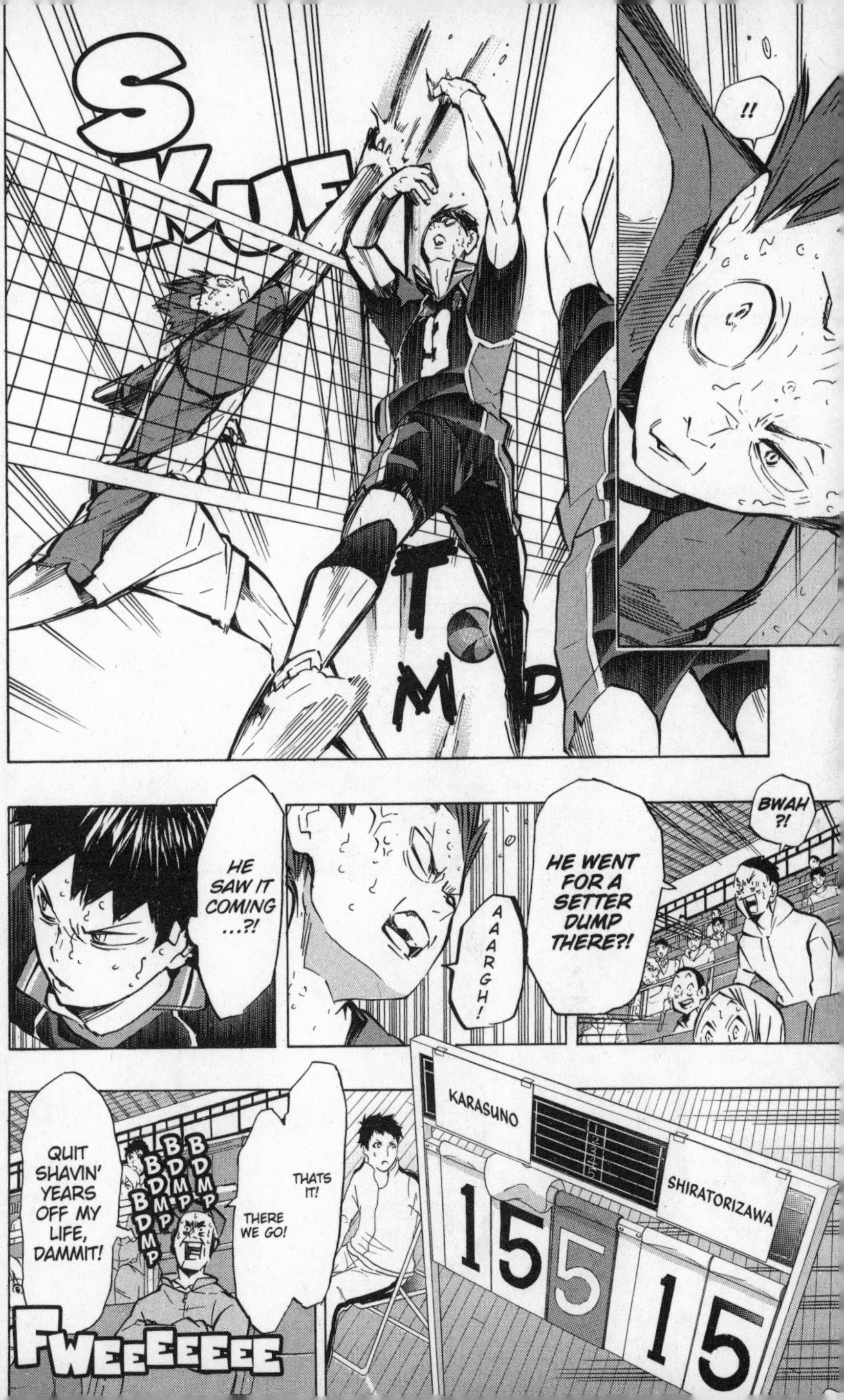

!!
SKUF
TOMP
BWAH?!
HE WENT FOR A SETTER DUMP THERE?!
AAAARGH!
HE SAW IT COMING...?!
KARASUNO
1 2 3 4 5
SHIRATORIZAWA
15 5 15
THATS IT!
THERE WE GO!
BDMP BDMP BDMP BDMP
QUIT SHAVIN' YEARS OFF MY LIFE, DAMMIT!
FWEEEEEEE

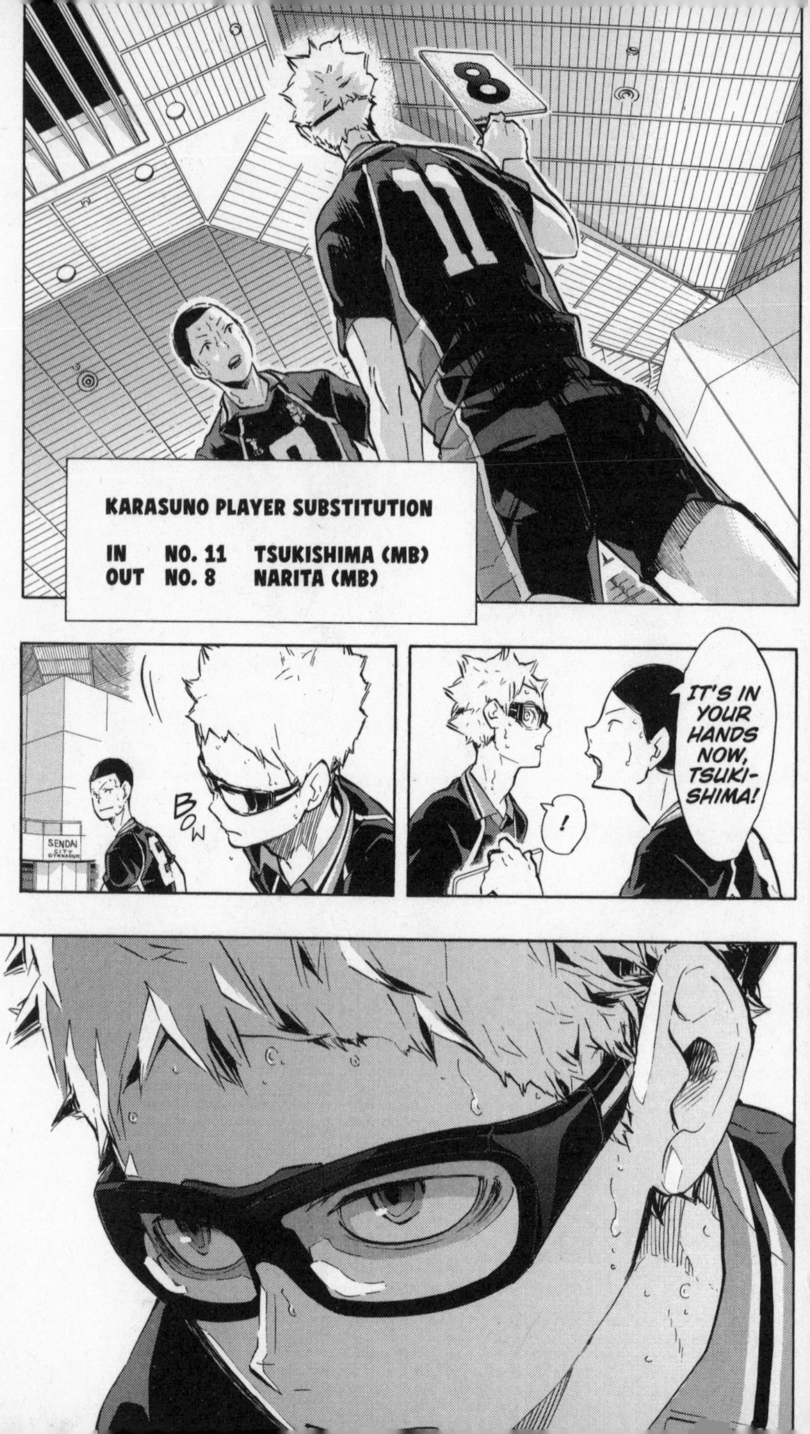
KARASUNO PLAYER SUBSTITUTION
IN NO. 11 TSUKISHIMA (MB)
OUT NO. 8 NARITA (MB)
IT'S IN YOUR HANDS NOW, TSUKI-SHIMA!
!
BOW
SENDAI CITY GYMNASIUM

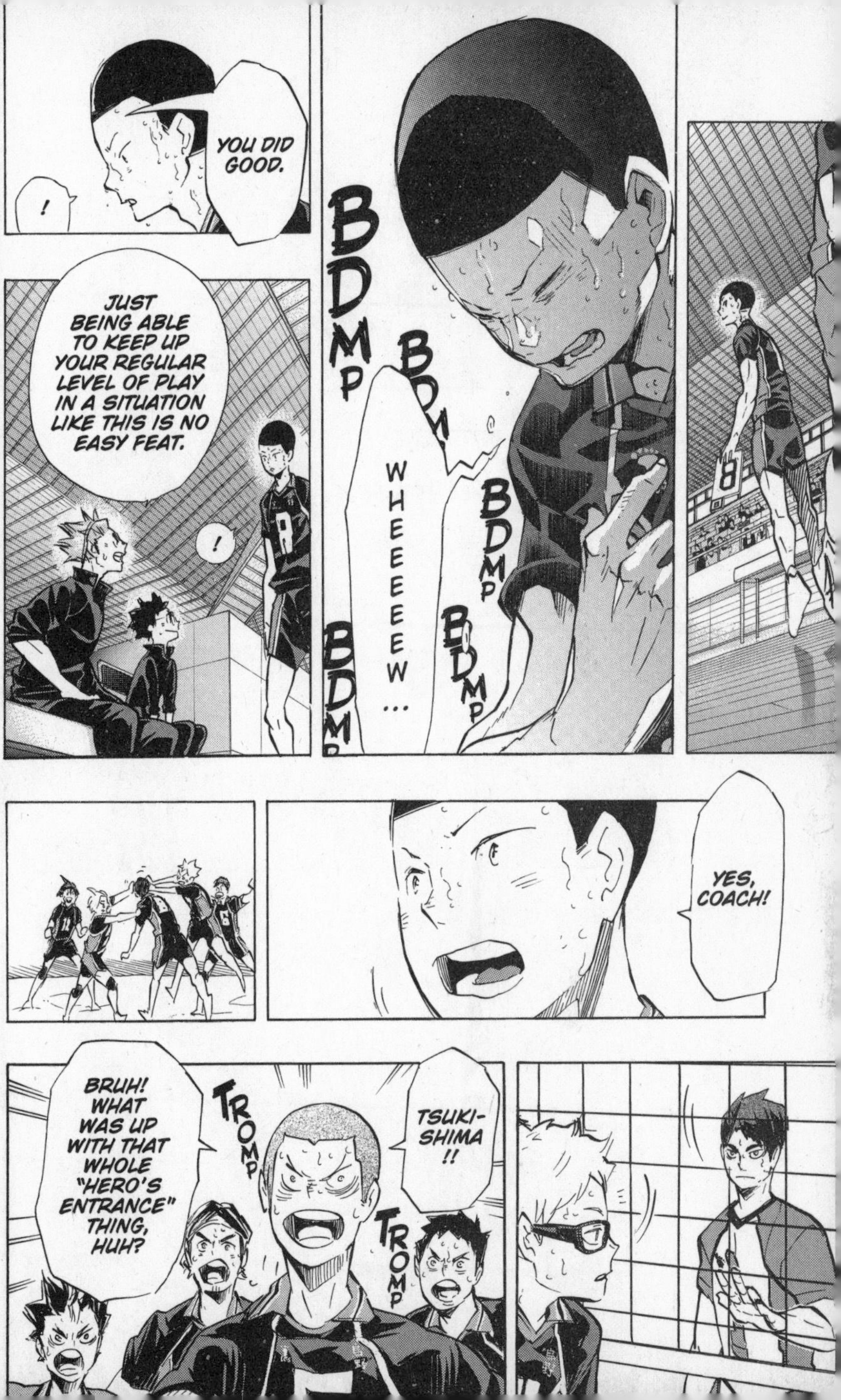
BDMP
BDMP
WHEEEEEEW...
BDMP
BDMP
BDMP
YOU DID GOOD.
!
JUST BEING ABLE TO KEEP UP YOUR REGULAR LEVEL OF PLAY IN A SITUATION LIKE THIS IS NO EASY FEAT.
!
YES, COACH!
TSUKI-SHIMA !!
TROMP
BRUH! WHAT WAS UP WITH THAT WHOLE "HERO'S ENTRANCE" THING, HUH?
TROMP

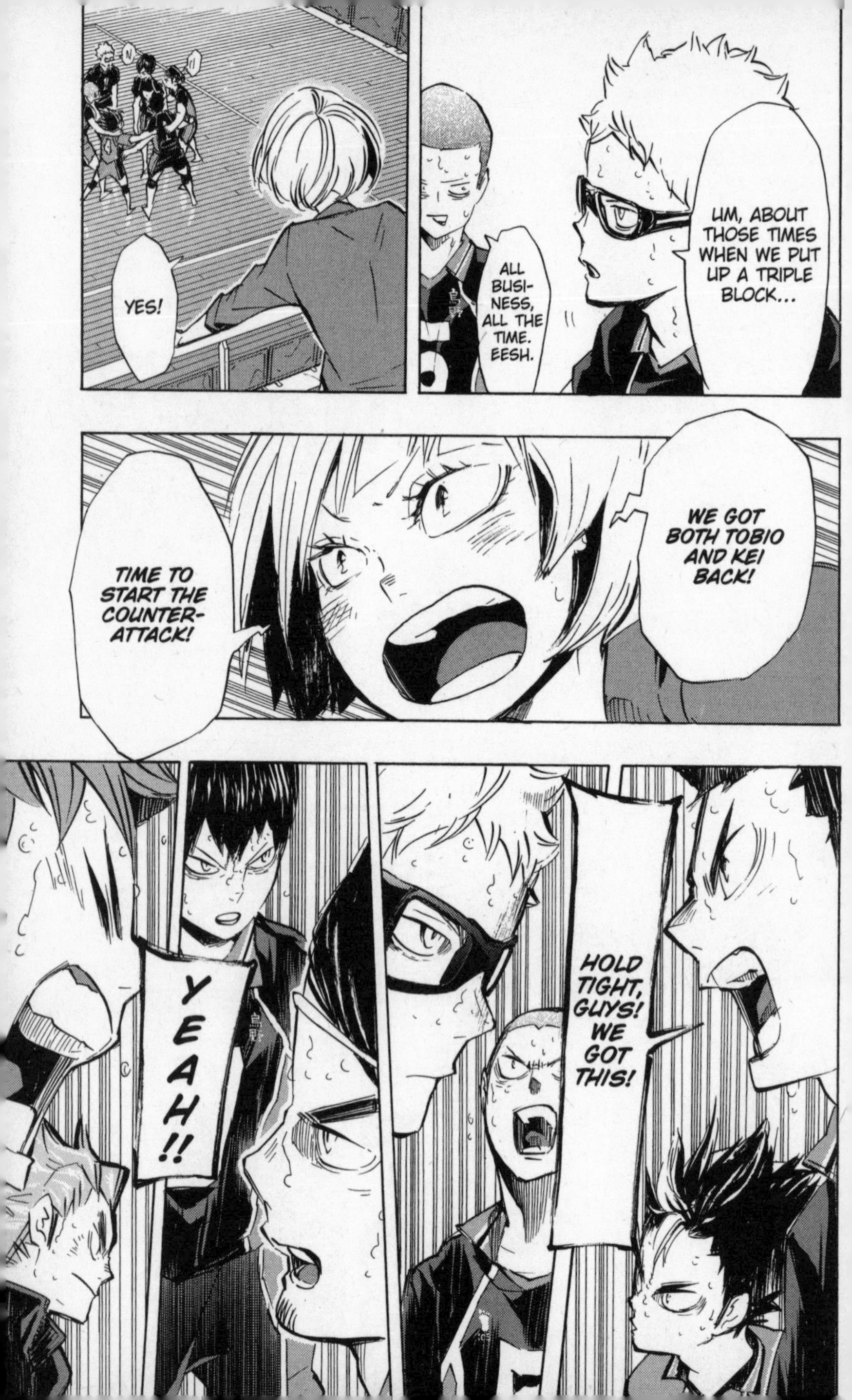
UM, ABOUT THOSE TIMES WHEN WE PUT UP A TRIPLE BLOCK...
ALL BUSINESS, ALL THE TIME. EESH.
YES!
WE GOT BOTH TOBIO AND KEI BACK!
TIME TO START THE COUNTER-ATTACK!
HOLD TIGHT, GUYS! WE GOT THIS!
YEAH!!

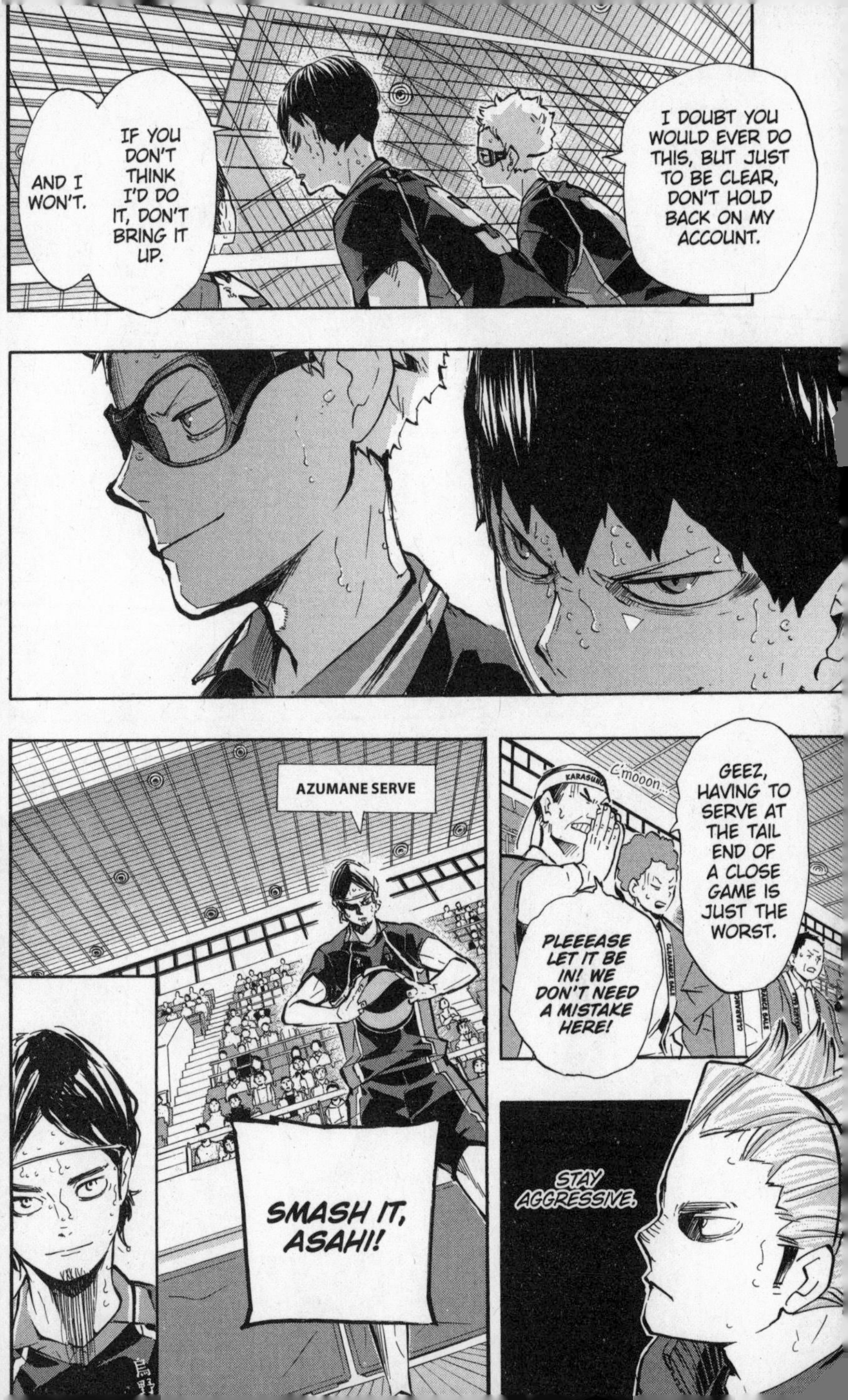

I DOUBT YOU WOULD EVER DO THIS, BUT JUST TO BE CLEAR, DON'T HOLD BACK ON MY ACCOUNT.
IF YOU DON'T THINK I'D DO IT, DON'T BRING IT UP.
AND I WON'T.
KARASUNO
C'mooon...
GEEZ, HAVING TO SERVE AT THE TAIL END OF A CLOSE GAME IS JUST THE WORST.
PLEEEASE LET IT BE IN! WE DON'T NEED A MISTAKE HERE!
STAY AGGRESSIVE.
AZUMANE SERVE
SMASH IT, ASAHI!

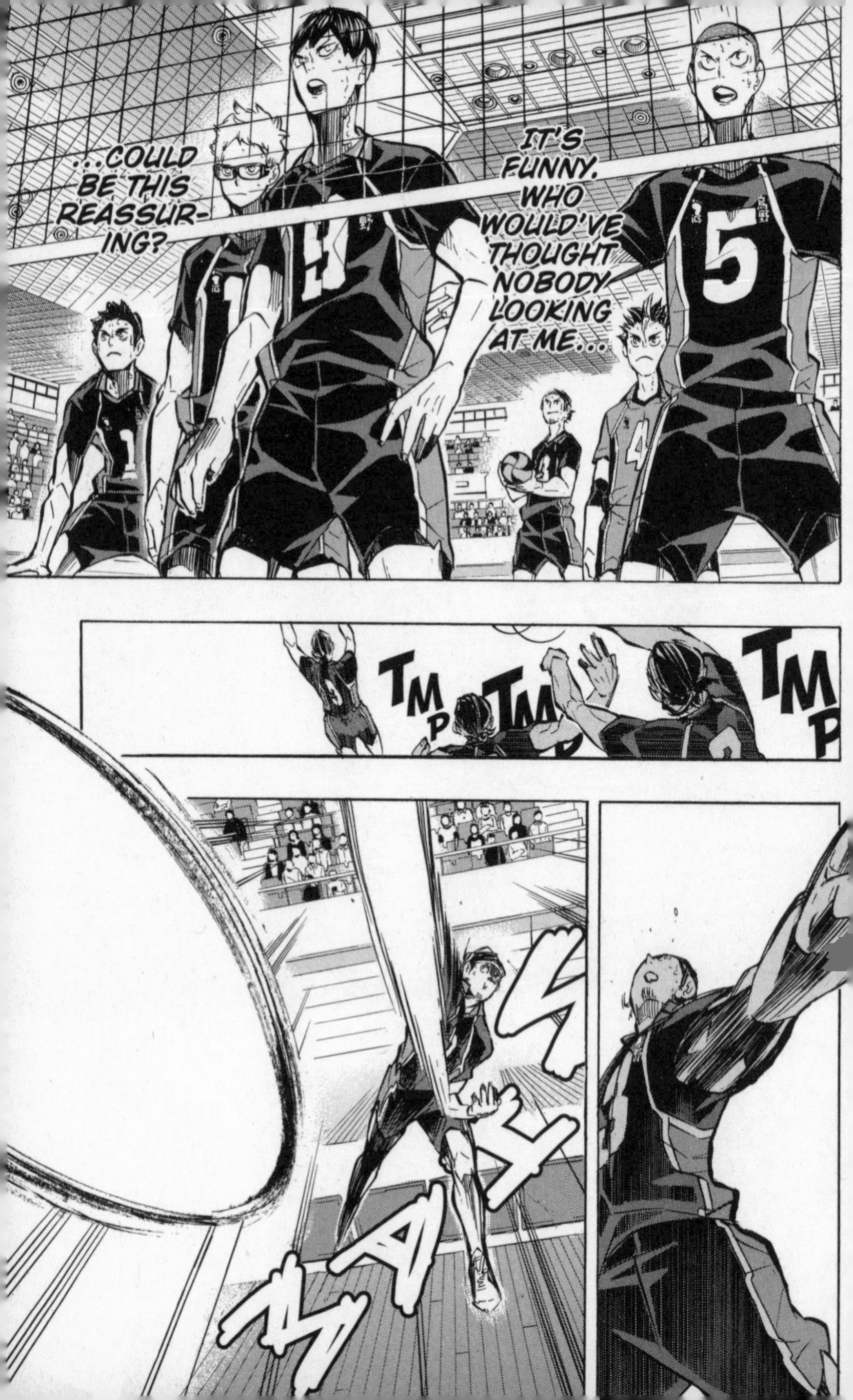
IT'S FUNNY. WHO WOULD'VE THOUGHT NOBODY LOOKING AT ME...
...COULD BE THIS REASSURING?
TMP TMP

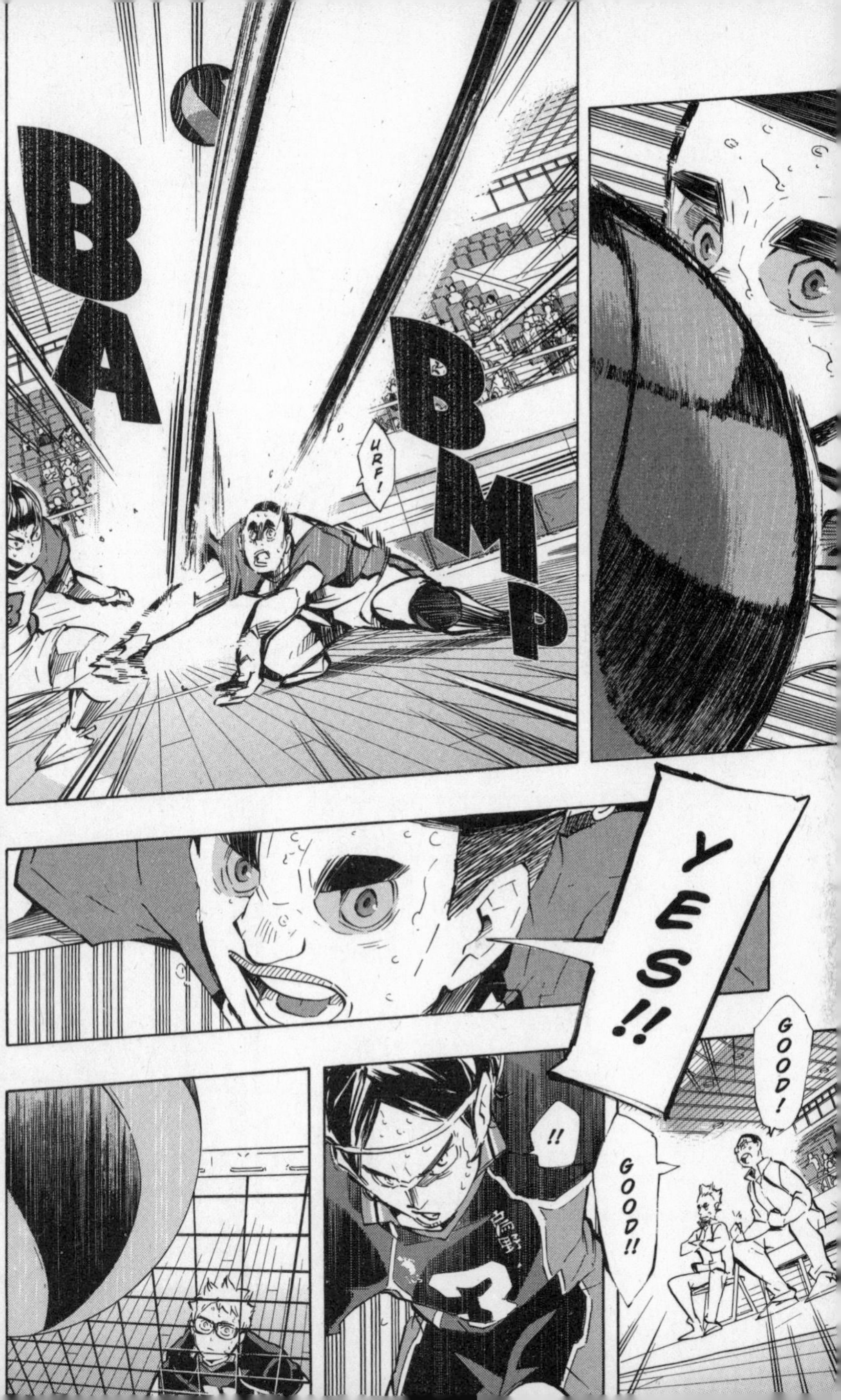
BA
BUMP
URF!
YES!!
GOOD!
GOOD!!
!!

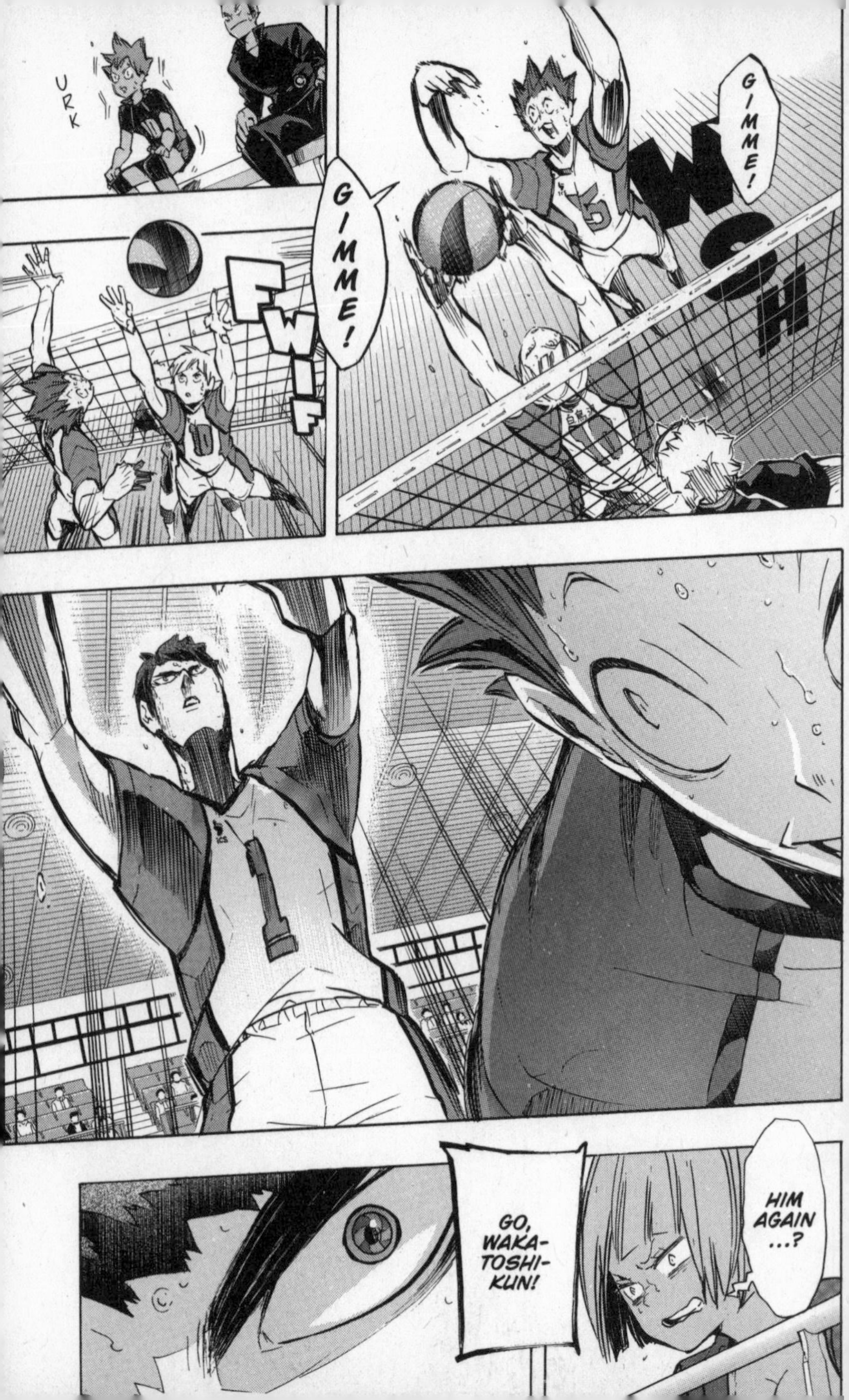
GIMME!
WOOSH
URK
GIMME!
FWIF
HIM AGAIN ...?
GO, WAKATOSHI-KUN!

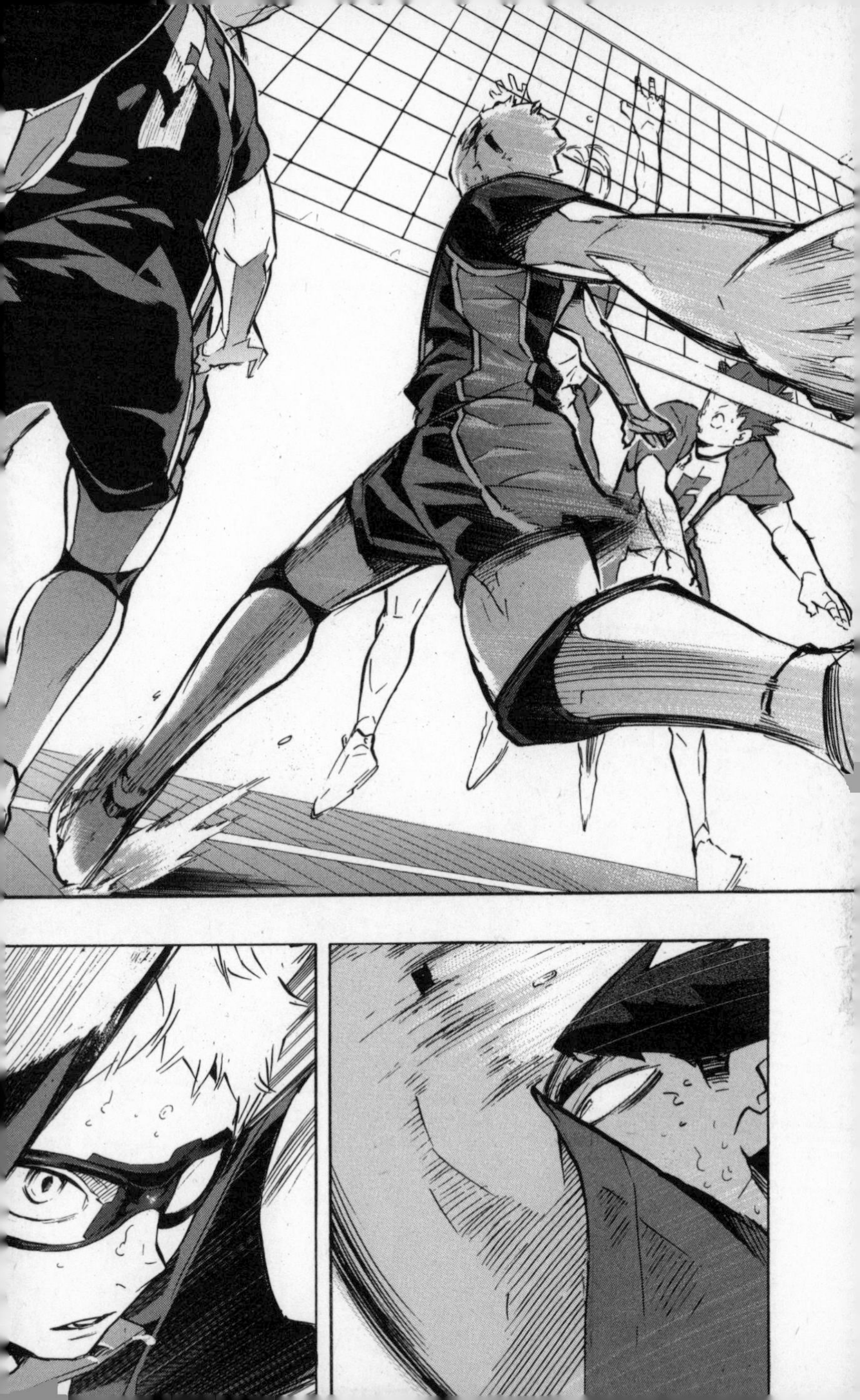

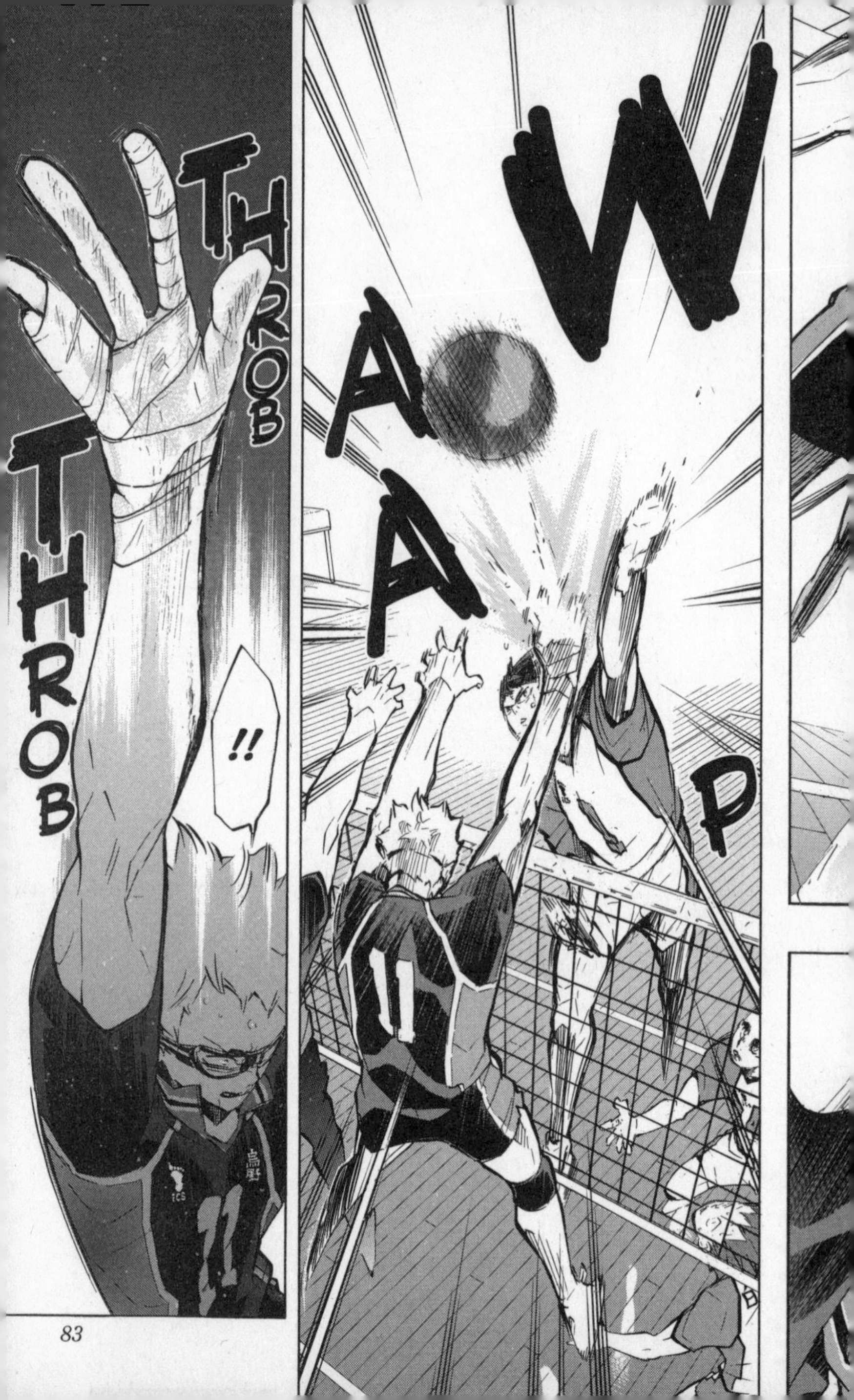
WAAP
THROB
THROB
!!

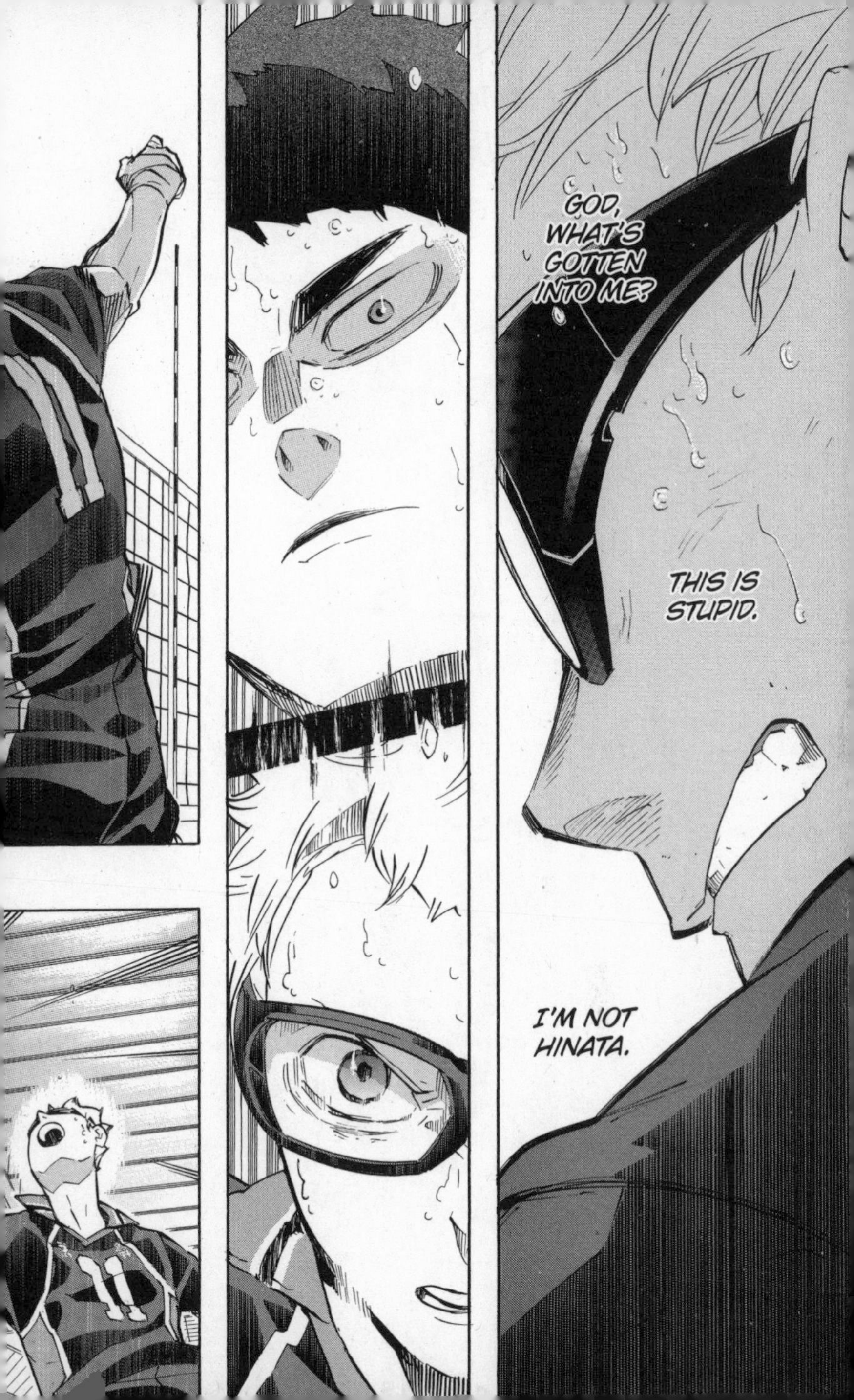
GOD, WHAT'S GOTTEN INTO ME?
THIS IS STUPID.
I'M NOT HINATA.

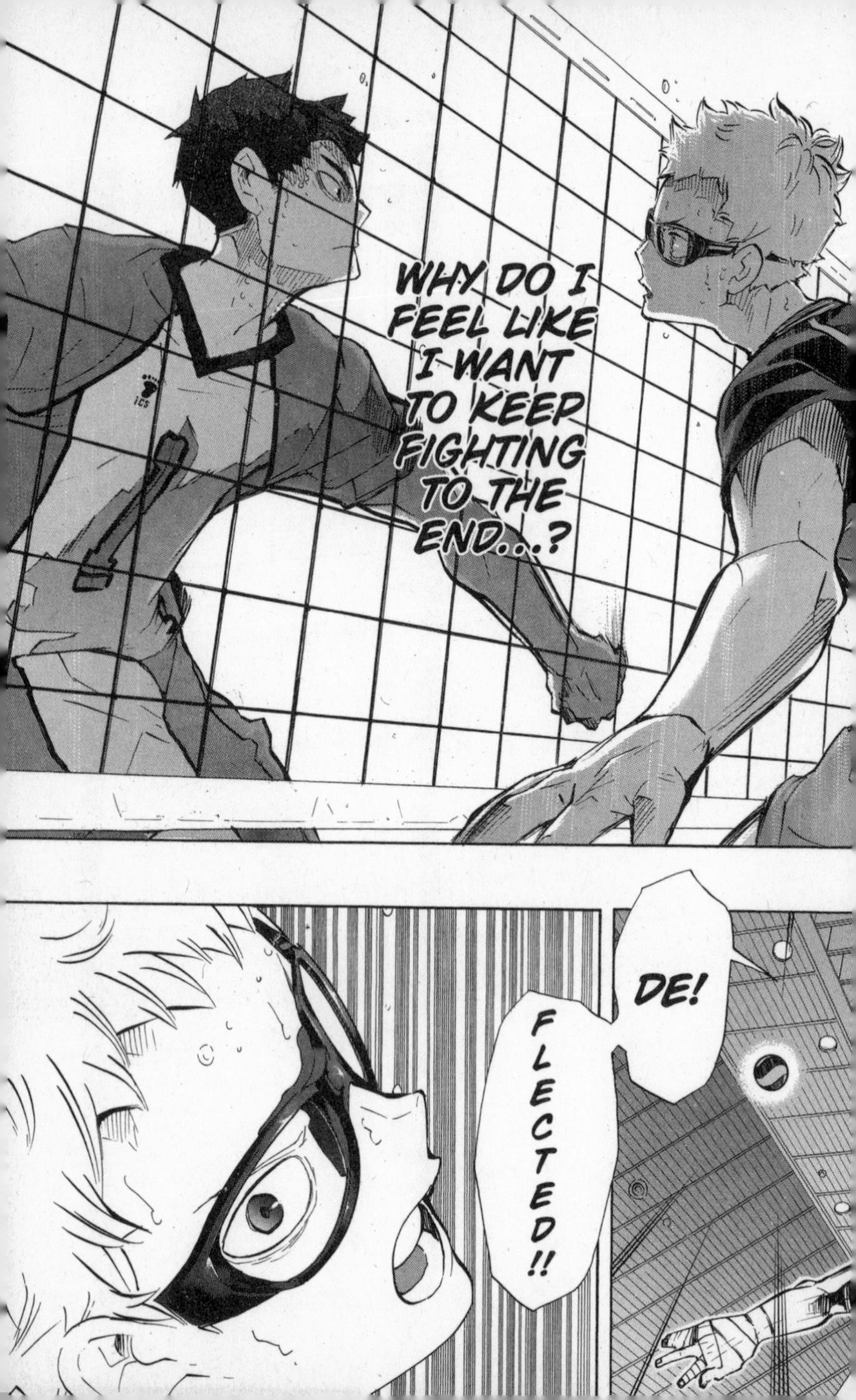
WHY DO I FEEL LIKE I WANT TO KEEP FIGHTING TO THE END...?
DE!
FLECTED!!

Intrusive Thoughts

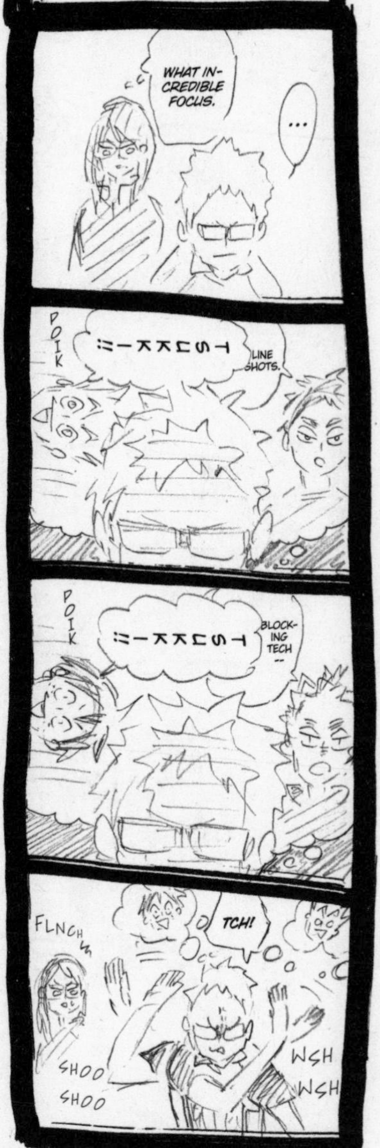
WHAT IN-CREDIBLE FOCUS.
...
LINE SHOTS.
TSUKKI--!!
POIK
BLOCKING TECH --
TSUKKI--!!
POIK
TCH!
FLNCH
WSH WSH
SHOO SHOO

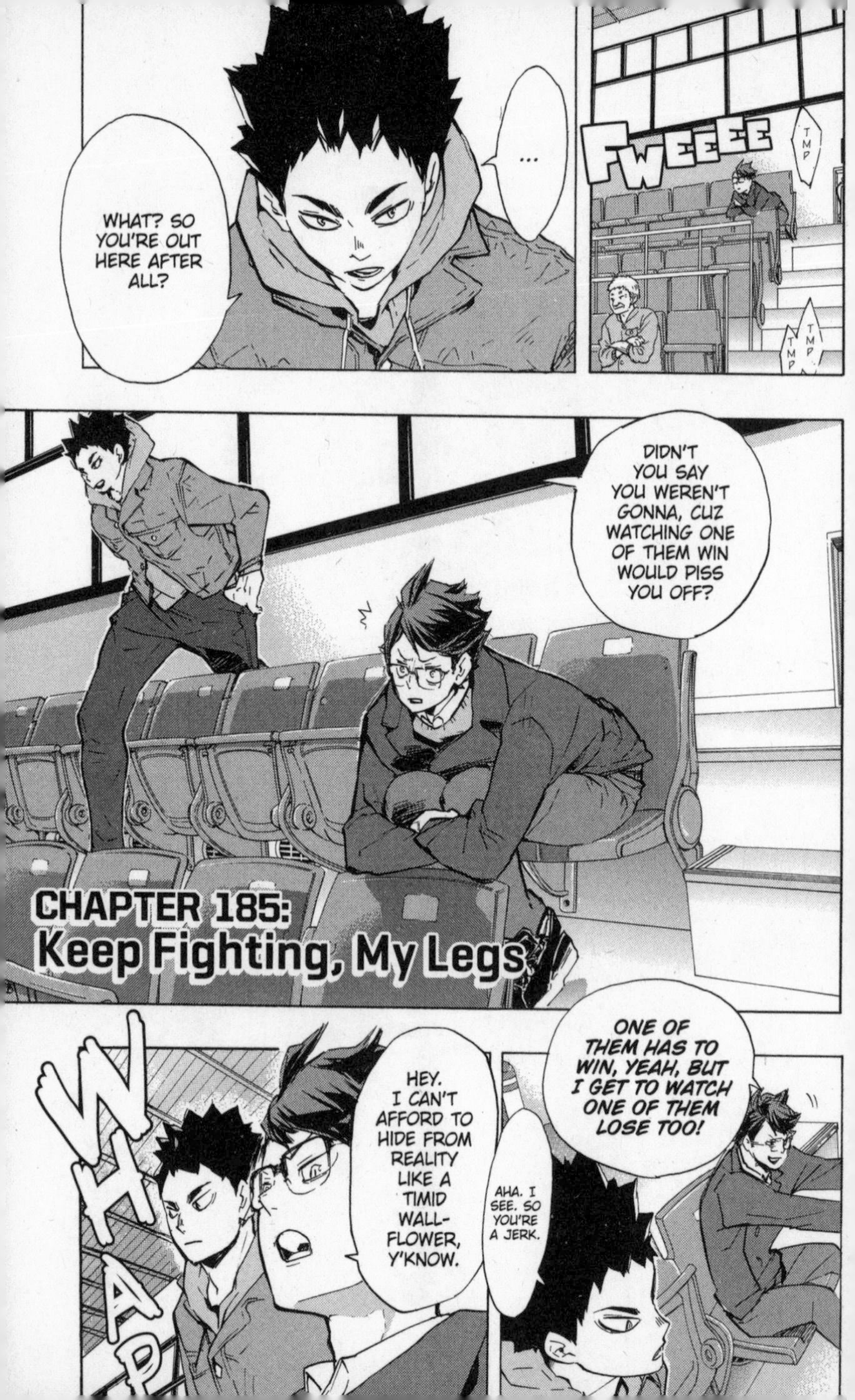
FWEEEE
TMP
TMP TMP TMP
...
WHAT? SO YOU'RE OUT HERE AFTER ALL?
DIDN'T YOU SAY YOU WEREN'T GONNA, CUZ WATCHING ONE OF THEM WIN WOULD PISS YOU OFF?
CHAPTER 185:
Keep Fighting, My Legs
ONE OF THEM HAS TO WIN, YEAH, BUT I GET TO WATCH ONE OF THEM LOSE TOO!
AHA. I SEE. SO YOU'RE A JERK.
HEY. I CAN'T AFFORD TO HIDE FROM REALITY LIKE A TIMID WALL-FLOWER, Y'KNOW.
WHAP

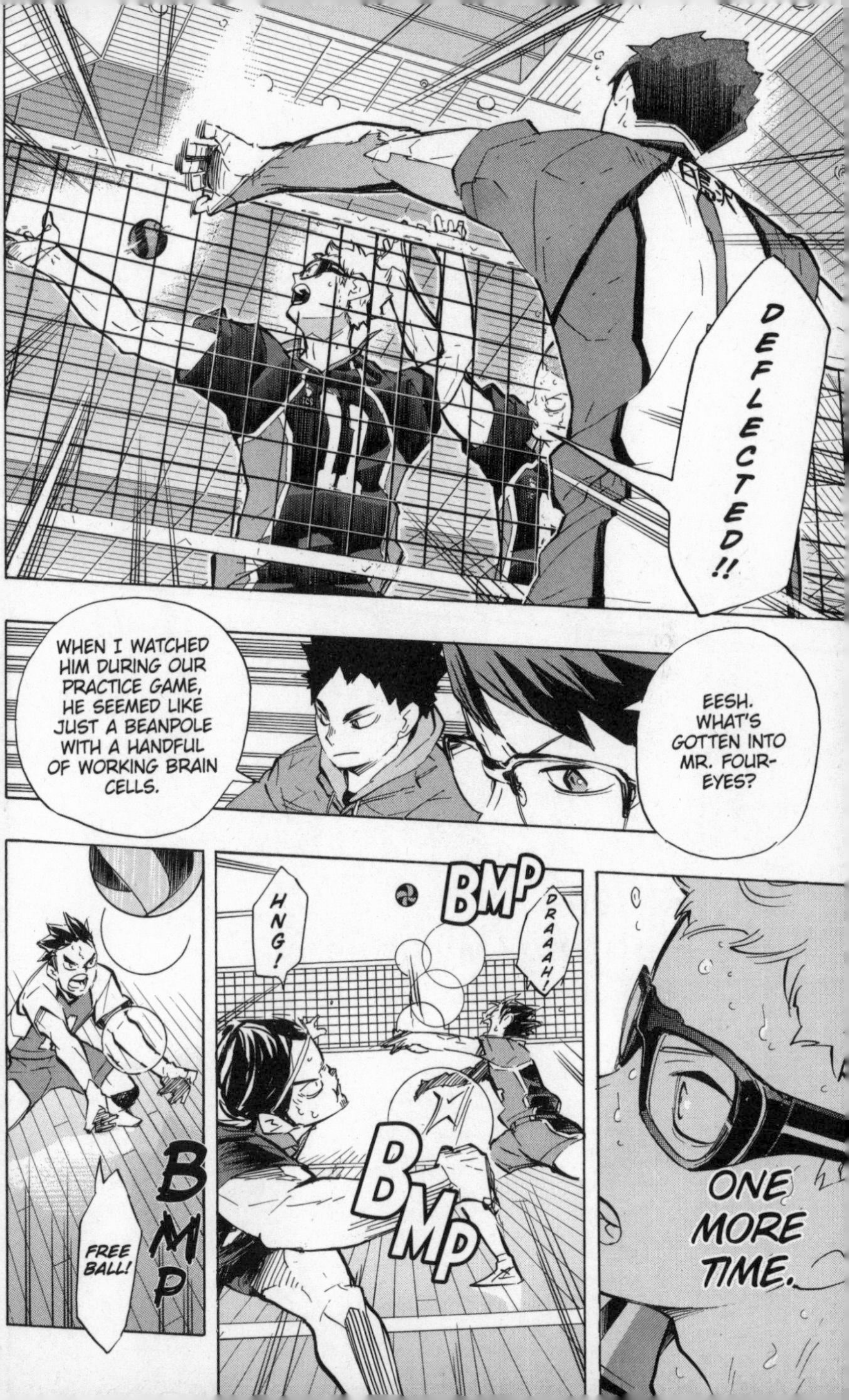
DEFLECTED!!
EESH. WHAT'S GOTTEN INTO MR. FOUR-EYES?
WHEN I WATCHED HIM DURING OUR PRACTICE GAME, HE SEEMED LIKE JUST A BEANPOLE WITH A HANDFUL OF WORKING BRAIN CELLS.
ONE MORE TIME.
BMP
DRAAAH!
HNG!
BMP
BMP
FREE BALL!

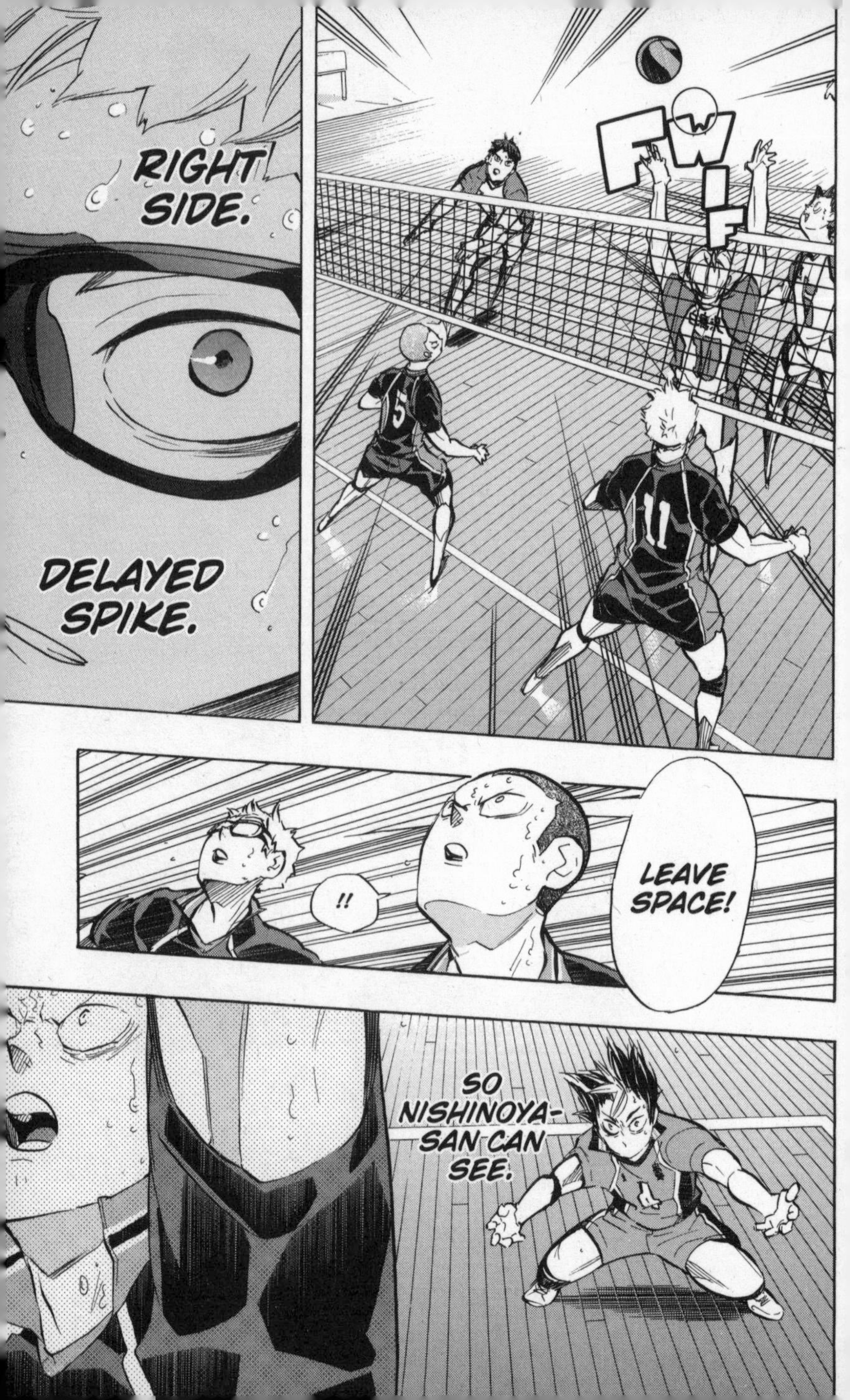
FWIF
RIGHT SIDE.
DELAYED SPIKE.
LEAVE SPACE!
!!
SO NISHINOYA-SAN CAN SEE.

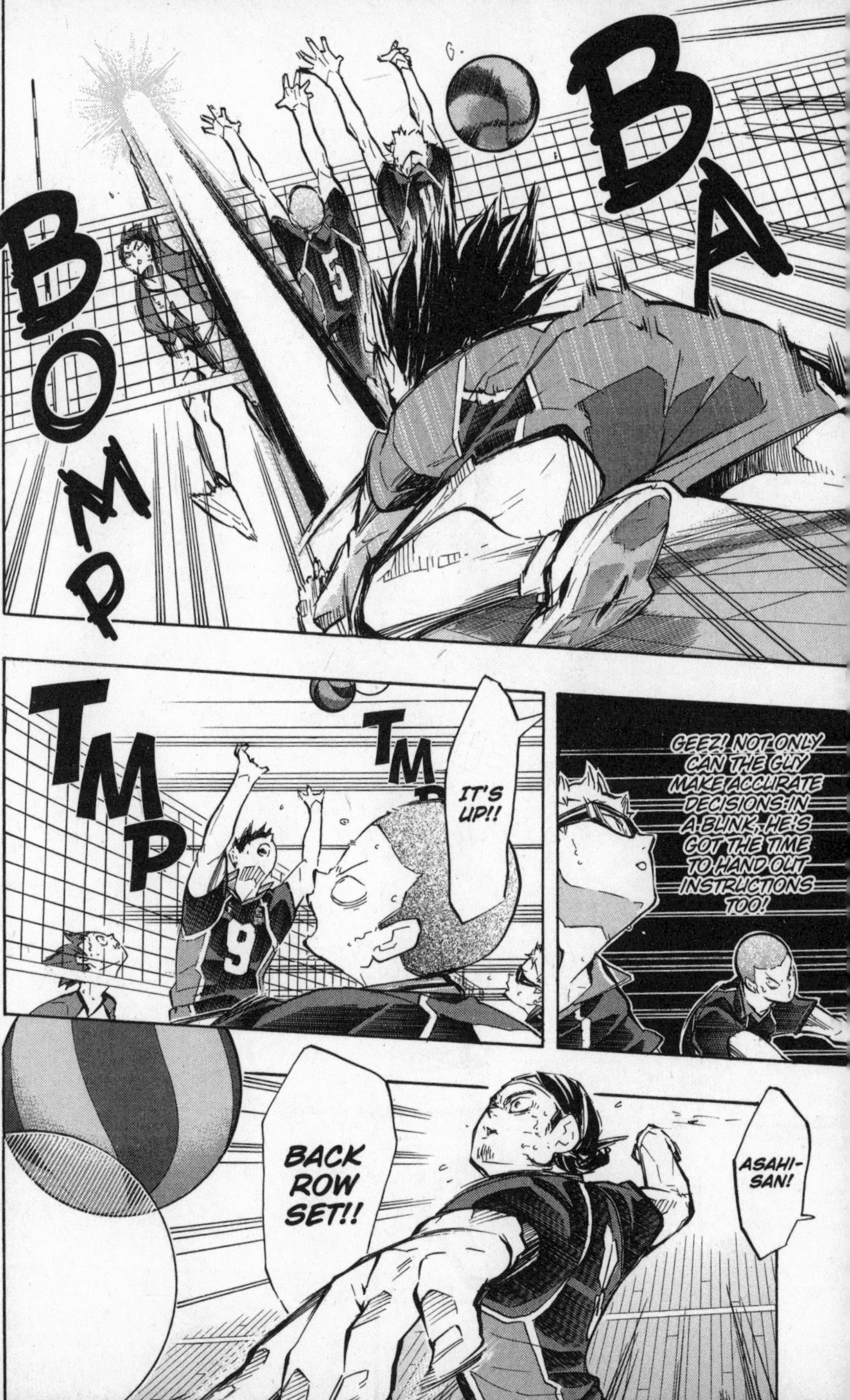
BA
BOMP
GEEZ! NOT ONLY CAN THE GUY MAKE ACCURATE DECISIONS IN A BLINK, HE'S GOT THE TIME TO HAND OUT INSTRUCTIONS TOO!
IT'S UP!!
TM
TMP
ASAHI-SAN!
BACK ROW SET!!

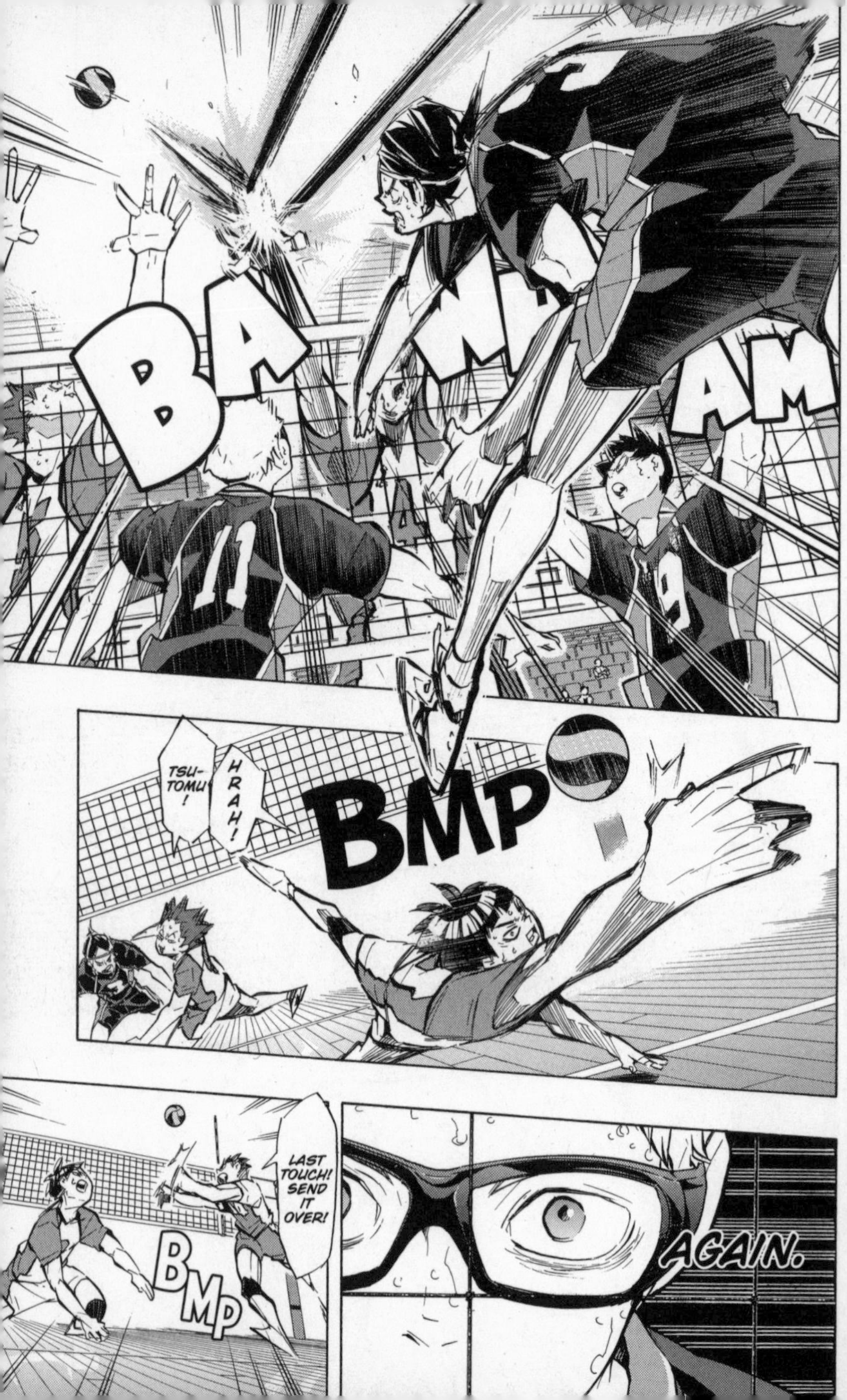
BAM! BAM
HRAH!
TSU-TOMU!
BMP
AGAIN.
LAST TOUCH! SEND IT OVER!
BMP

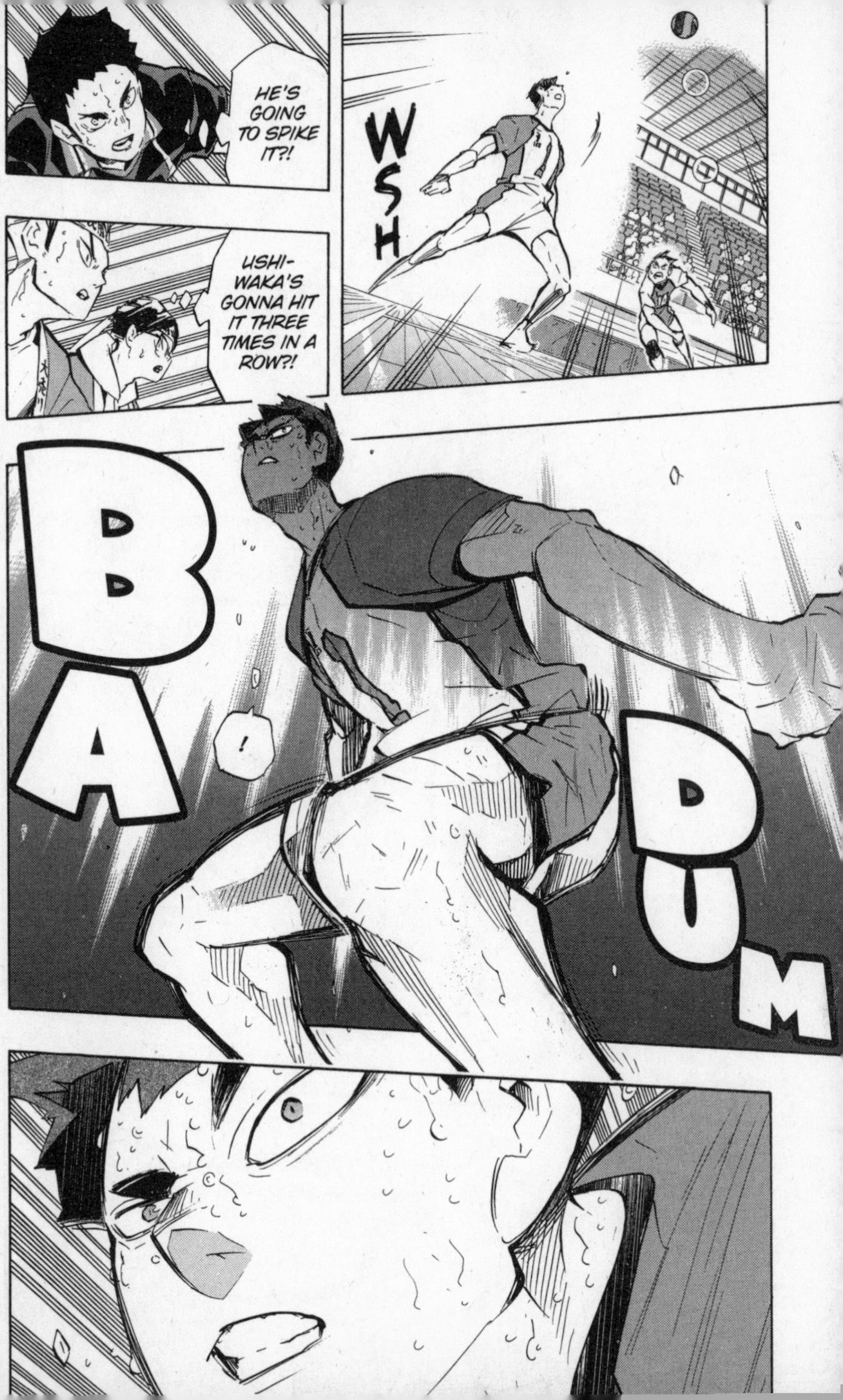
WSH
HE'S GOING TO SPIKE IT?!
USHI-WAKA'S GONNA HIT IT THREE TIMES IN A ROW?!
BA DUM
!

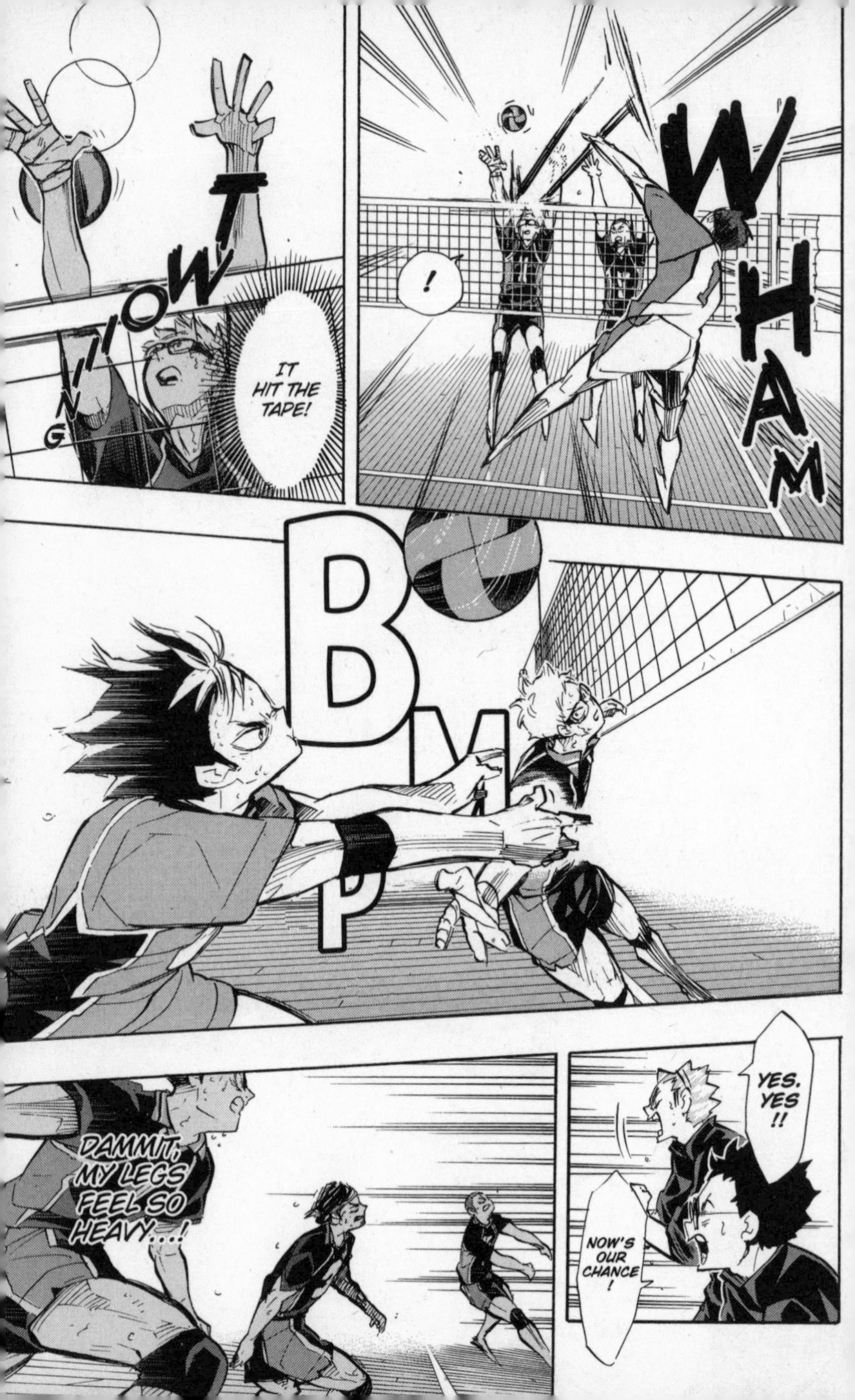
WHAM
!
IT HIT THE TAPE!
BUMP
YES. YES!!
NOW'S OUR CHANCE!
DAMMIT, MY LEGS FEEL SO HEAVY...!

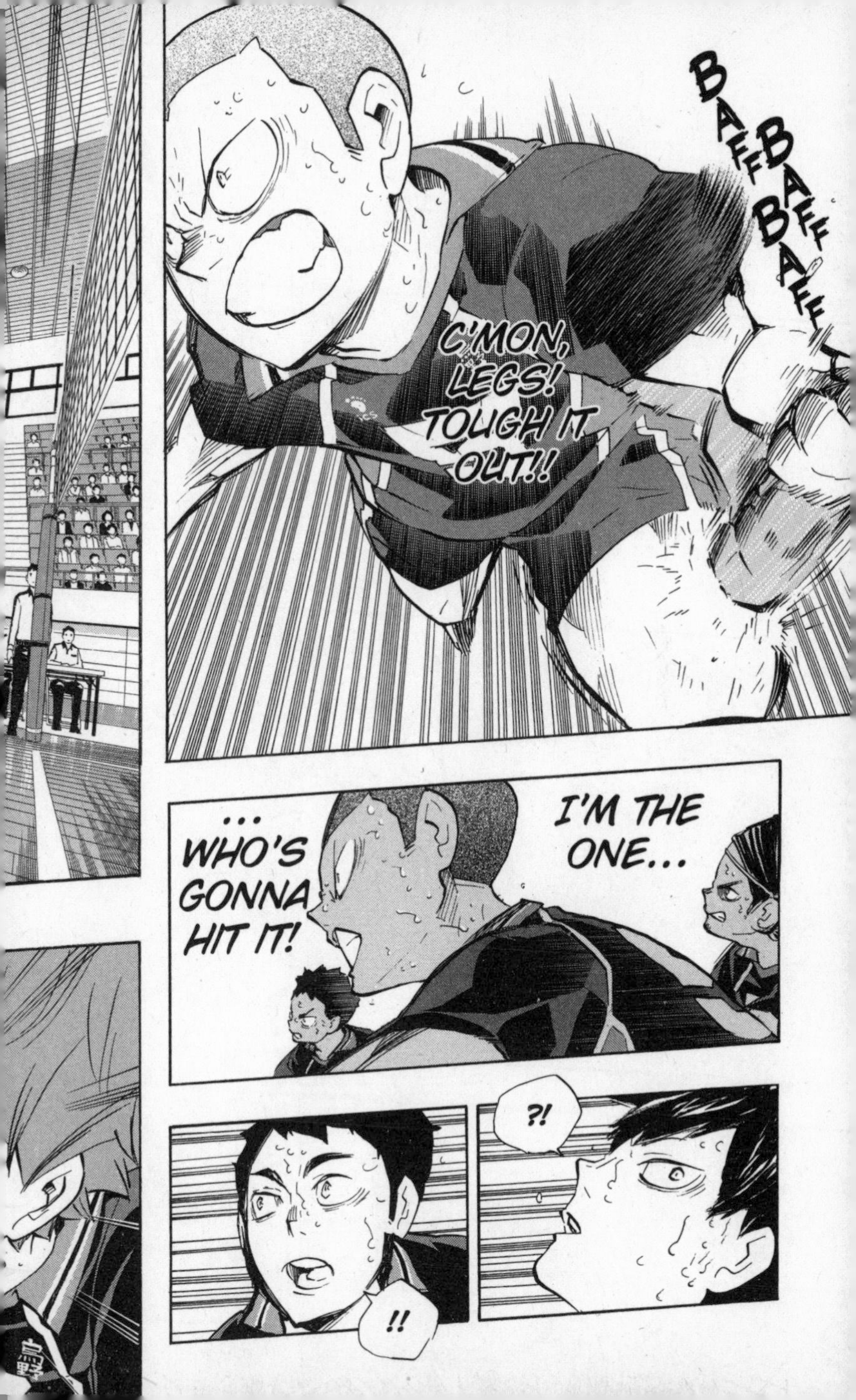
BAFF BAFF BAFF
C'MON, LEGS! TOUGH IT OUT!!
I'M THE ONE...
... WHO'S GONNA HIT IT!
?!
!!

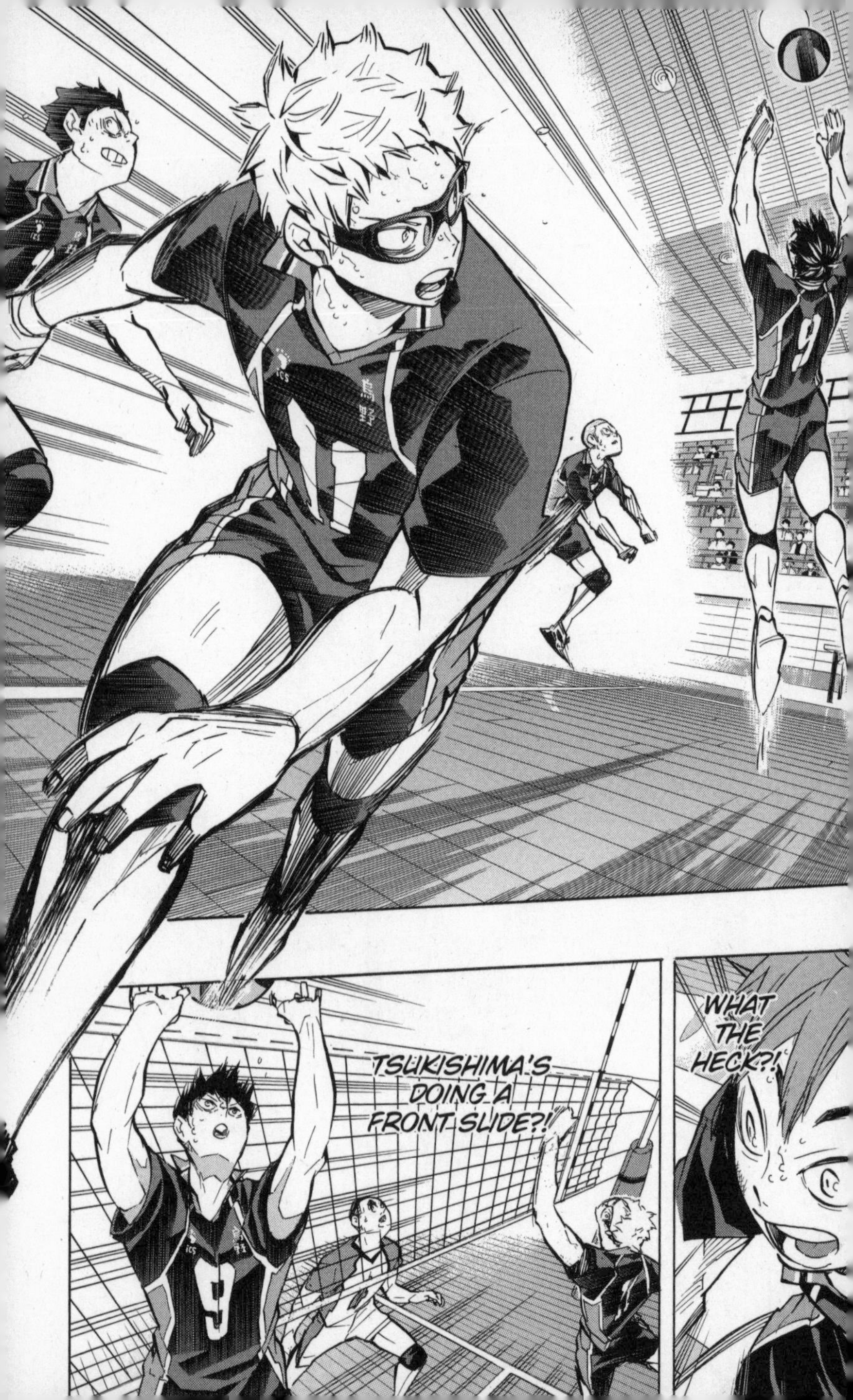
WHAT THE HECK?!
TSUKISHIMA'S DOING A FRONT SLIDE?!

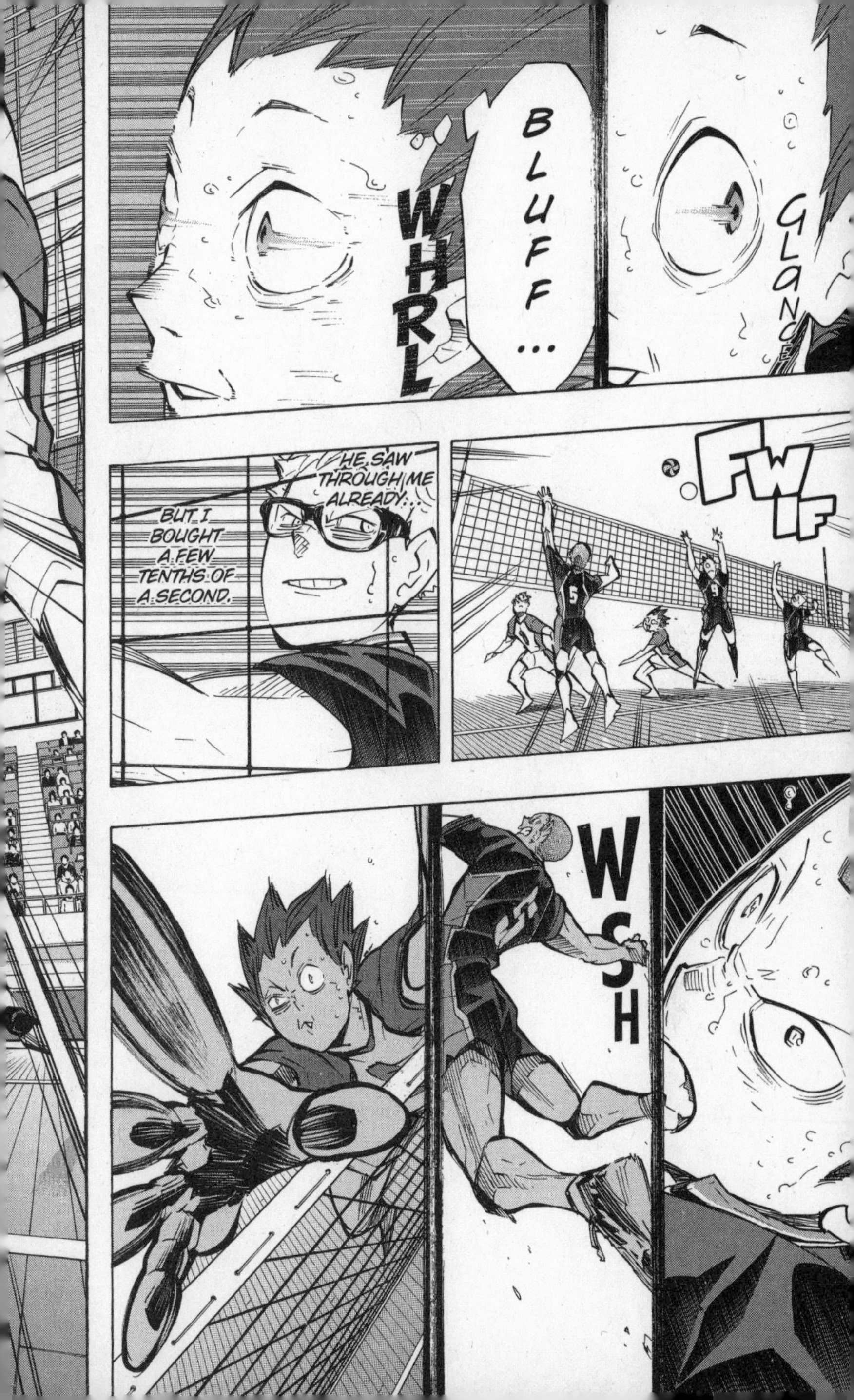
GLANCE
BLUFF...
WHRL
FWIF
HE SAW THROUGH ME ALREADY...
BUT I BOUGHT A FEW TENTHS OF A SECOND.
WSH

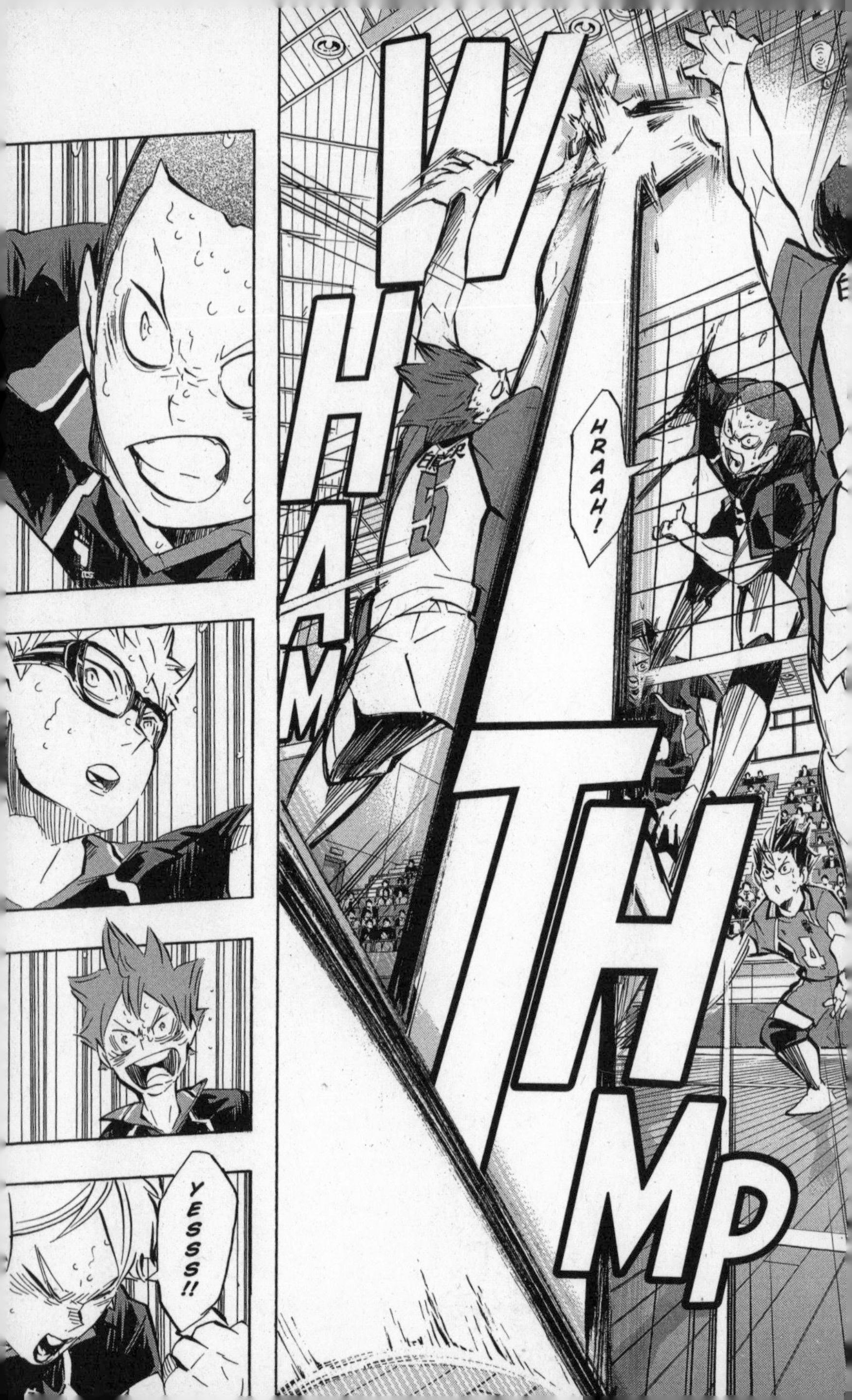
WHAM
HRAAH!
THMP
YESSS!!

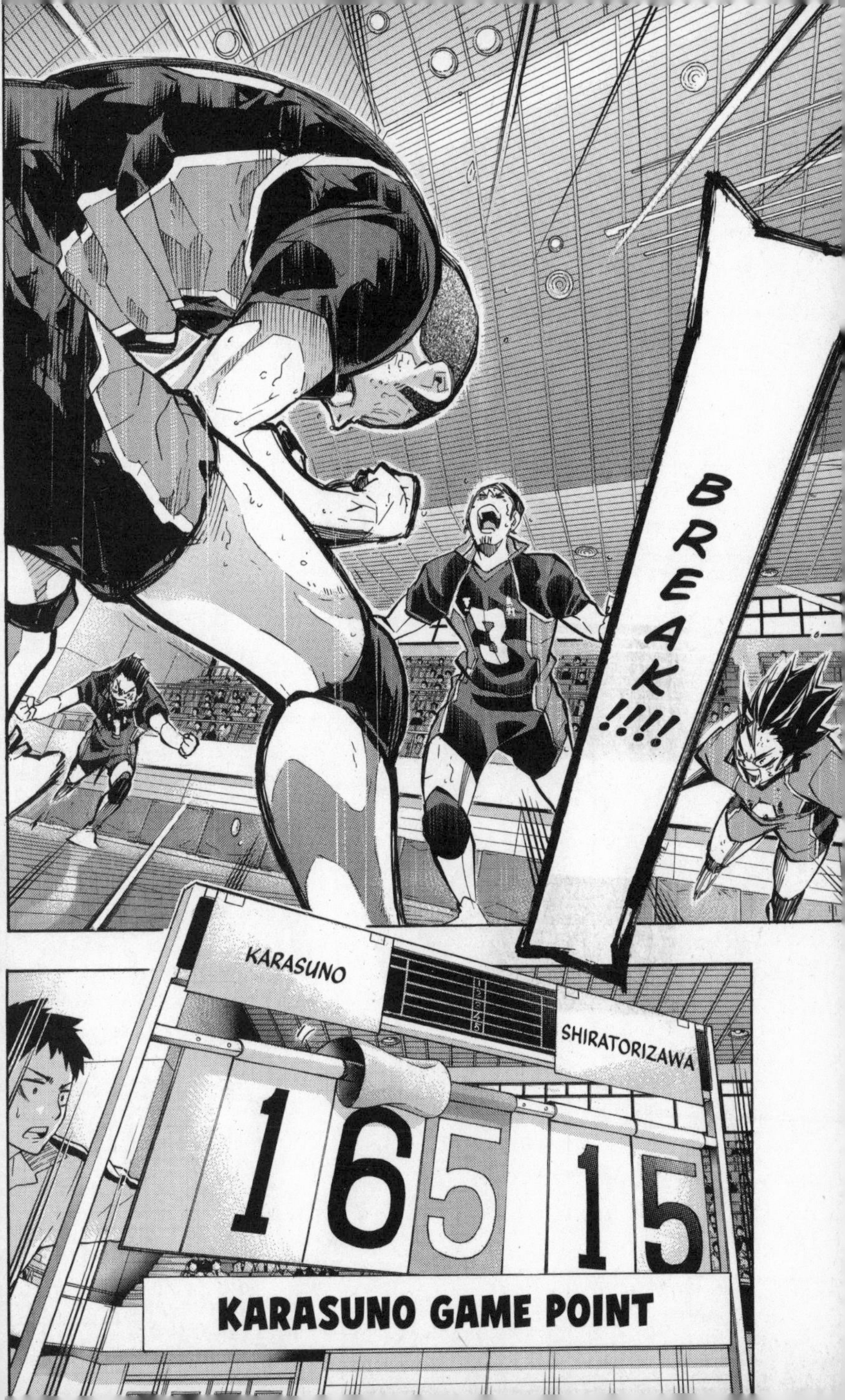
BREAK!!!!
KARASUNO
SHIRATORIZAWA
16 5 15
KARASUNO GAME POINT

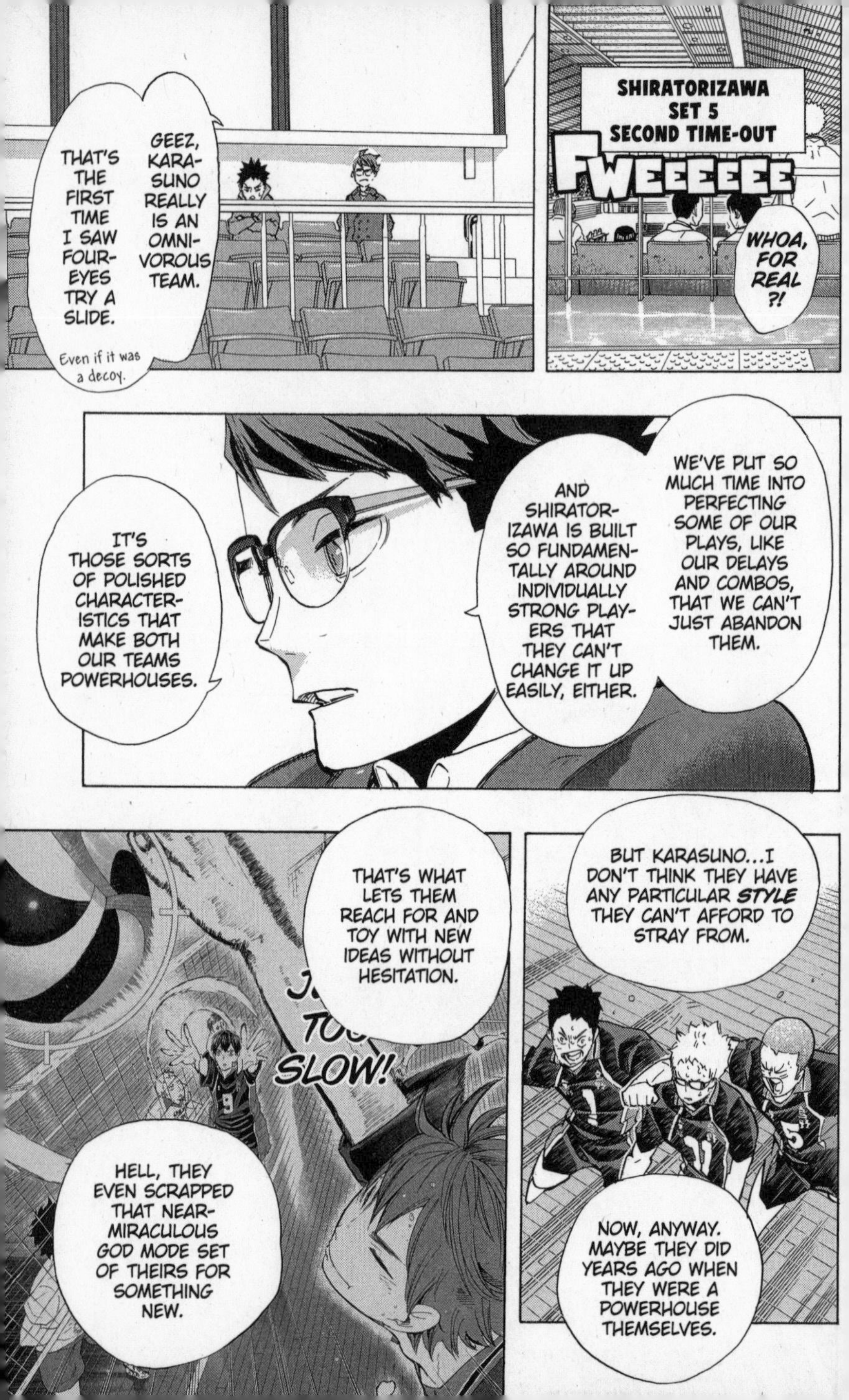
SHIRATORIZAWA SET 5 SECOND TIME-OUT
FWEEEEEE
WHOA, FOR REAL?!
GEEZ, KARASUNO REALLY IS AN OMNIVOROUS TEAM.
THAT'S THE FIRST TIME I SAW FOUR-EYES TRY A SLIDE.
Even if it was a decoy.
WE'VE PUT SO MUCH TIME INTO PERFECTING SOME OF OUR PLAYS, LIKE OUR DELAYS AND COMBOS, THAT WE CAN'T JUST ABANDON THEM.
AND SHIRATORIZAWA IS BUILT SO FUNDAMENTALLY AROUND INDIVIDUALLY STRONG PLAYERS THAT THEY CAN'T CHANGE IT UP EASILY, EITHER.
IT'S THOSE SORTS OF POLISHED CHARACTERISTICS THAT MAKE BOTH OUR TEAMS POWERHOUSES.
BUT KARASUNO...I DON'T THINK THEY HAVE ANY PARTICULAR STYLE THEY CAN'T AFFORD TO STRAY FROM.
NOW, ANYWAY. MAYBE THEY DID YEARS AGO WHEN THEY WERE A POWERHOUSE THEMSELVES.
THAT'S WHAT LETS THEM REACH FOR AND TOY WITH NEW IDEAS WITHOUT HESITATION.
SLOW!
HELL, THEY EVEN SCRAPPED THAT NEAR-MIRACULOUS GOD MODE SET OF THEIRS FOR SOMETHING NEW.

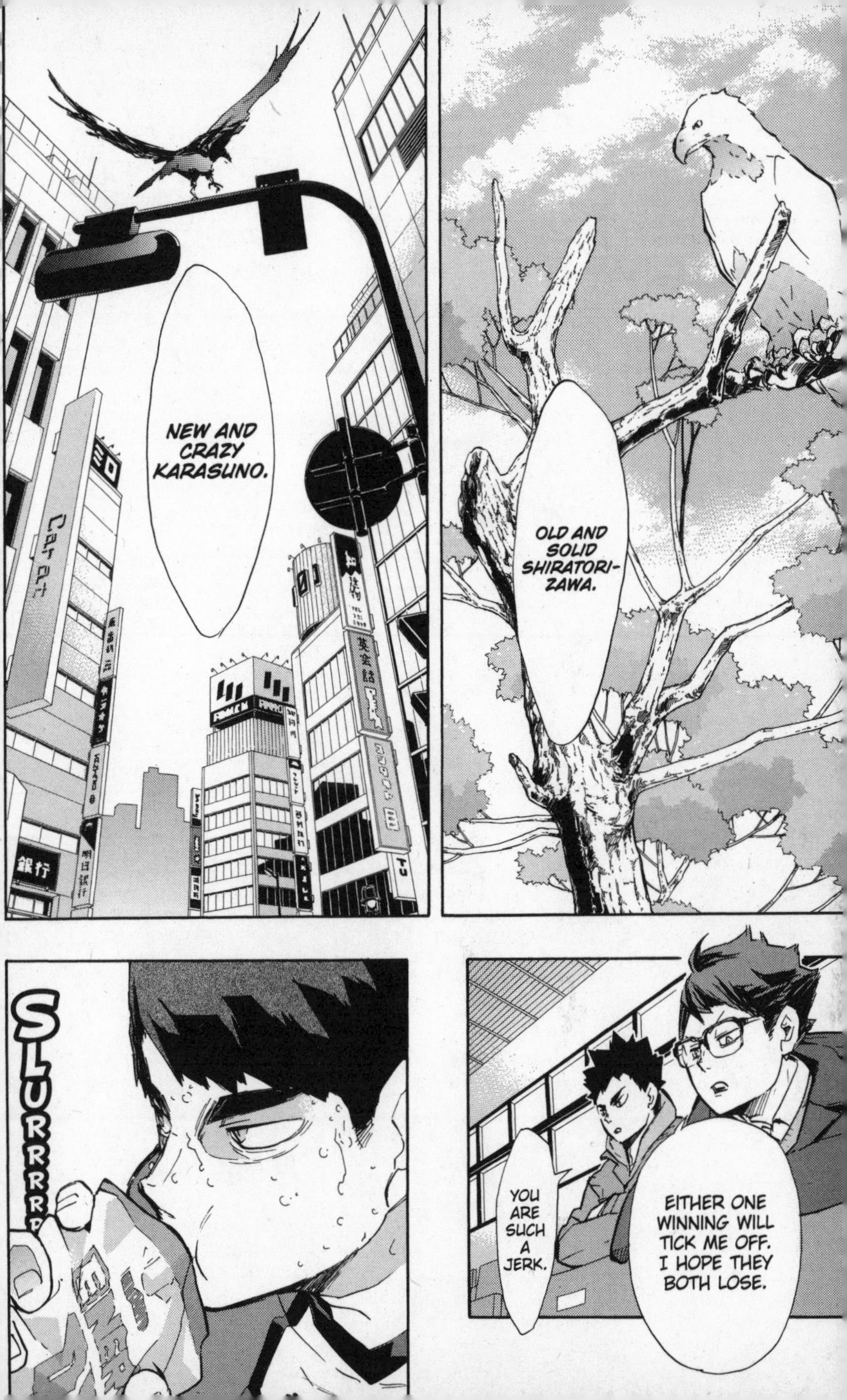
OLD AND SOLID SHIRATORI-ZAWA.
NEW AND CRAZY KARASUNO.
EITHER ONE WINNING WILL TICK ME OFF. I HOPE THEY BOTH LOSE.
YOU ARE SUCH A JERK.
SLURRRP

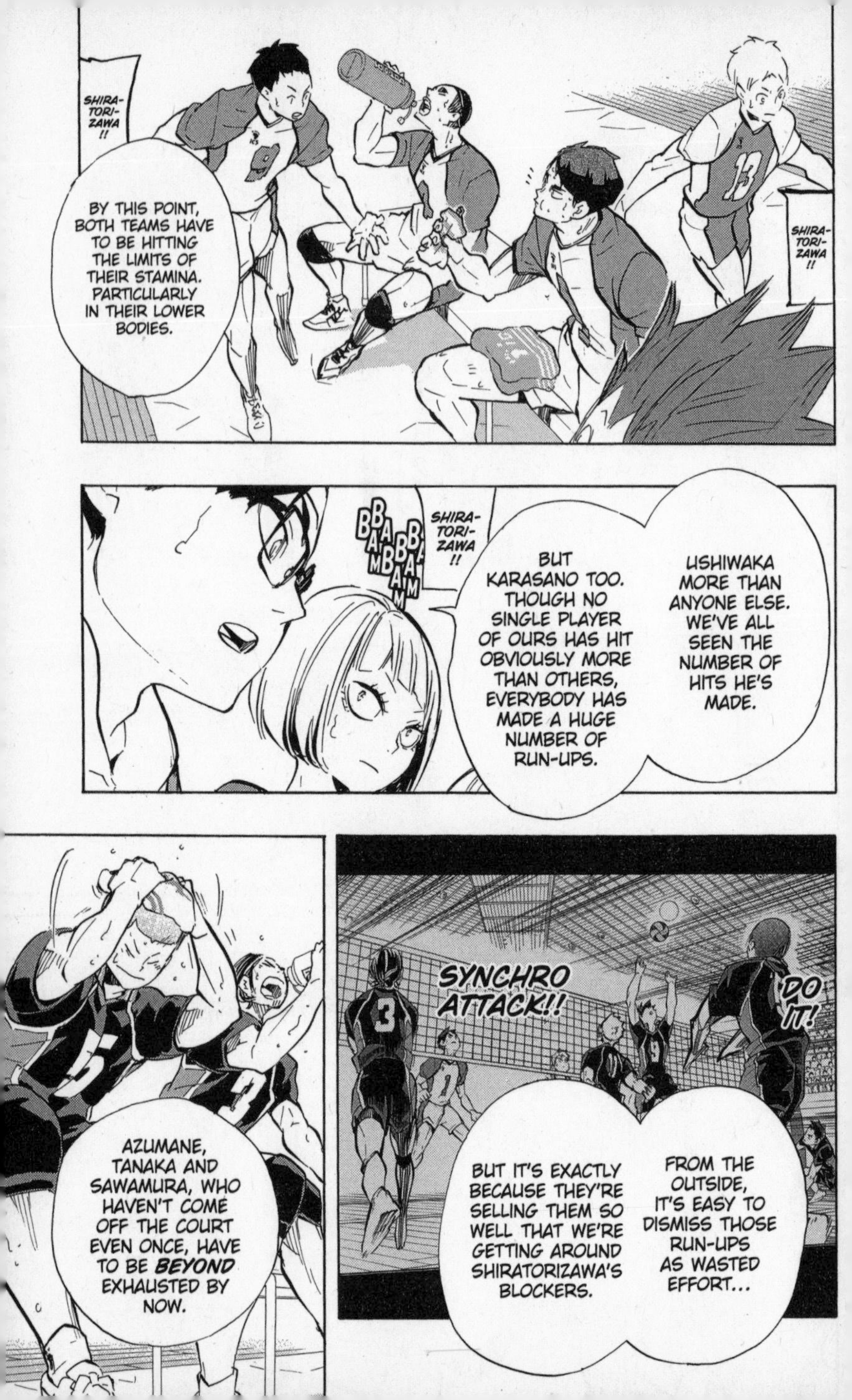

SHIRA-TORI-ZAWA!!
SHIRA-TORI-ZAWA!!
BY THIS POINT, BOTH TEAMS HAVE TO BE HITTING THE LIMITS OF THEIR STAMINA. PARTICULARLY IN THEIR LOWER BODIES.
USHIWAKA MORE THAN ANYONE ELSE. WE'VE ALL SEEN THE NUMBER OF HITS HE'S MADE.
BUT KARASANO TOO. THOUGH NO SINGLE PLAYER OF OURS HAS HIT OBVIOUSLY MORE THAN OTHERS, EVERYBODY HAS MADE A HUGE NUMBER OF RUN-UPS.
SHIRA-TORI-ZAWA!!
BBAM BBAM
DO IT!
SYNCHRO ATTACK!!
FROM THE OUTSIDE, IT'S EASY TO DISMISS THOSE RUN-UPS AS WASTED EFFORT...
BUT IT'S EXACTLY BECAUSE THEY'RE SELLING THEM SO WELL THAT WE'RE GETTING AROUND SHIRATORIZAWA'S BLOCKERS.
AZUMANE, TANAKA AND SAWAMURA, WHO HAVEN'T COME OFF THE COURT EVEN ONCE, HAVE TO BE *BEYOND* EXHAUSTED BY NOW.

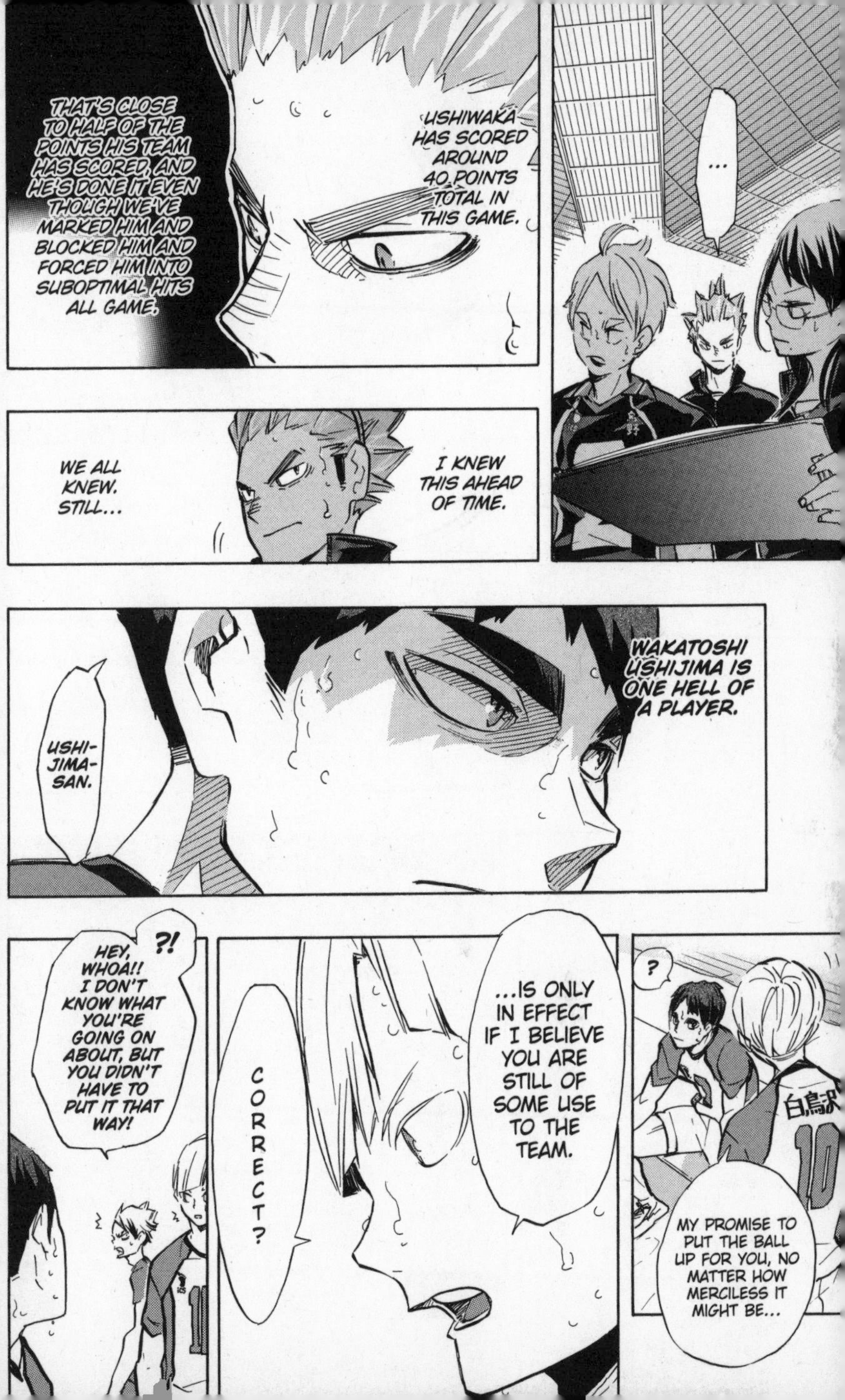
...
USHIWAKA HAS SCORED AROUND 40 POINTS TOTAL IN THIS GAME.
THAT'S CLOSE TO HALF OF THE POINTS HIS TEAM HAS SCORED, AND HE'S DONE IT EVEN THOUGH WE'VE MARKED HIM AND BLOCKED HIM AND FORCED HIM INTO SUBOPTIMAL HITS ALL GAME.
I KNEW THIS AHEAD OF TIME.
WE ALL KNEW. STILL...
WAKATOSHI USHIJIMA IS ONE HELL OF A PLAYER.
USHI-JIMA-SAN.
?
MY PROMISE TO PUT THE BALL UP FOR YOU, NO MATTER HOW MERCILESS IT MIGHT BE...
...IS ONLY IN EFFECT IF I BELIEVE YOU ARE STILL OF SOME USE TO THE TEAM.
CORRECT?
?!
HEY, WHOA!! I DON'T KNOW WHAT YOU'RE GOING ON ABOUT, BUT YOU DIDN'T HAVE TO PUT IT THAT WAY!

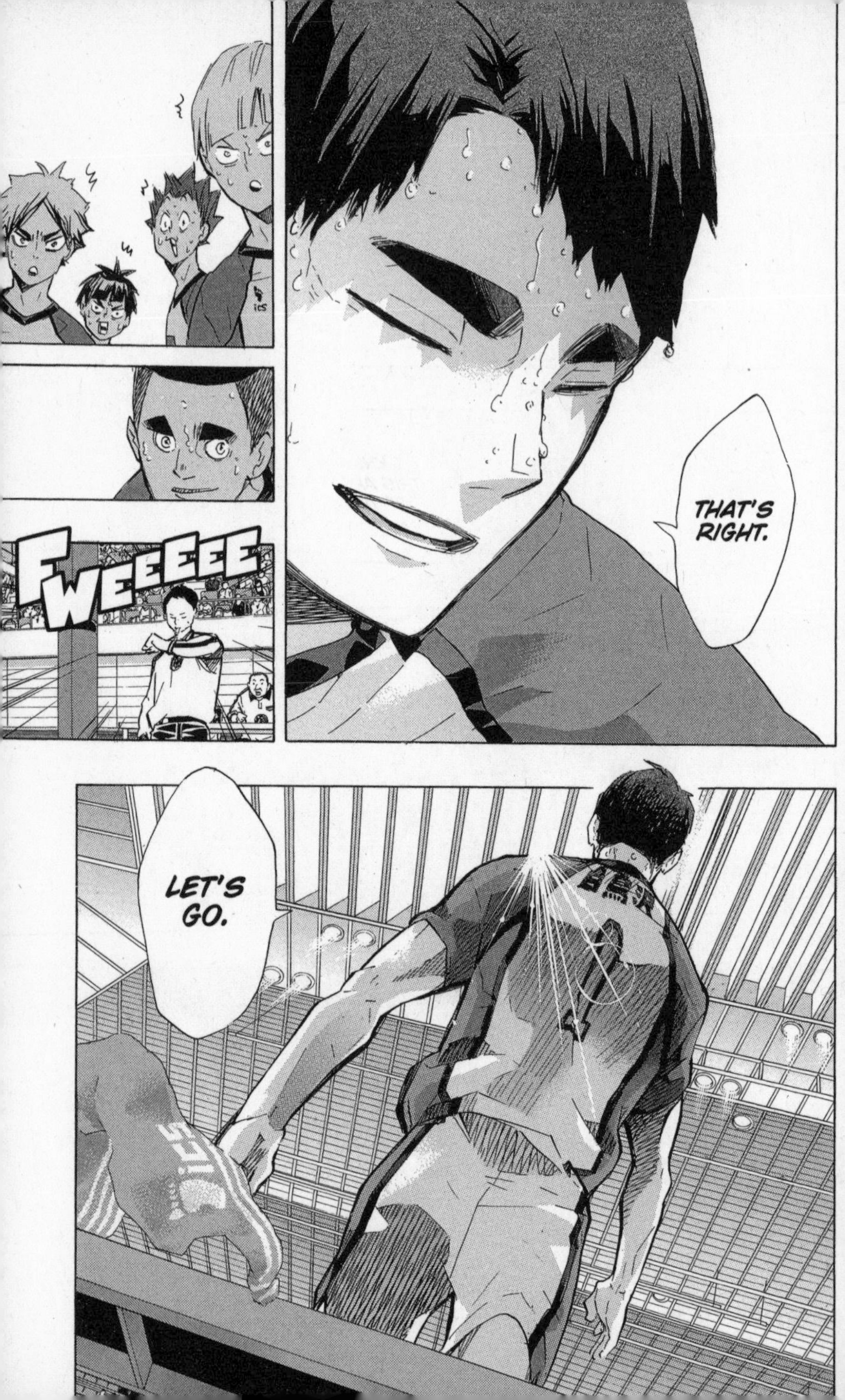
THAT'S RIGHT.
FWEEEEE
LET'S GO.

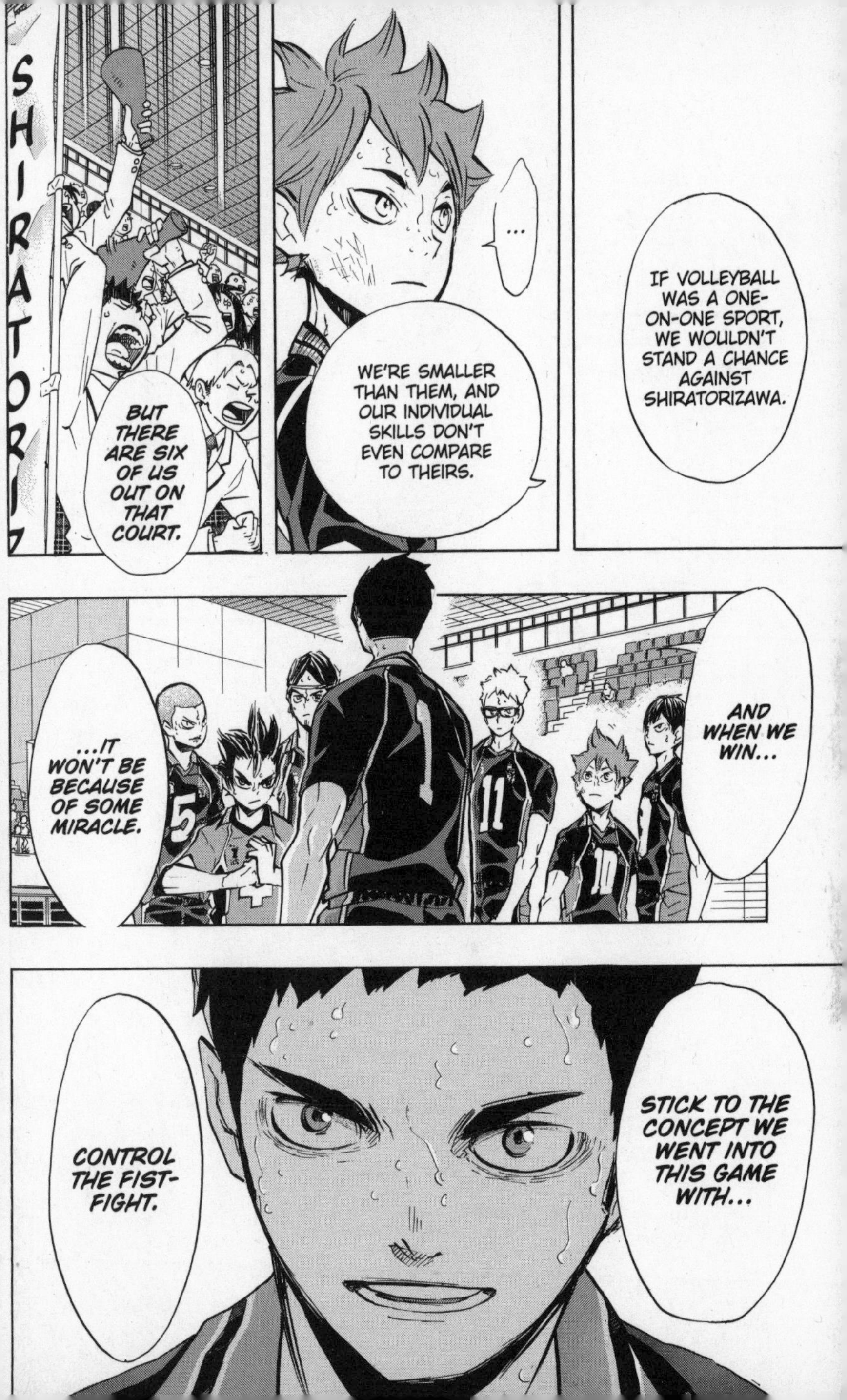
IF VOLLEYBALL WAS A ONE-ON-ONE SPORT, WE WOULDN'T STAND A CHANCE AGAINST SHIRATORIZAWA.
...
WE'RE SMALLER THAN THEM, AND OUR INDIVIDUAL SKILLS DON'T EVEN COMPARE TO THEIRS.
SHIRATORI
BUT THERE ARE SIX OF US OUT ON THAT COURT.
AND WHEN WE WIN...
...IT WON'T BE BECAUSE OF SOME MIRACLE.
STICK TO THE CONCEPT WE WENT INTO THIS GAME WITH...
CONTROL THE FIST-FIGHT.

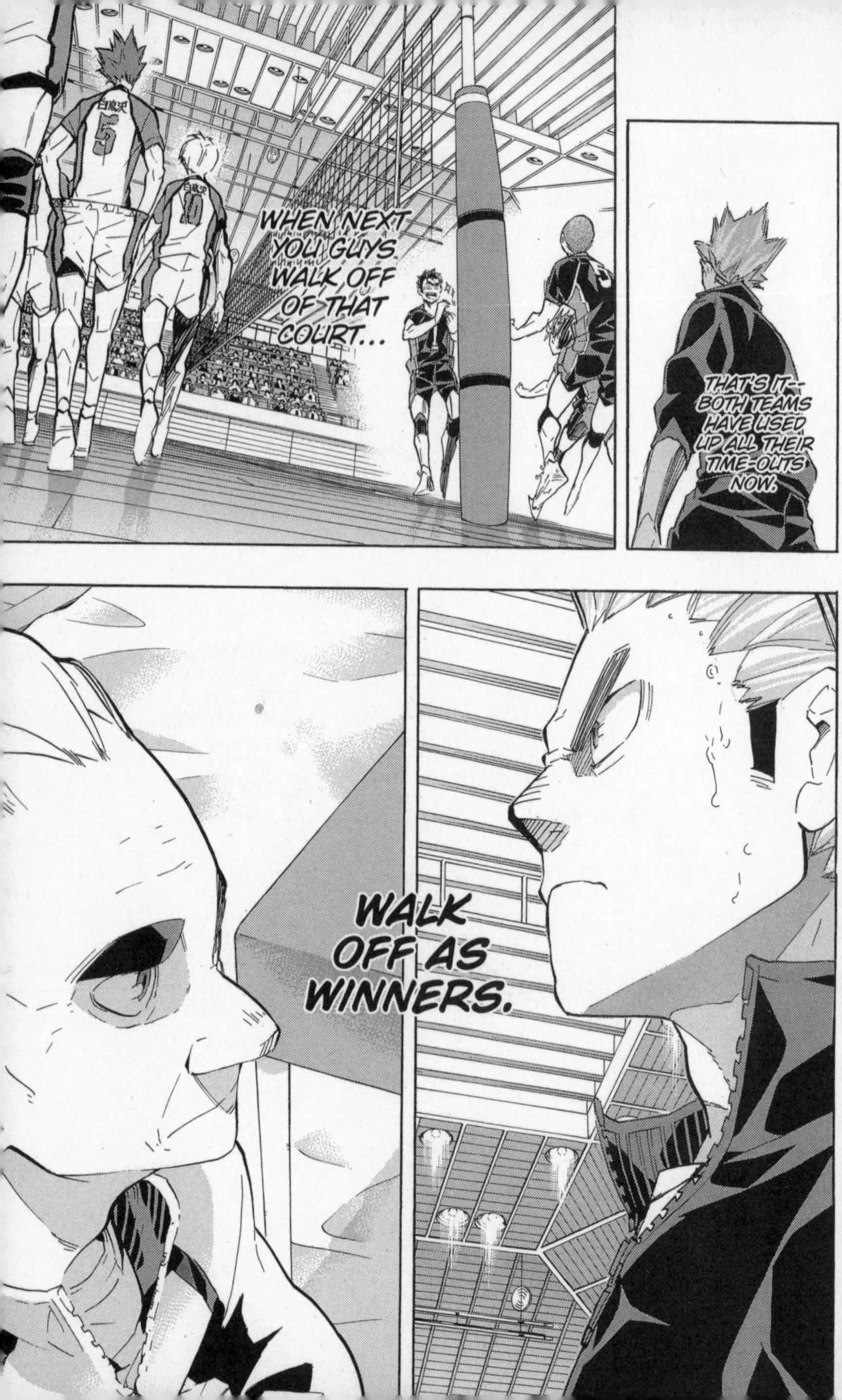
THAT'S IT-- BOTH TEAMS HAVE USED UP ALL THEIR TIME-OUTS NOW.
WHEN NEXT YOU GUYS WALK OFF OF THAT COURT...
WALK OFF AS WINNERS.

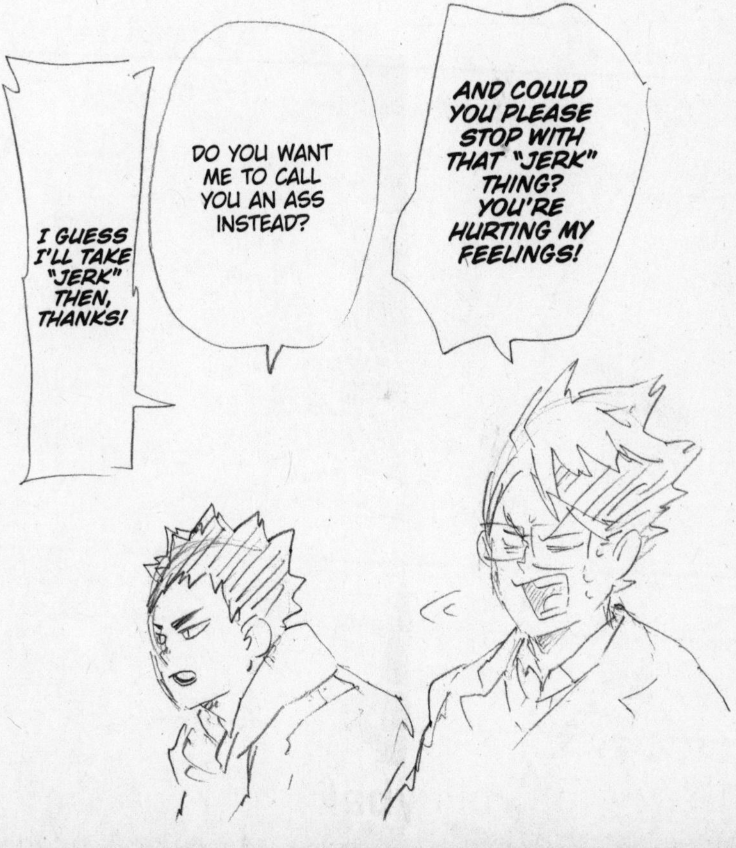
AND COULD YOU PLEASE STOP WITH THAT "JERK" THING? YOU'RE HURTING MY FEELINGS!
DO YOU WANT ME TO CALL YOU AN ASS INSTEAD?
I GUESS I'LL TAKE "JERK" THEN, THANKS!

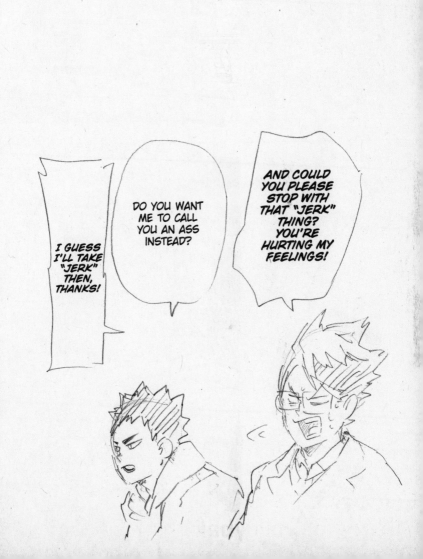

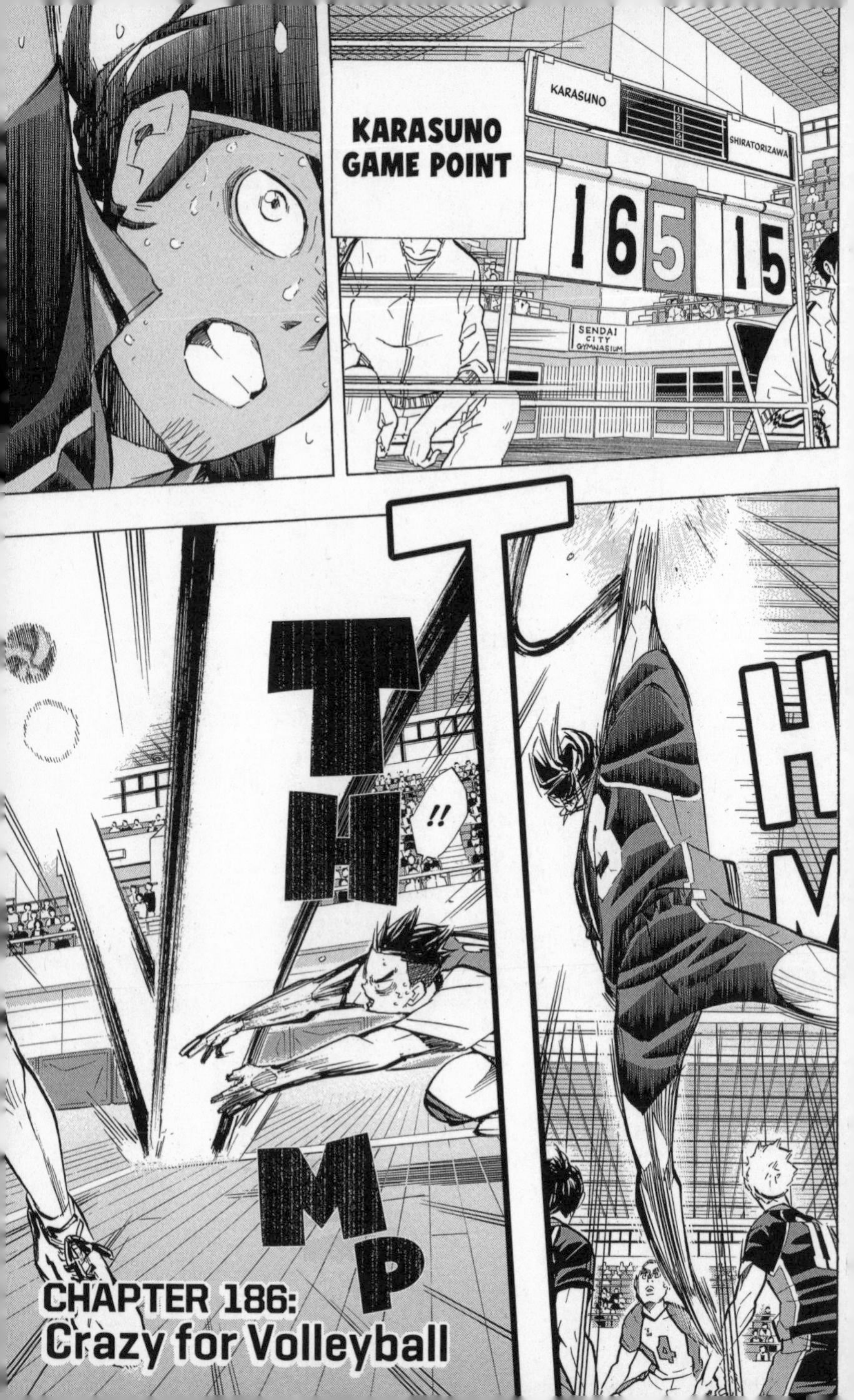
KARASUNO GAME POINT
KARASUNO
SHIRATORIZAWA
16 5 15
SENDAI CITY GYMNASIUM
THMP
!!
CHAPTER 186:
Crazy for Volleyball

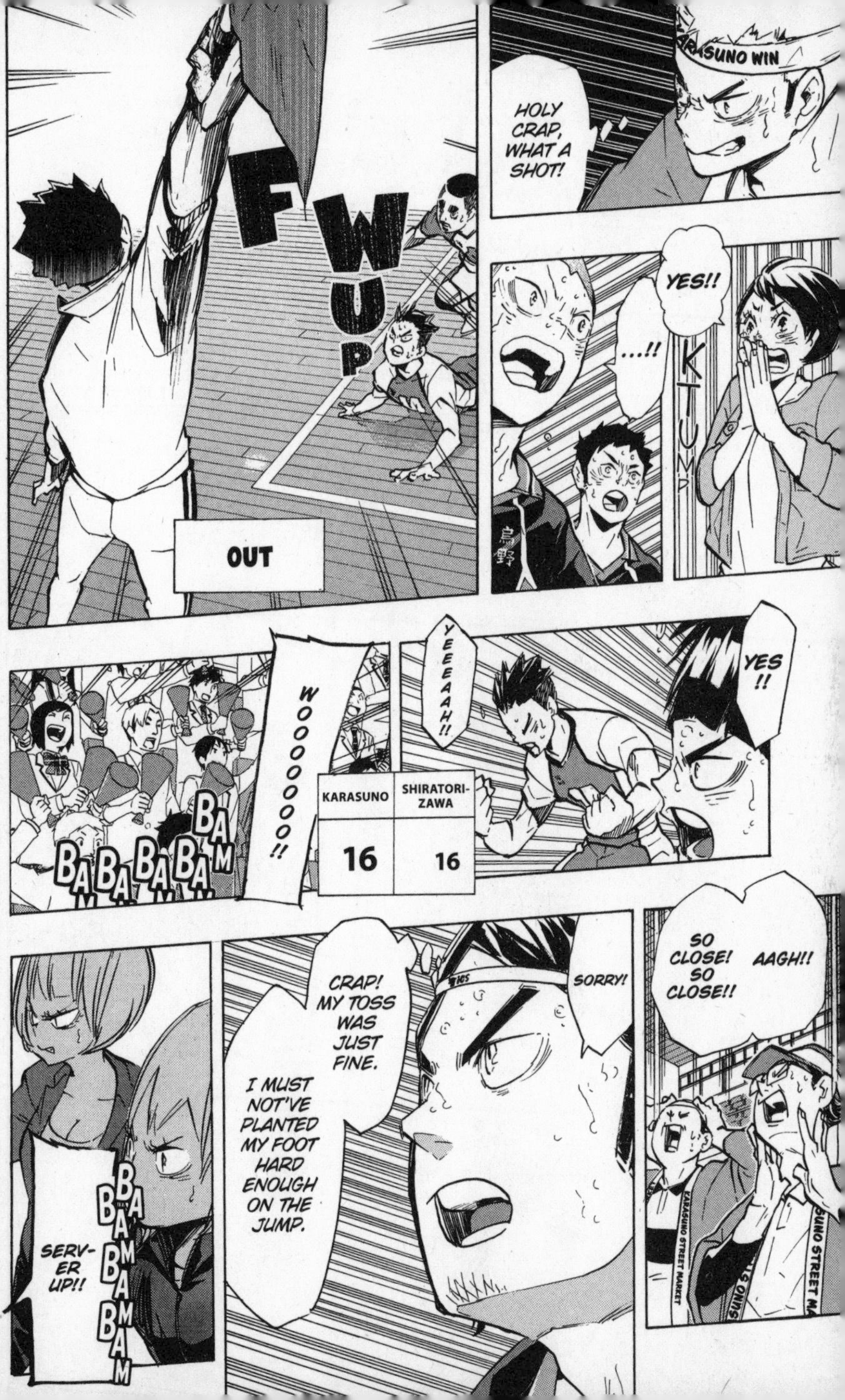
KARASUNO WIN
HOLY CRAP, WHAT A SHOT!
YES!!
...!!
KTUMP
FWUP
OUT
YES !!
YEEEAAAH!!
KARASUNO 16
SHIRATORIZAWA 16
WOOOOOOOOO!!
BABABABABAM
SO CLOSE! SO CLOSE!!
AAGH!!
KARASUNO STREET MARKET
SORRY!
CRAP! MY TOSS WAS JUST FINE.
I MUST NOT'VE PLANTED MY FOOT HARD ENOUGH ON THE JUMP.
SERVER UP!!
BABABAMBAMBAM

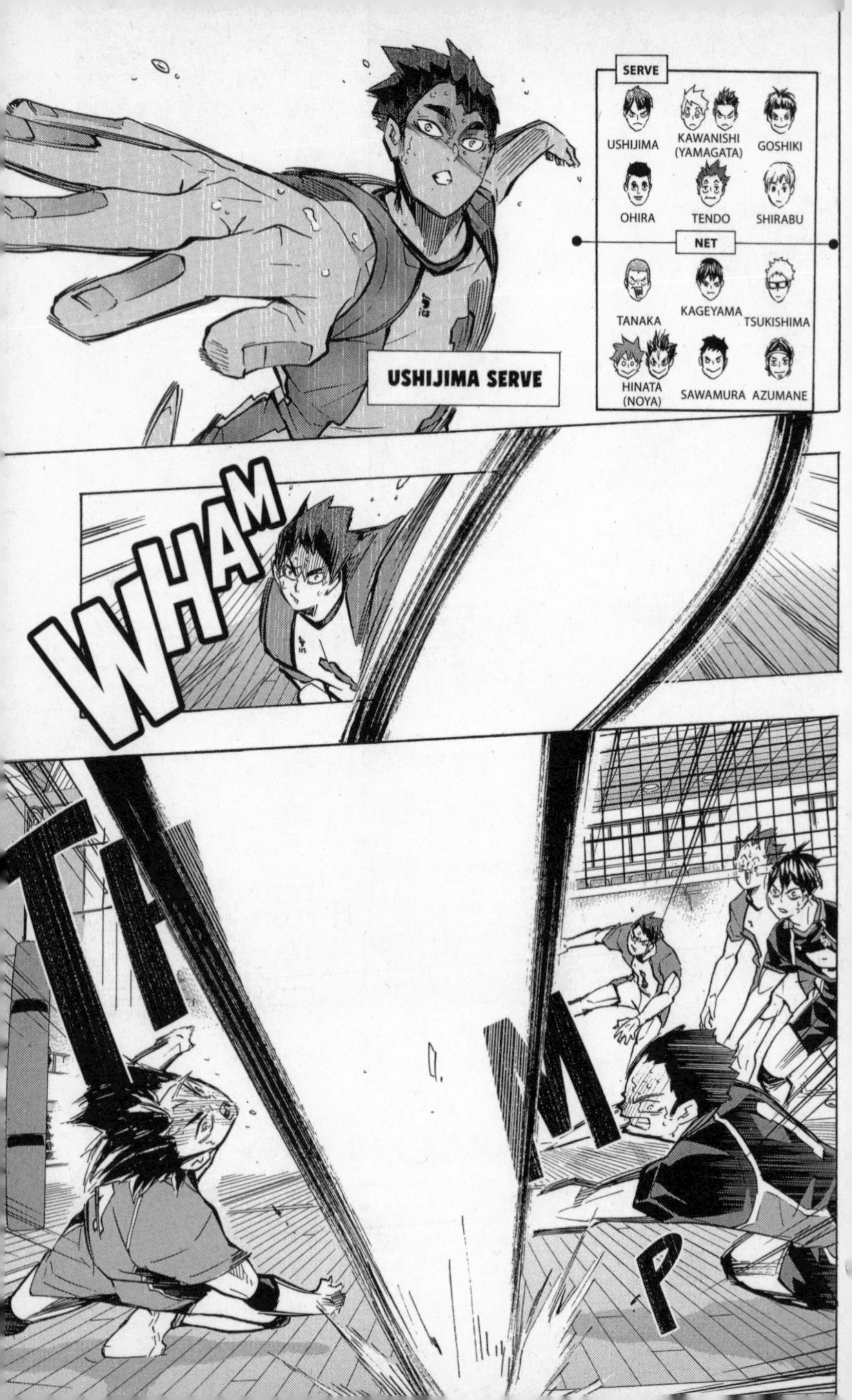

SERVE
USHIJIMA
KAWANISHI (YAMAGATA)
GOSHIKI
OHIRA
TENDO
SHIRABU
NET
TANAKA
KAGEYAMA
TSUKISHIMA
HINATA (NOYA)
SAWAMURA
AZUMANE
USHIJIMA SERVE
WHAM
THMP

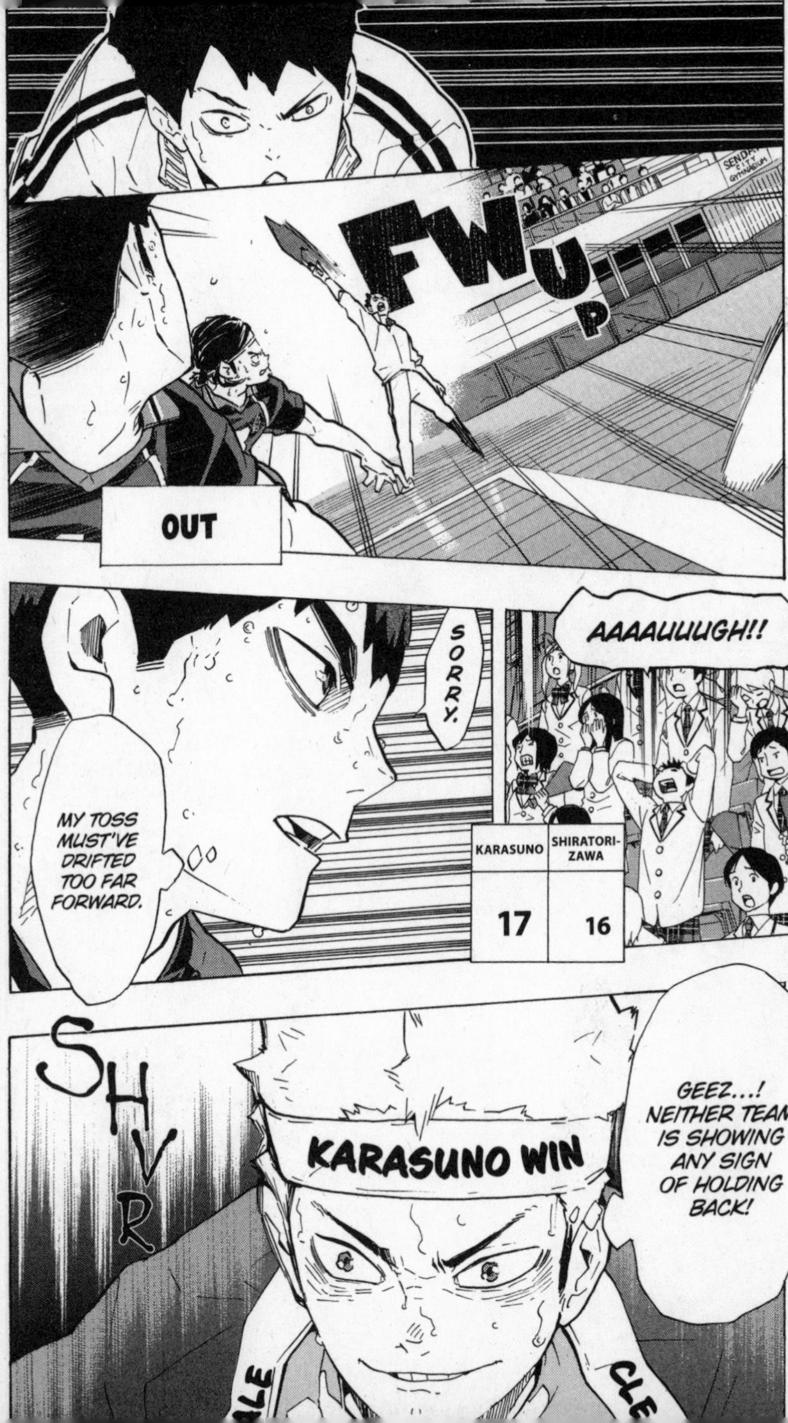
SENDAI CITY GYMNASIUM
FWUP
OUT
AAAAUUUGH!!
KARASUNO 17
SHIRATORIZAWA 16
SORRY.
MY TOSS MUST'VE DRIFTED TOO FAR FORWARD.
GEEZ...! NEITHER TEAM IS SHOWING ANY SIGN OF HOLDING BACK!
KARASUNO WIN
SHVR

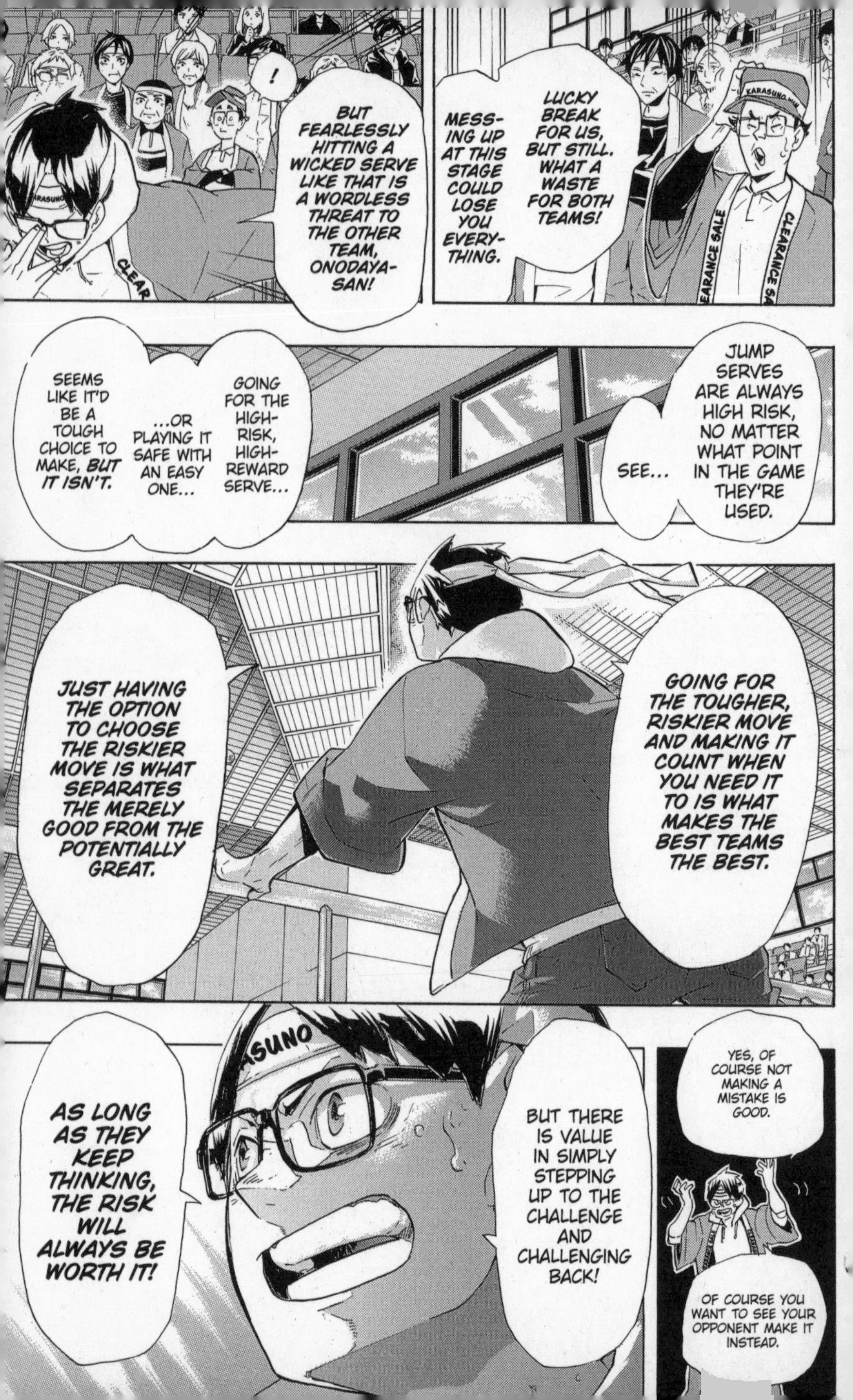
LUCKY BREAK FOR US, BUT STILL. WHAT A WASTE FOR BOTH TEAMS!
MESSING UP AT THIS STAGE COULD LOSE YOU EVERYTHING.
CLEARANCE SALE
!
BUT FEARLESSLY HITTING A WICKED SERVE LIKE THAT IS A WORDLESS THREAT TO THE OTHER TEAM, ONODAYA-SAN!
JUMP SERVES ARE ALWAYS HIGH RISK, NO MATTER WHAT POINT IN THE GAME THEY'RE USED.
SEE...
GOING FOR THE HIGH-RISK, HIGH-REWARD SERVE...
...OR PLAYING IT SAFE WITH AN EASY ONE...
SEEMS LIKE IT'D BE A TOUGH CHOICE TO MAKE, BUT IT ISN'T.
GOING FOR THE TOUGHER, RISKIER MOVE AND MAKING IT COUNT WHEN YOU NEED IT TO IS WHAT MAKES THE BEST TEAMS THE BEST.
JUST HAVING THE OPTION TO CHOOSE THE RISKIER MOVE IS WHAT SEPARATES THE MERELY GOOD FROM THE POTENTIALLY GREAT.
YES, OF COURSE NOT MAKING A MISTAKE IS GOOD.
OF COURSE YOU WANT TO SEE YOUR OPPONENT MAKE IT INSTEAD.
BUT THERE IS VALUE IN SIMPLY STEPPING UP TO THE CHALLENGE AND CHALLENGING BACK!
AS LONG AS THEY KEEP THINKING, THE RISK WILL ALWAYS BE WORTH IT!

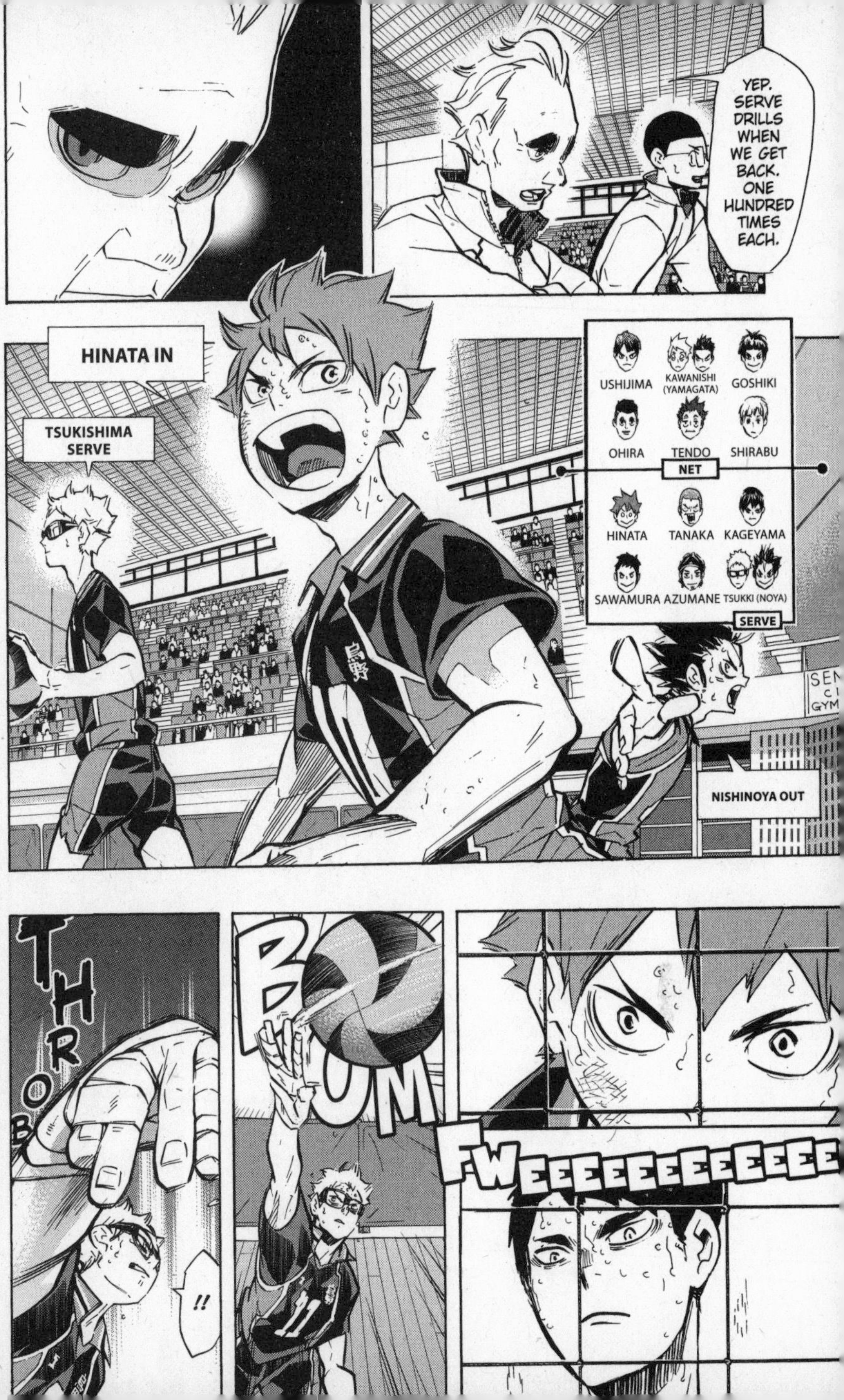
YEP. SERVE DRILLS WHEN WE GET BACK. ONE HUNDRED TIMES EACH.
USHIJIMA
KAWANISHI (YAMAGATA)
GOSHIKI
OHIRA
TENDO
SHIRABU
NET
HINATA
TANAKA
KAGEYAMA
SAWAMURA
AZUMANE
TSUKKI (NOYA)
SERVE
NISHINOYA OUT
HINATA IN
TSUKISHIMA SERVE
SEN
CI
GYM
FWEEEEEEEEEEEE
BOOM
THROB
!!

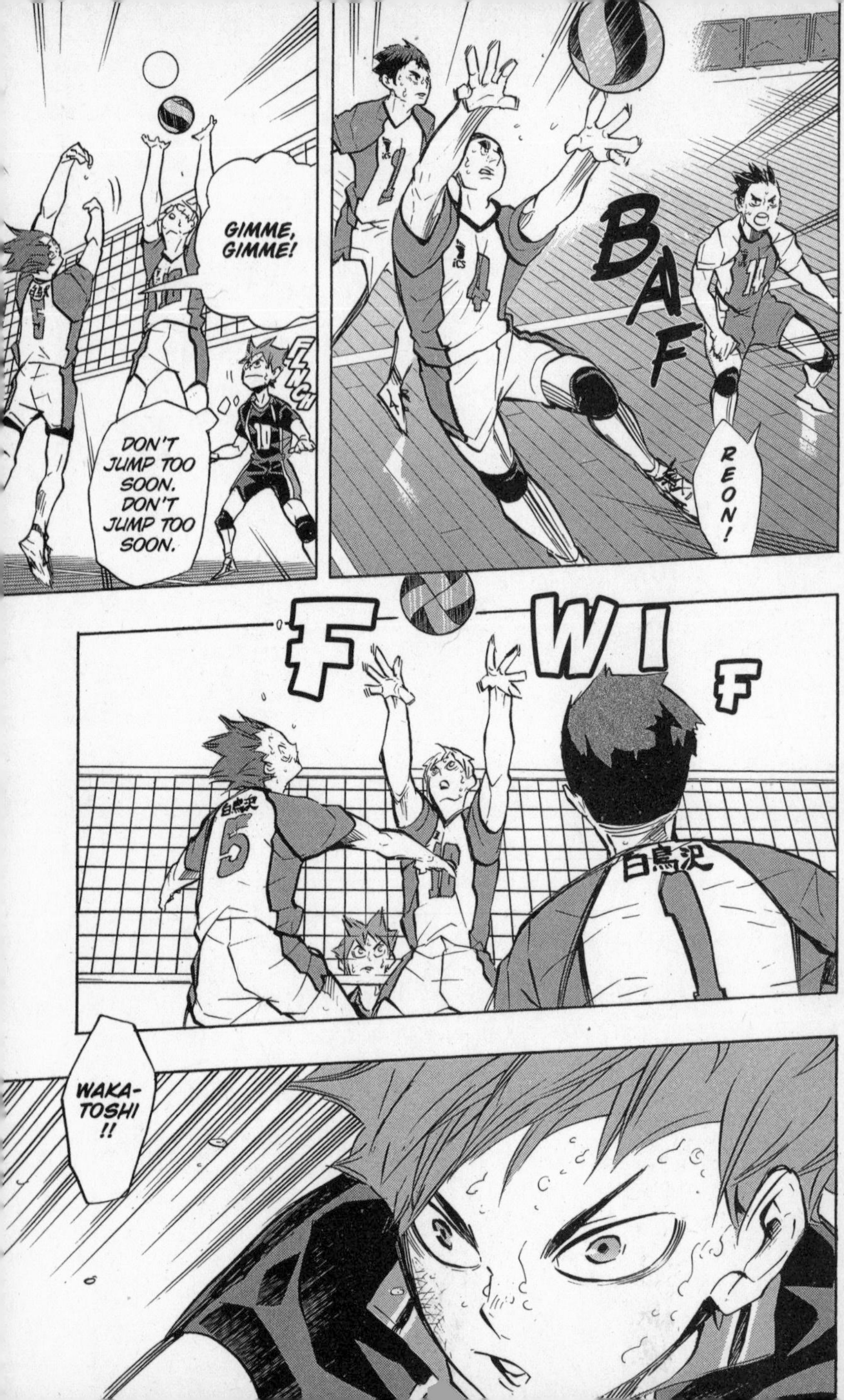

BAF
REON!
GIMME, GIMME!
FLINCH
DON'T JUMP TOO SOON. DON'T JUMP TOO SOON.
FWIF
WAKA-TOSHI!!

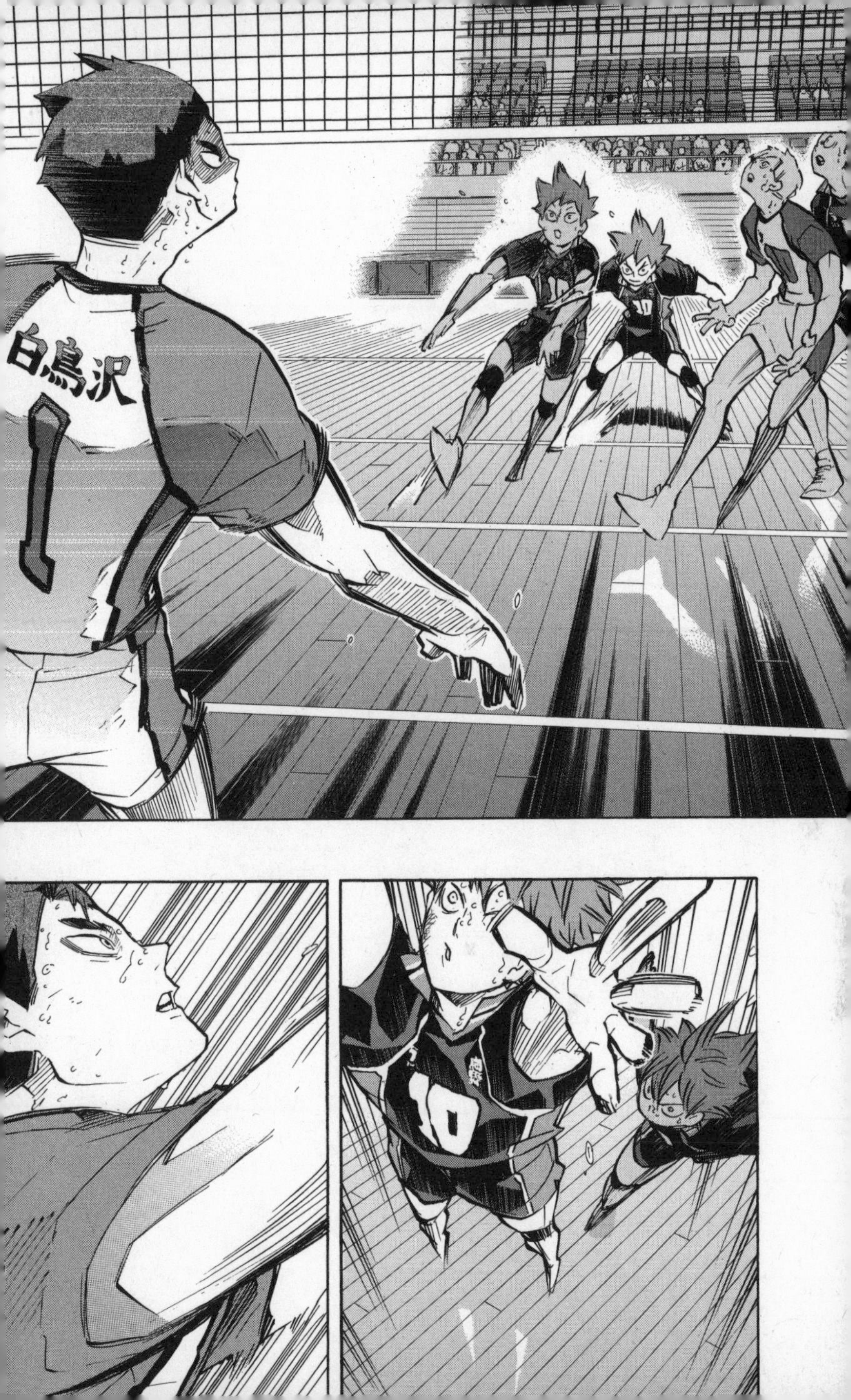
白鳥沢

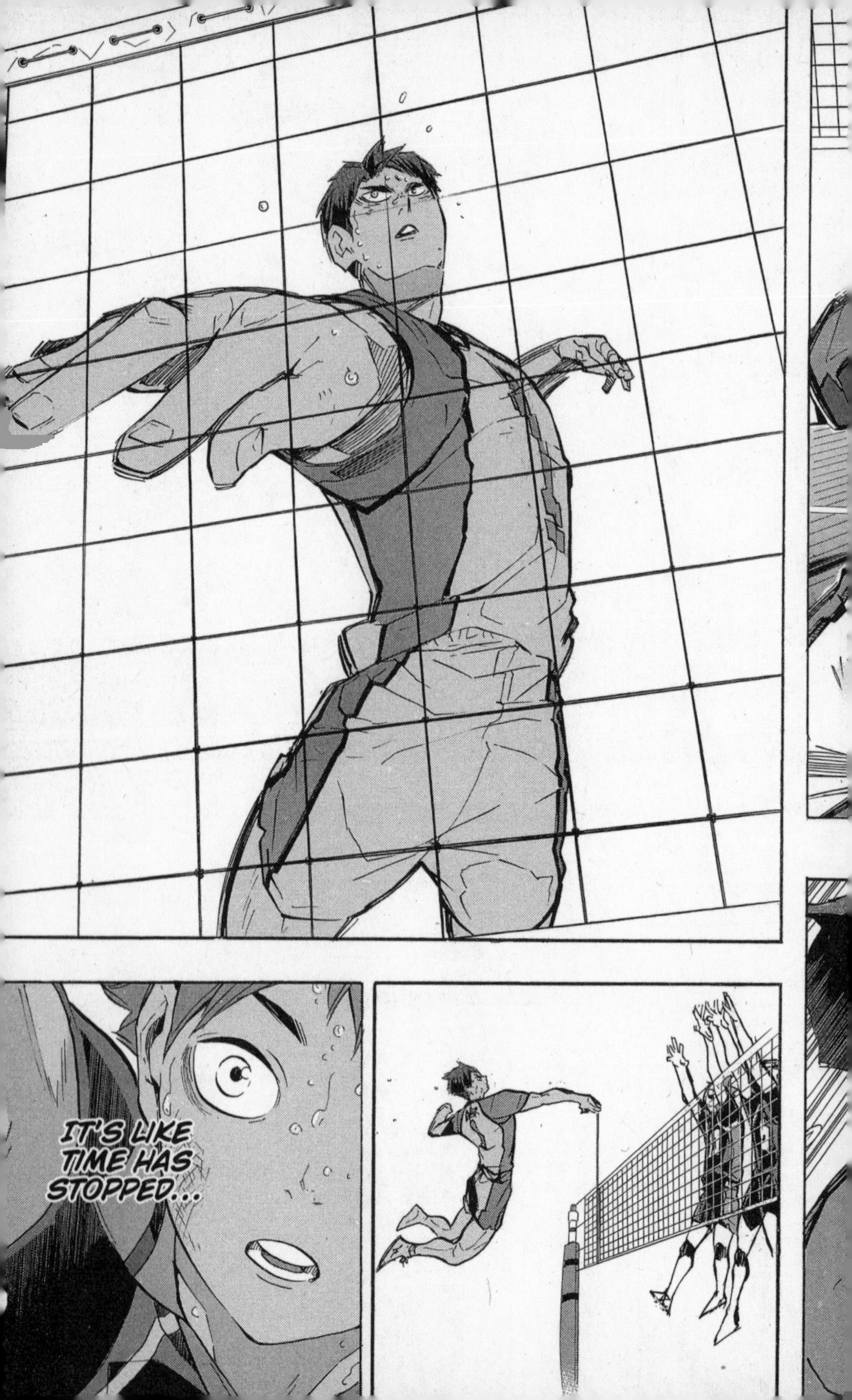
IT'S LIKE TIME HAS STOPPED...

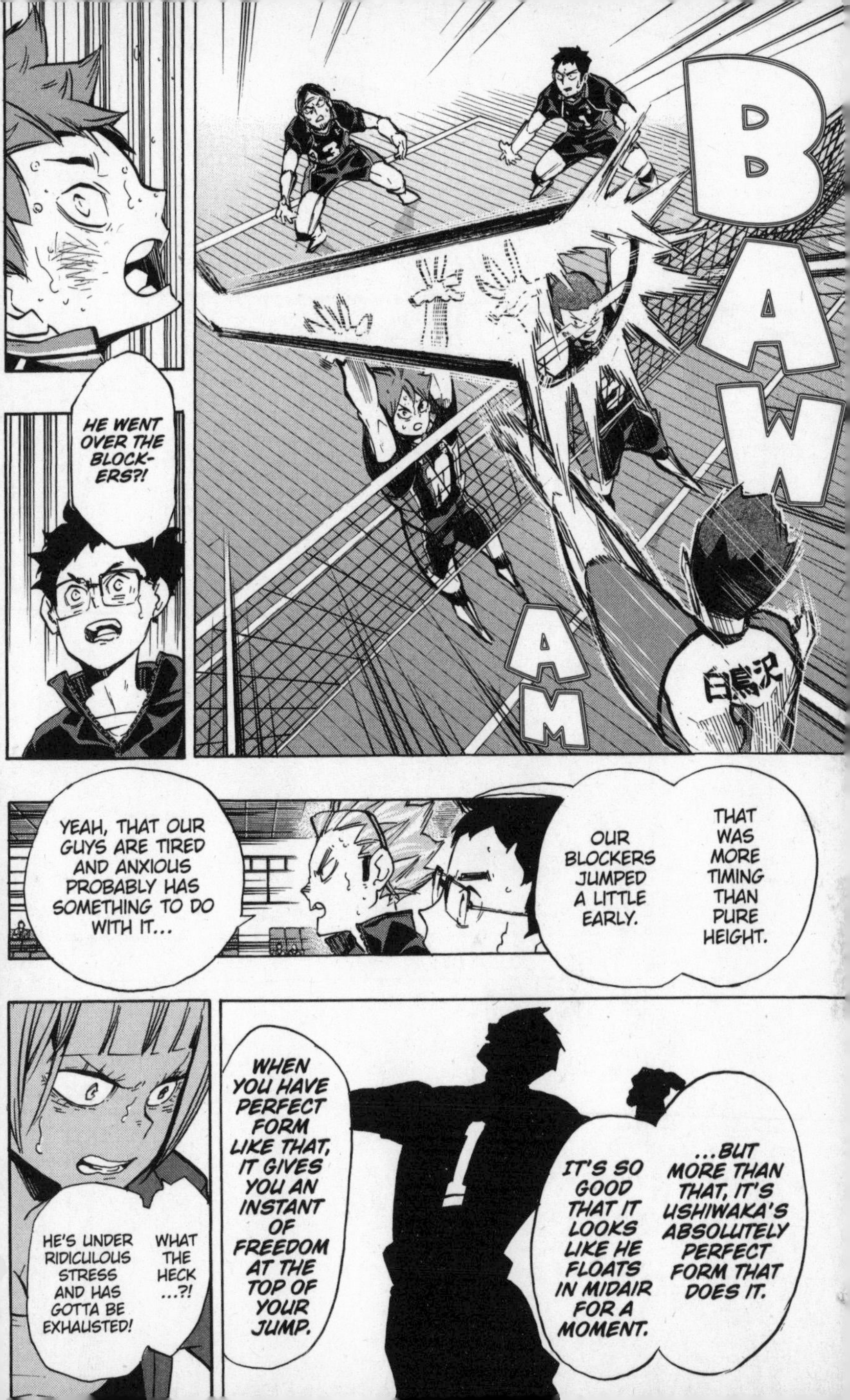
BAWAM
白鳥沢
HE WENT OVER THE BLOCKERS?!
THAT WAS MORE TIMING THAN PURE HEIGHT.
OUR BLOCKERS JUMPED A LITTLE EARLY.
YEAH, THAT OUR GUYS ARE TIRED AND ANXIOUS PROBABLY HAS SOMETHING TO DO WITH IT...
...BUT MORE THAN THAT, IT'S USHIWAKA'S ABSOLUTELY PERFECT FORM THAT DOES IT.
IT'S SO GOOD THAT IT LOOKS LIKE HE FLOATS IN MIDAIR FOR A MOMENT.
WHEN YOU HAVE PERFECT FORM LIKE THAT, IT GIVES YOU AN INSTANT OF FREEDOM AT THE TOP OF YOUR JUMP.
WHAT THE HECK...?!
HE'S UNDER RIDICULOUS STRESS AND HAS GOTTA BE EXHAUSTED!

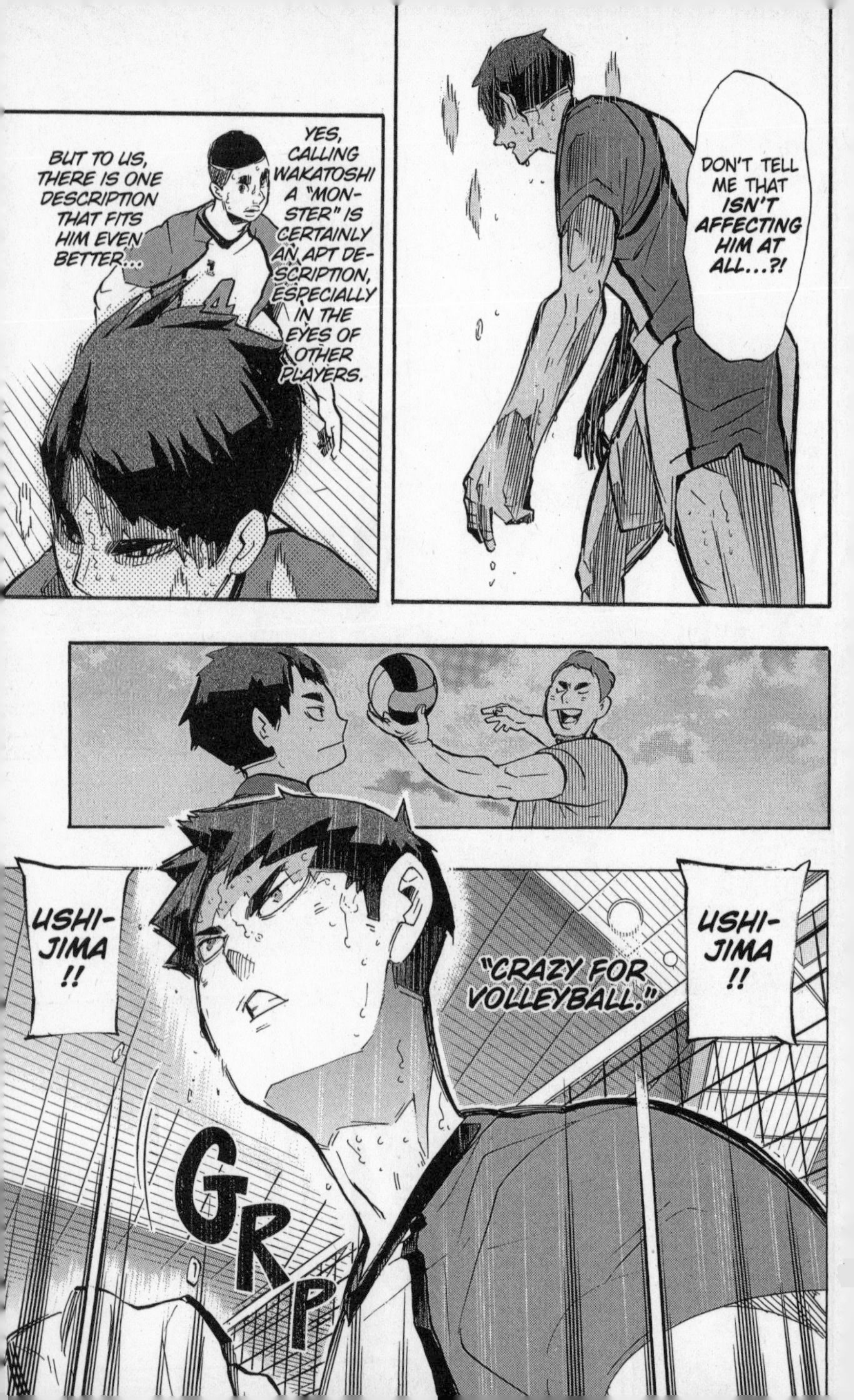

DON'T TELL ME THAT ISN'T AFFECTING HIM AT ALL...?!
YES, CALLING WAKATOSHI A "MONSTER" IS CERTAINLY AN APT DESCRIPTION, ESPECIALLY IN THE EYES OF OTHER PLAYERS.
BUT TO US, THERE IS ONE DESCRIPTION THAT FITS HIM EVEN BETTER...
USHIJIMA!!
"CRAZY FOR VOLLEYBALL."
USHIJIMA!!
GRP

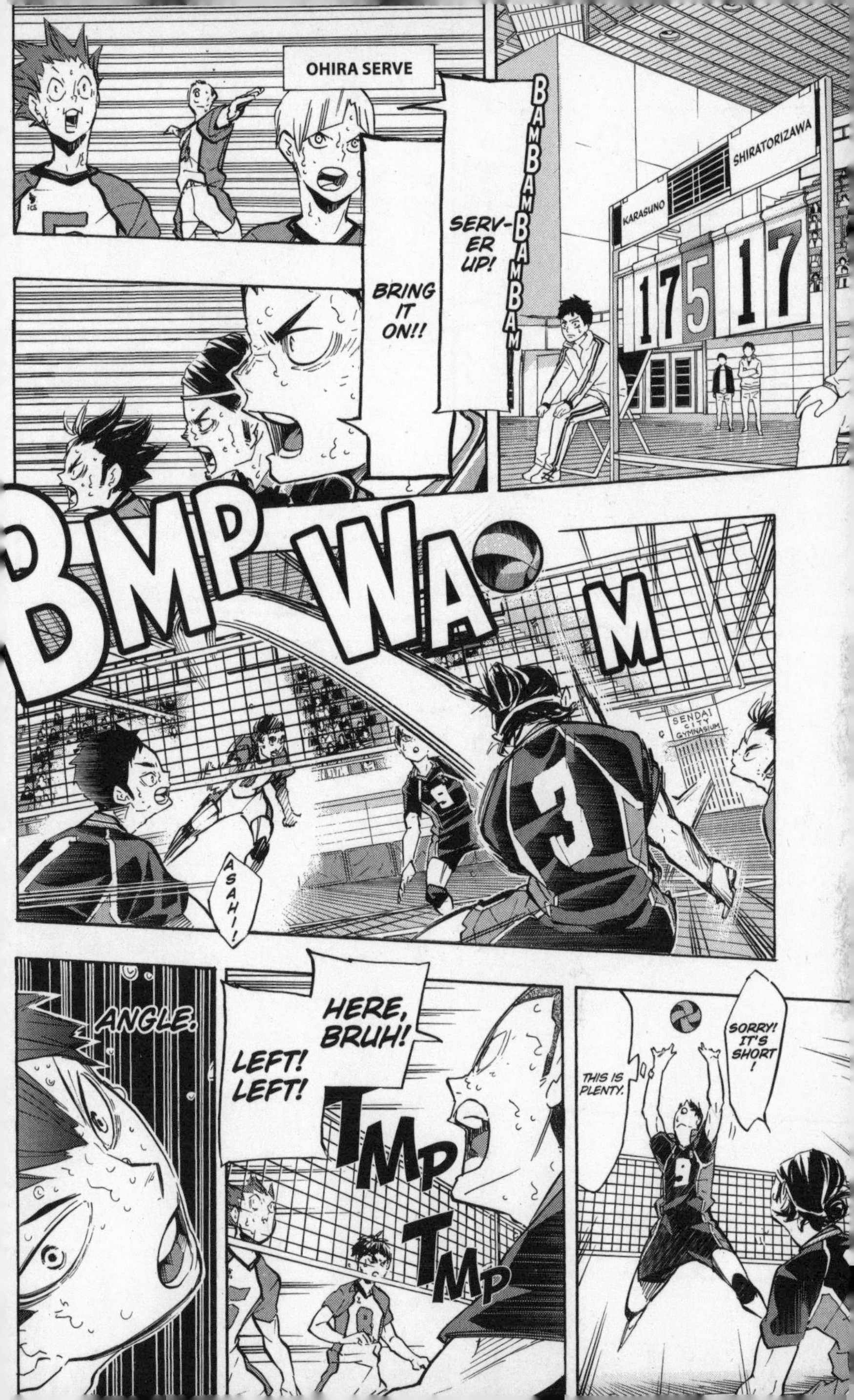
SHIRATORIZAWA
KARASUNO
17 5 17
BAMBAMBAMBAM
OHIRA SERVE
SERV-ER UP!
BRING IT ON!!
BMP
WAM
SENDAI CITY GYMNASIUM
ASAHI!
SORRY! IT'S SHORT!
THIS IS PLENTY.
HERE, BRUH!
LEFT! LEFT!
TMP TMP
ANGLE.

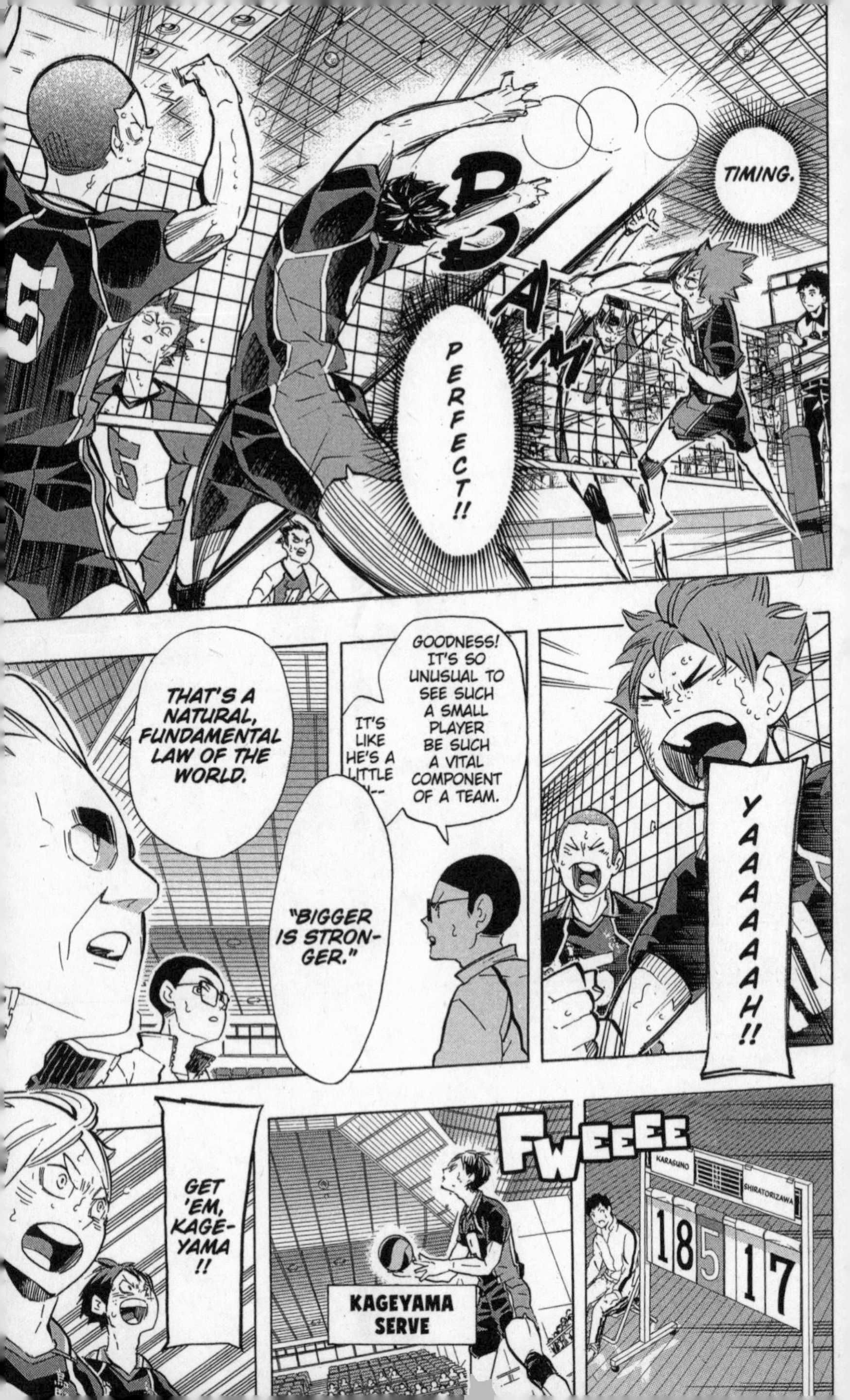

TIMING.
BAM
PERFECT!!
YAAAAAAAH!!
GOODNESS! IT'S SO UNUSUAL TO SEE SUCH A SMALL PLAYER BE SUCH A VITAL COMPONENT OF A TEAM.
IT'S LIKE HE'S A LITTLE --
THAT'S A NATURAL, FUNDAMENTAL LAW OF THE WORLD.
"BIGGER IS STRONGER."
FWEEEE
KARASUNO
SHIRATORIZAWA
18 5 17
KAGEYAMA SERVE
GET 'EM, KAGEYAMA!!

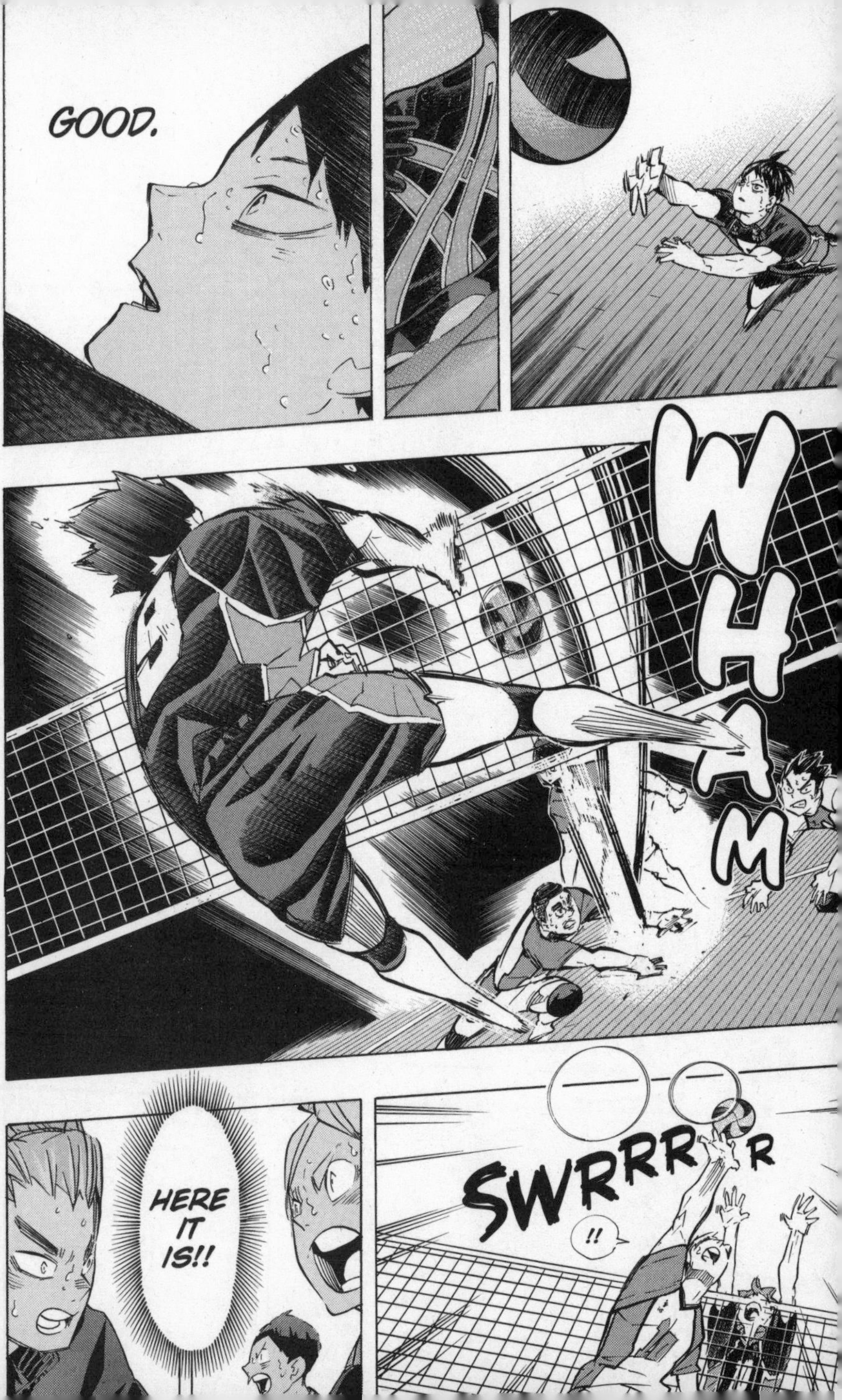
GOOD.
WHAM
SWRRRR
!!
HERE IT IS!!

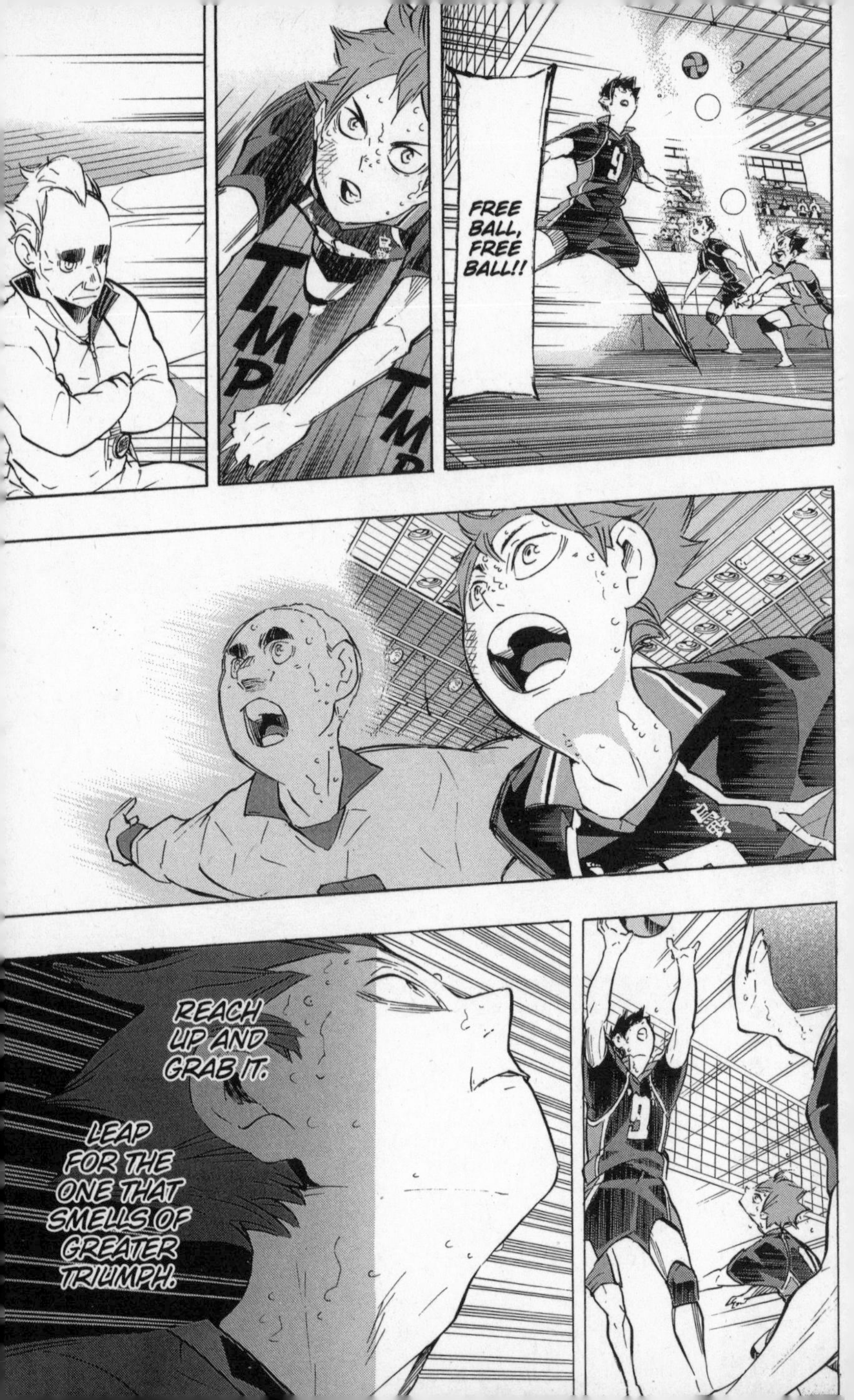
FREE BALL, FREE BALL!!
TMP
TMP
REACH UP AND GRAB IT.
LEAP FOR THE ONE THAT SMELLS OF GREATER TRIUMPH.

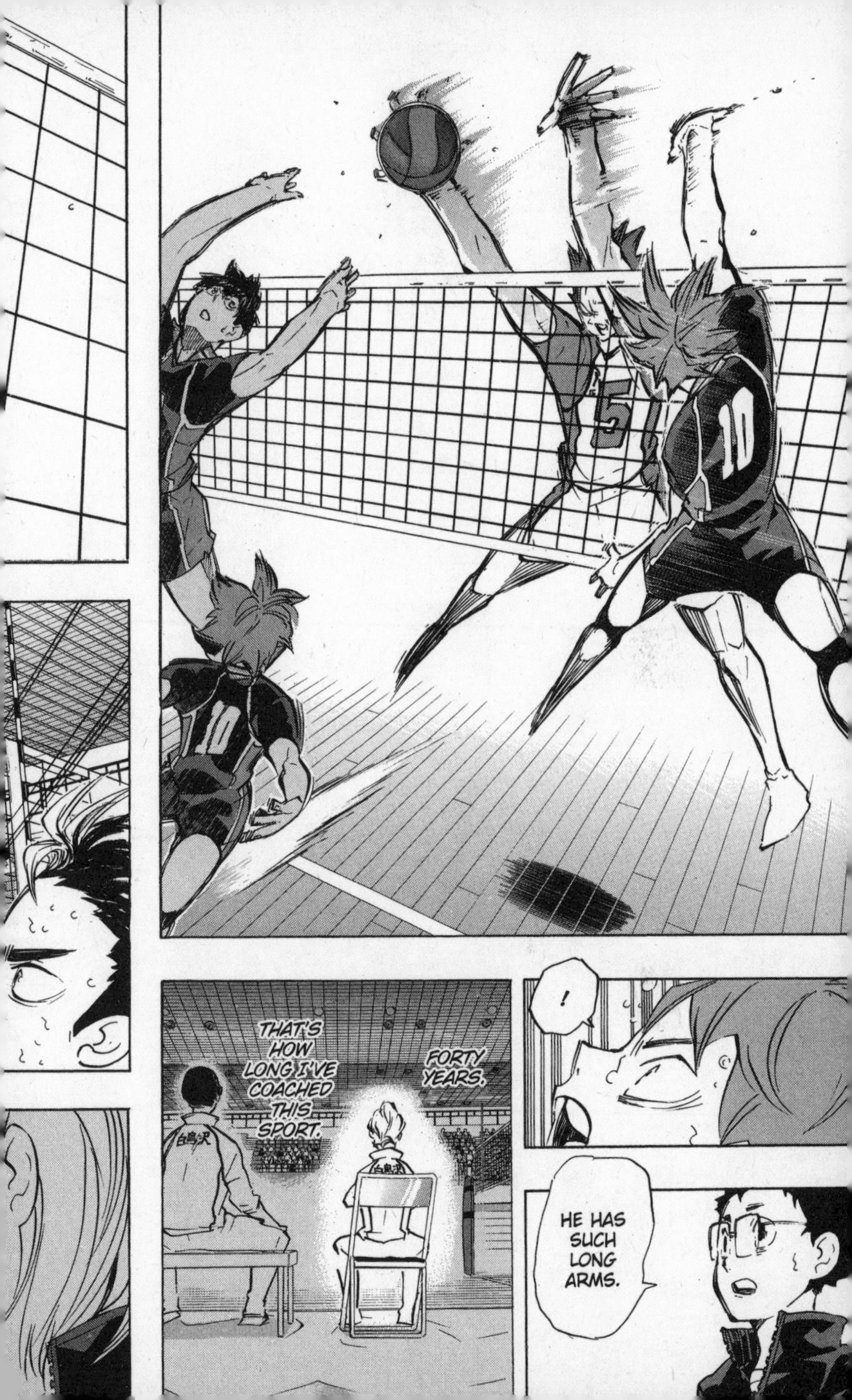
!
HE HAS SUCH LONG ARMS.
FORTY YEARS.
THAT'S HOW LONG I'VE COACHED THIS SPORT.

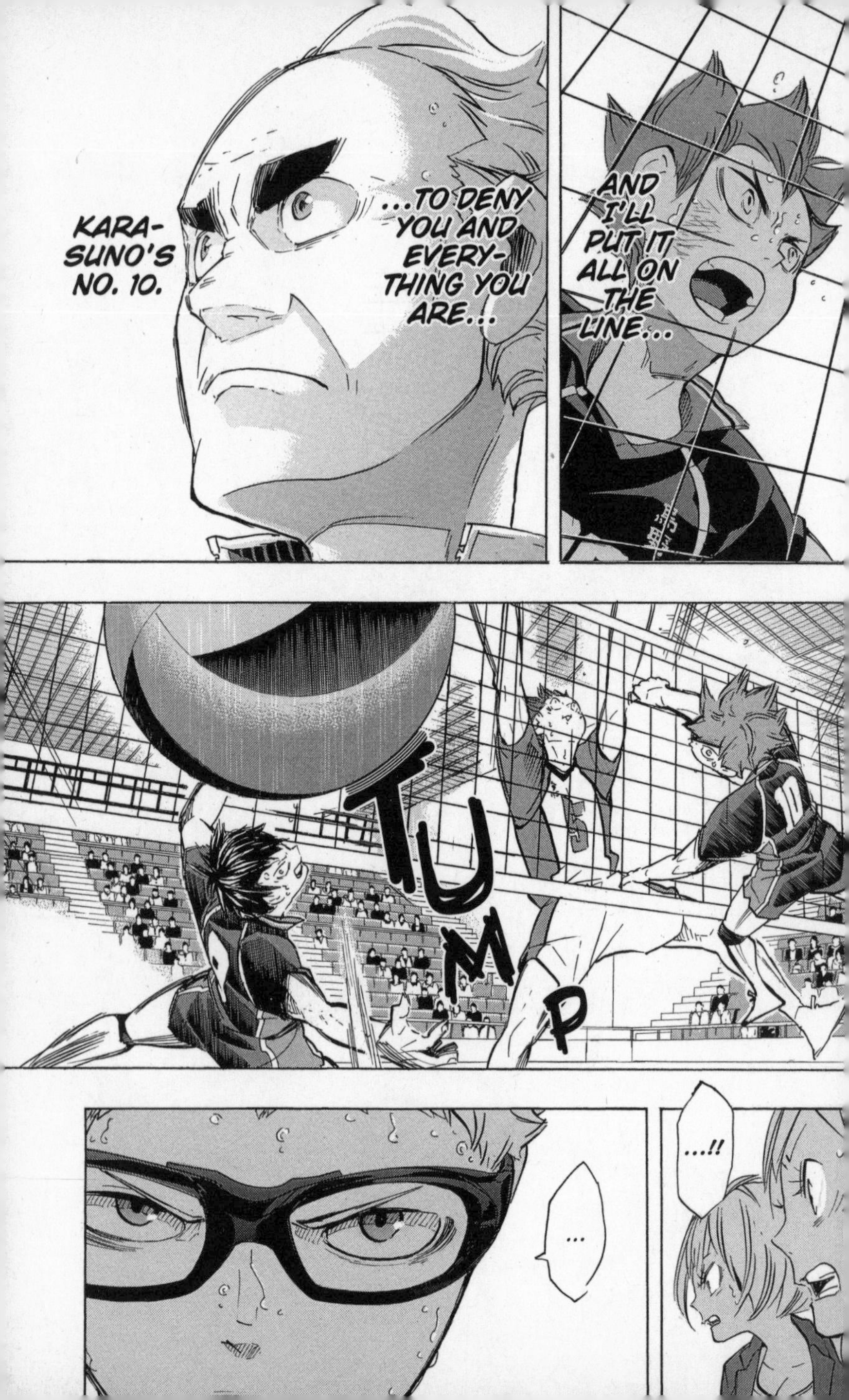
AND I'LL PUT IT ALL ON THE LINE...
...TO DENY YOU AND EVERY-THING YOU ARE...
KARA-SUNO'S NO. 10.
TUMP
...!!
...

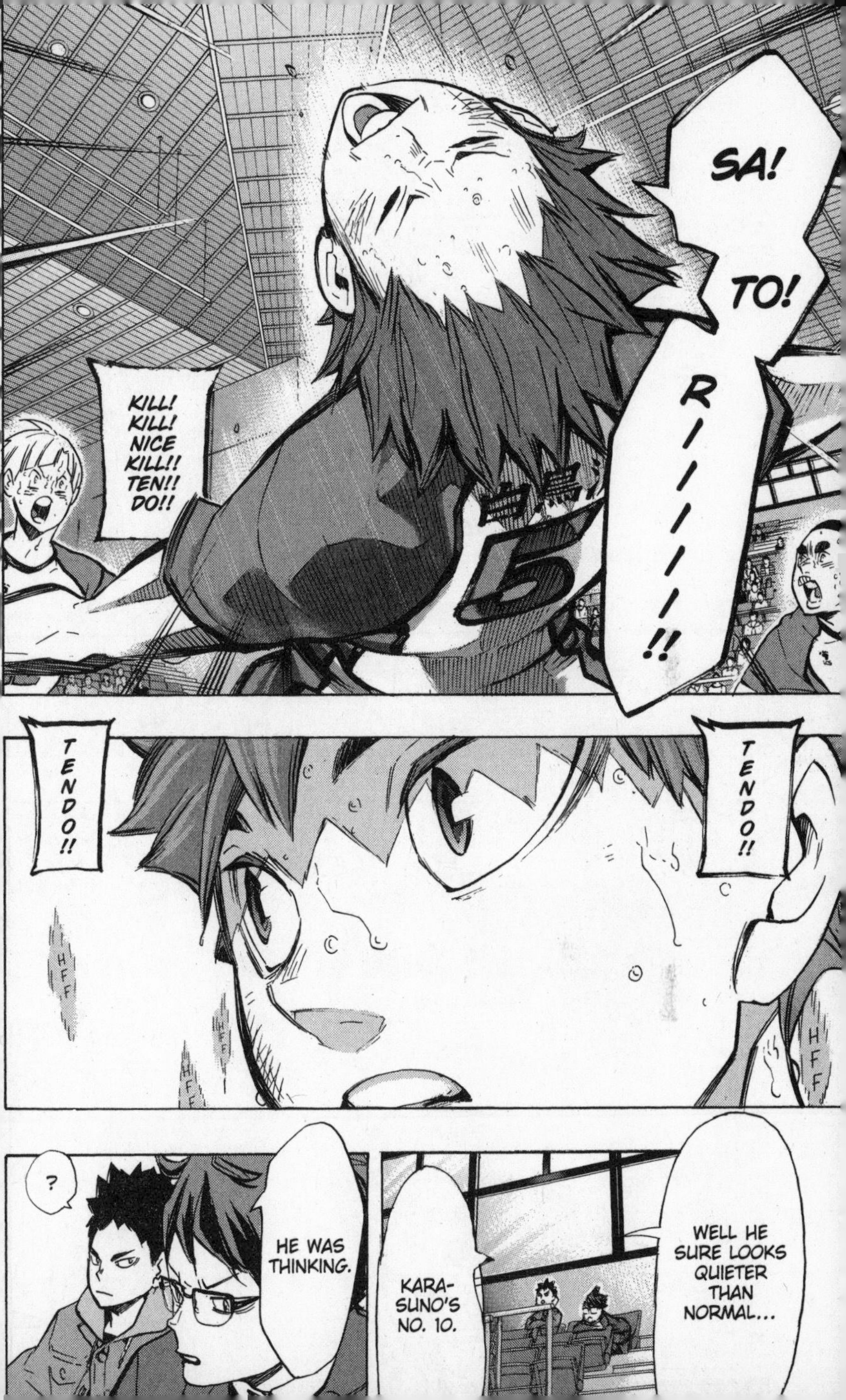
SA! TO! RIIIII!!
KILL! KILL! NICE KILL!! TEN!! DO!!
TENDO!!
TENDO!!
HFF
HFF
HFF
HFF
WELL HE SURE LOOKS QUIETER THAN NORMAL...
KARA-SUNO'S NO. 10.
HE WAS THINKING.
?

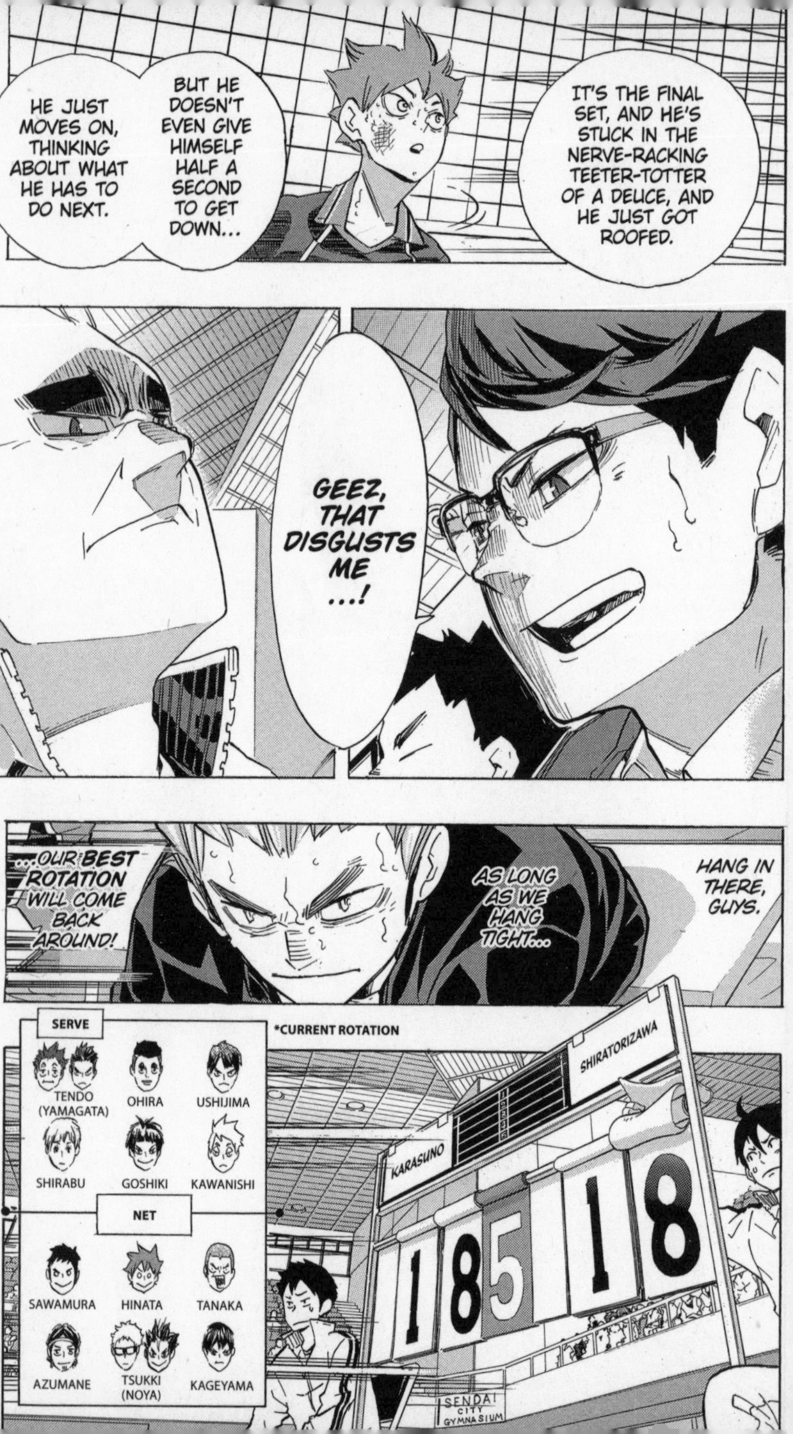

IT'S THE FINAL SET, AND HE'S STUCK IN THE NERVE-RACKING TEETER-TOTTER OF A DEUCE, AND HE JUST GOT ROOFED.
BUT HE DOESN'T EVEN GIVE HIMSELF HALF A SECOND TO GET DOWN...
HE JUST MOVES ON, THINKING ABOUT WHAT HE HAS TO DO NEXT.
GEEZ, THAT DISGUSTS ME ...!
HANG IN THERE, GUYS.
AS LONG AS WE HANG TIGHT...
...OUR BEST ROTATION WILL COME BACK AROUND!
SHIRATORIZAWA
KARASUNO
18 5 18
SENDAI CITY GYMNASIUM
*CURRENT ROTATION
SERVE
TENDO (YAMAGATA)
OHIRA
USHIJIMA
SHIRABU
GOSHIKI
KAWANISHI
NET
SAWAMURA
HINATA
TANAKA
AZUMANE
TSUKKI (NOYA)
KAGEYAMA

CHAPTER 187: Midday Moon

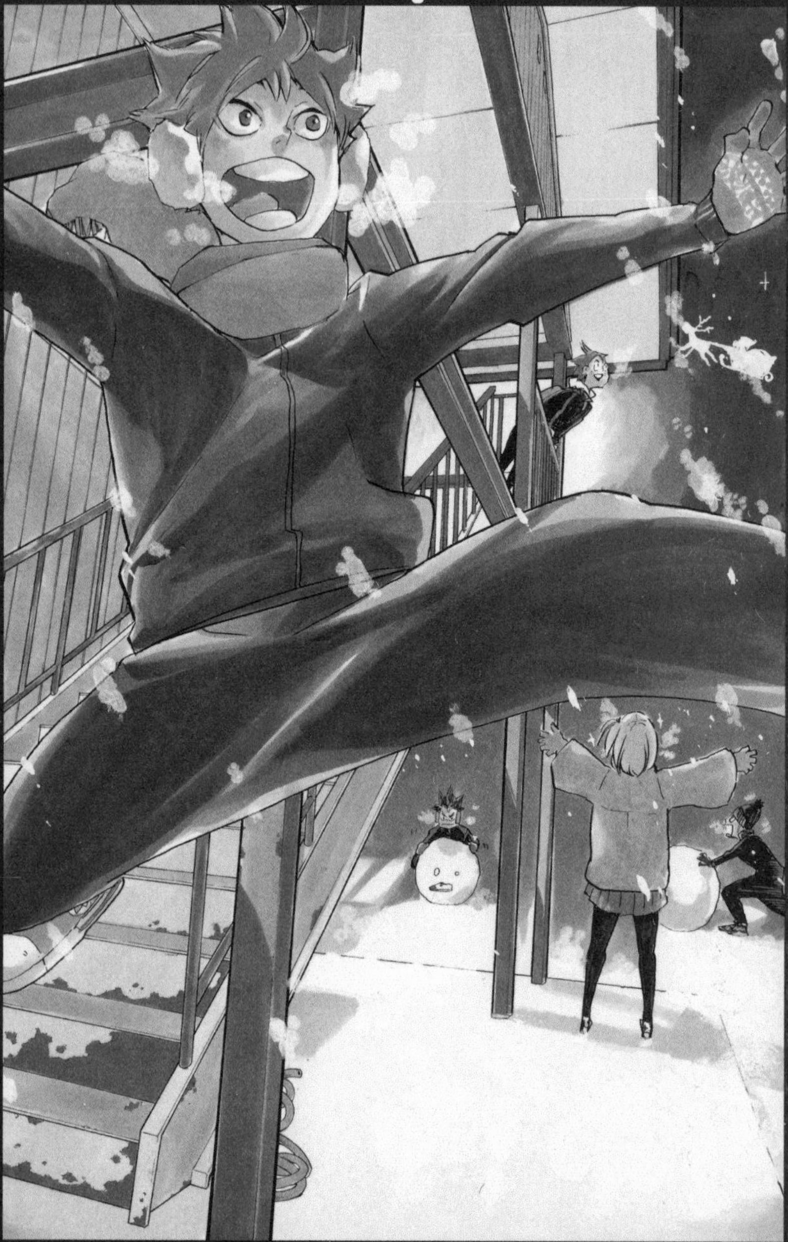

HAIKYU!!

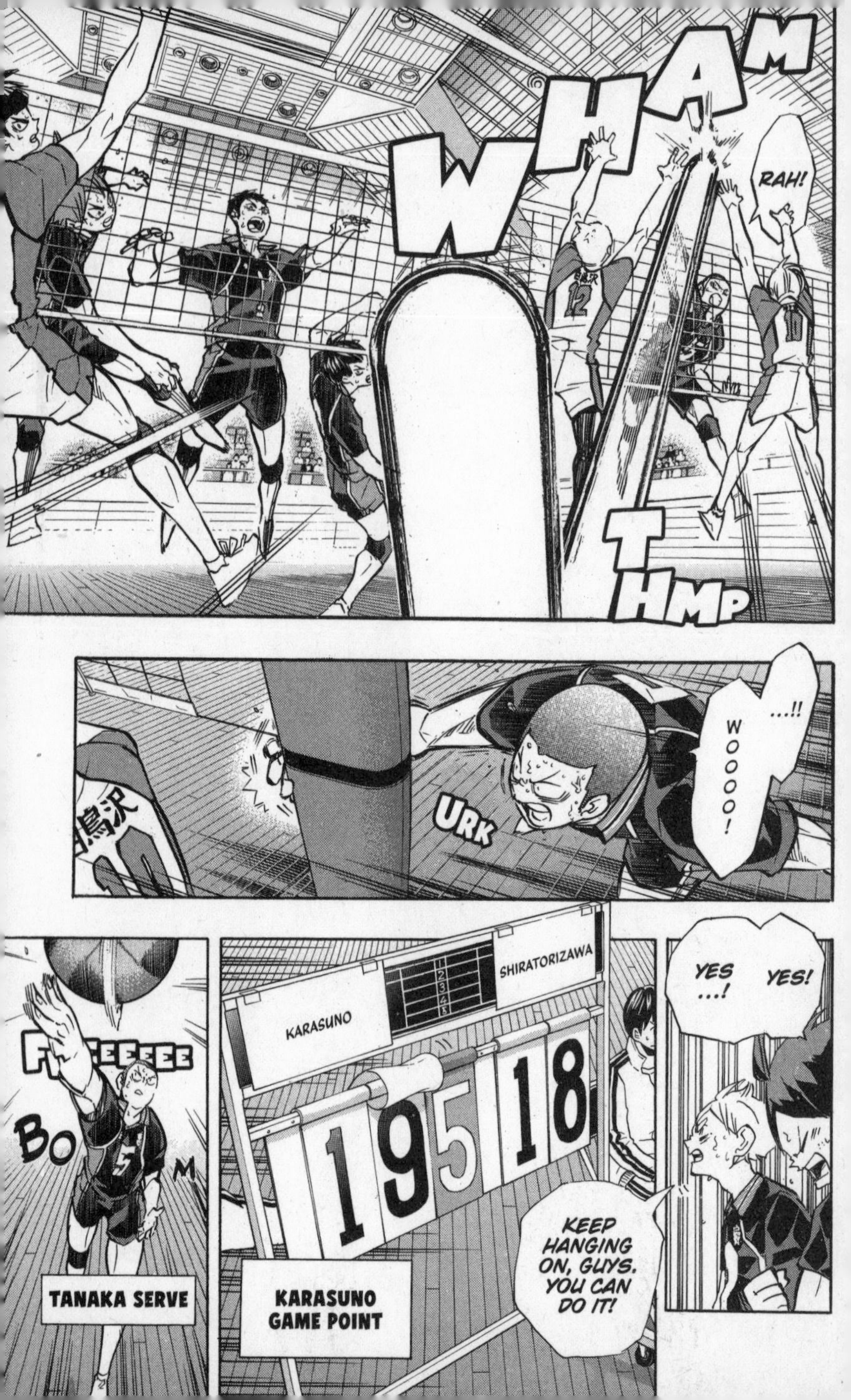
RAH!
WHAM
THMP
...!!
WOOOOO!
URK
YES!
YES ...!
KEEP HANGING ON, GUYS. YOU CAN DO IT!
SHIRATORIZAWA
KARASUNO
19
18
KARASUNO GAME POINT
BOOM
TANAKA SERVE

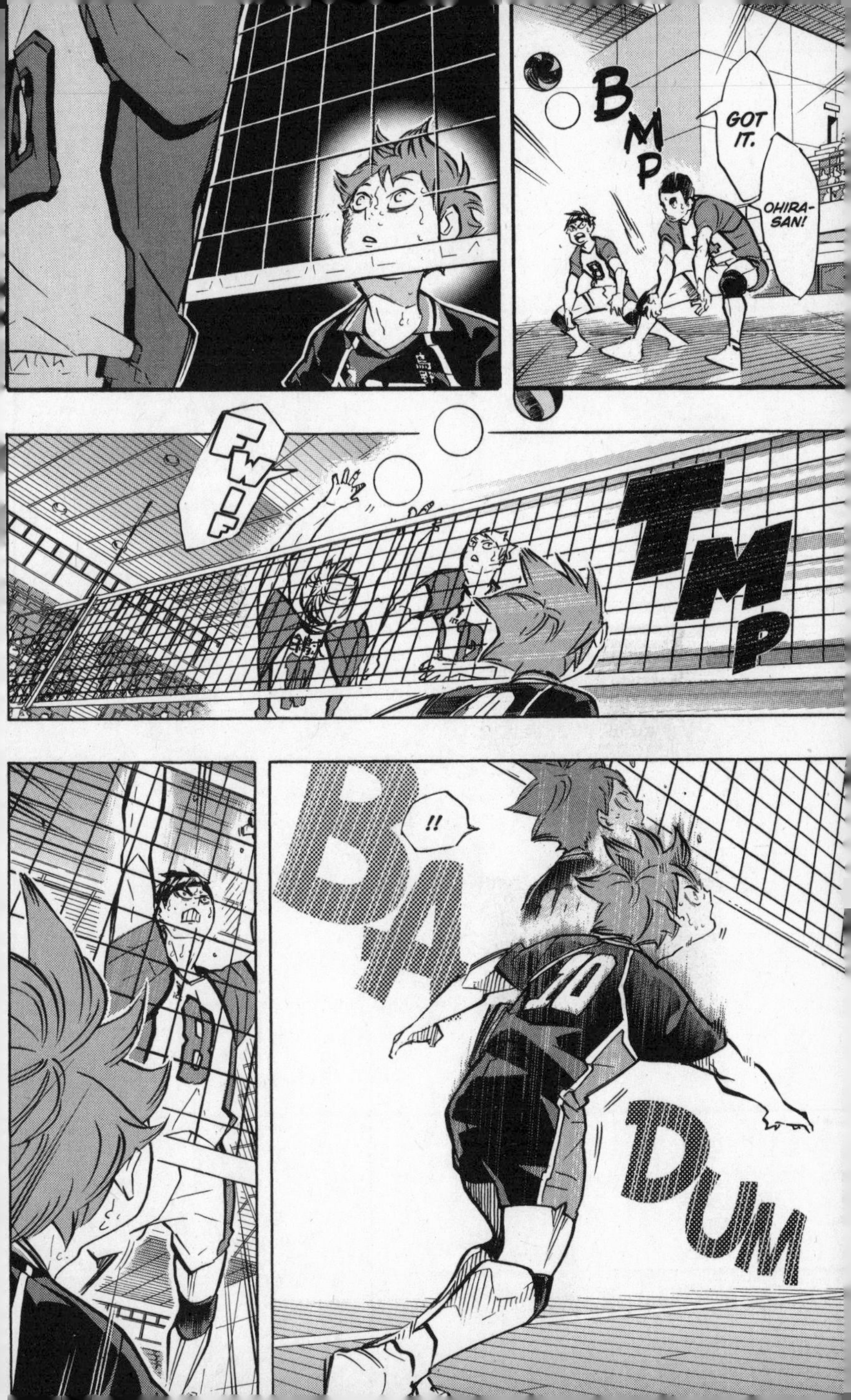
BMP
GOT IT.
OHIRA-SAN!
FWIP
TMP
!!
BA
DUM

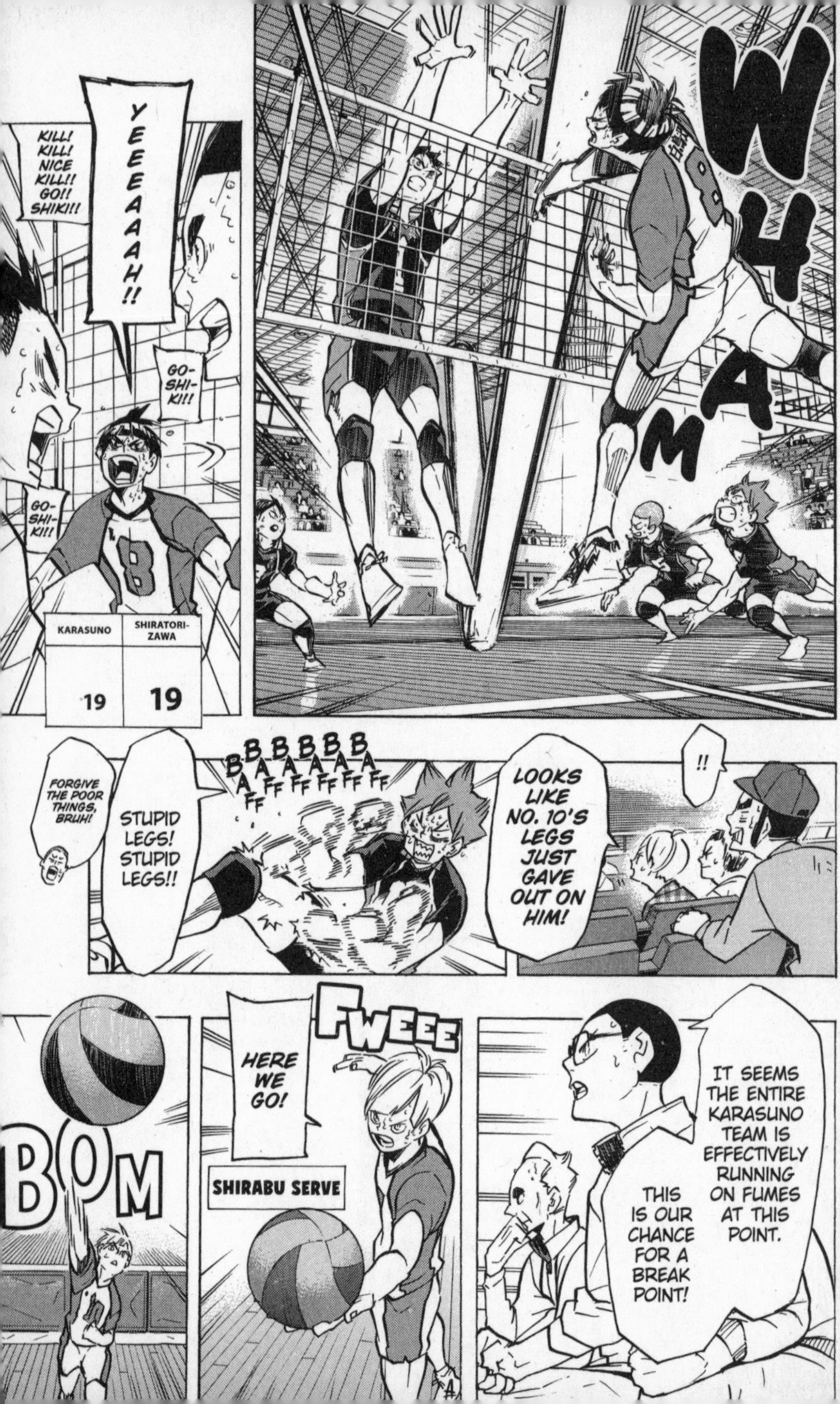
WHAM
YEEEAAAAH!!
KILL! KILL! NICE KILL!! GO!! SHIKI!!
GO-SHIKI!!
GO-SHIKI!!
KARASUNO
SHIRATORI-ZAWA
19
19
!!
LOOKS LIKE NO. 10'S LEGS JUST GAVE OUT ON HIM!
BBBBBB AAAAAA FFFFFF FFFFFF
STUPID LEGS! STUPID LEGS!!
FORGIVE THE POOR THINGS, BRUH!
IT SEEMS THE ENTIRE KARASUNO TEAM IS EFFECTIVELY RUNNING ON FUMES AT THIS POINT.
THIS IS OUR CHANCE FOR A BREAK POINT!
FWEEE
HERE WE GO!
SHIRABU SERVE
BOM

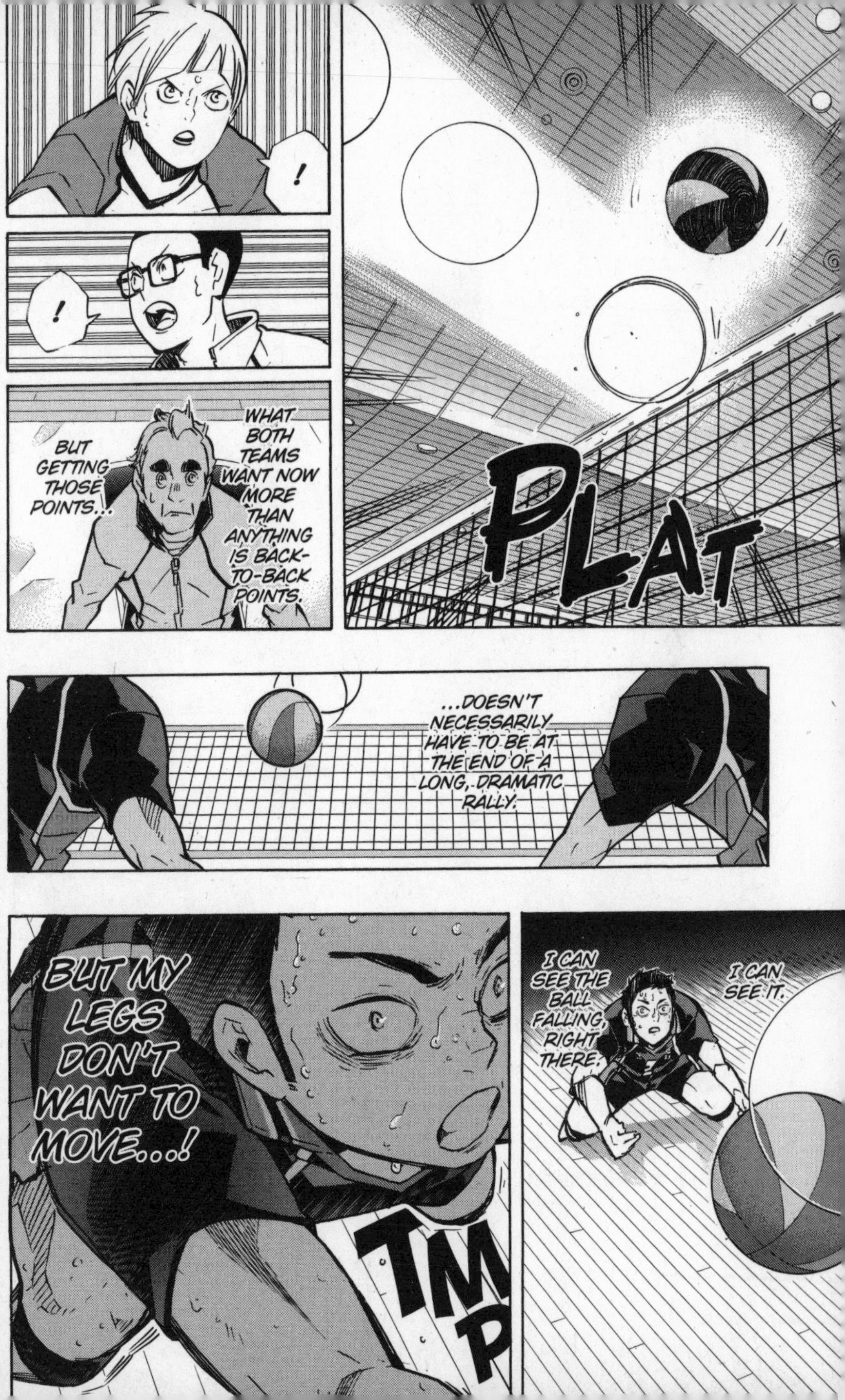
PLAT
!
!
WHAT BOTH TEAMS WANT NOW MORE THAN ANYTHING IS BACK-TO-BACK POINTS.
BUT GETTING THOSE POINTS...
...DOESN'T NECESSARILY HAVE TO BE AT THE END OF A LONG, DRAMATIC RALLY.
I CAN SEE IT.
I CAN SEE THE BALL FALLING, RIGHT THERE.
BUT MY LEGS DON'T WANT TO MOVE...!

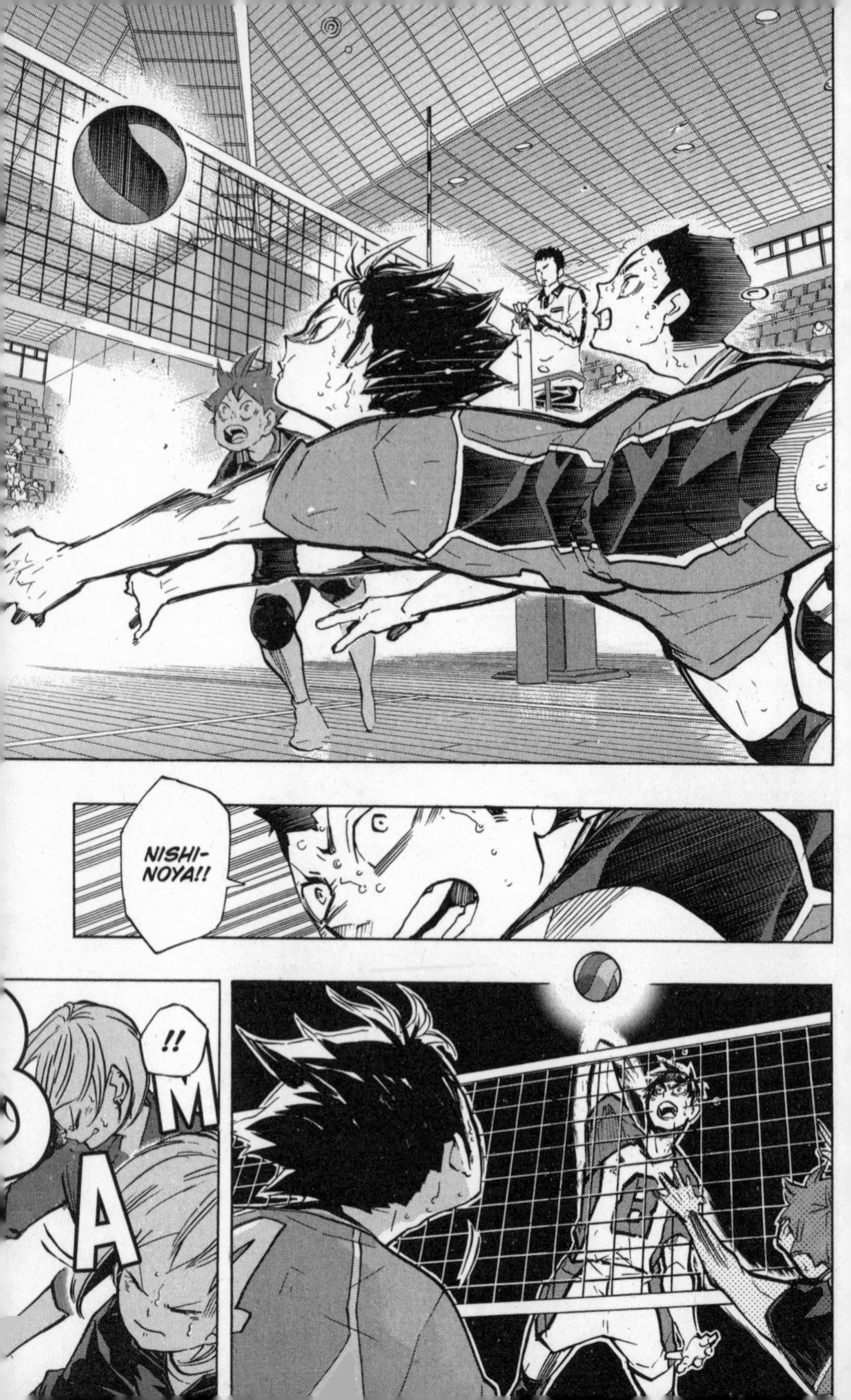
NISHI-NOYA!!
!!
M
A

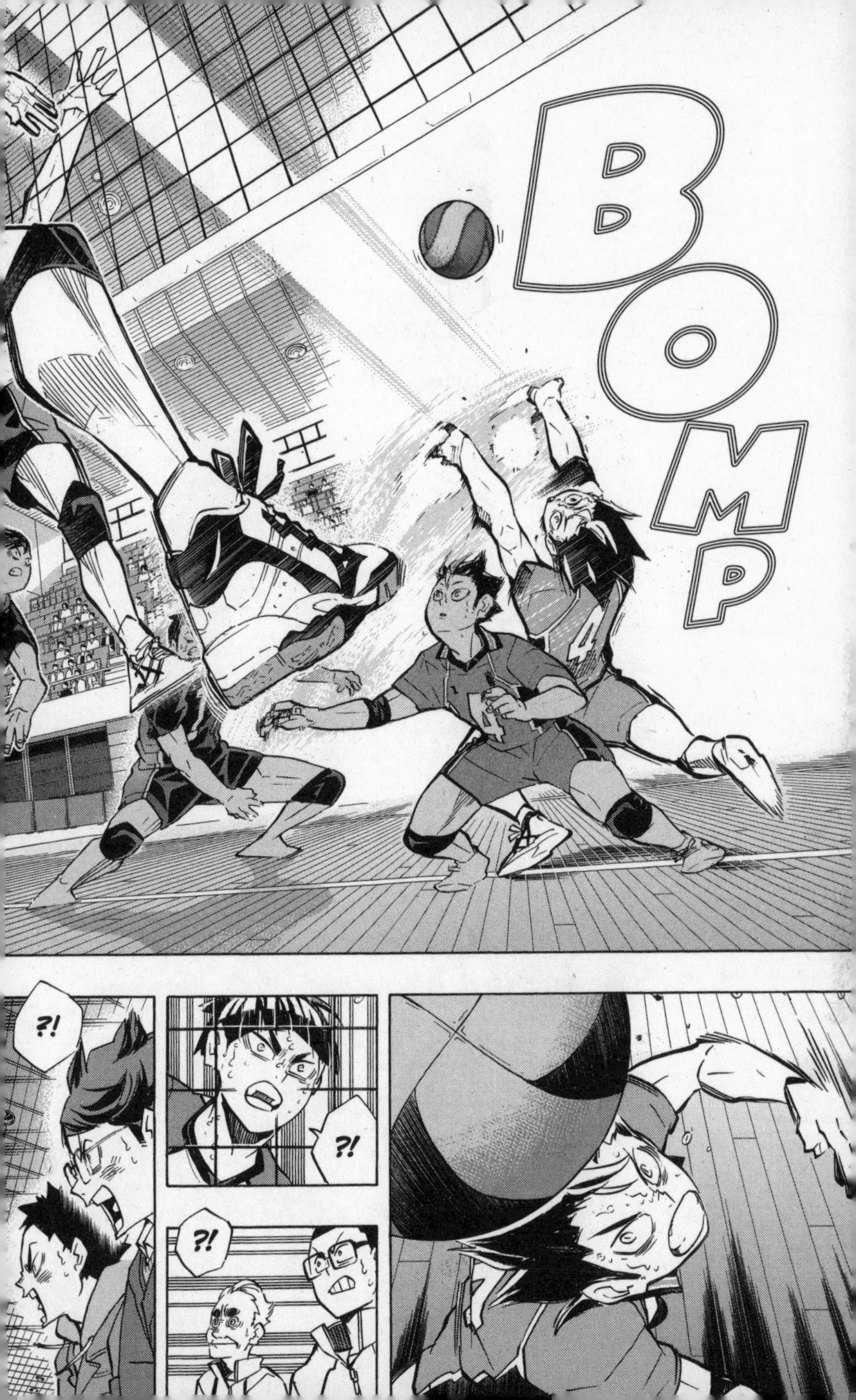
BOMP
?!
?!
?!

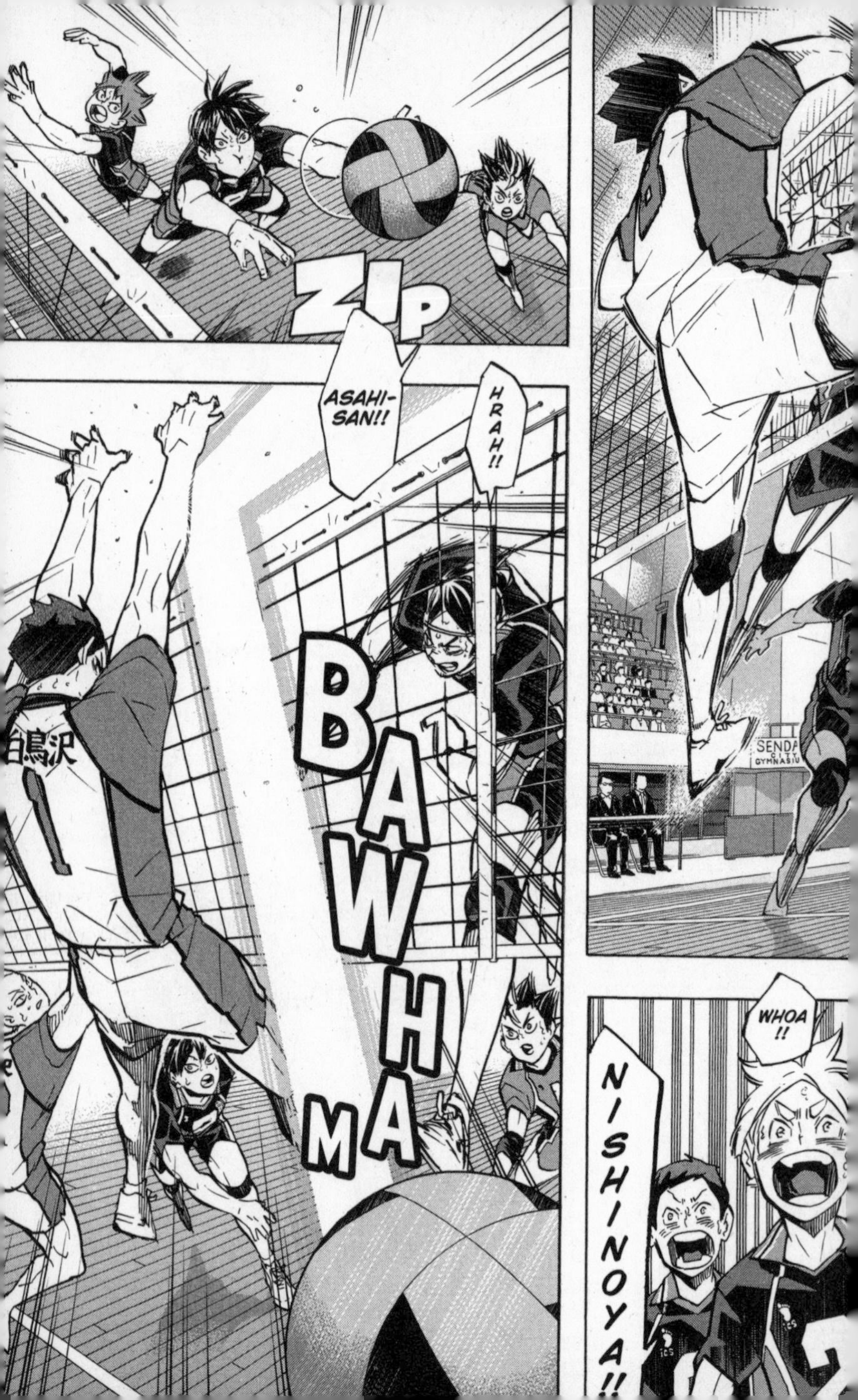
ZIP
ASAHI-SAN!!
HRAH!!
BAWHAM
WHOA!!
NISHINOYA!!

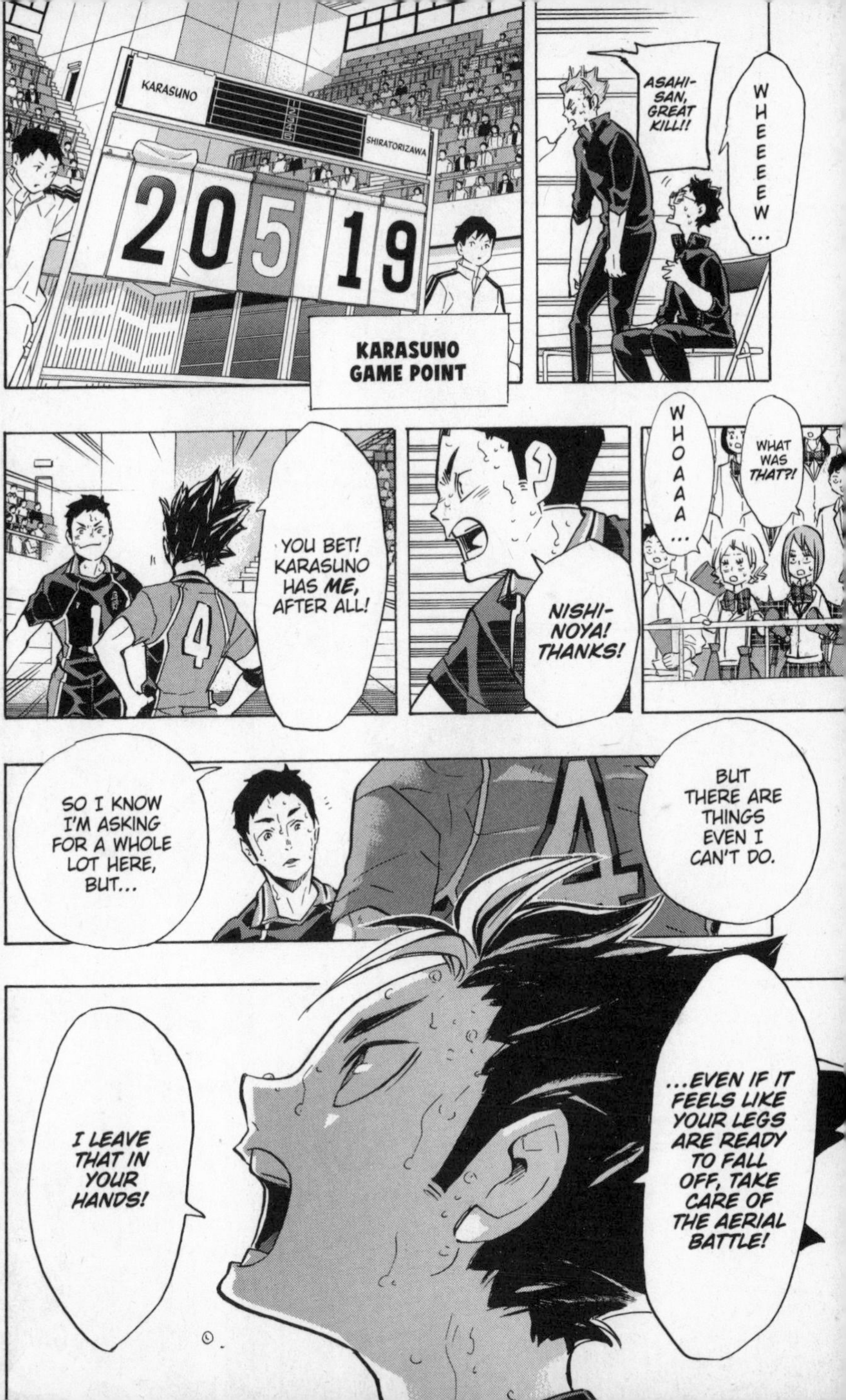
ASAHI-SAN, GREAT KILL!!
WHEEEEEW...
KARASUNO
SHIRATORIZAWA
20 5 19
KARASUNO GAME POINT
WHAT WAS THAT?!
WHOAAA...
NISHINOYA! THANKS!
YOU BET! KARASUNO HAS ME, AFTER ALL!
BUT THERE ARE THINGS EVEN I CAN'T DO.
SO I KNOW I'M ASKING FOR A WHOLE LOT HERE, BUT...
...EVEN IF IT FEELS LIKE YOUR LEGS ARE READY TO FALL OFF, TAKE CARE OF THE AERIAL BATTLE!
I LEAVE THAT IN YOUR HANDS!

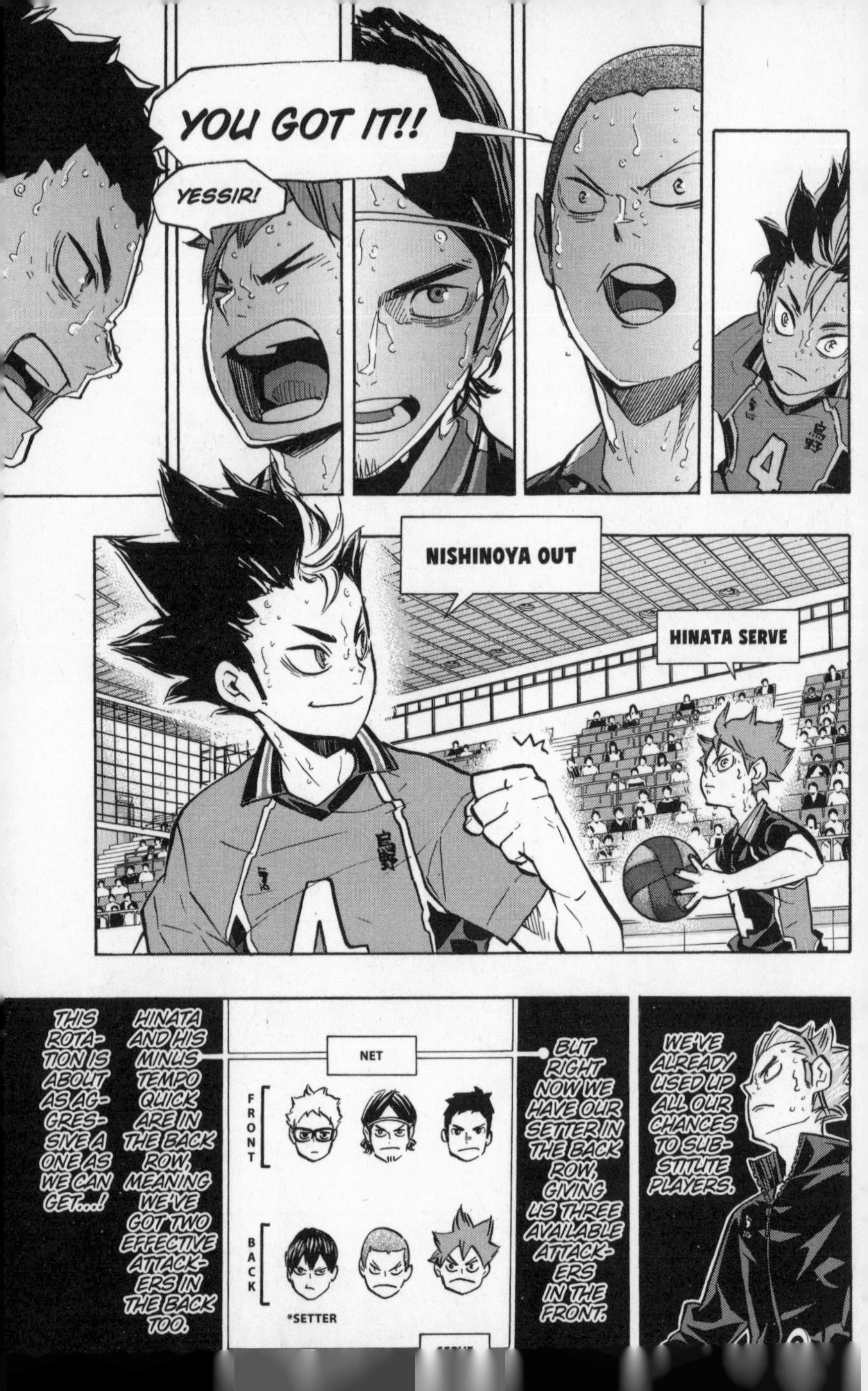
YOU GOT IT!!
YESSIR!
NISHINOYA OUT
HINATA SERVE
WE'VE ALREADY USED UP ALL OUR CHANCES TO SUBSTITUTE PLAYERS.
BUT RIGHT NOW WE HAVE OUR SETTER IN THE BACK ROW, GIVING US THREE AVAILABLE ATTACKERS IN THE FRONT.
NET
FRONT
BACK
*SETTER
HINATA AND HIS MINUS TEMPO QUICK ARE IN THE BACK ROW, MEANING WE'VE GOT TWO EFFECTIVE ATTACKERS IN THE BACK TOO.
THIS ROTATION IS ABOUT AS AGGRESSIVE A ONE AS WE CAN GET...!

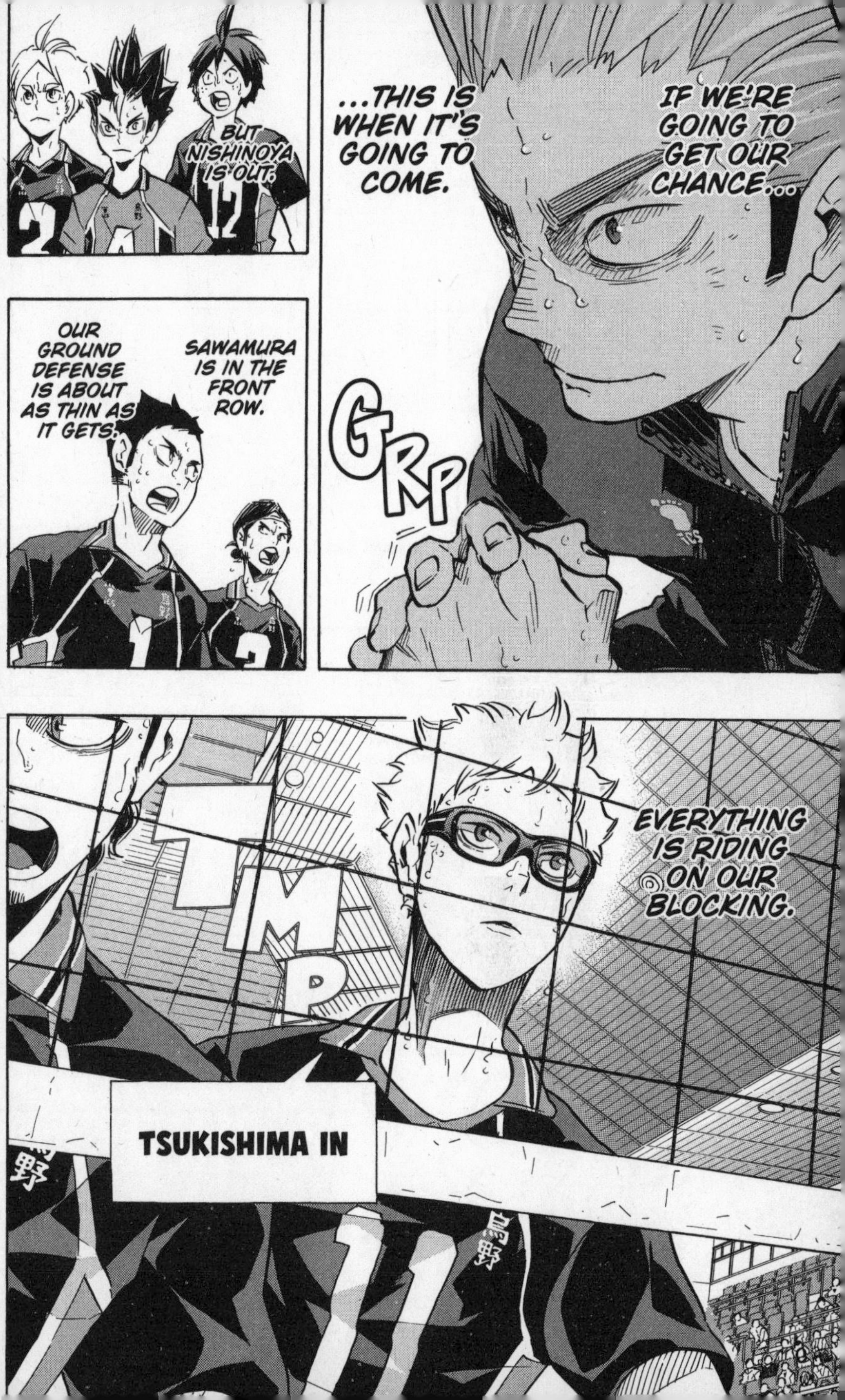
IF WE'RE GOING TO GET OUR CHANCE...
...THIS IS WHEN IT'S GOING TO COME.
GRP
BUT NISHINOYA IS OUT.
SAWAMURA IS IN THE FRONT ROW.
OUR GROUND DEFENSE IS ABOUT AS THIN AS IT GETS.
EVERYTHING IS RIDING ON OUR BLOCKING.
TMP
TSUKISHIMA IN

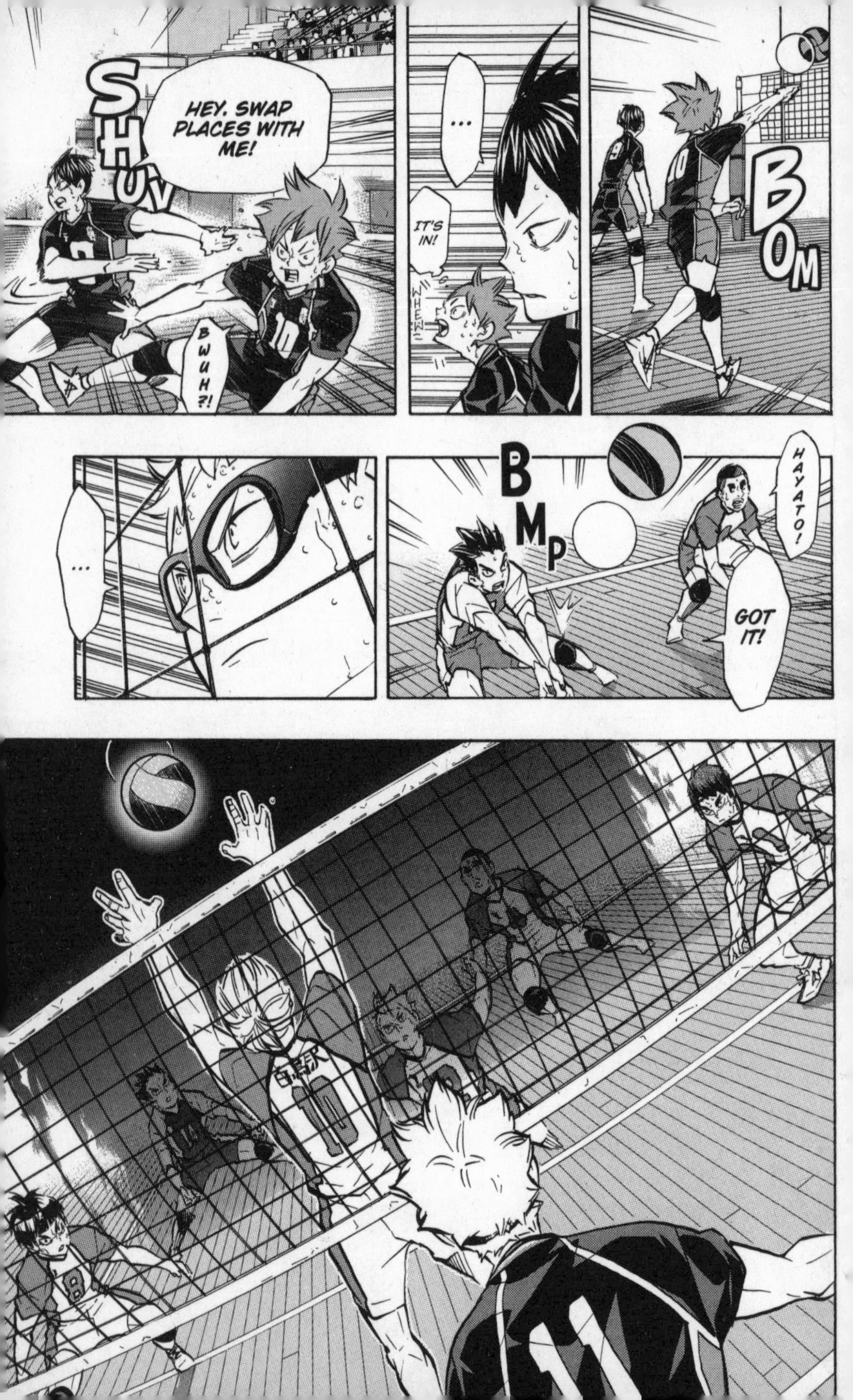
BOM
...
IT'S IN!
WHEW
HEY. SWAP PLACES WITH ME!
SHUV
BWUH?!
HAYATO!
GOT IT!
BMP
...

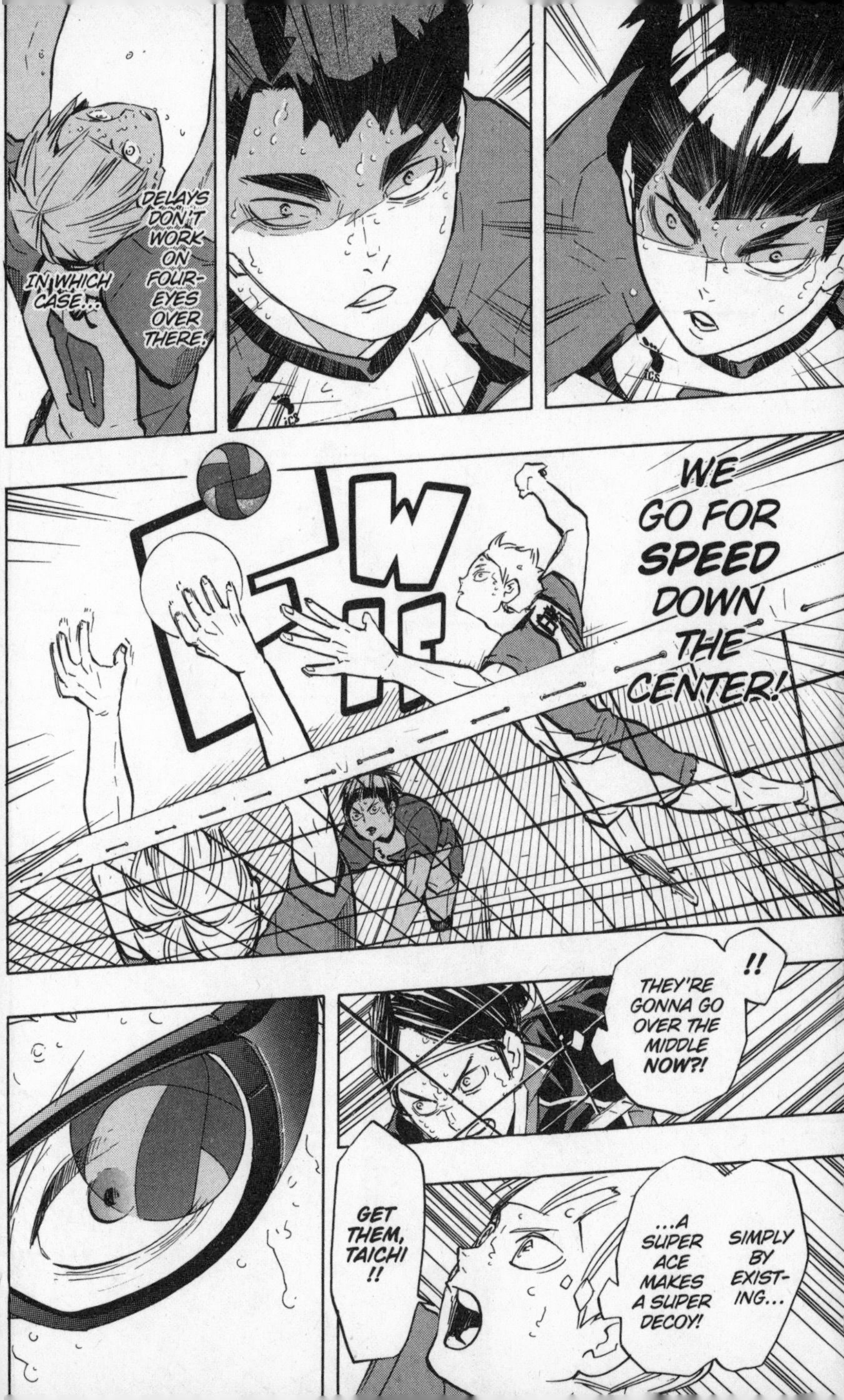
DELAYS DON'T WORK ON FOUR-EYES OVER THERE.
IN WHICH CASE...
WE GO FOR SPEED DOWN THE CENTER!
!!
THEY'RE GONNA GO OVER THE MIDDLE NOW?!
SIMPLY BY EXIST-ING...
...A SUPER ACE MAKES A SUPER DECOY!
GET THEM, TAICHI!!

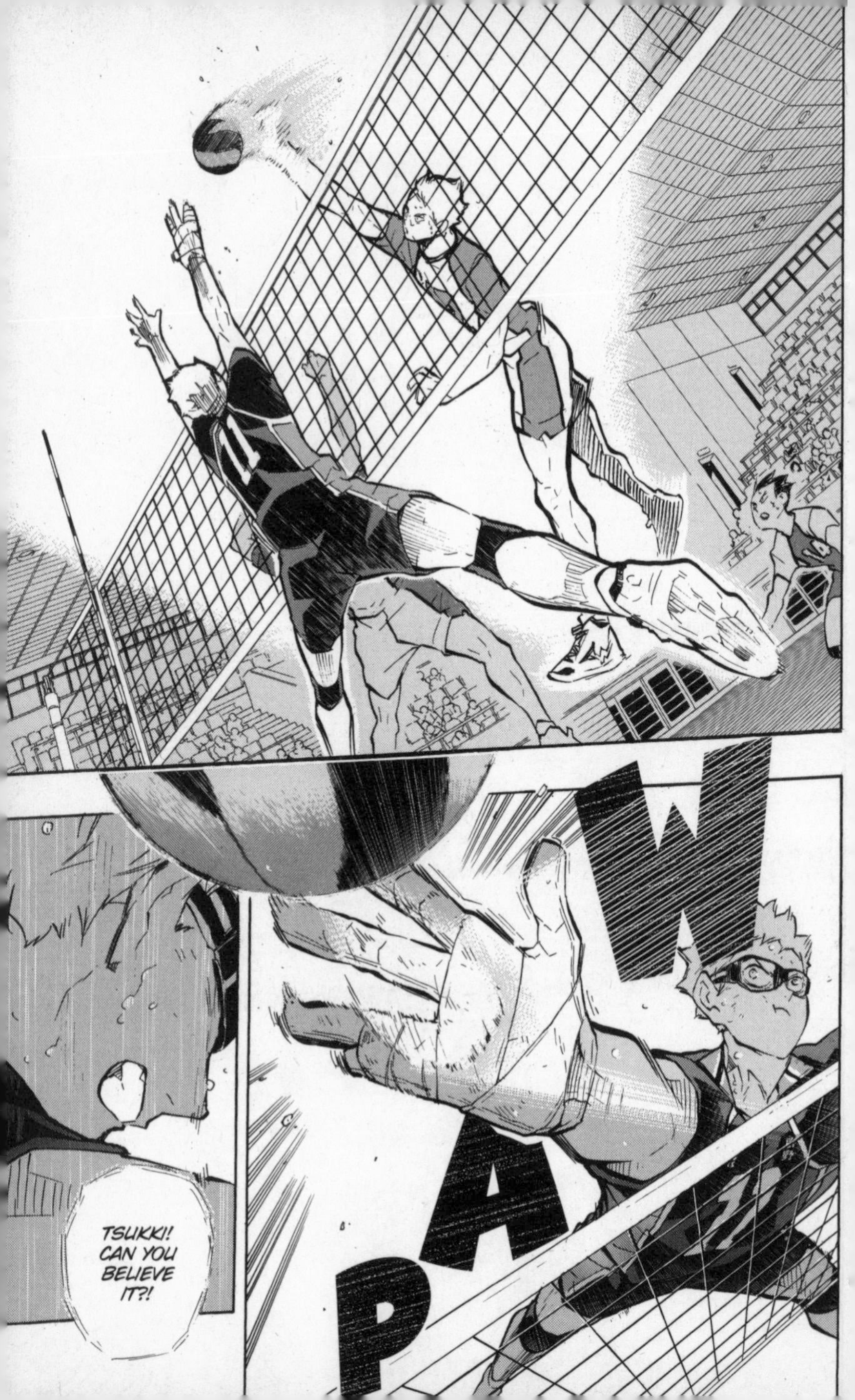

PAW
TSUKKI! CAN YOU BELIEVE IT?!

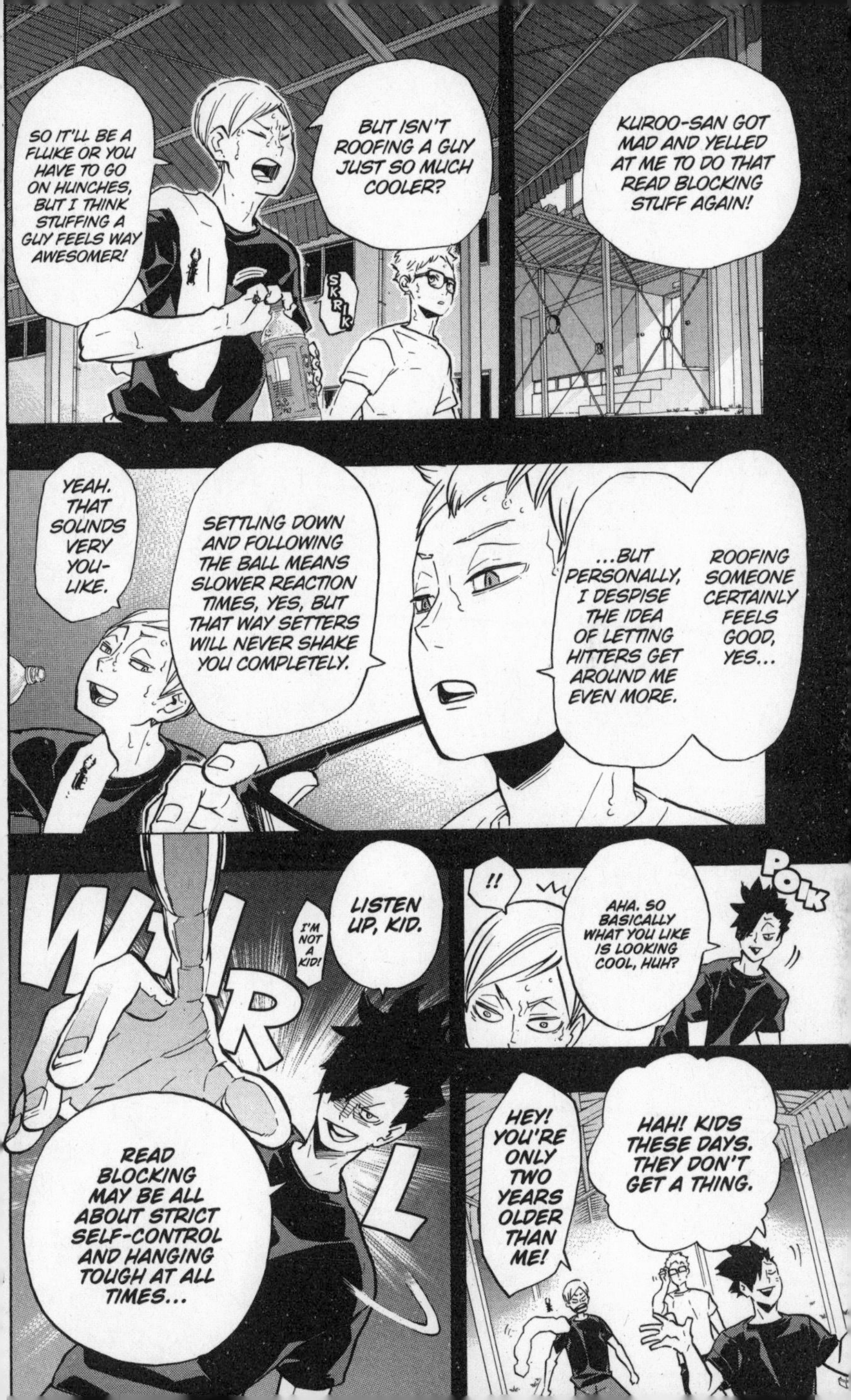
KUROO-SAN GOT MAD AND YELLED AT ME TO DO THAT READ BLOCKING STUFF AGAIN!
BUT ISN'T ROOFING A GUY JUST SO MUCH COOLER?
SO IT'LL BE A FLUKE OR YOU HAVE TO GO ON HUNCHES, BUT I THINK STUFFING A GUY FEELS WAY AWESOMER!
SKRIK
ROOFING SOMEONE CERTAINLY FEELS GOOD, YES...
...BUT PERSONALLY, I DESPISE THE IDEA OF LETTING HITTERS GET AROUND ME EVEN MORE.
SETTLING DOWN AND FOLLOWING THE BALL MEANS SLOWER REACTION TIMES, YES, BUT THAT WAY SETTERS WILL NEVER SHAKE YOU COMPLETELY.
YEAH. THAT SOUNDS VERY YOU-LIKE.
POIK
AHA. SO BASICALLY WHAT YOU LIKE IS LOOKING COOL, HUH?
!!
HAH! KIDS THESE DAYS. THEY DON'T GET A THING.
HEY! YOU'RE ONLY TWO YEARS OLDER THAN ME!
LISTEN UP, KID.
I'M NOT A KID!
WHIRL
READ BLOCKING MAY BE ALL ABOUT STRICT SELF-CONTROL AND HANGING TOUGH AT ALL TIMES...

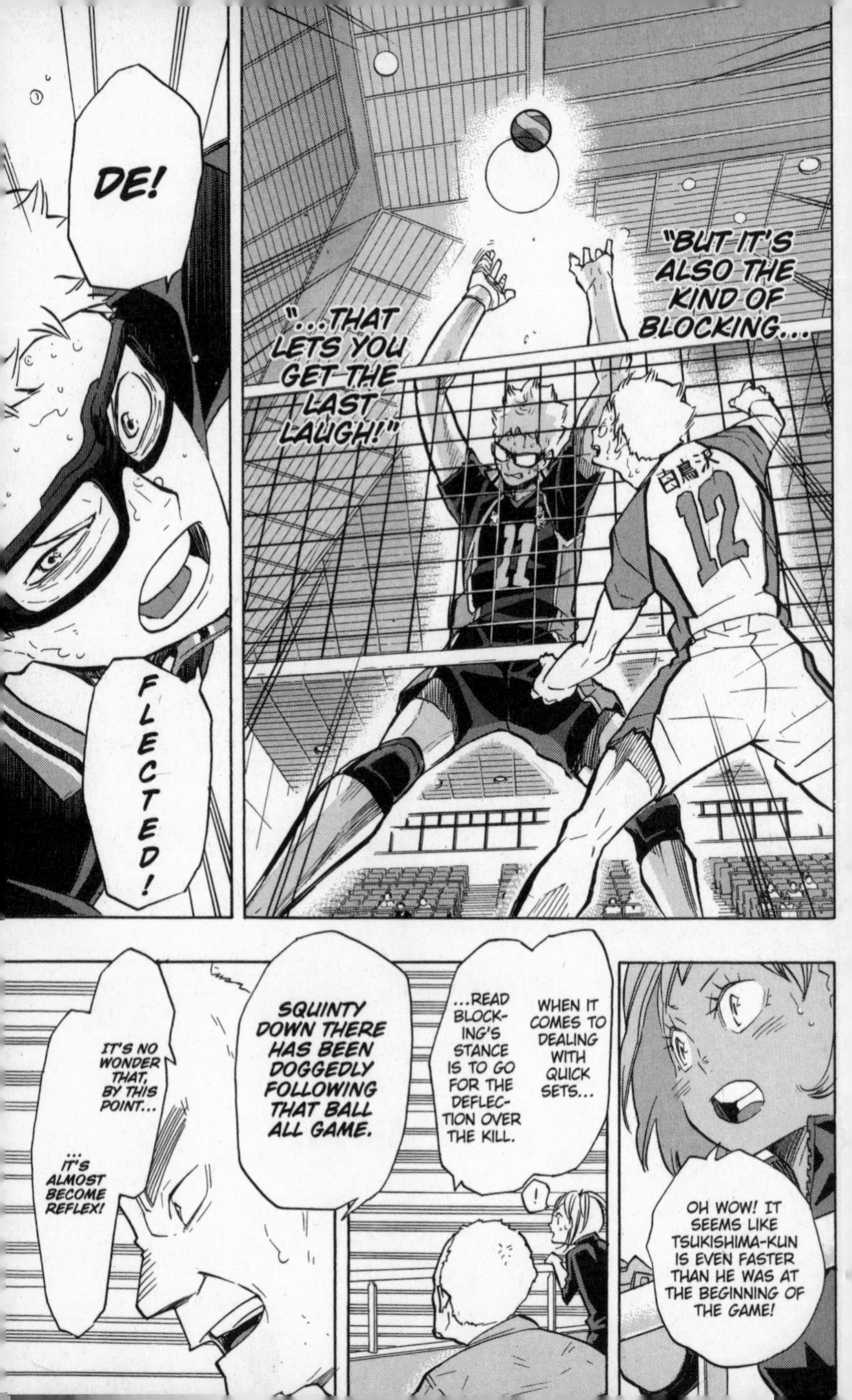
"BUT IT'S ALSO THE KIND OF BLOCKING...
"...THAT LETS YOU GET THE LAST LAUGH!"
DE!
FLECTED!
OH WOW! IT SEEMS LIKE TSUKISHIMA-KUN IS EVEN FASTER THAN HE WAS AT THE BEGINNING OF THE GAME!
WHEN IT COMES TO DEALING WITH QUICK SETS...
...READ BLOCKING'S STANCE IS TO GO FOR THE DEFLECTION OVER THE KILL.
SQUINTY DOWN THERE HAS BEEN DOGGEDLY FOLLOWING THAT BALL ALL GAME.
!
IT'S NO WONDER THAT, BY THIS POINT...
...IT'S ALMOST BECOME REFLEX!

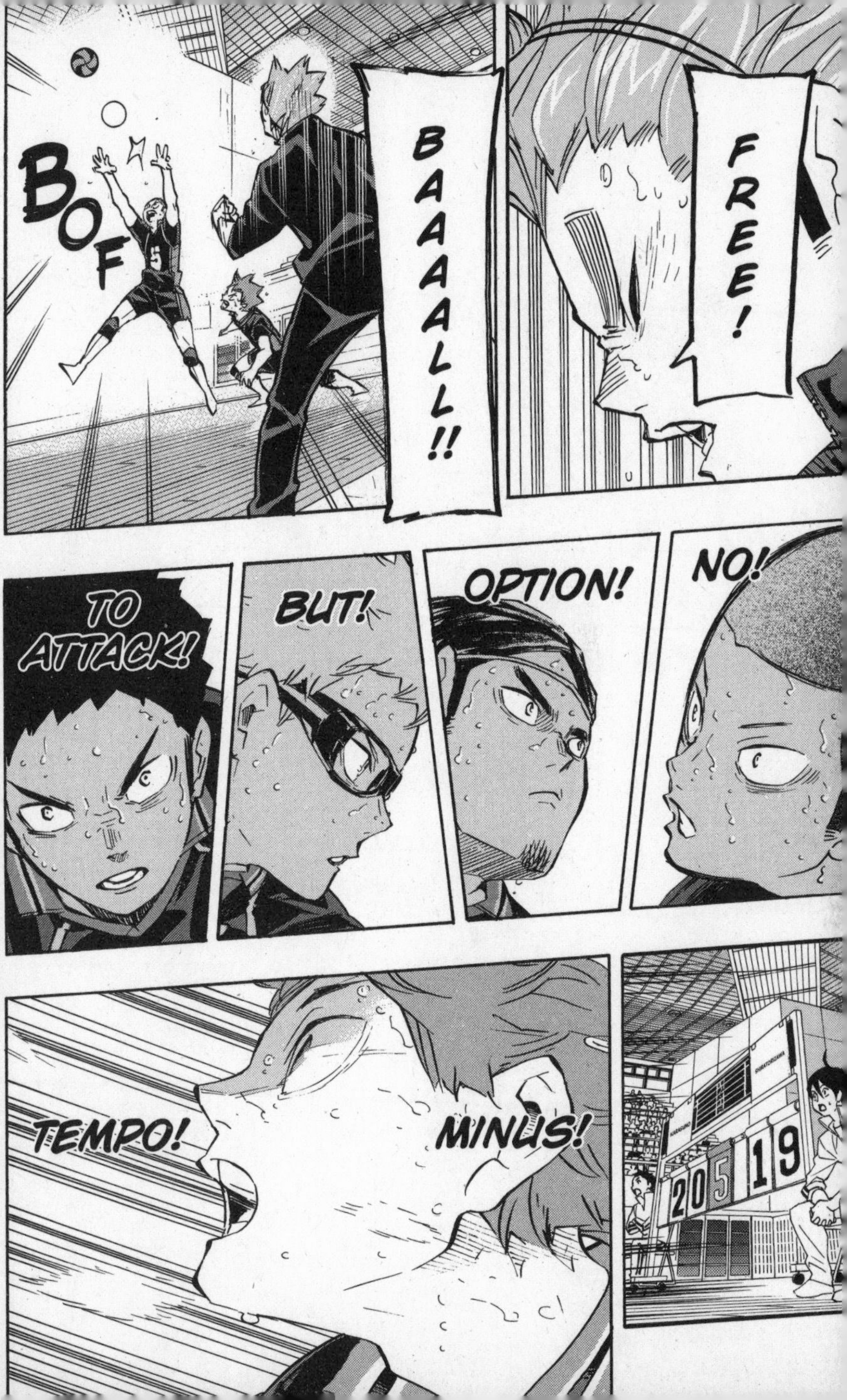
FREE!
BAAAAALL!!
BOF
NO!
OPTION!
BUT!
TO ATTACK!
20
5
19
MINUS!
TEMPO!

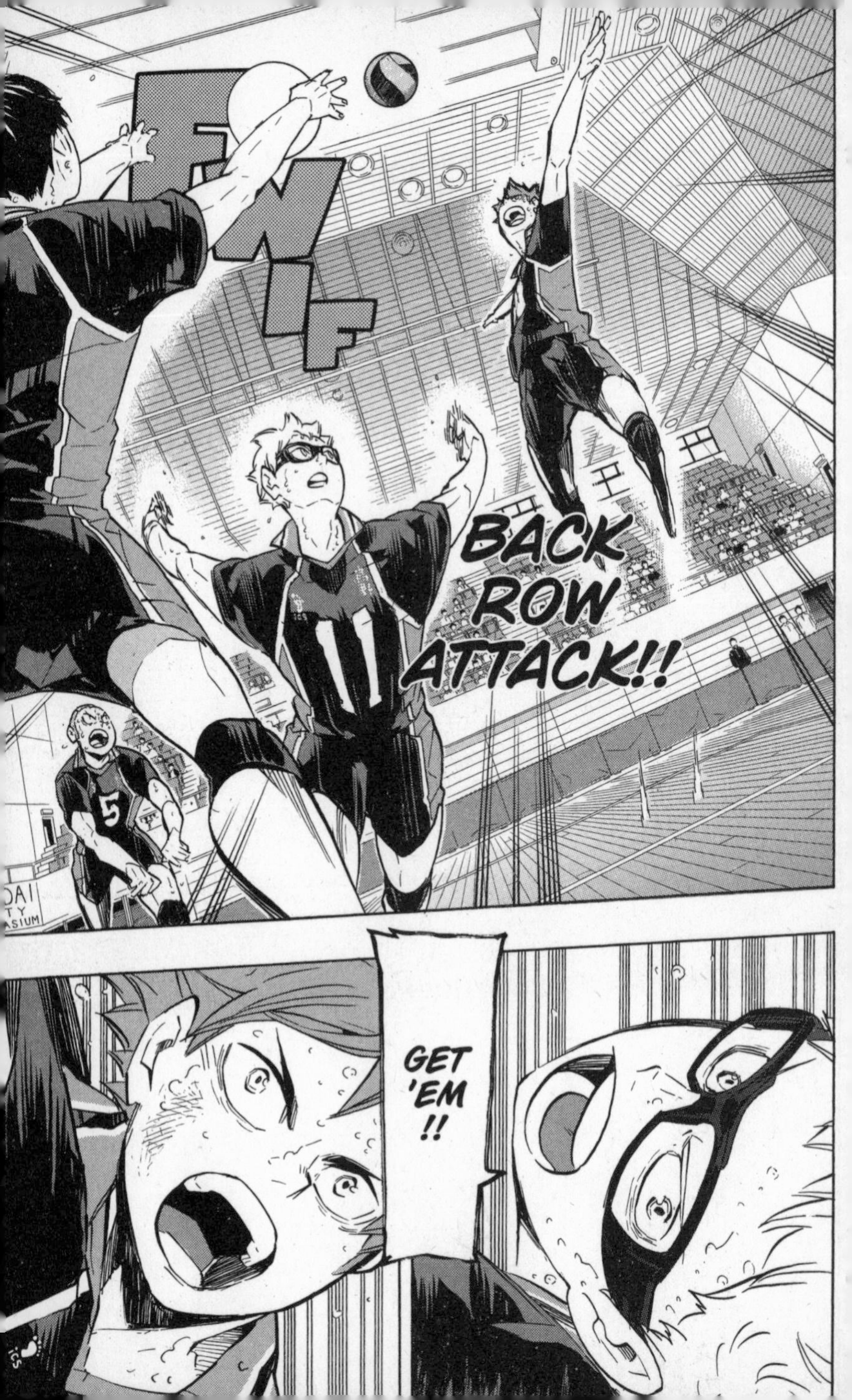
FWIF
BACK ROW ATTACK!!
GET 'EM!!

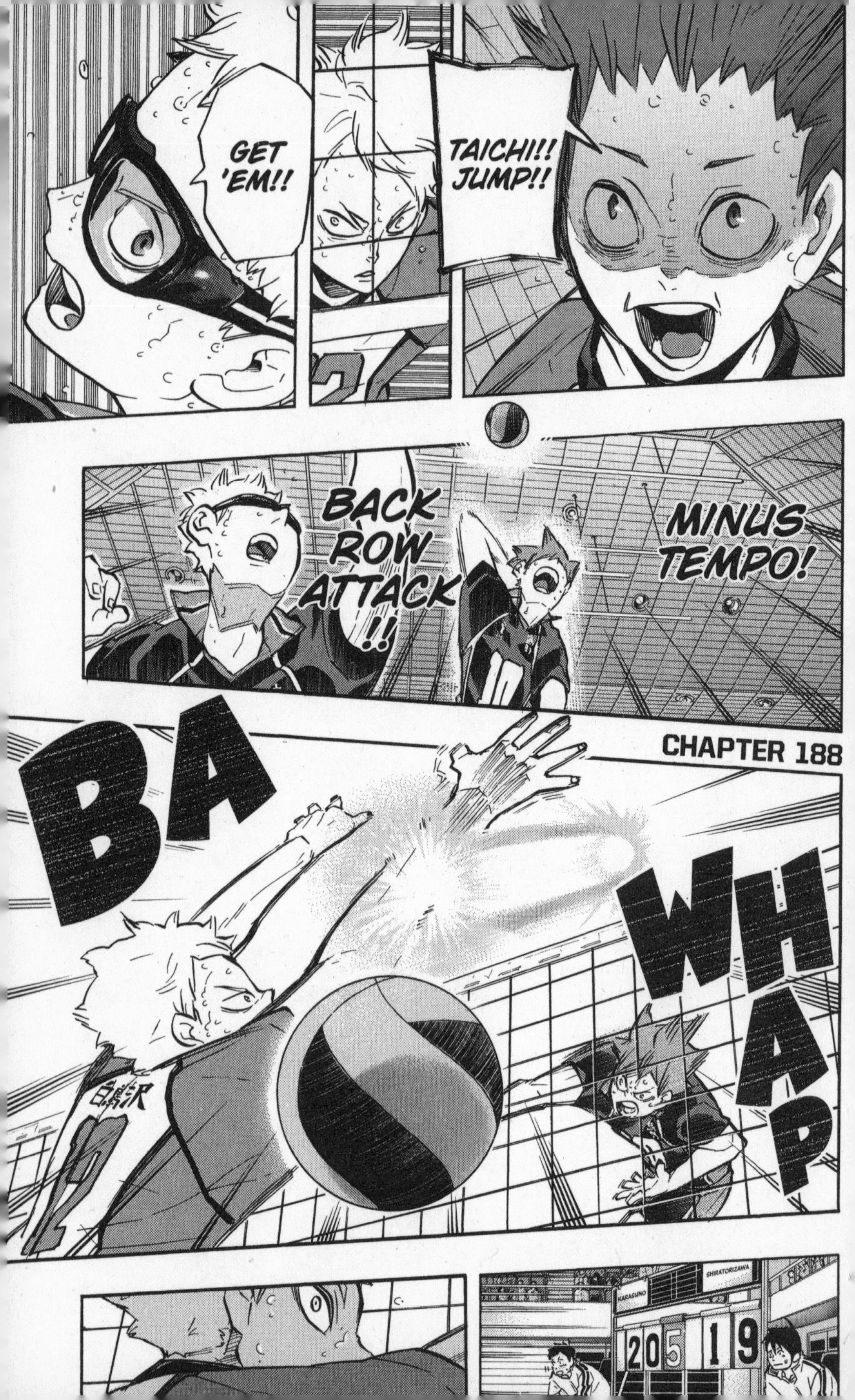
TAICHI!! JUMP!!
GET 'EM!!
MINUS TEMPO!
BACK ROW ATTACK!!
CHAPTER 188
BA
WHAP
白鳥沢
SHIRATORIZAWA
KARASUNO
20 5 19

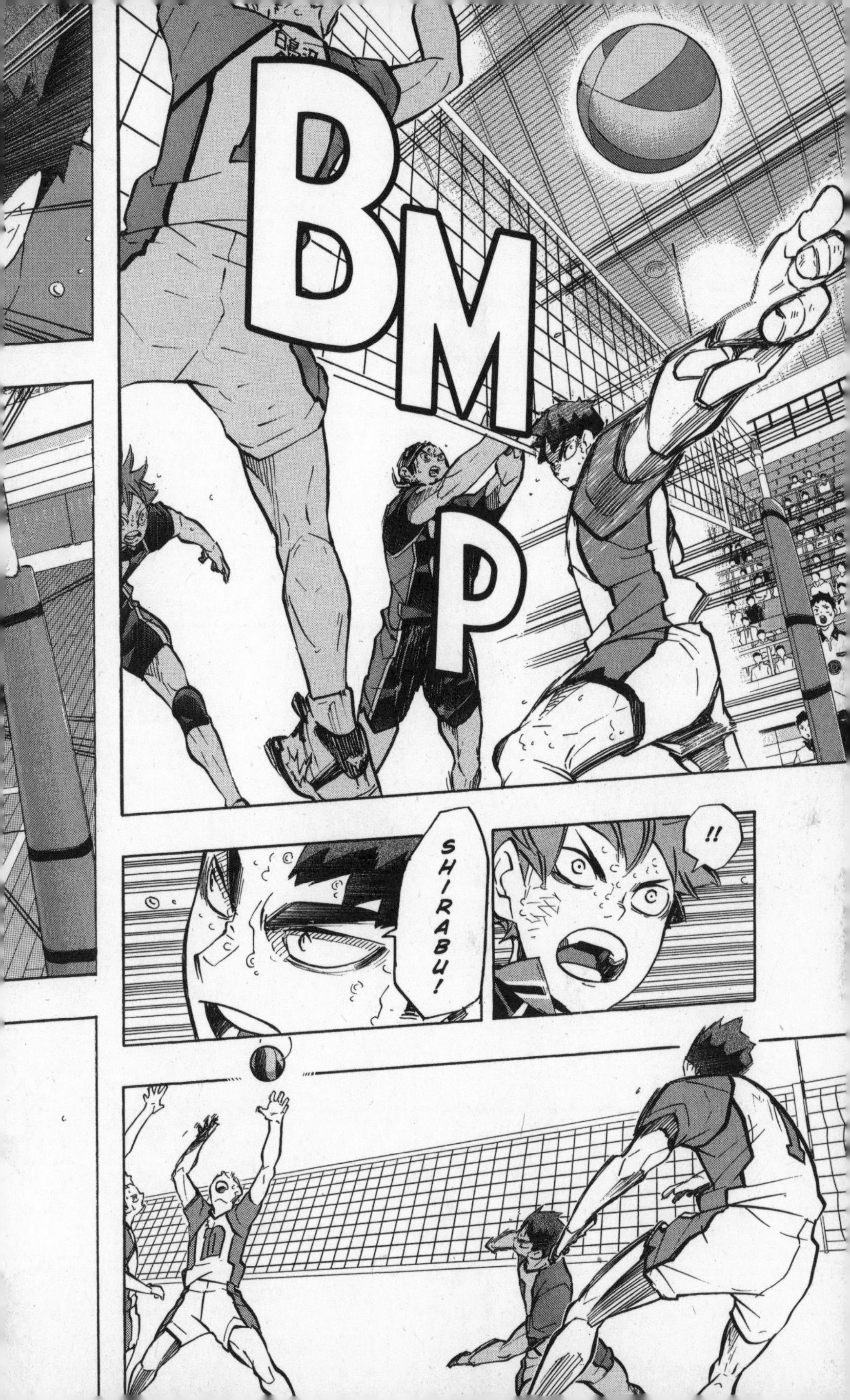
BMP
!!
SHIRABU!

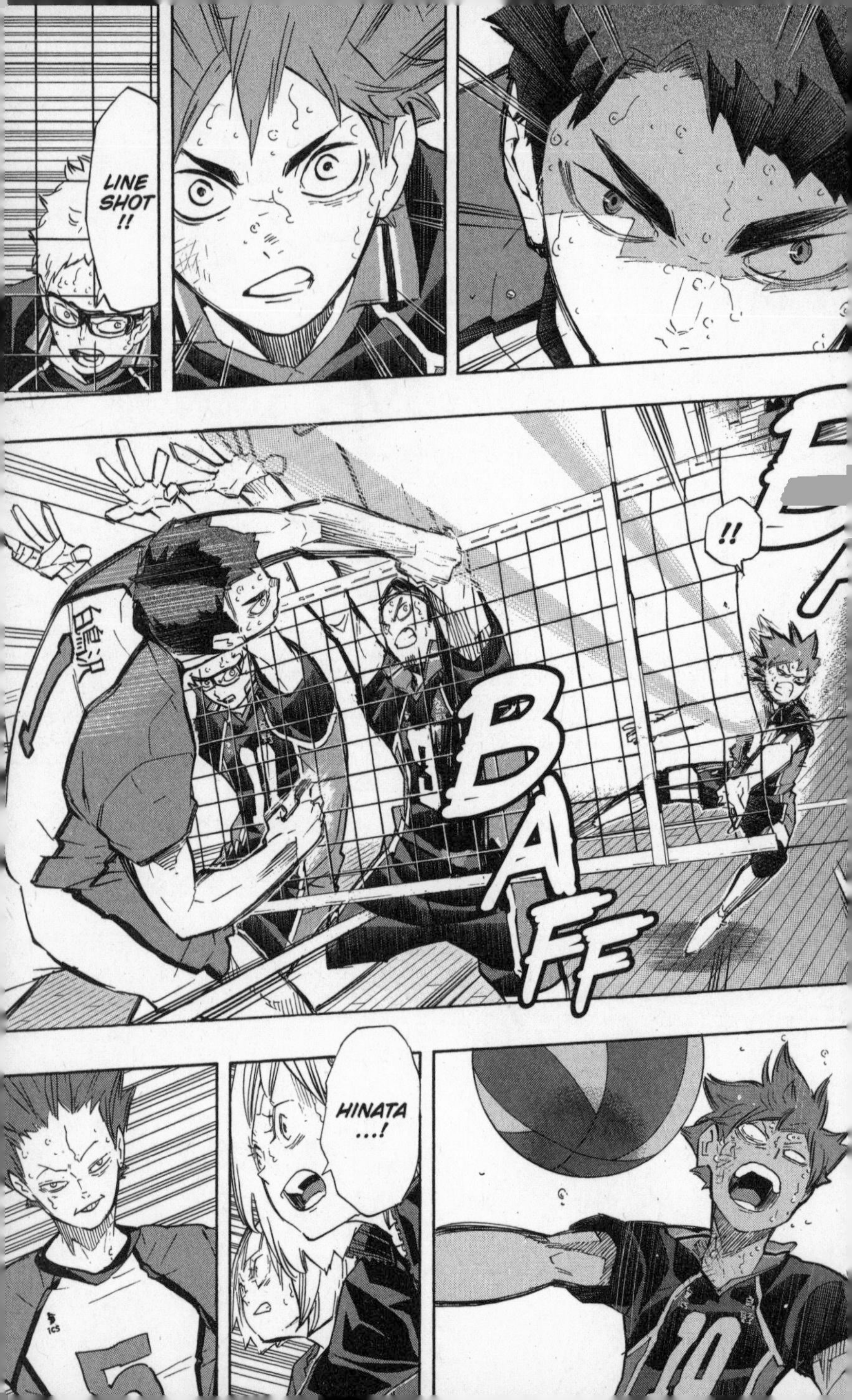
LINE SHOT !!
!!
BAFF
HINATA ...!

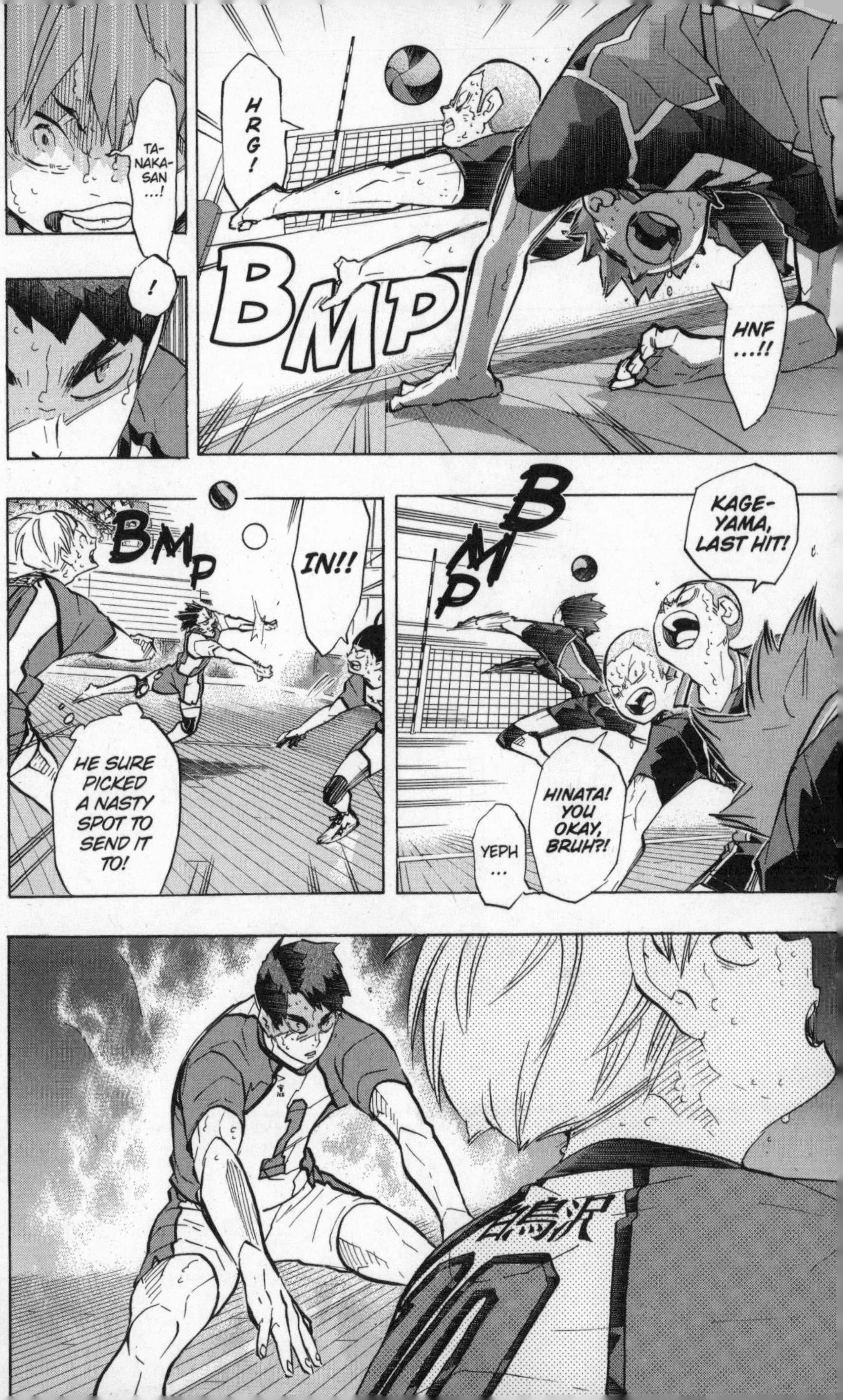
HRG!
BMP
HNF ...!!
TA-NAKA-SAN ...!
!
KAGE-YAMA, LAST HIT!
BMP
HINATA! YOU OKAY, BRUH?!
YEPH ...
IN!!
BMP
HE SURE PICKED A NASTY SPOT TO SEND IT TO!
白鳥沢

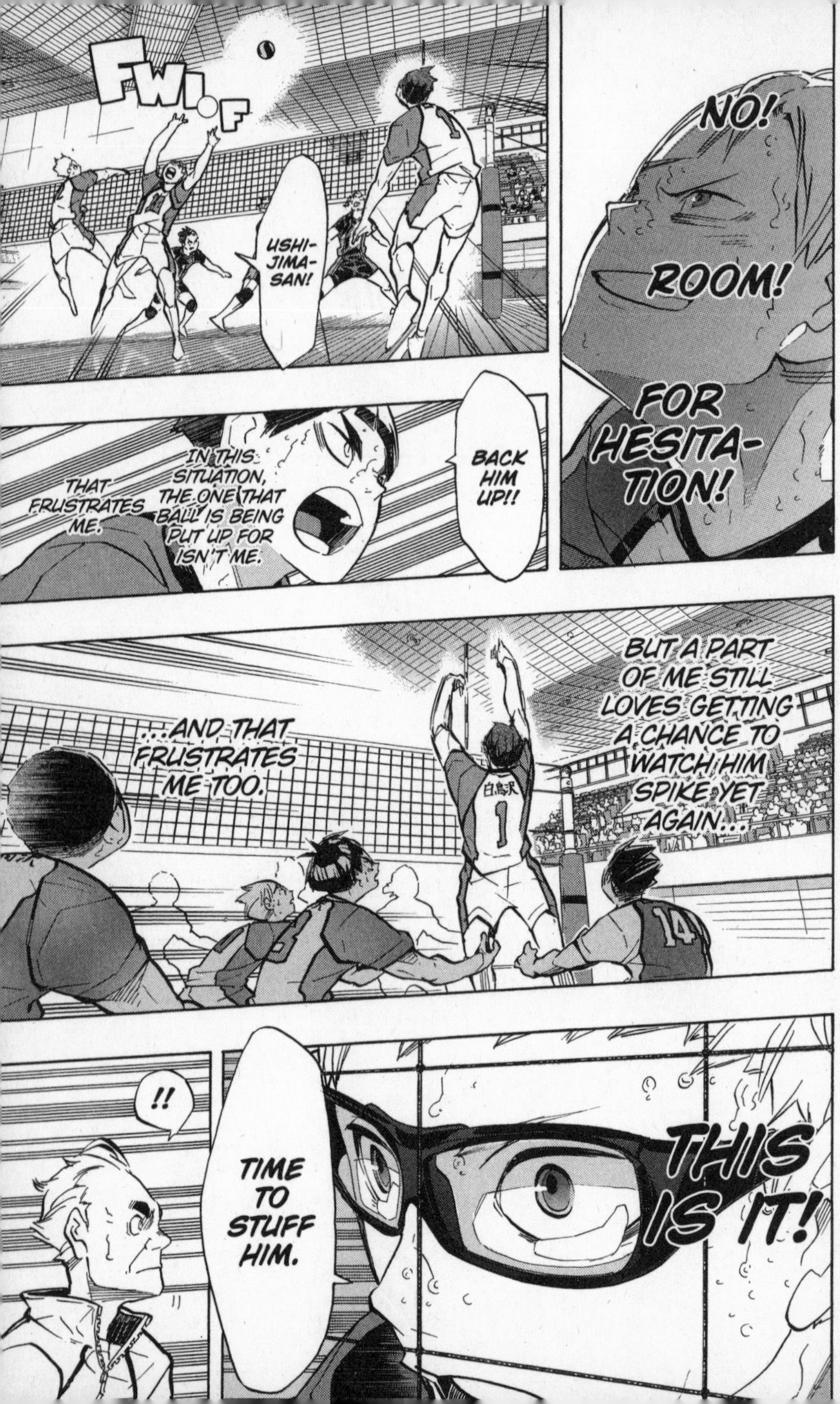
NO! ROOM! FOR HESITATION!
FWI F
USHIJIMA-SAN!
BACK HIM UP!!
IN THIS SITUATION, THE ONE THAT BALL IS BEING PUT UP FOR ISN'T ME.
THAT FRUSTRATES ME.
BUT A PART OF ME STILL LOVES GETTING A CHANCE TO WATCH HIM SPIKE YET AGAIN...
...AND THAT FRUSTRATES ME TOO.
白鳥沢
THIS IS IT!
TIME TO STUFF HIM.
!!

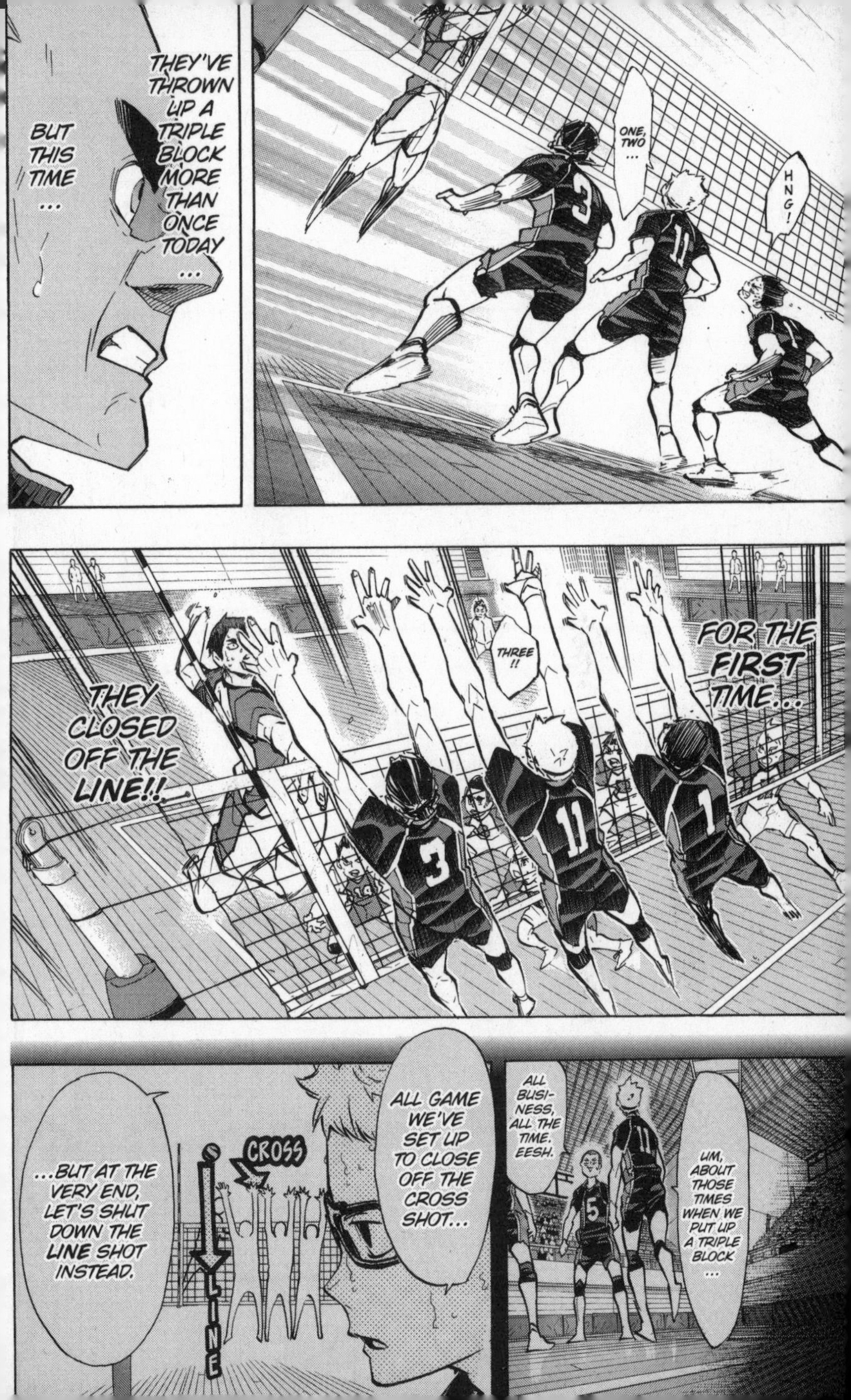
ONE, TWO ...
HNG!
THEY'VE THROWN UP A TRIPLE BLOCK MORE THAN ONCE TODAY ...
BUT THIS TIME ...
FOR THE FIRST TIME...
THREE!!
THEY CLOSED OFF THE LINE!!
UM, ABOUT THOSE TIMES WHEN WE PUT UP A TRIPLE BLOCK ...
ALL BUSINESS, ALL THE TIME. EESH.
ALL GAME WE'VE SET UP TO CLOSE OFF THE CROSS SHOT...
CROSS
LINE
...BUT AT THE VERY END, LET'S SHUT DOWN THE LINE SHOT INSTEAD.

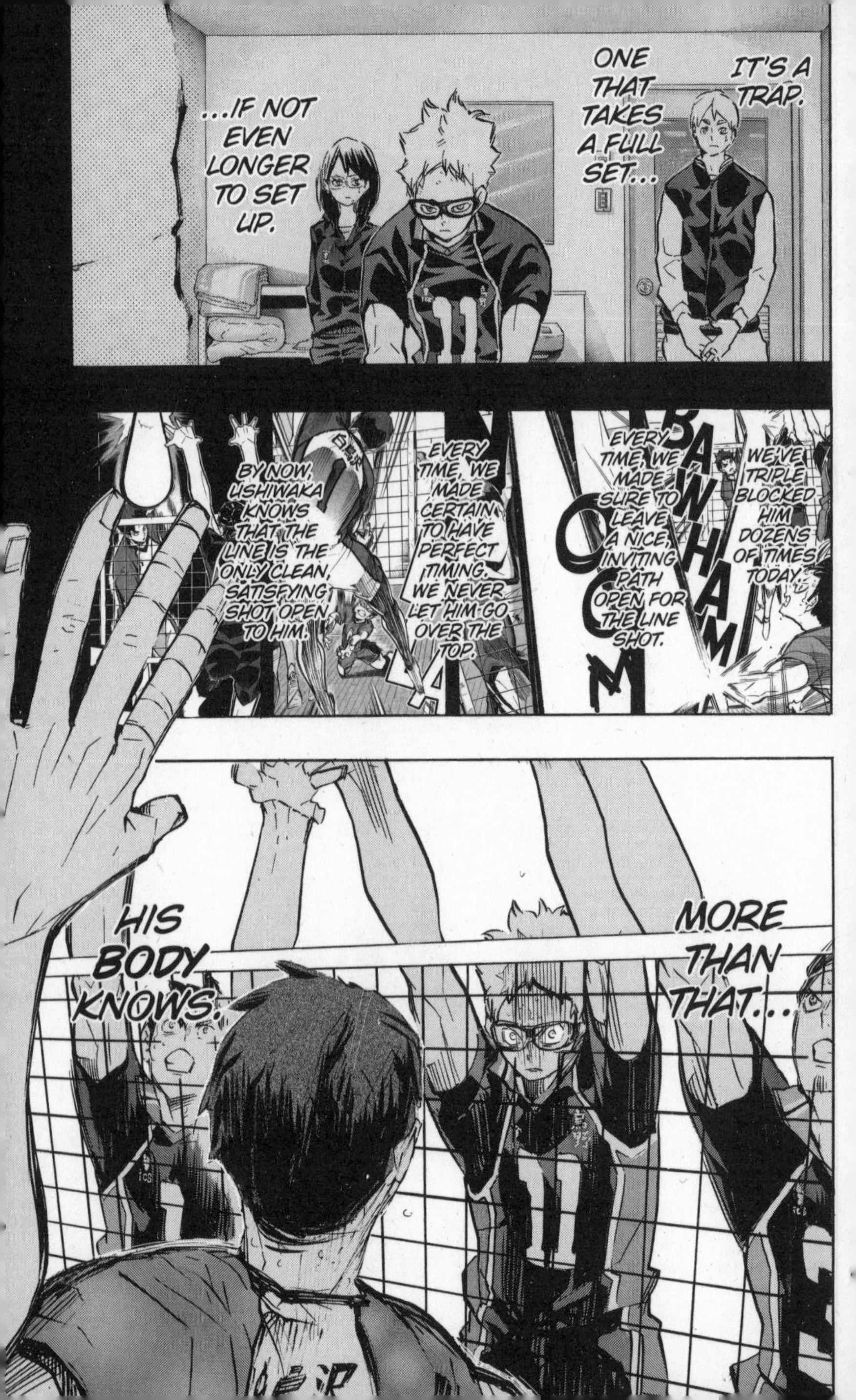
IT'S A TRAP.
ONE THAT TAKES A FULL SET...
...IF NOT EVEN LONGER TO SET UP.
WE'VE TRIPLE BLOCKED HIM DOZENS OF TIMES TODAY.
EVERY TIME, WE MADE SURE TO LEAVE A NICE, INVITING PATH OPEN FOR THE LINE SHOT.
BAWHAM
EVERY TIME, WE MADE CERTAIN TO HAVE PERFECT TIMING. WE NEVER LET HIM GO OVER THE TOP.
BY NOW, USHIWAKA KNOWS THAT THE LINE IS THE ONLY CLEAN, SATISFYING SHOT OPEN TO HIM.
MORE THAN THAT...
HIS BODY KNOWS.

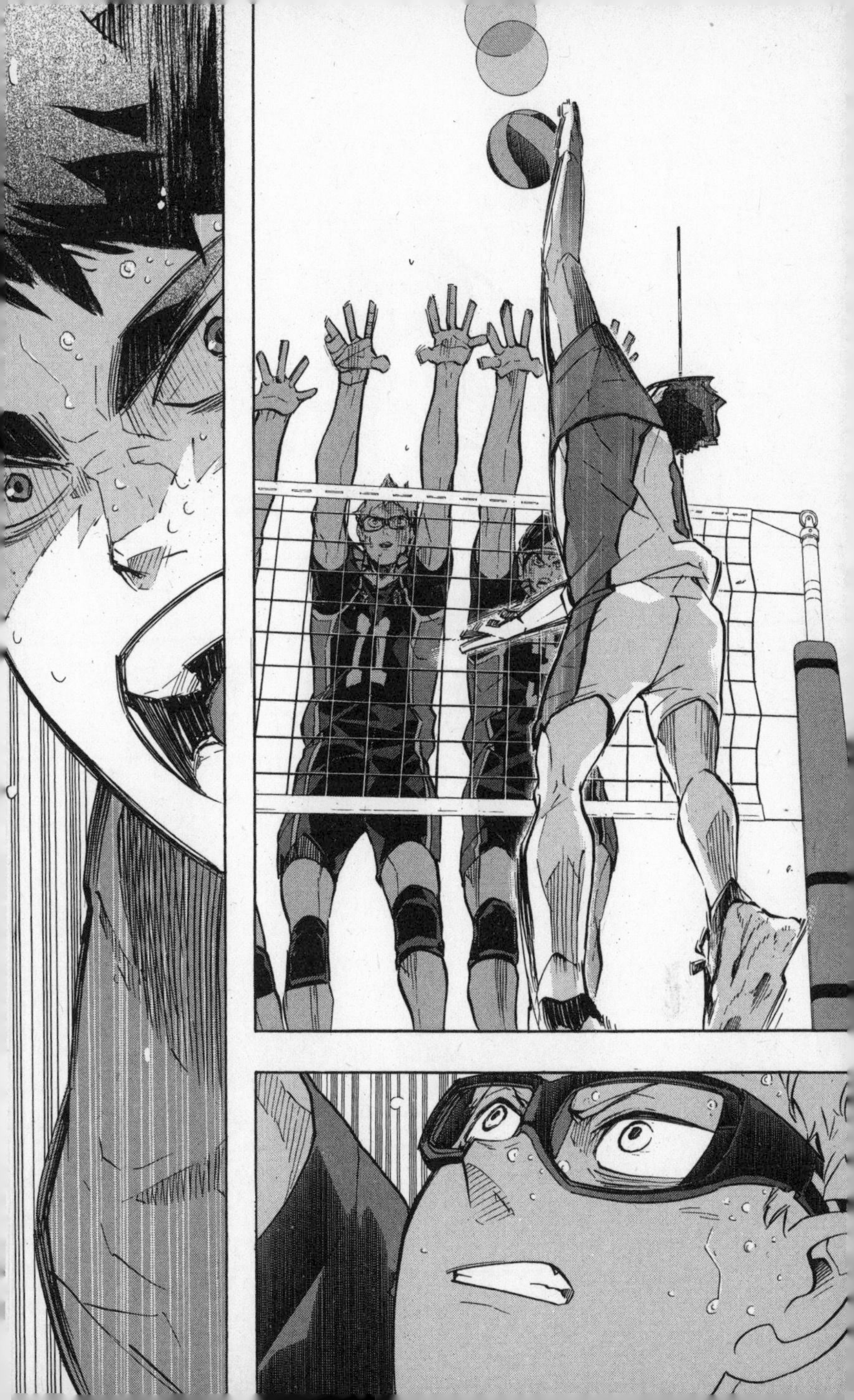

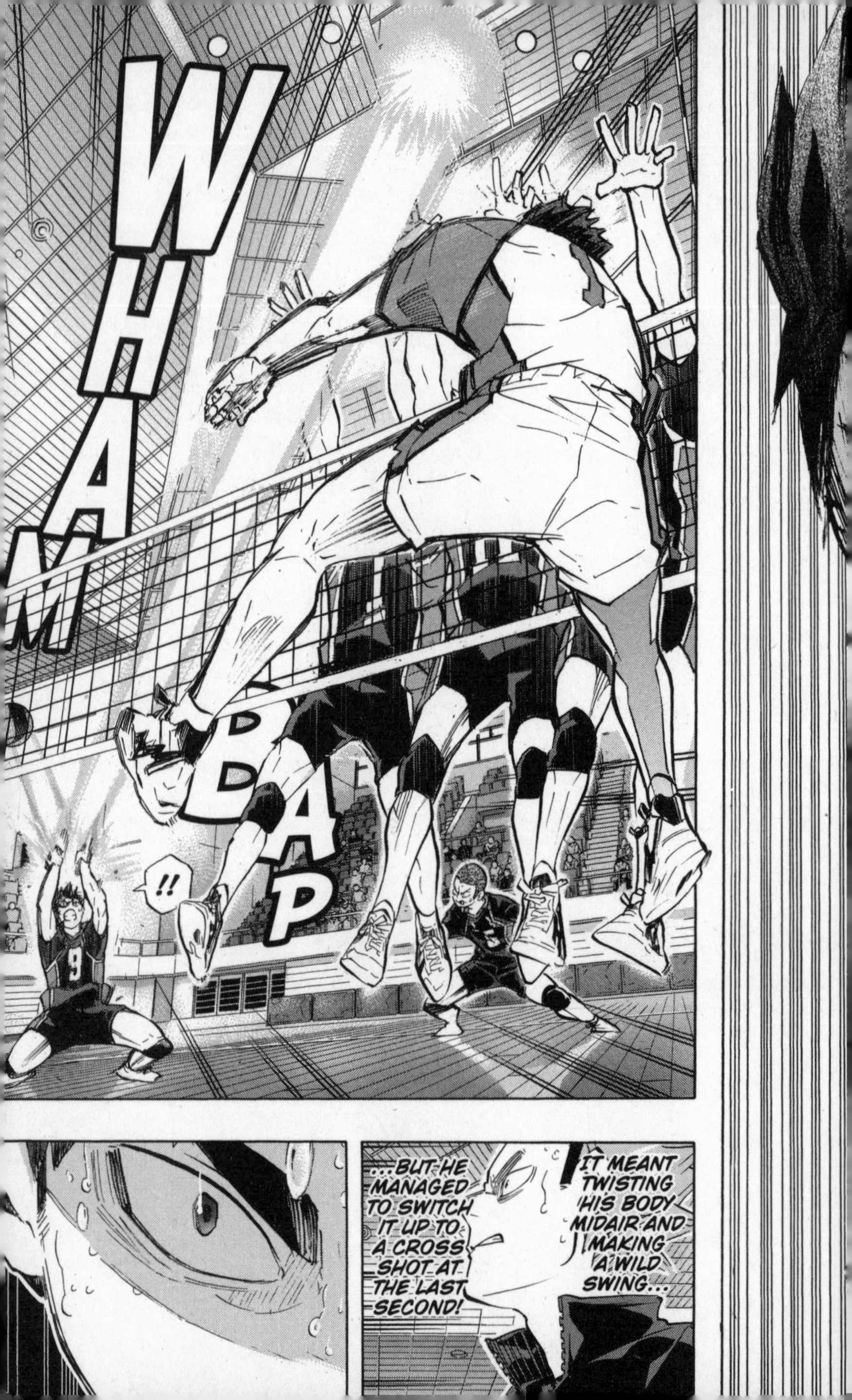
WHAM
DDAP
!!
IT MEANT TWISTING HIS BODY MIDAIR AND MAKING A WILD SWING...
...BUT HE MANAGED TO SWITCH IT UP TO A CROSS SHOT AT THE LAST SECOND!

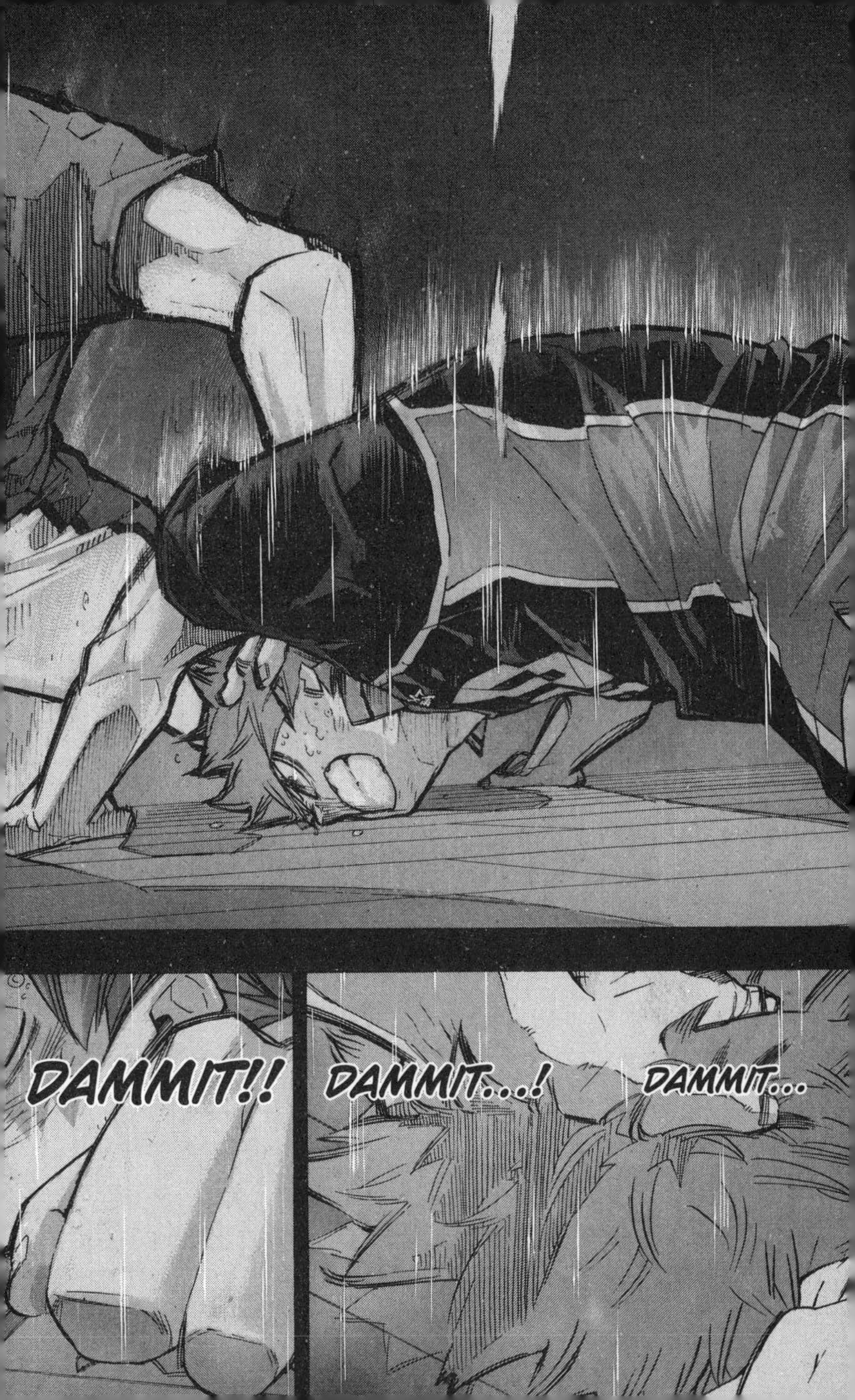
DAMMIT...
DAMMIT...!
DAMMIT!!

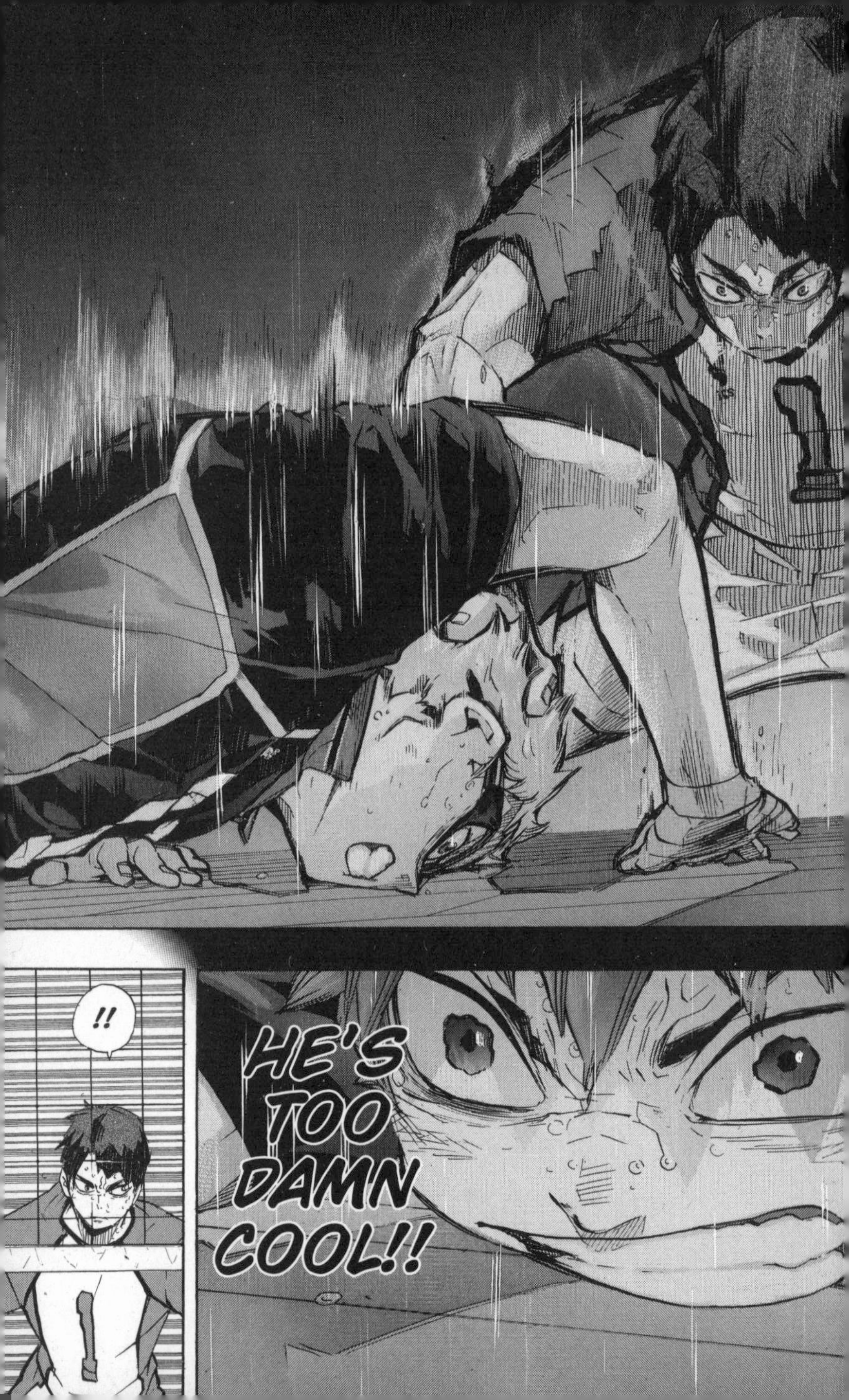
HE'S TOO DAMN COOL!!
!!

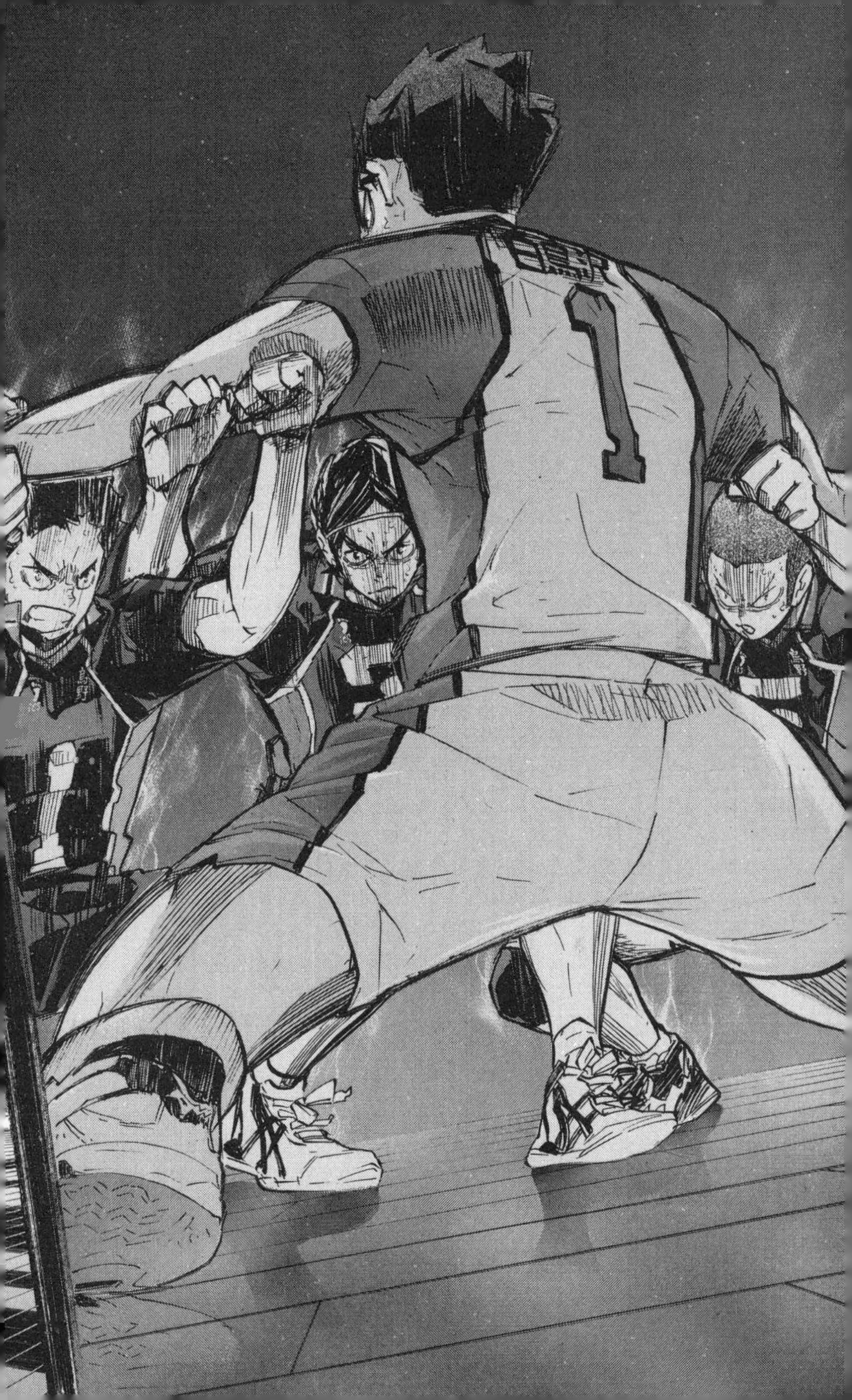

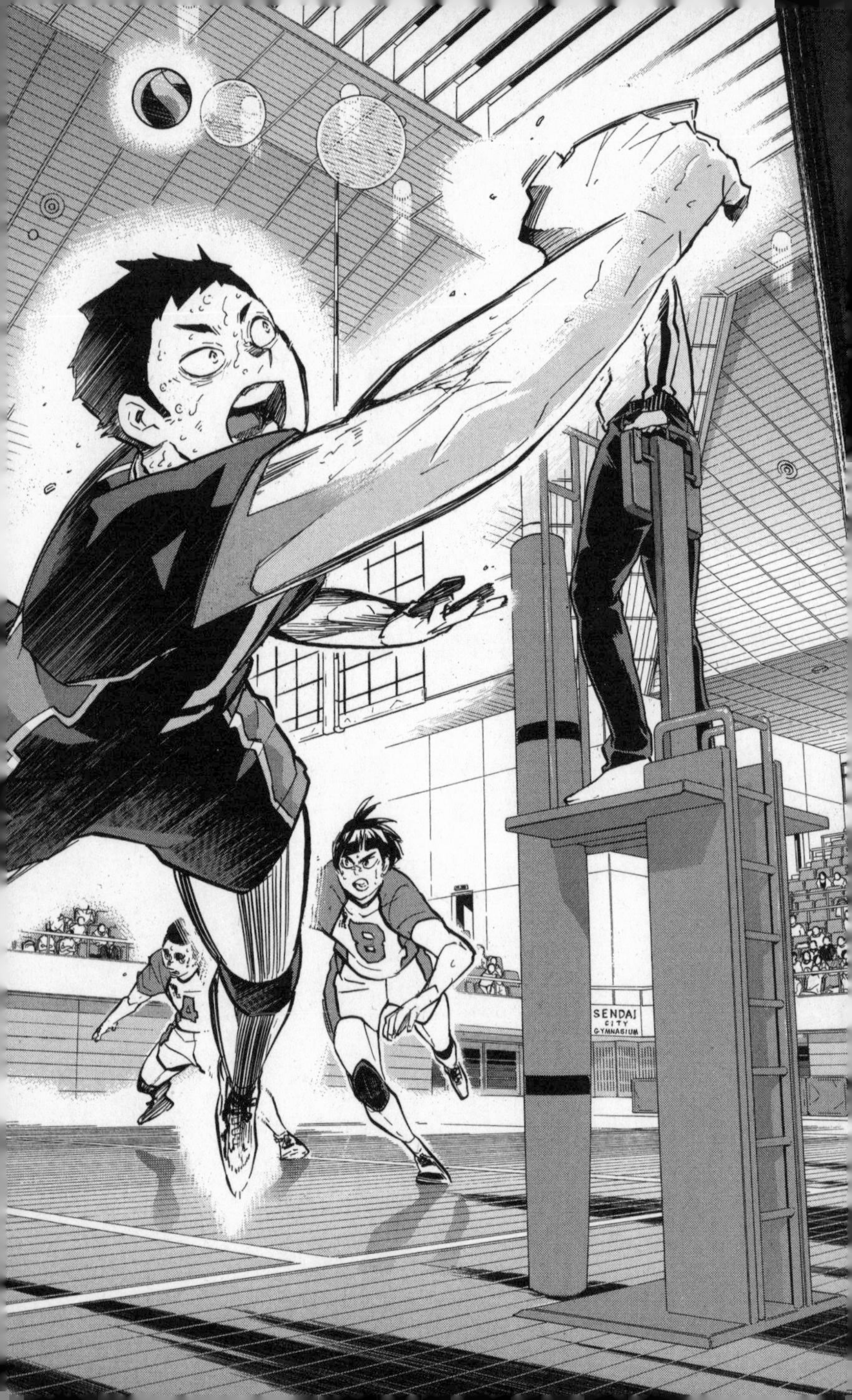
SENDAI
CITY
GYMNASIUM

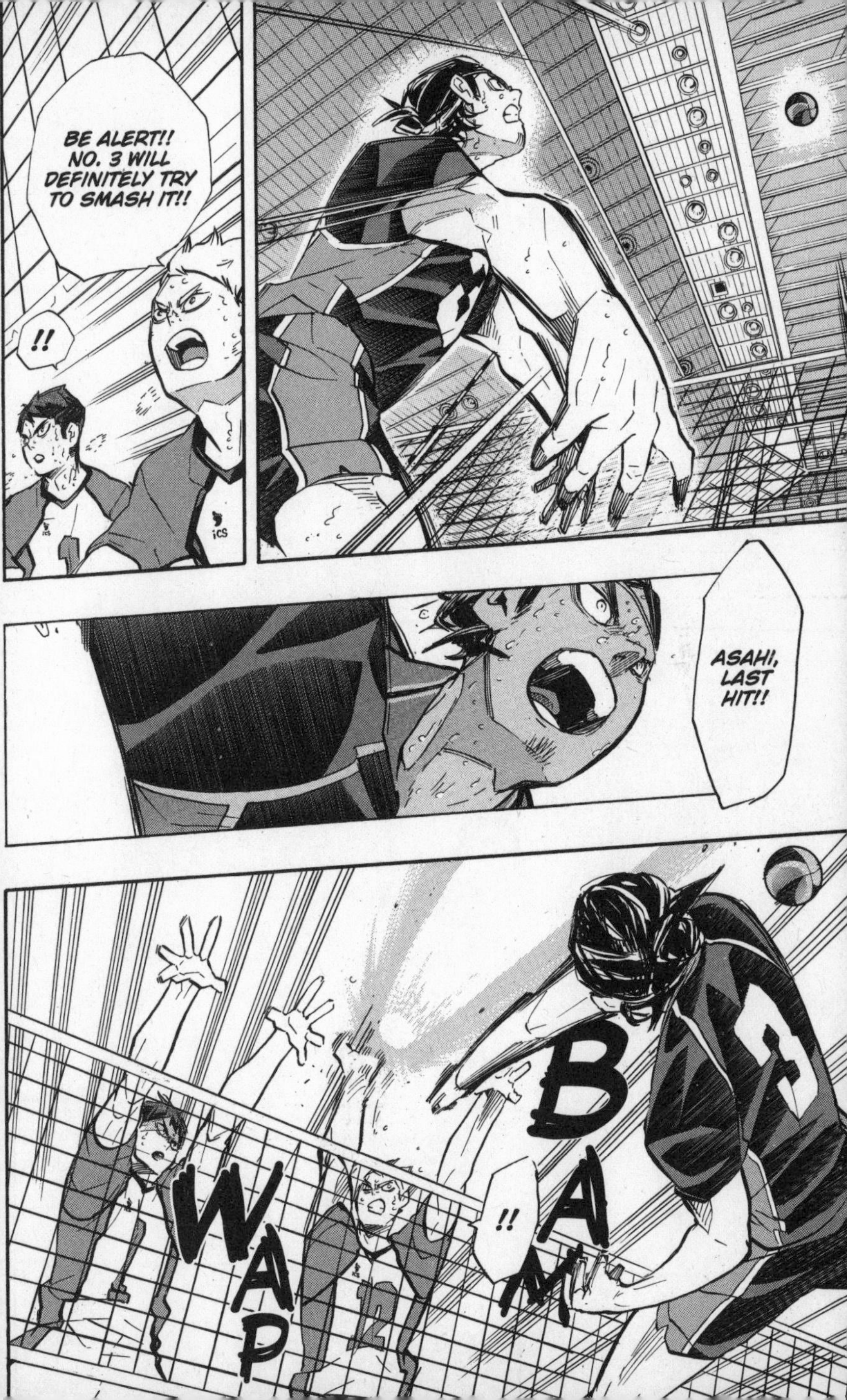
BE ALERT!! NO. 3 WILL DEFINITELY TRY TO SMASH IT!!
!!
ASAHI, LAST HIT!!
BAM
!!
WAP

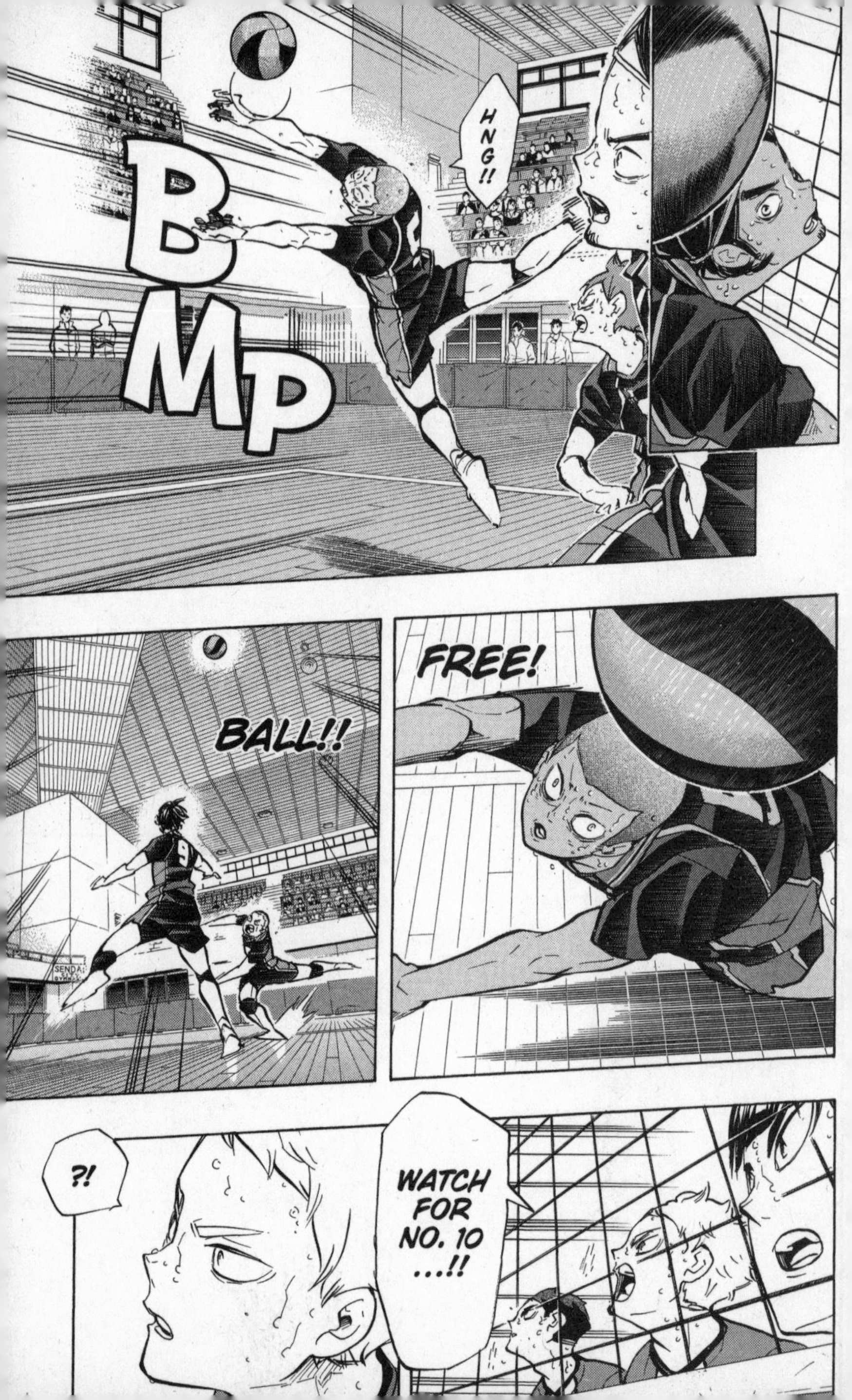
HNG!!
BMP
FREE!
BALL!!
WATCH FOR NO. 10 ...!!
?!

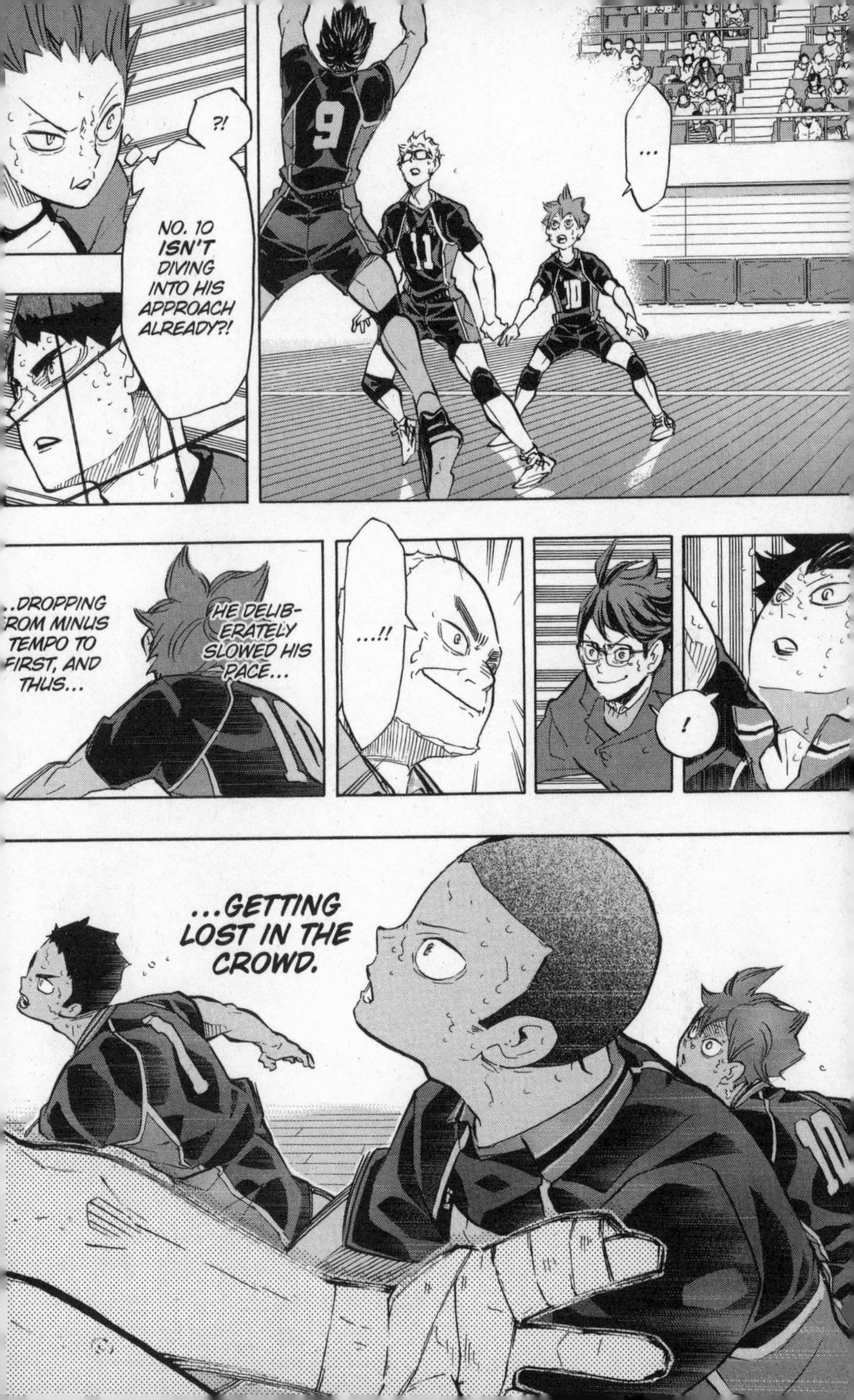
...
?!
NO. 10 ISN'T DIVING INTO HIS APPROACH ALREADY?!
!
...!!
HE DELIB-ERATELY SLOWED HIS PACE...
..DROPPING FROM MINUS TEMPO TO FIRST, AND THUS...
...GETTING LOST IN THE CROWD.

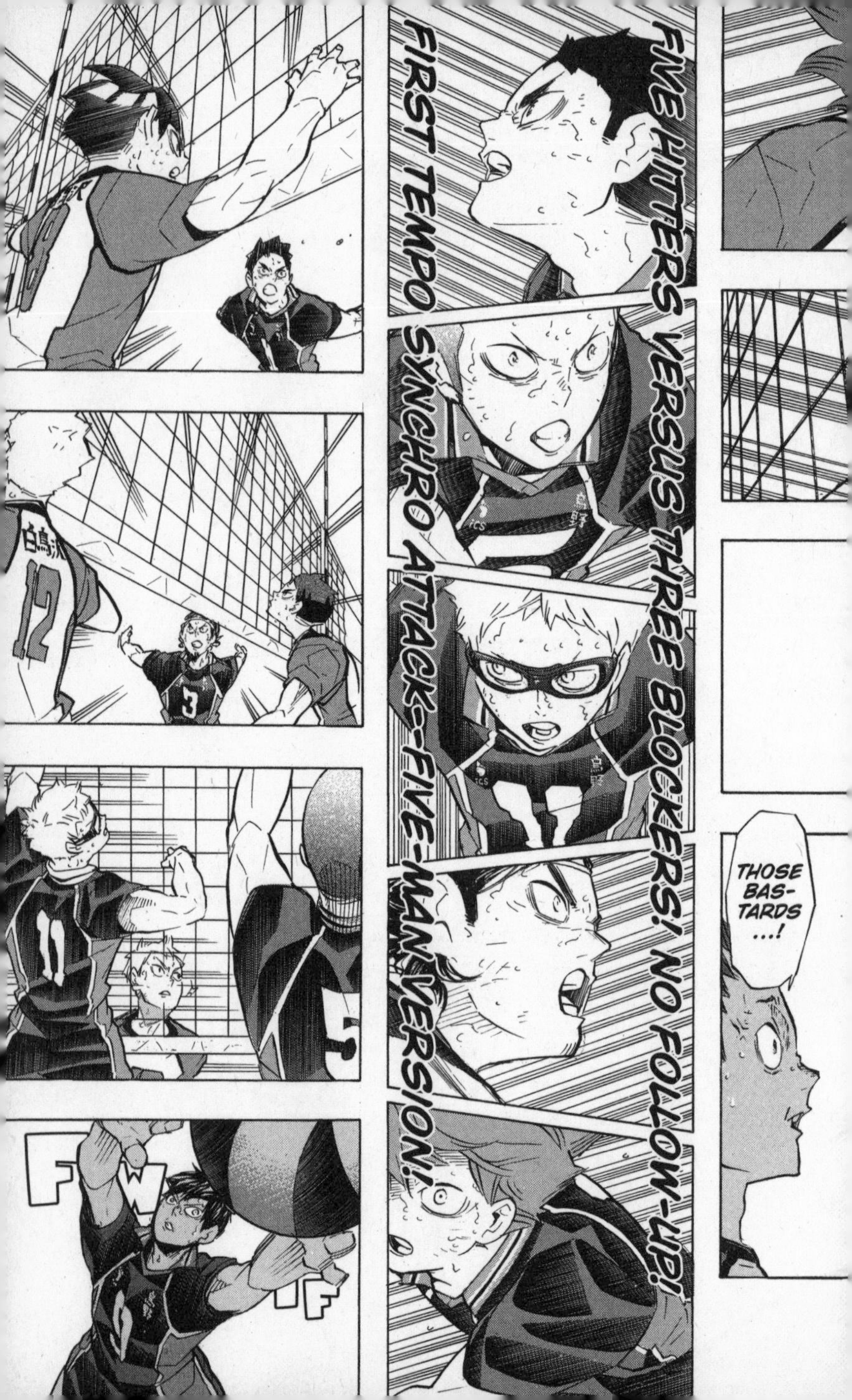

THOSE BASTARDS...!
FIVE HITTERS VERSUS THREE BLOCKERS! NO FOLLOW-UP!
FIRST TEMPO SYNCHRO ATTACK--FIVE-MAN VERSION!
FWF

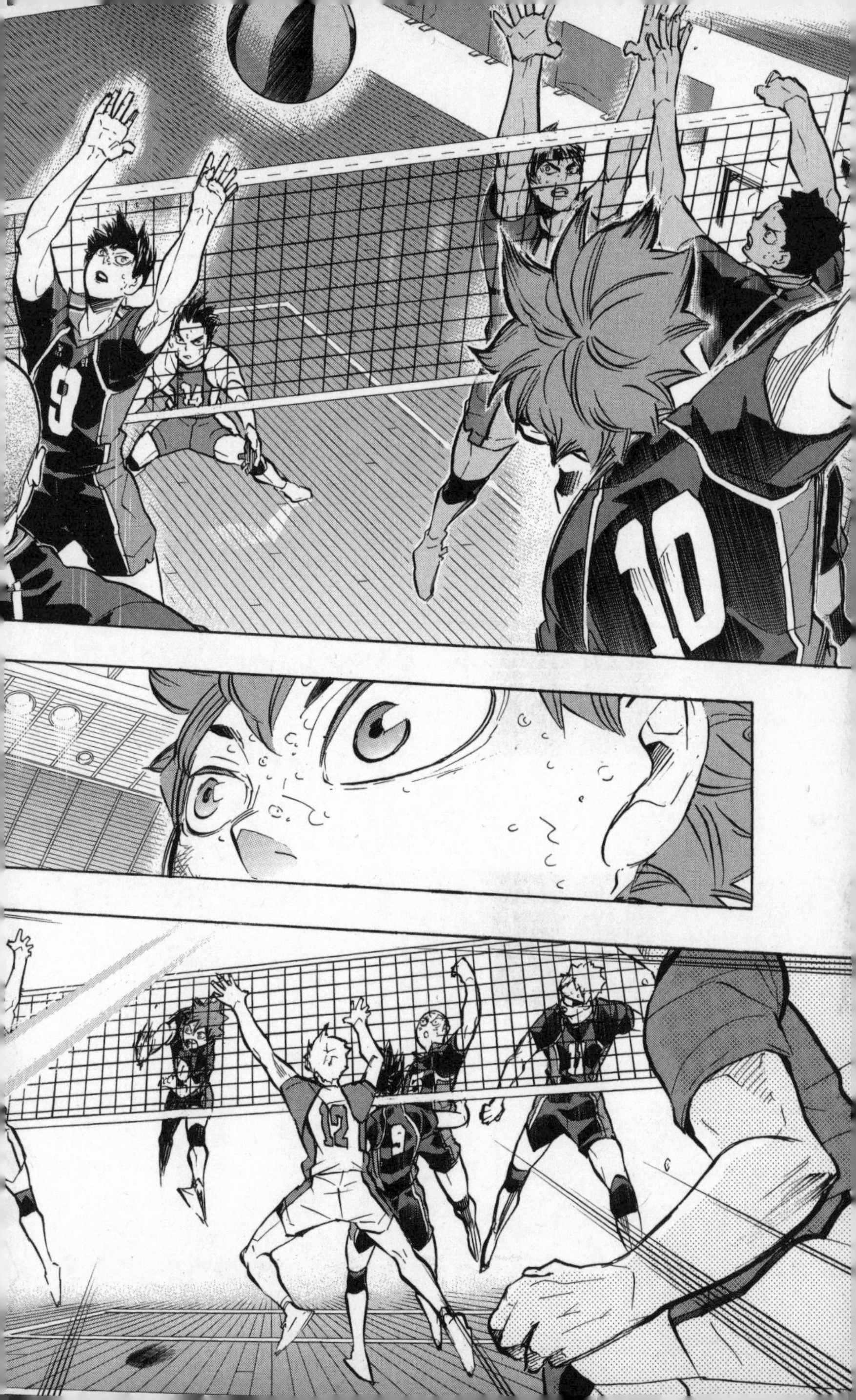

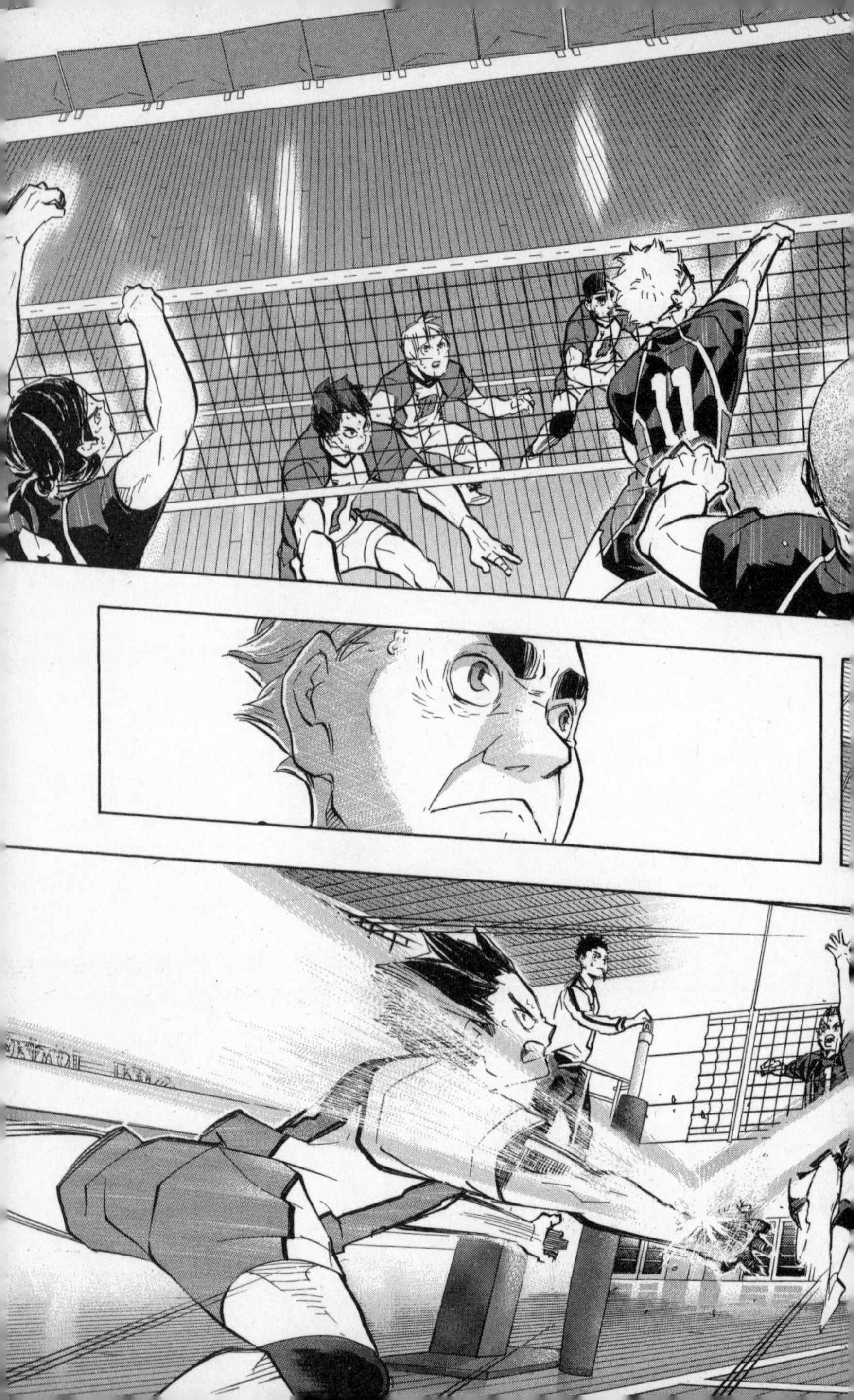

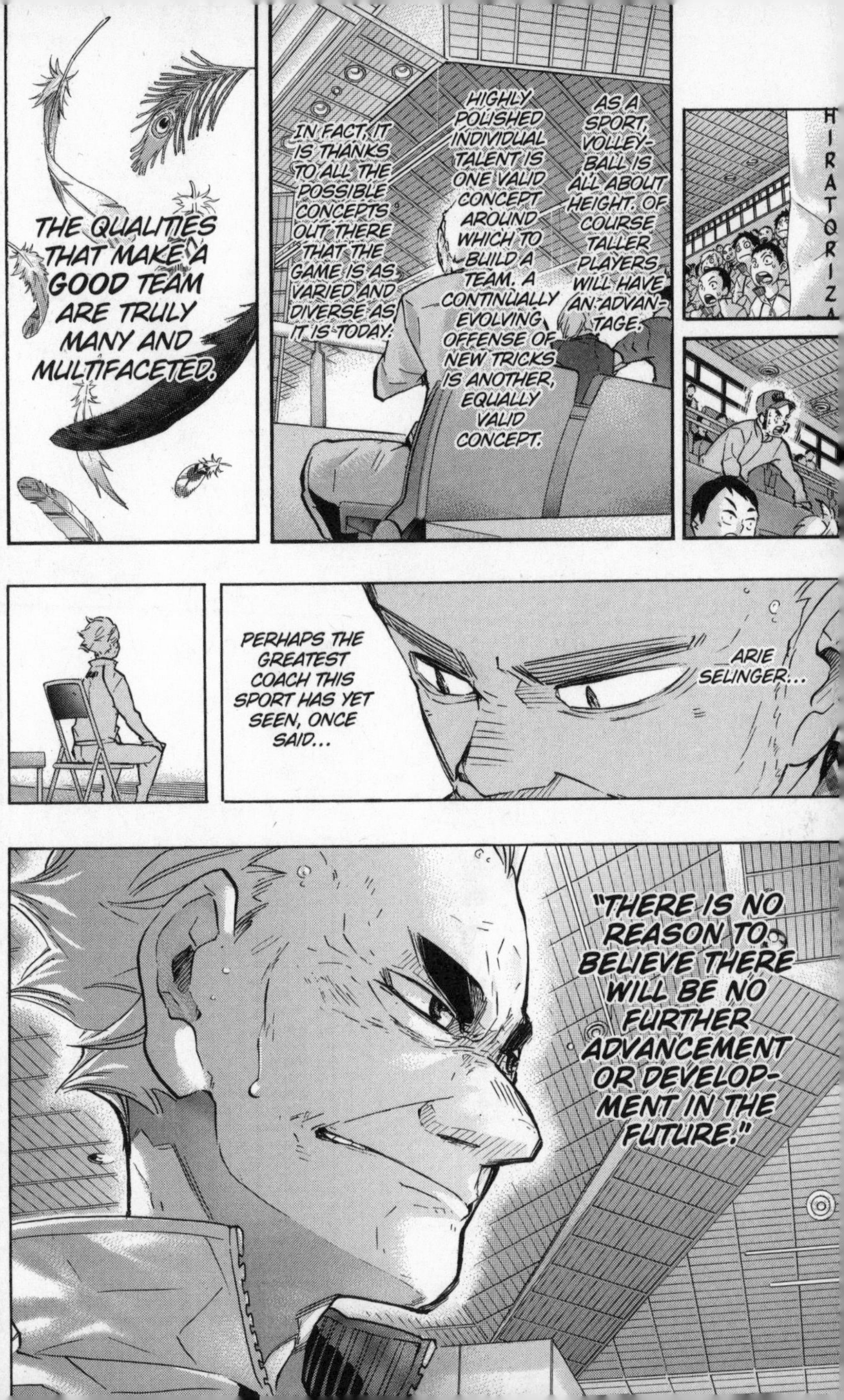
HIRATORIZA
AS A SPORT, VOLLEY-BALL IS ALL ABOUT HEIGHT. OF COURSE TALLER PLAYERS WILL HAVE AN ADVAN-TAGE.
HIGHLY POLISHED INDIVIDUAL TALENT IS ONE VALID CONCEPT AROUND WHICH TO BUILD A TEAM. A CONTINUALLY EVOLVING OFFENSE OF NEW TRICKS IS ANOTHER, EQUALLY VALID CONCEPT.
IN FACT, IT IS THANKS TO ALL THE POSSIBLE CONCEPTS OUT THERE THAT THE GAME IS AS VARIED AND DIVERSE AS IT IS TODAY.
THE QUALITIES THAT MAKE A GOOD TEAM ARE TRULY MANY AND MULTIFACETED.
ARIE SELINGER...
PERHAPS THE GREATEST COACH THIS SPORT HAS YET SEEN, ONCE SAID...
"THERE IS NO REASON TO BELIEVE THERE WILL BE NO FURTHER ADVANCEMENT OR DEVELOP-MENT IN THE FUTURE."

CHAPTER 188: A Battle of Concepts

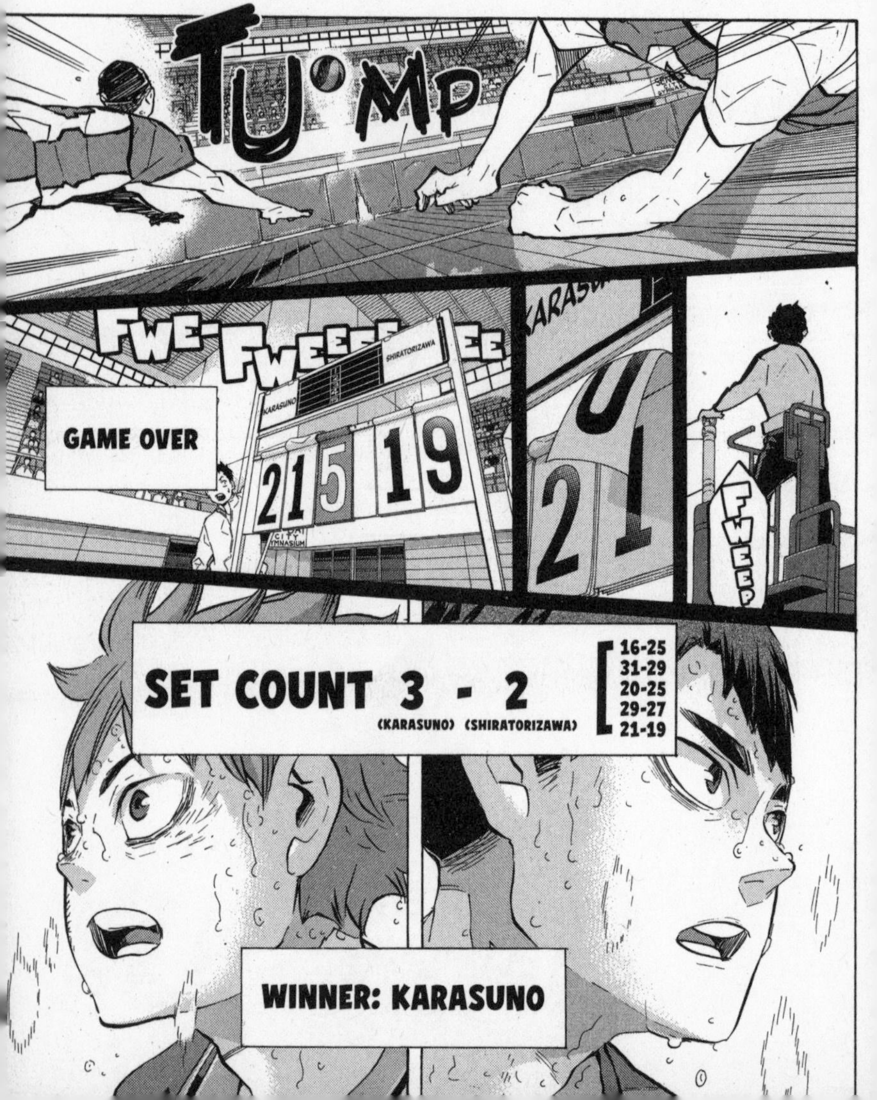
TUMP
FWEEP
21
FWE-FWEEEEEEE
SHIRATORIZAWA
KARASUNO
21
5
19
GAME OVER
SET COUNT 3 - 2
(KARASUNO) (SHIRATORIZAWA)
16-25
31-29
20-25
29-27
21-19
WINNER: KARASUNO

HAIKYU!!

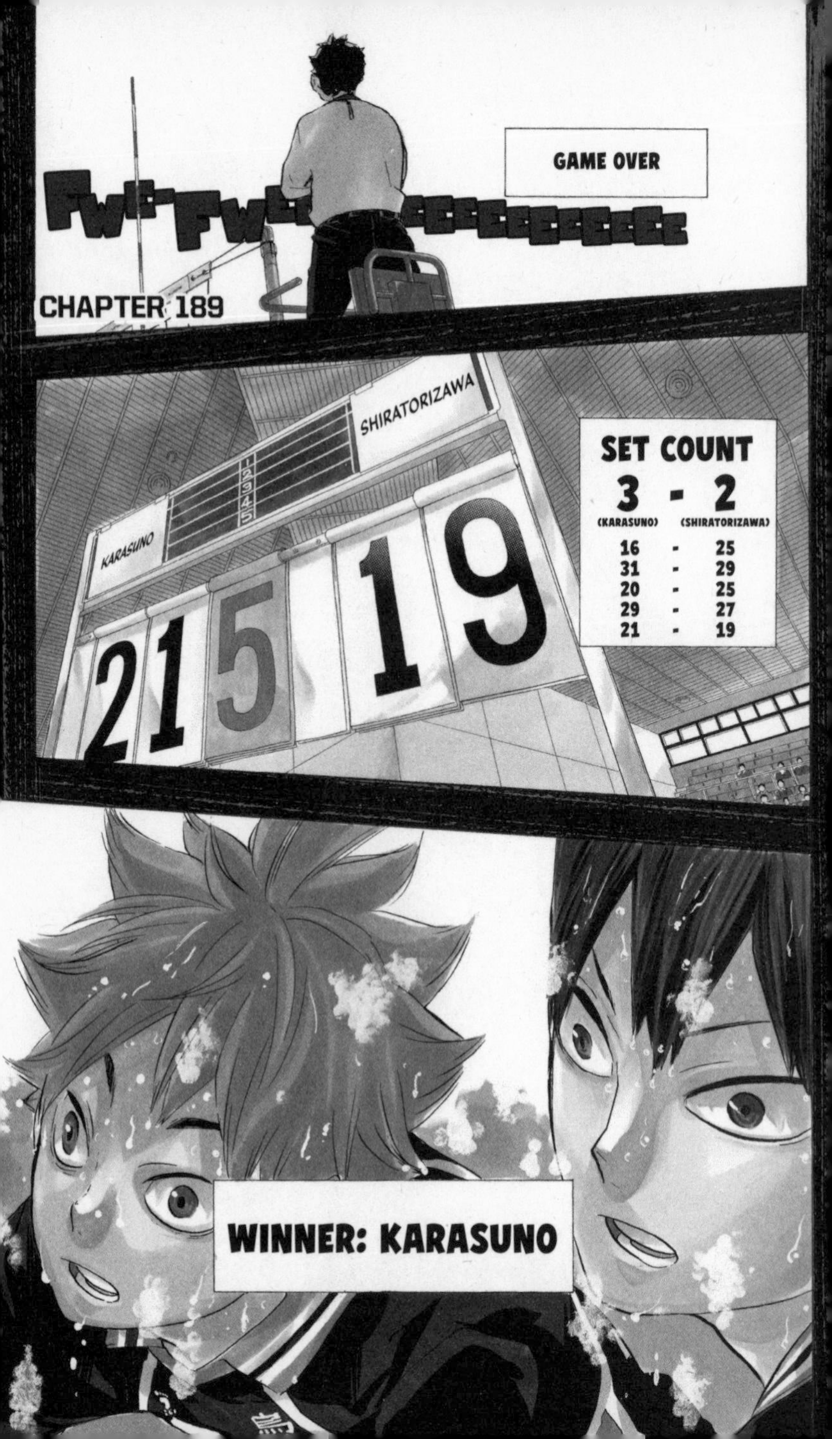
GAME OVER
FWE-FWEEEEEEEEEEEEEEE
CHAPTER 189
SET COUNT
3 - 2
(KARASUNO) (SHIRATORIZAWA)
16 - 25
31 - 29
20 - 25
29 - 27
21 - 19
SHIRATORIZAWA
KARASUNO
21 5 19
WINNER: KARASUNO

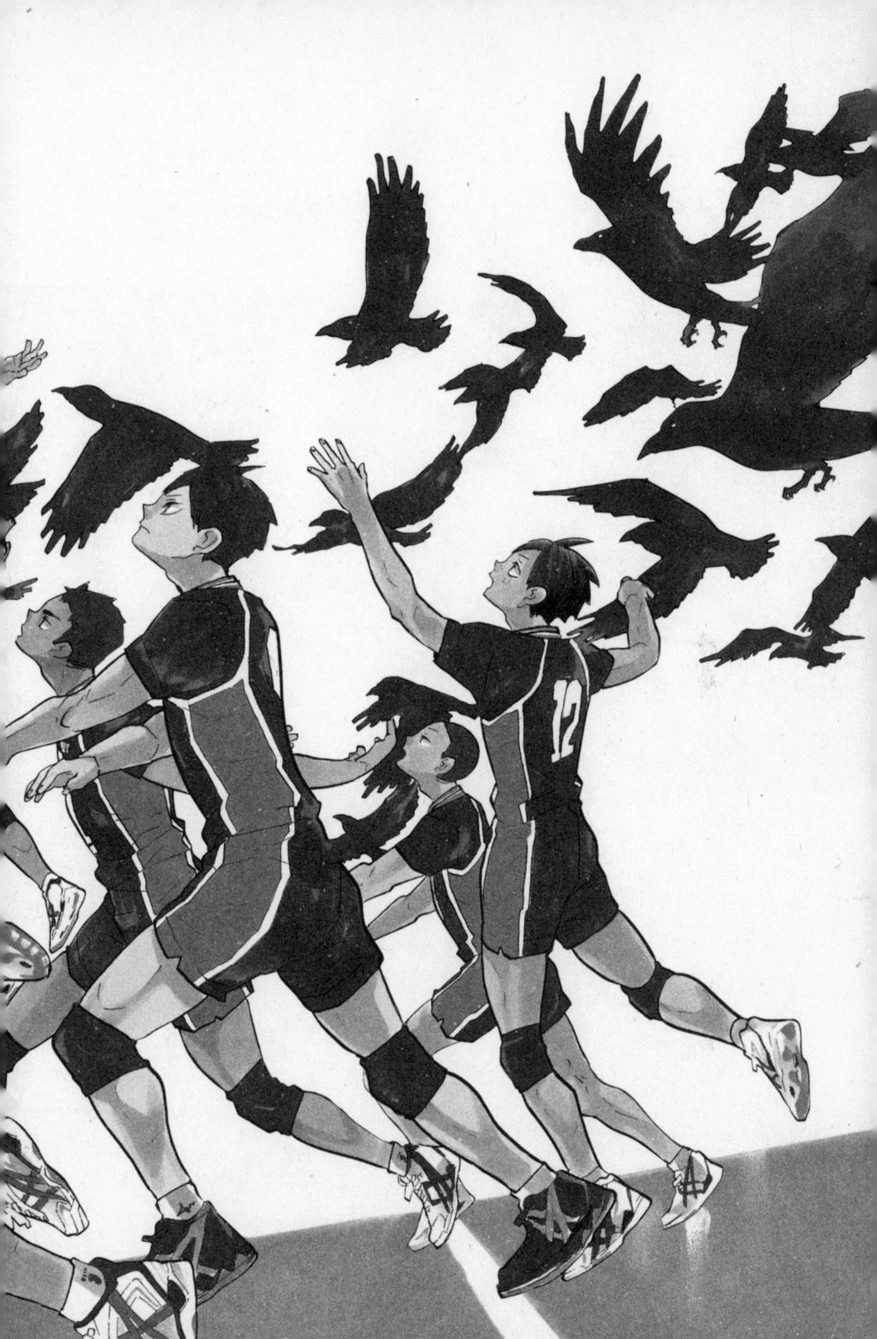

CHAPTER 189: Declaration of War: Part 2

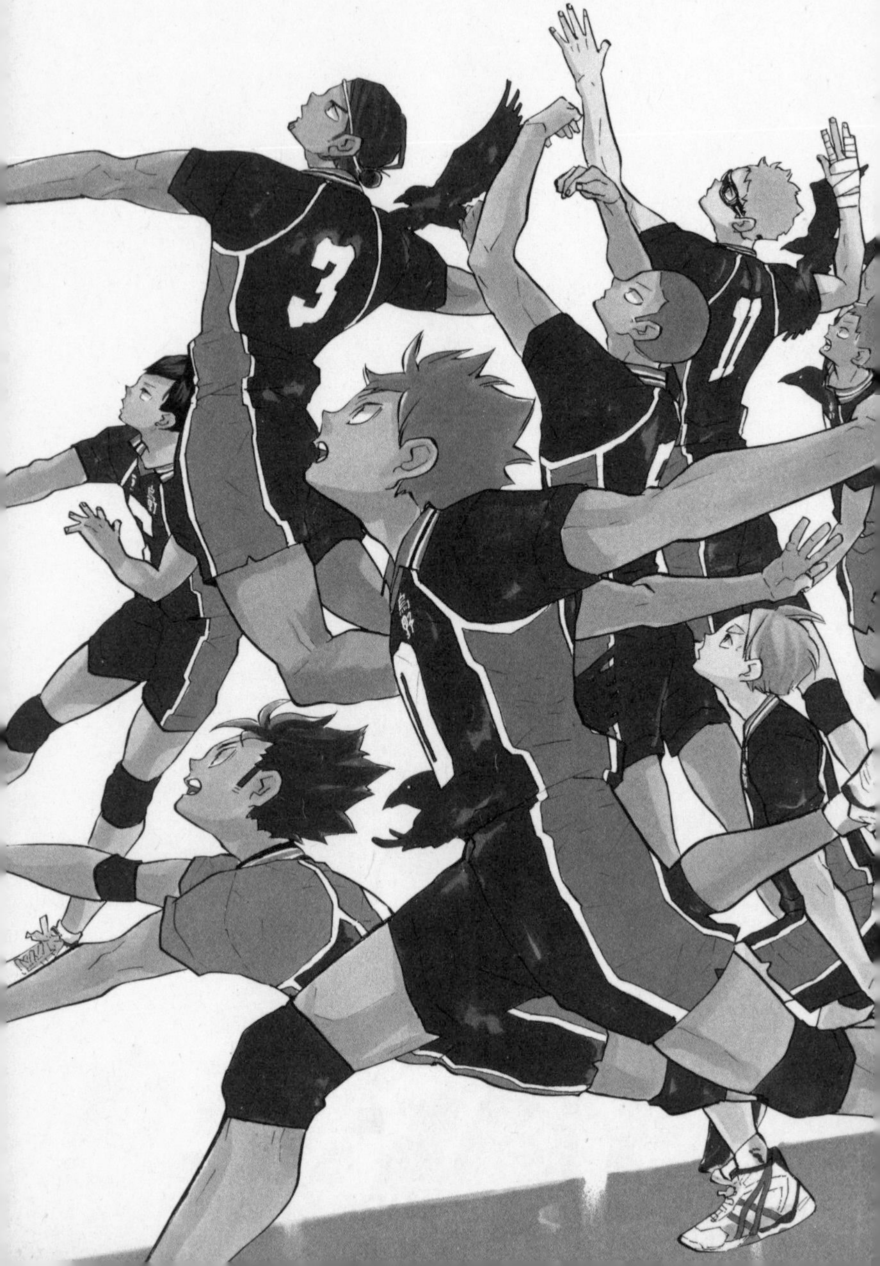

HAIKYU!!

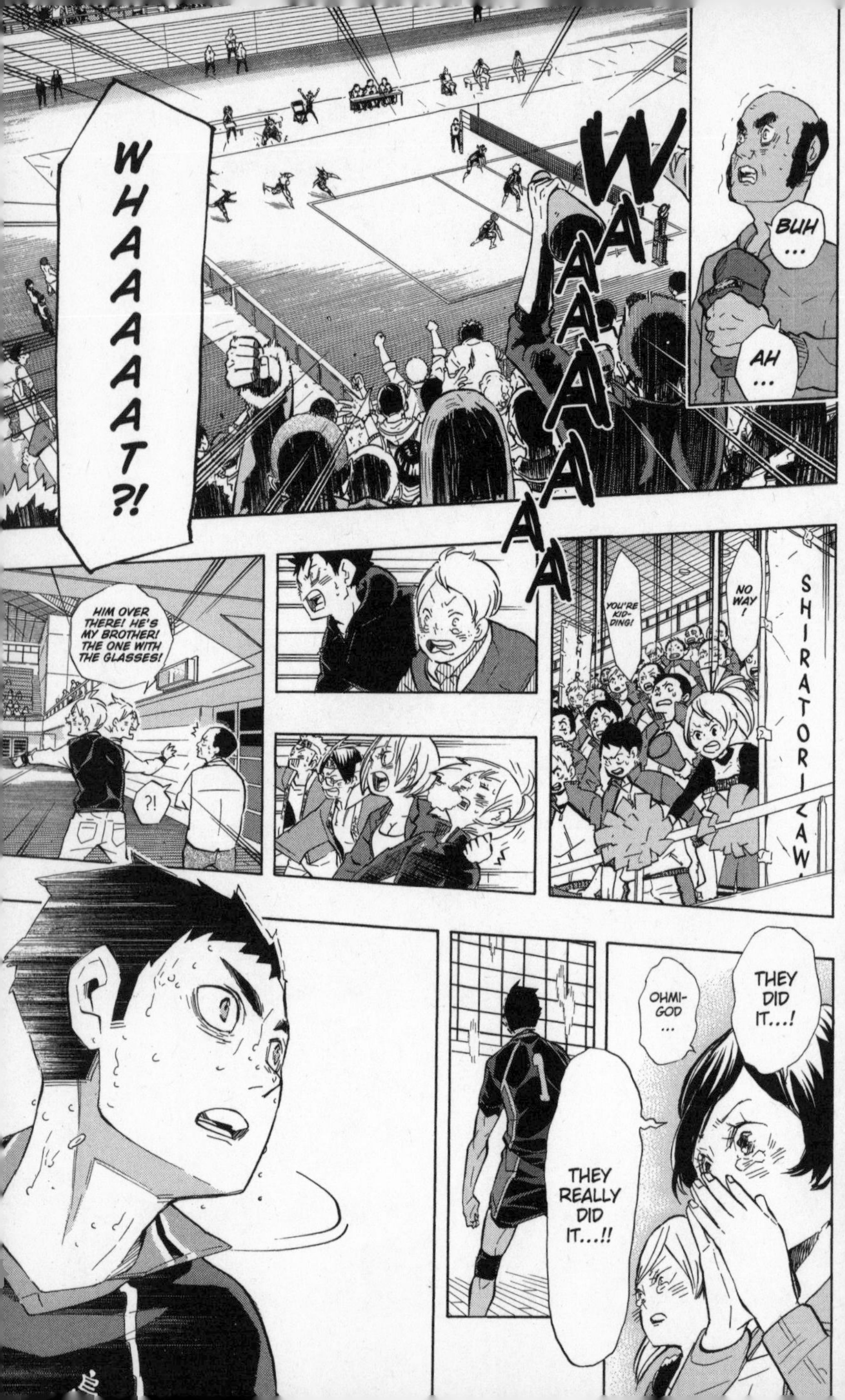
BUH ...
AH ...
WAAAAAAAAA
WHAAAAAAAT?!
SHIRATORIZAWA!
NO WAY!
YOU'RE KID-DING!
HIM OVER THERE! HE'S MY BROTHER! THE ONE WITH THE GLASSES!
?!
THEY DID IT...!
OHMI-GOD ...
THEY REALLY DID IT...!!

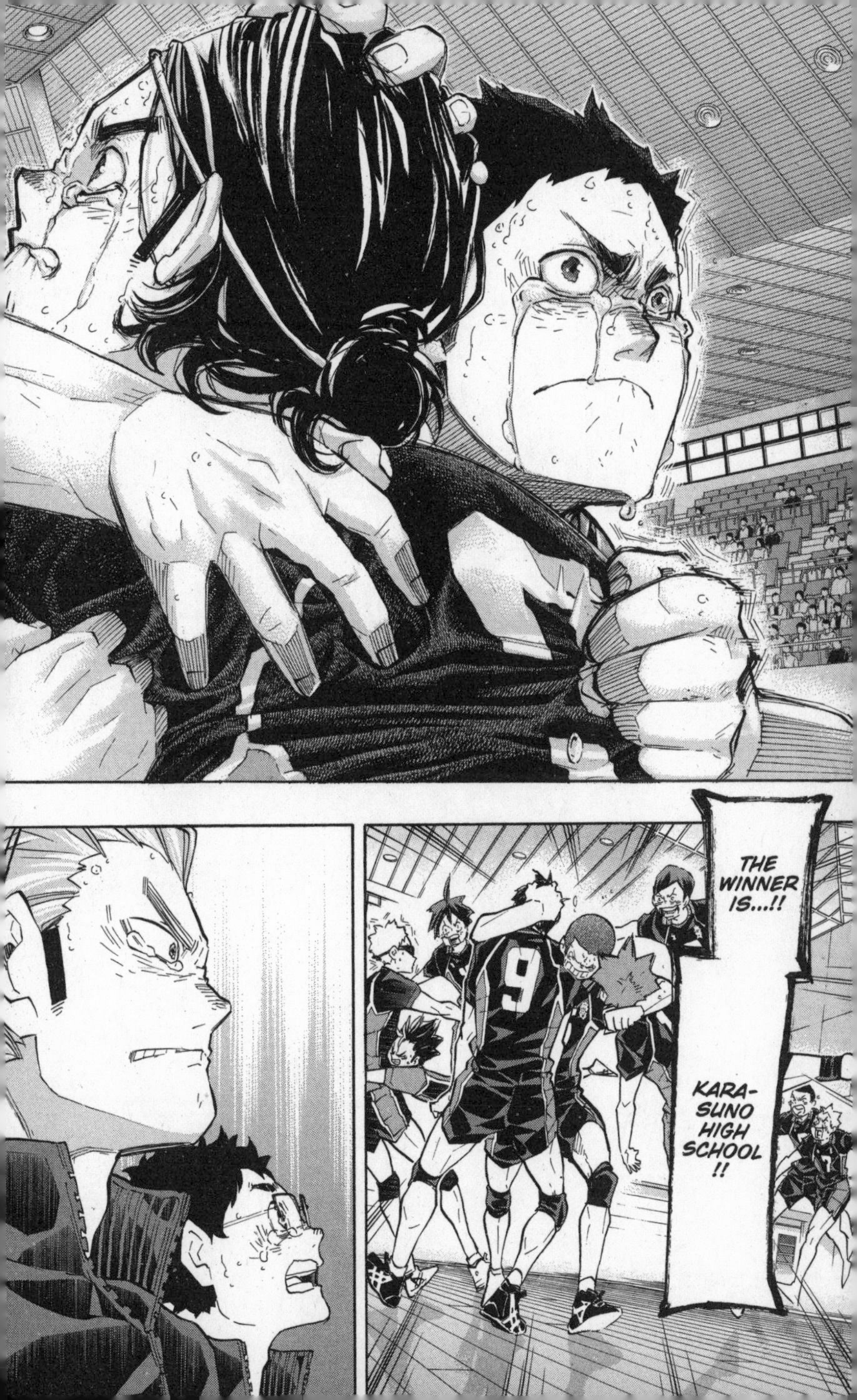
THE WINNER IS...!!
KARA-SUNO HIGH SCHOOL!!

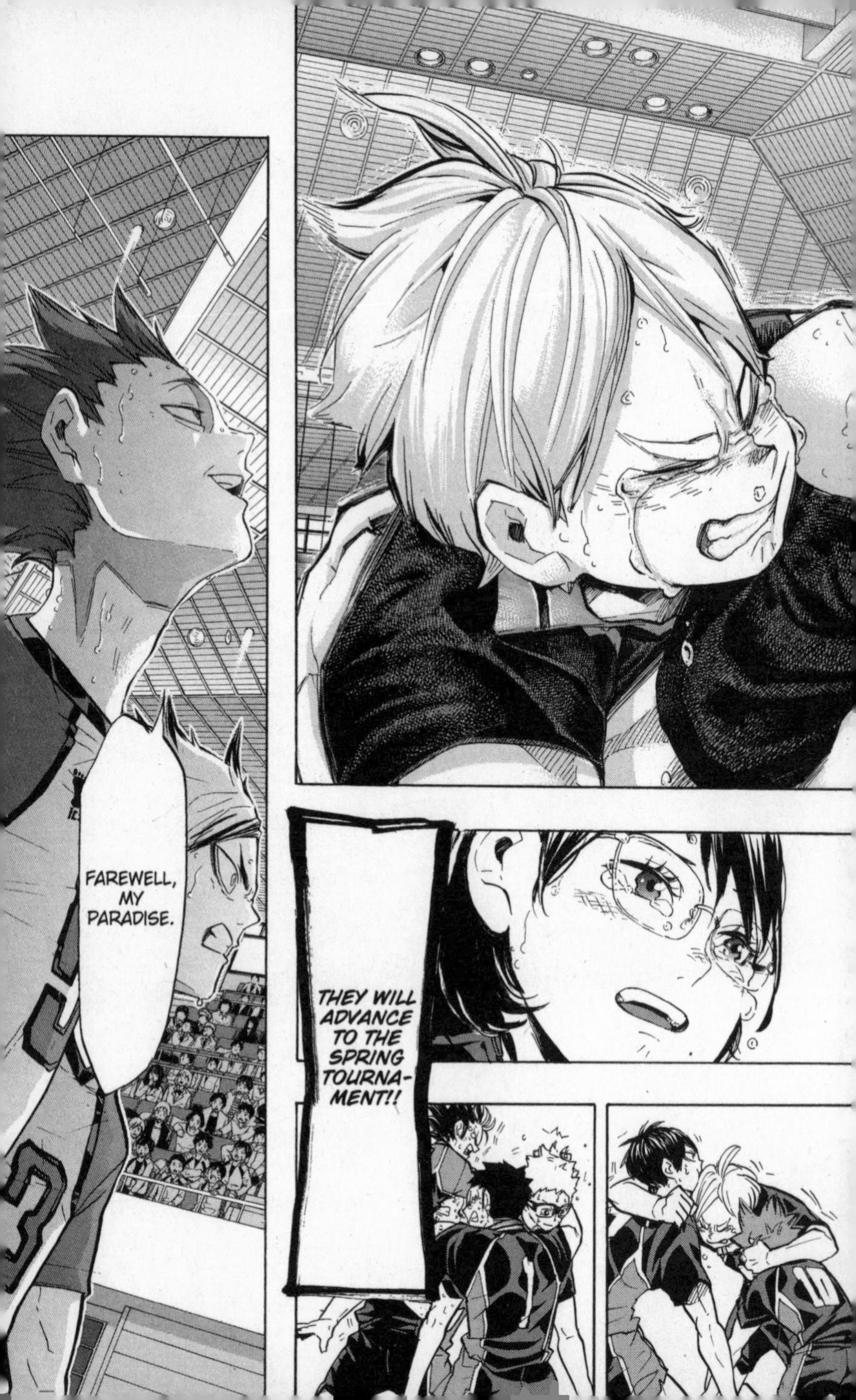
THEY WILL ADVANCE TO THE SPRING TOURNAMENT!!
FAREWELL, MY PARADISE.

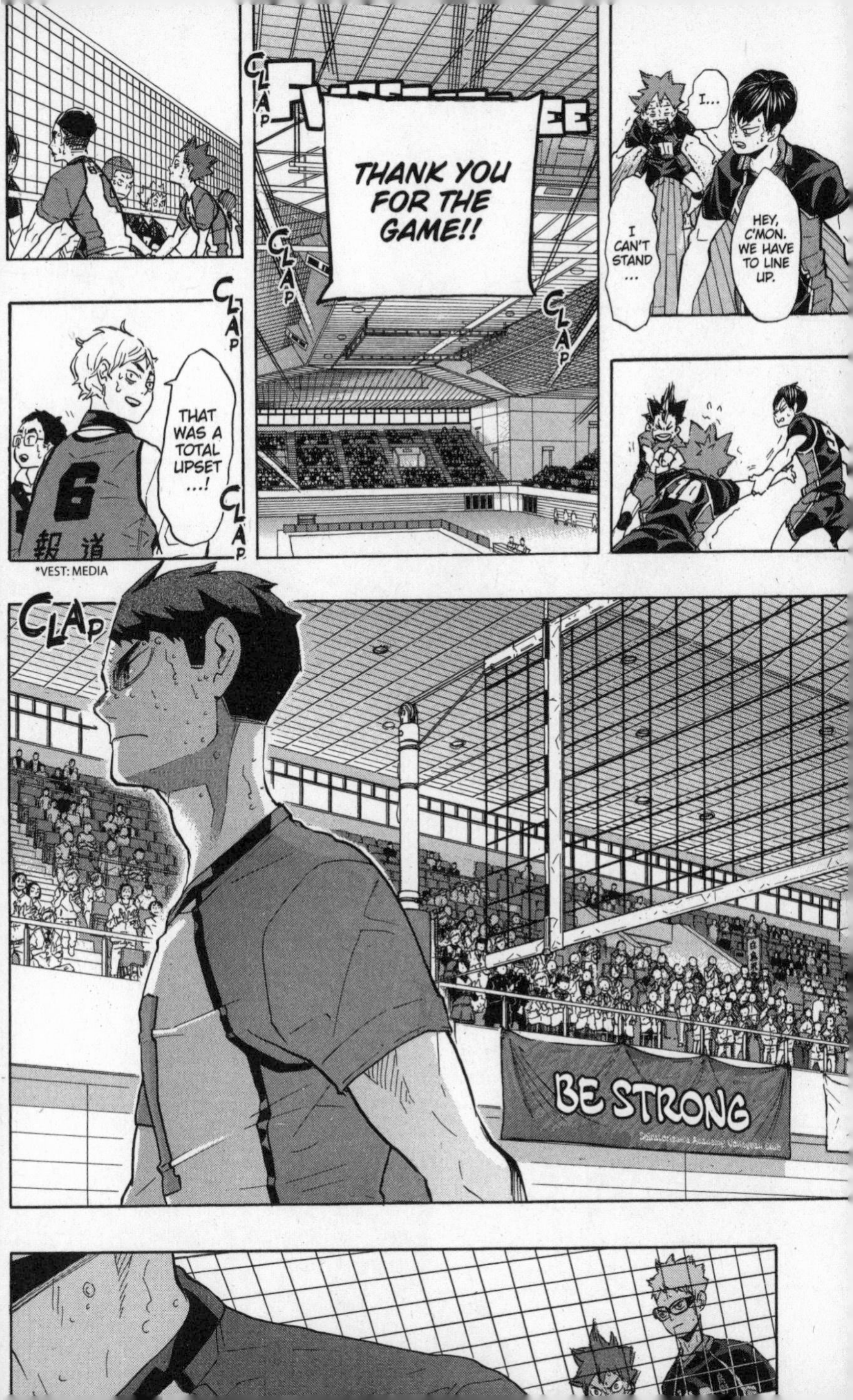
I...
I CAN'T STAND ...
HEY, C'MON. WE HAVE TO LINE UP.
CLAP
CLAP
THANK YOU FOR THE GAME!!
CLAP
CLAP
THAT WAS A TOTAL UPSET ...!
CLAP
報道
*VEST: MEDIA
CLAP
BE STRONG

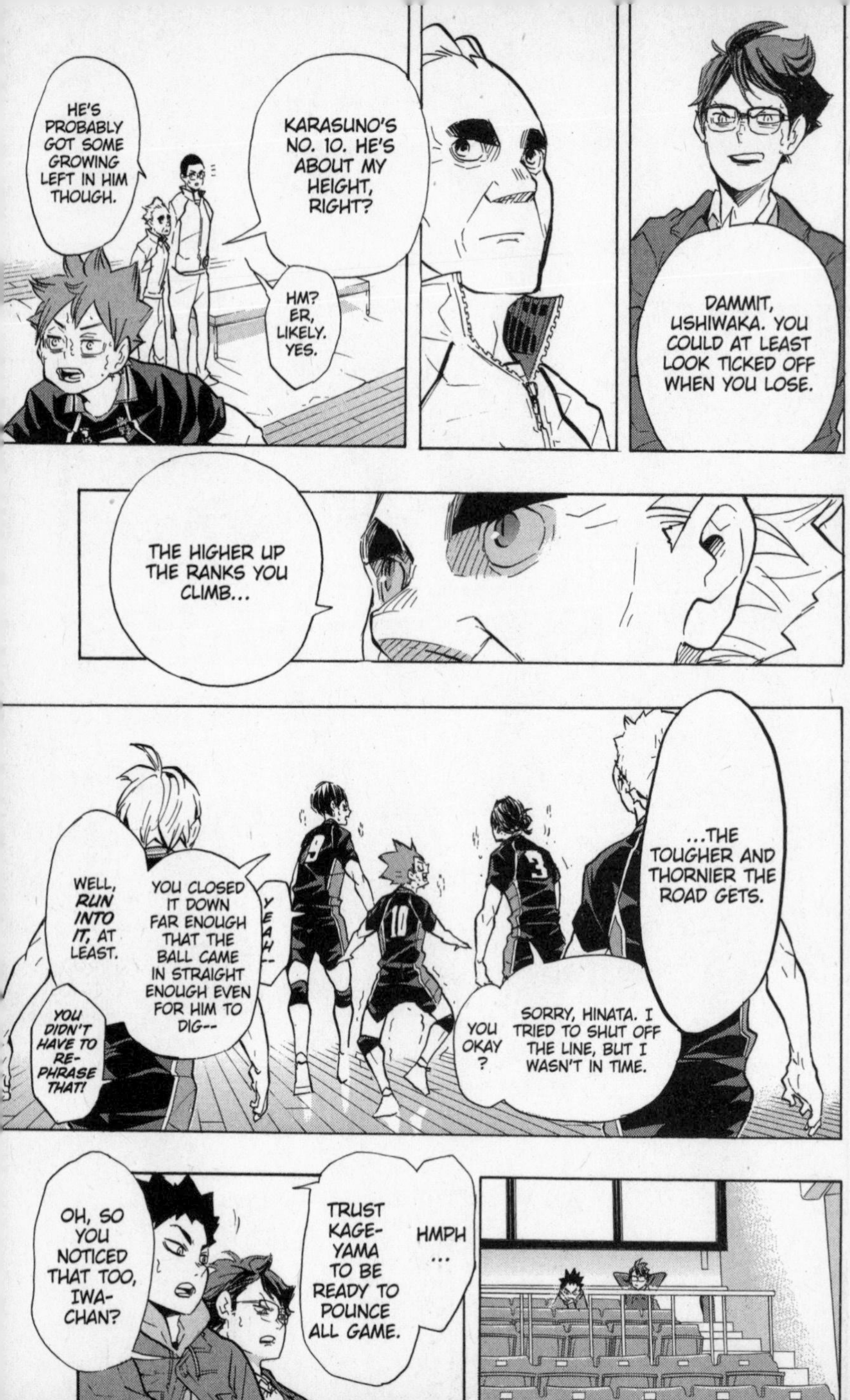
DAMMIT, USHIWAKA. YOU COULD AT LEAST LOOK TICKED OFF WHEN YOU LOSE.
KARASUNO'S NO. 10. HE'S ABOUT MY HEIGHT, RIGHT?
HM? ER, LIKELY. YES.
HE'S PROBABLY GOT SOME GROWING LEFT IN HIM THOUGH.
THE HIGHER UP THE RANKS YOU CLIMB...
...THE TOUGHER AND THORNIER THE ROAD GETS.
SORRY, HINATA. I TRIED TO SHUT OFF THE LINE, BUT I WASN'T IN TIME.
YOU OKAY?
YEAH--
YOU CLOSED IT DOWN FAR ENOUGH THAT THE BALL CAME IN STRAIGHT ENOUGH EVEN FOR HIM TO DIG--
WELL, *RUN INTO IT*, AT LEAST.
YOU DIDN'T HAVE TO RE-PHRASE THAT!
HMPH...
TRUST KAGE-YAMA TO BE READY TO POUNCE ALL GAME.
OH, SO YOU NOTICED THAT TOO, IWA-CHAN?

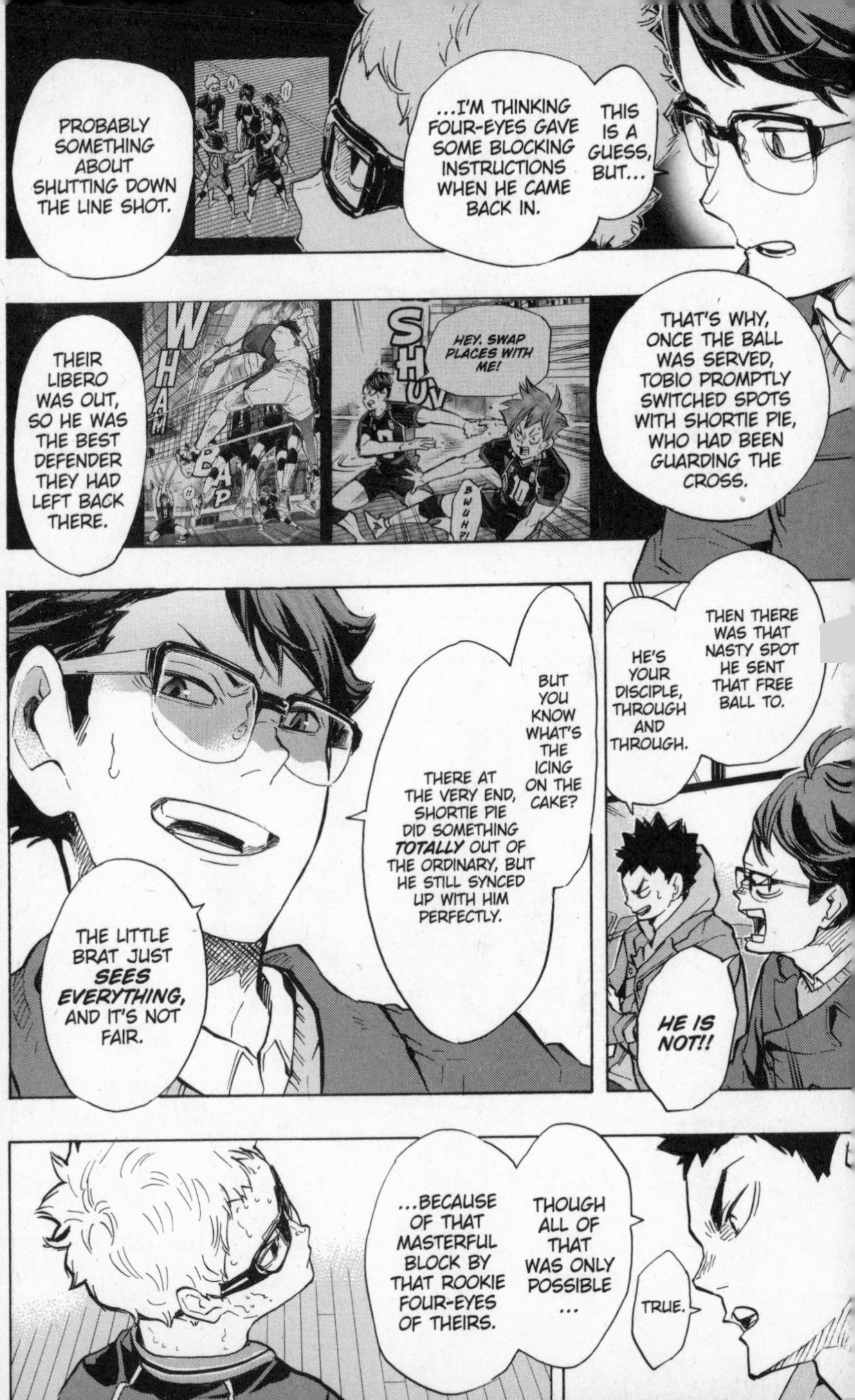
THIS IS A GUESS, BUT...
...I'M THINKING FOUR-EYES GAVE SOME BLOCKING INSTRUCTIONS WHEN HE CAME BACK IN.
PROBABLY SOMETHING ABOUT SHUTTING DOWN THE LINE SHOT.
THAT'S WHY, ONCE THE BALL WAS SERVED, TOBIO PROMPTLY SWITCHED SPOTS WITH SHORTIE PIE, WHO HAD BEEN GUARDING THE CROSS.
SHUV
HEY. SWAP PLACES WITH ME!
BWUH?!
WHAM
BAP
THEIR LIBERO WAS OUT, SO HE WAS THE BEST DEFENDER THEY HAD LEFT BACK THERE.
THEN THERE WAS THAT NASTY SPOT HE SENT THAT FREE BALL TO.
HE'S YOUR DISCIPLE, THROUGH AND THROUGH.
HE IS NOT!!
BUT YOU KNOW WHAT'S THE ICING ON THE CAKE?
THERE AT THE VERY END, SHORTIE PIE DID SOMETHING TOTALLY OUT OF THE ORDINARY, BUT HE STILL SYNCED UP WITH HIM PERFECTLY.
THE LITTLE BRAT JUST SEES EVERYTHING, AND IT'S NOT FAIR.
TRUE.
THOUGH ALL OF THAT WAS ONLY POSSIBLE...
...BECAUSE OF THAT MASTERFUL BLOCK BY THAT ROOKIE FOUR-EYES OF THEIRS.

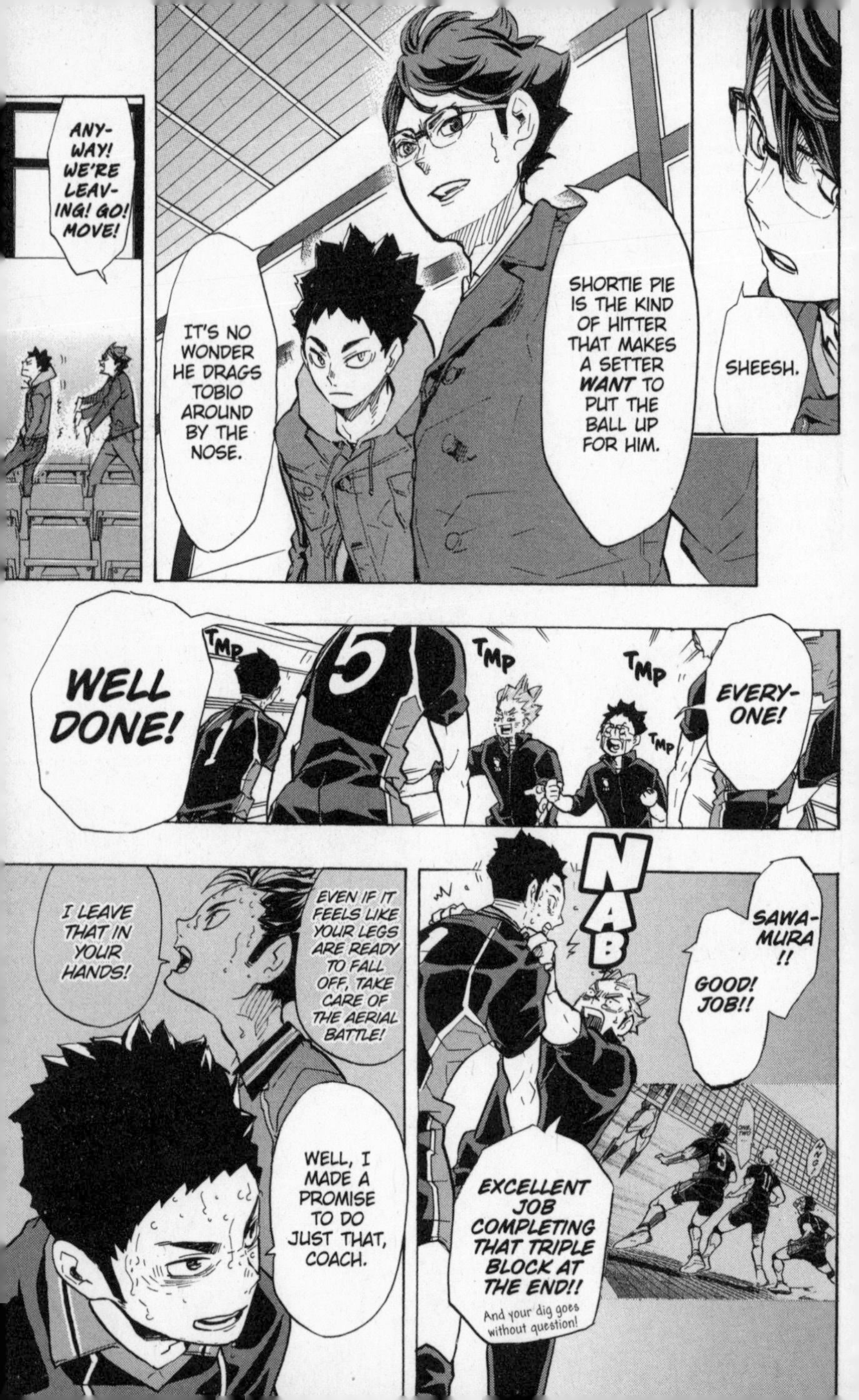
SHEESH.
SHORTIE PIE IS THE KIND OF HITTER THAT MAKES A SETTER WANT TO PUT THE BALL UP FOR HIM.
IT'S NO WONDER HE DRAGS TOBIO AROUND BY THE NOSE.
ANY-WAY! WE'RE LEAV-ING! GO! MOVE!
EVERY-ONE!
TMP
TMP
TMP
TMP
WELL DONE!
SAWA-MURA !!
GOOD! JOB!!
NAB
EXCELLENT JOB COMPLETING THAT TRIPLE BLOCK AT THE END!!
And your dig goes without question!
EVEN IF IT FEELS LIKE YOUR LEGS ARE READY TO FALL OFF, TAKE CARE OF THE AERIAL BATTLE!
I LEAVE THAT IN YOUR HANDS!
WELL, I MADE A PROMISE TO DO JUST THAT, COACH.

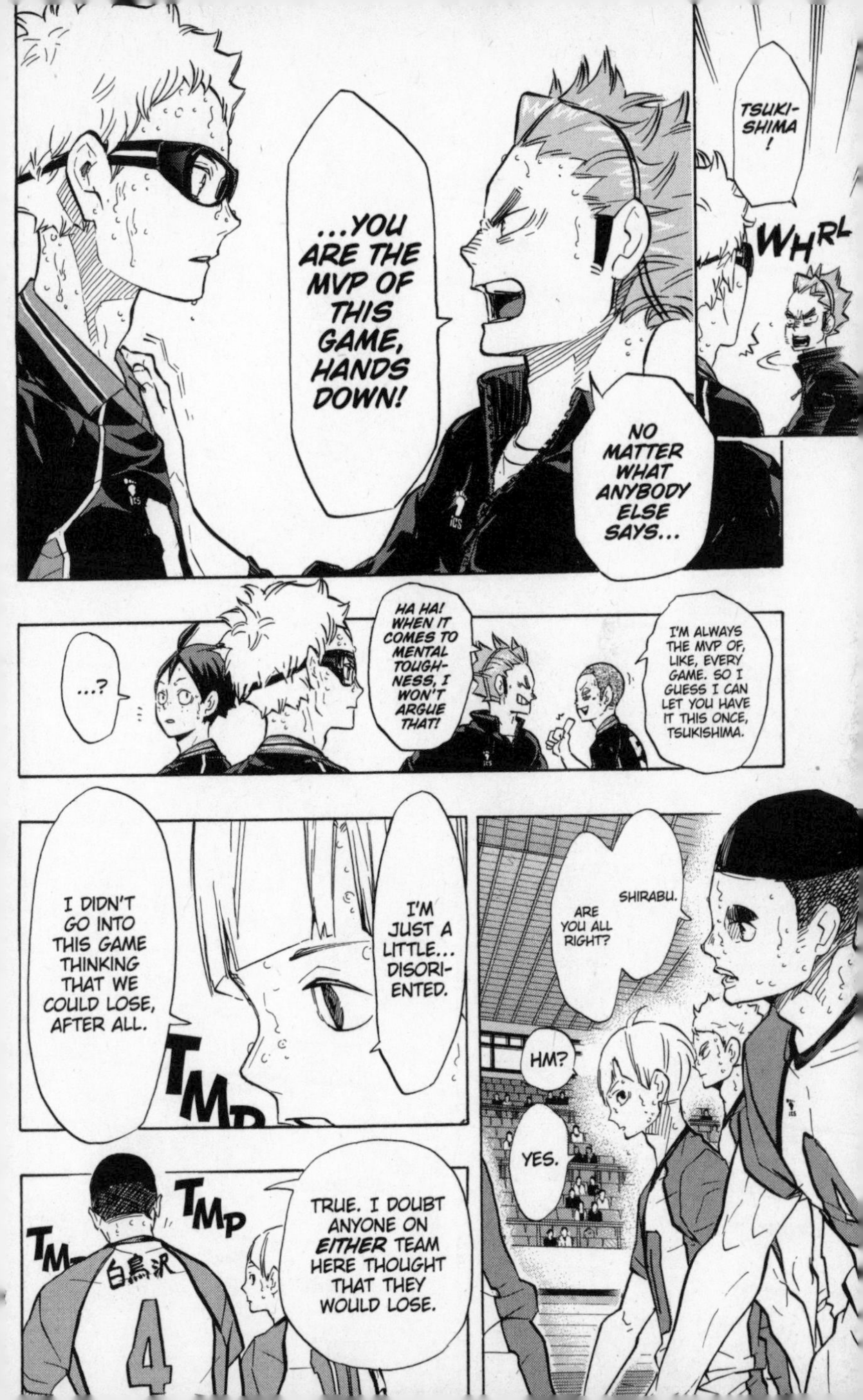
TSUKISHIMA!
WHRL
NO MATTER WHAT ANYBODY ELSE SAYS...
...YOU ARE THE MVP OF THIS GAME, HANDS DOWN!
I'M ALWAYS THE MVP OF, LIKE, EVERY GAME. SO I GUESS I CAN LET YOU HAVE IT THIS ONCE, TSUKISHIMA.
HA HA! WHEN IT COMES TO MENTAL TOUGHNESS, I WON'T ARGUE THAT!
...?
SHIRABU.
ARE YOU ALL RIGHT?
HM?
YES.
I'M JUST A LITTLE... DISORIENTED.
I DIDN'T GO INTO THIS GAME THINKING THAT WE COULD LOSE, AFTER ALL.
TMP
TRUE. I DOUBT ANYONE ON EITHER TEAM HERE THOUGHT THAT THEY WOULD LOSE.
TMP
TM-
白鳥沢
4

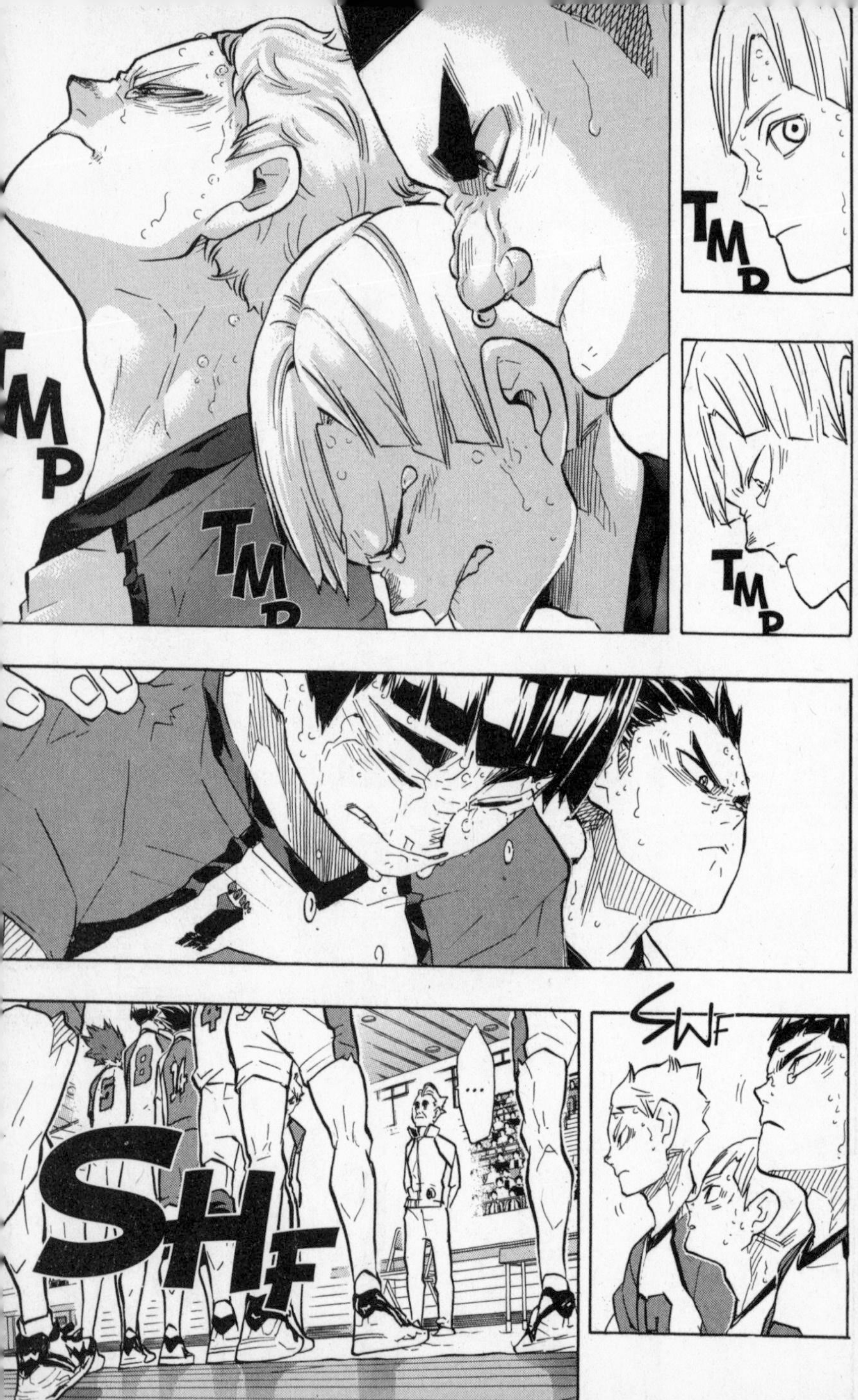
TMP
TMP
TMP
TMP
SWF
...
SHF

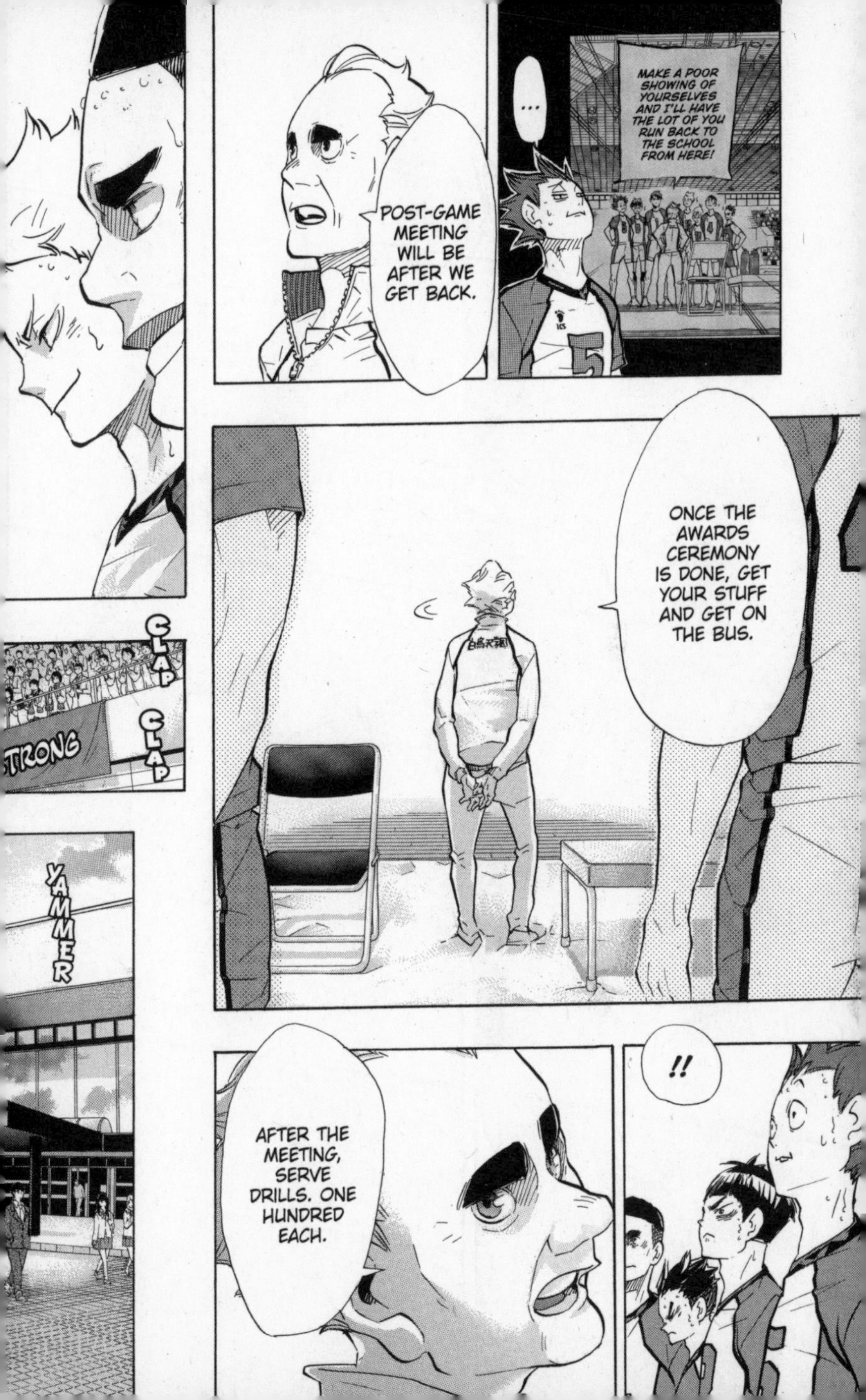
MAKE A POOR SHOWING OF YOURSELVES AND I'LL HAVE THE LOT OF YOU RUN BACK TO THE SCHOOL FROM HERE!
...
POST-GAME MEETING WILL BE AFTER WE GET BACK.
ONCE THE AWARDS CEREMONY IS DONE, GET YOUR STUFF AND GET ON THE BUS.
CLAP
CLAP
STRONG
!!
AFTER THE MEETING, SERVE DRILLS. ONE HUNDRED EACH.
YAMMER

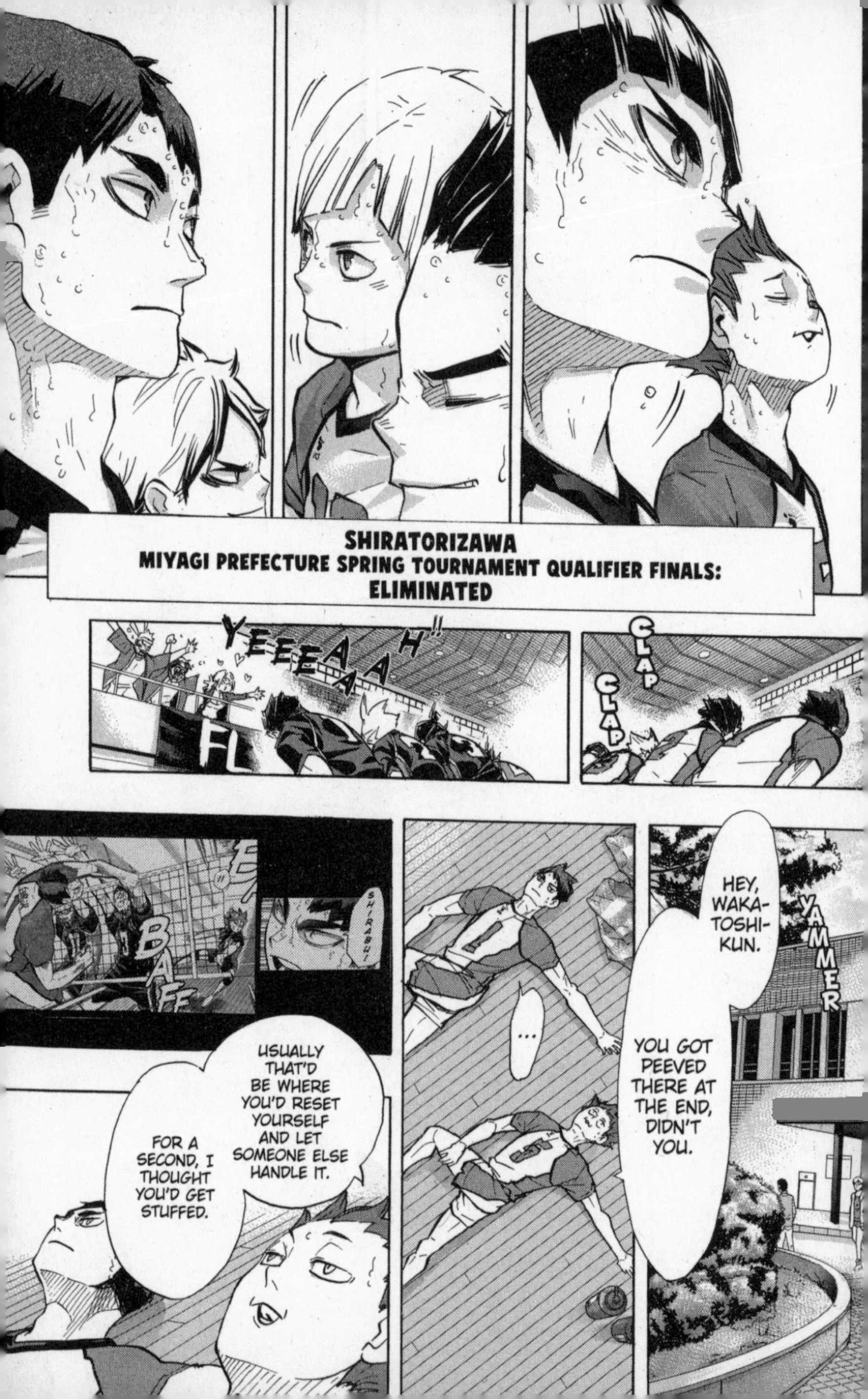
SHIRATORIZAWA
MIYAGI PREFECTURE SPRING TOURNAMENT QUALIFIER FINALS:
ELIMINATED
CLAP CLAP
YEEEAAAH!!
YAMMER
HEY, WAKA-TOSHI-KUN.
YOU GOT PEEVED THERE AT THE END, DIDN'T YOU.
...
SHIRABU!
BAFF
USUALLY THAT'D BE WHERE YOU'D RESET YOURSELF AND LET SOMEONE ELSE HANDLE IT.
FOR A SECOND, I THOUGHT YOU'D GET STUFFED.

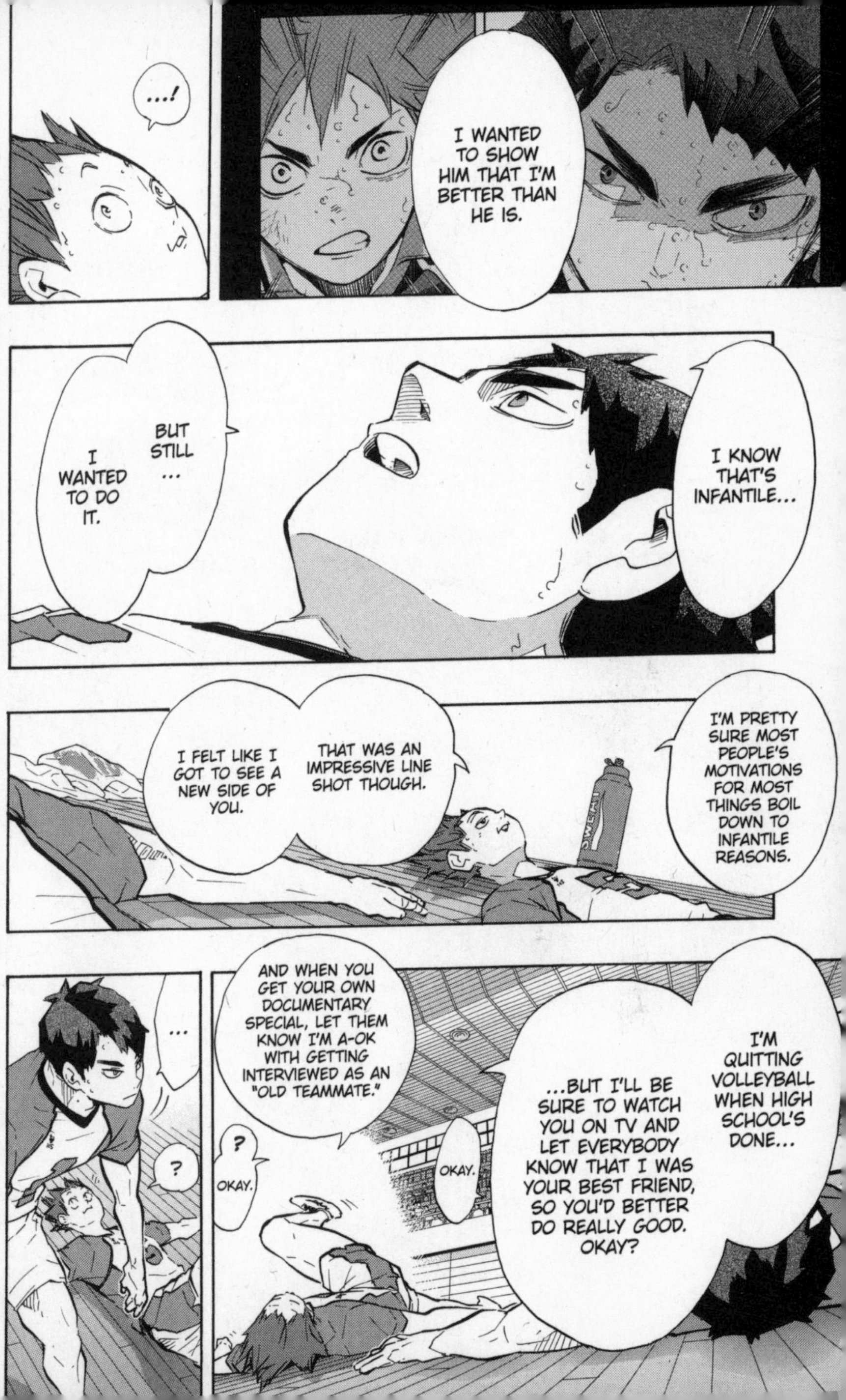
I WANTED TO SHOW HIM THAT I'M BETTER THAN HE IS.
...!
I KNOW THAT'S INFANTILE...
BUT STILL...
I WANTED TO DO IT.
I'M PRETTY SURE MOST PEOPLE'S MOTIVATIONS FOR MOST THINGS BOIL DOWN TO INFANTILE REASONS.
THAT WAS AN IMPRESSIVE LINE SHOT THOUGH.
I FELT LIKE I GOT TO SEE A NEW SIDE OF YOU.
I'M QUITTING VOLLEYBALL WHEN HIGH SCHOOL'S DONE...
...BUT I'LL BE SURE TO WATCH YOU ON TV AND LET EVERYBODY KNOW THAT I WAS YOUR BEST FRIEND, SO YOU'D BETTER DO REALLY GOOD. OKAY?
OKAY.
AND WHEN YOU GET YOUR OWN DOCUMENTARY SPECIAL, LET THEM KNOW I'M A-OK WITH GETTING INTERVIEWED AS AN "OLD TEAMMATE."
?
OKAY.
...
?

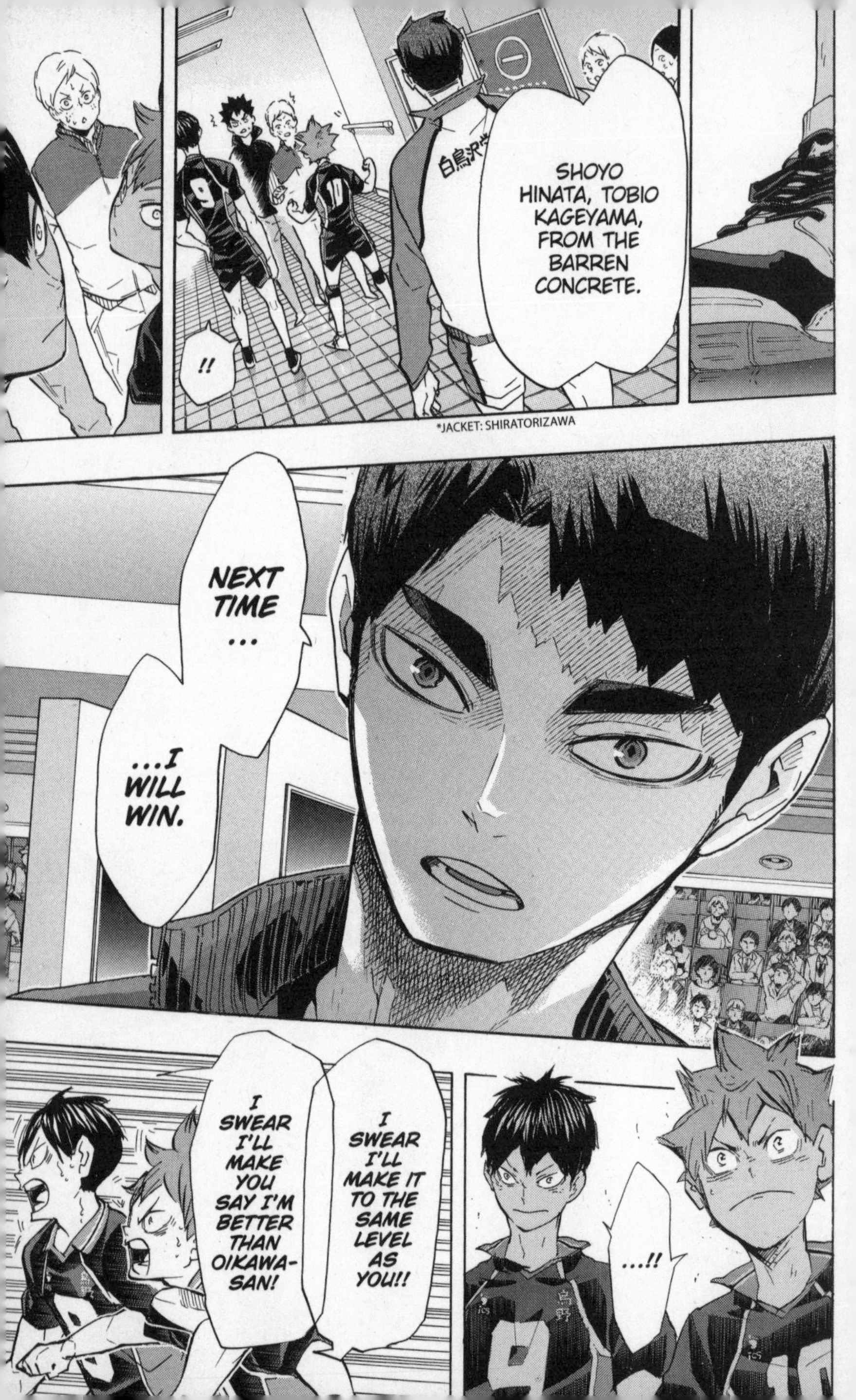
SHOYO HINATA, TOBIO KAGEYAMA, FROM THE BARREN CONCRETE.
!!
*JACKET: SHIRATORIZAWA
NEXT TIME...
...I WILL WIN.
...!!
I SWEAR I'LL MAKE IT TO THE SAME LEVEL AS YOU!!
I SWEAR I'LL MAKE YOU SAY I'M BETTER THAN OIKAWA-SAN!

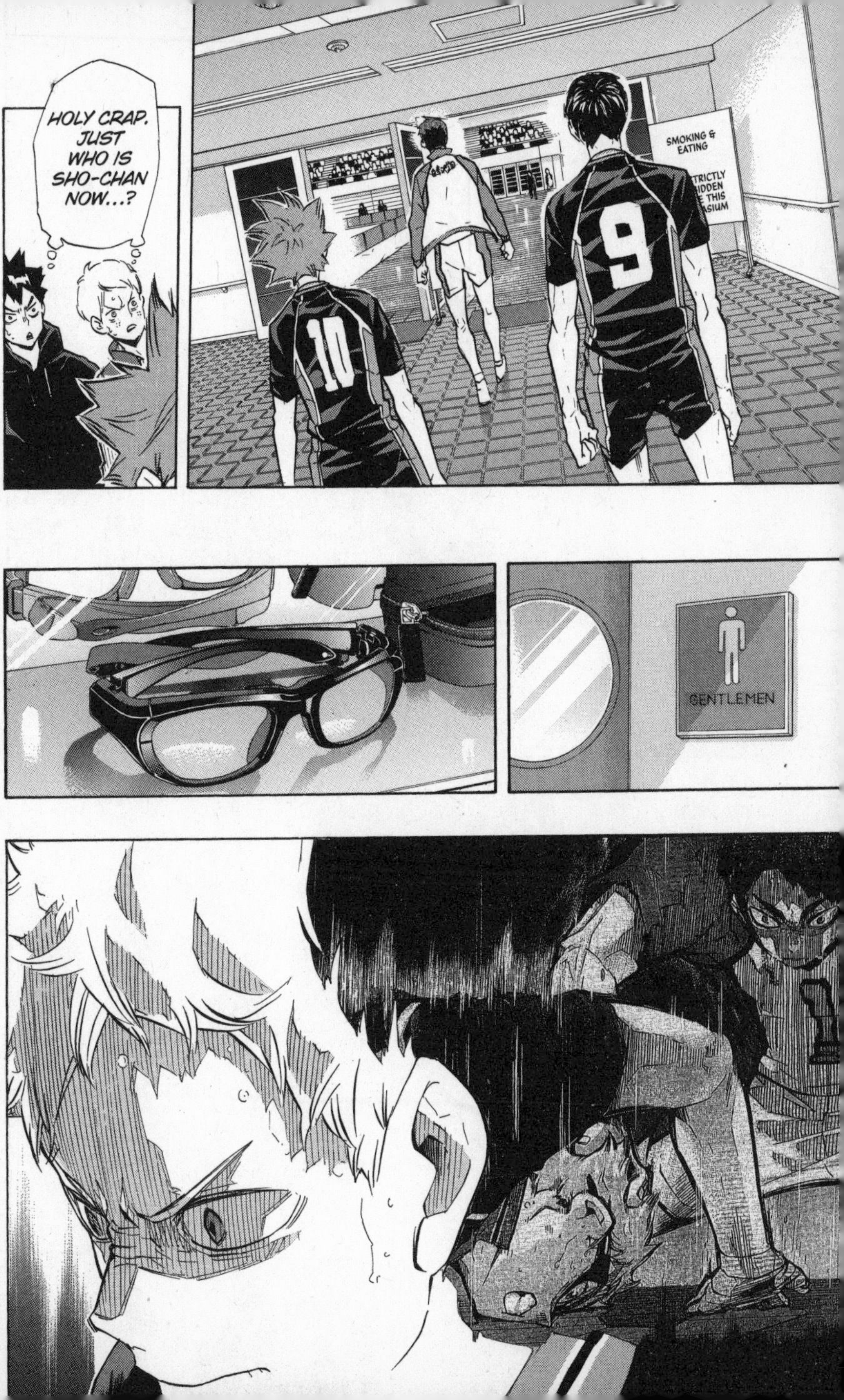
SMOKING & EATING
HOLY CRAP. JUST WHO IS SHO-CHAN NOW...?
GENTLEMEN

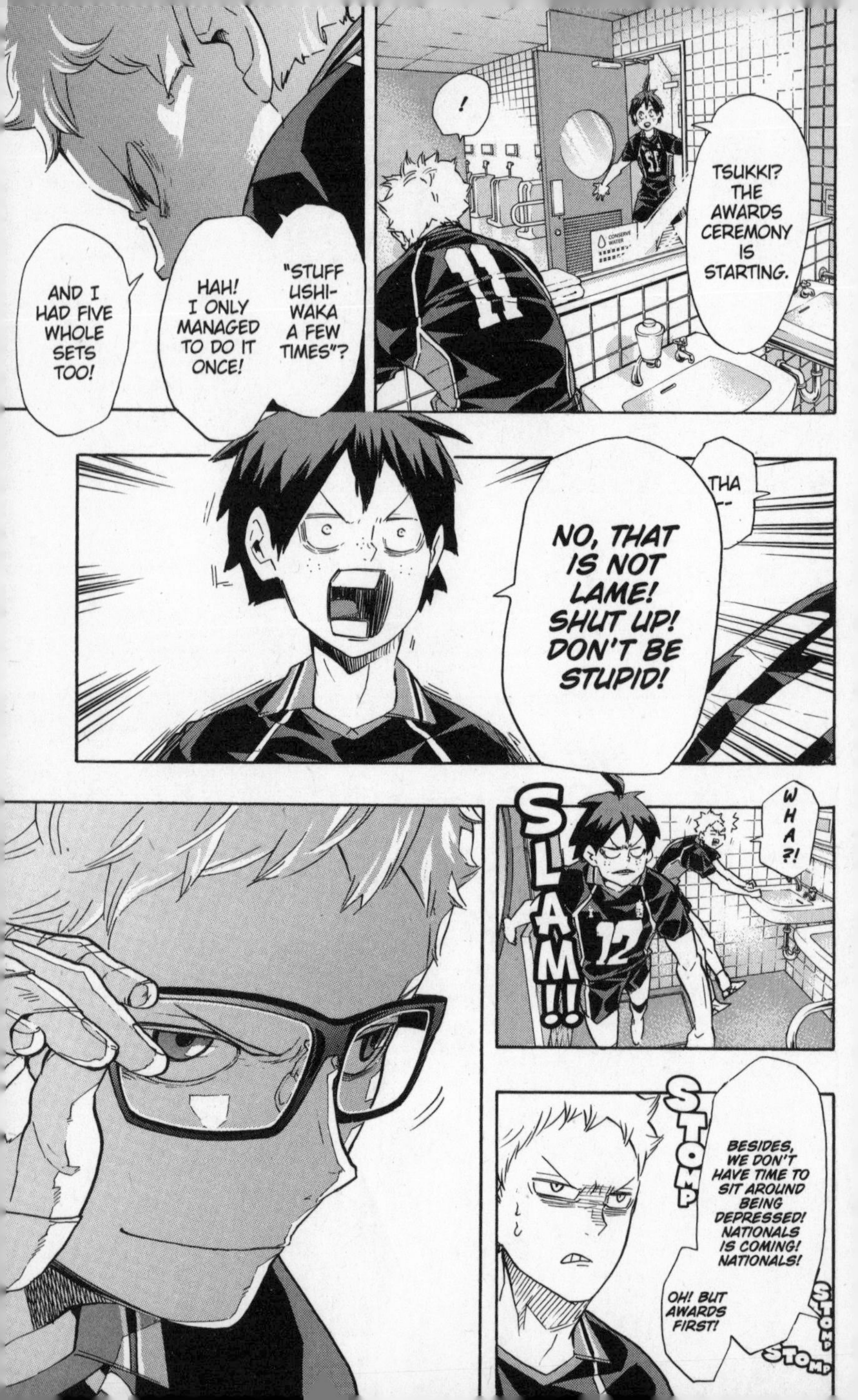
TSUKKI? THE AWARDS CEREMONY IS STARTING.
!
CONSERVE WATER
"STUFF USHIWAKA A FEW TIMES"?
HAH! I ONLY MANAGED TO DO IT ONCE!
AND I HAD FIVE WHOLE SETS TOO!
THA--
NO, THAT IS NOT LAME! SHUT UP! DON'T BE STUPID!
WHA?!
SLAM!!
STOMP
BESIDES, WE DON'T HAVE TIME TO SIT AROUND BEING DEPRESSED! NATIONALS IS COMING! NATIONALS!
OH! BUT AWARDS FIRST!
STOMP
STOMP

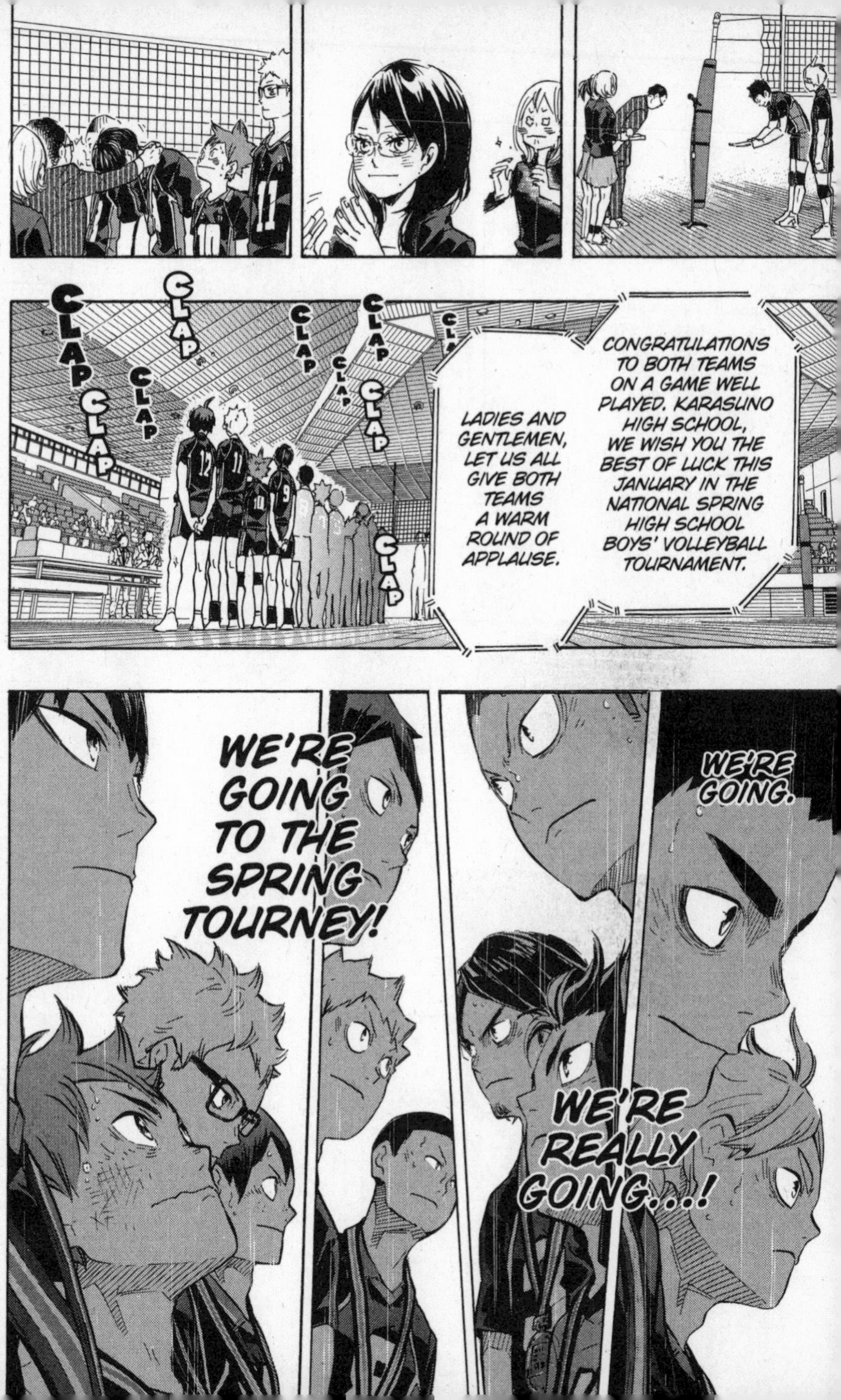
CONGRATULATIONS TO BOTH TEAMS ON A GAME WELL PLAYED. KARASUNO HIGH SCHOOL, WE WISH YOU THE BEST OF LUCK THIS JANUARY IN THE NATIONAL SPRING HIGH SCHOOL BOYS' VOLLEYBALL TOURNAMENT.
LADIES AND GENTLEMEN, LET US ALL GIVE BOTH TEAMS A WARM ROUND OF APPLAUSE.
CLAP
CLAP
CLAP
CLAP
CLAP
CLAP
CLAP
CLAP
CLAP
CLAP
WE'RE GOING.
WE'RE REALLY GOING...!
WE'RE GOING TO THE SPRING TOURNEY!

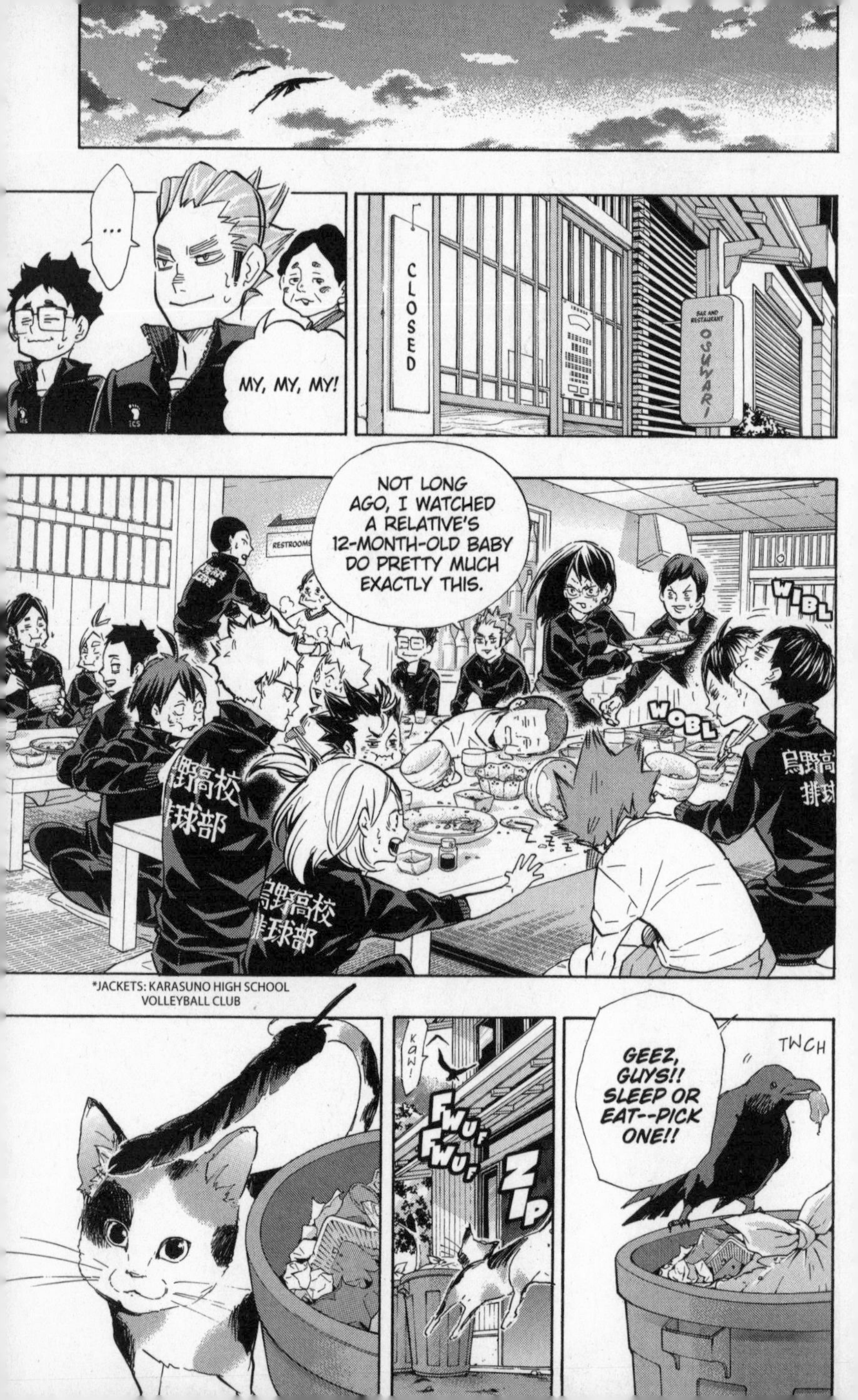
CLOSED
BAR AND RESTAURANT
OSUWARI
...
MY, MY, MY!
NOT LONG AGO, I WATCHED A RELATIVE'S 12-MONTH-OLD BABY DO PRETTY MUCH EXACTLY THIS.
RESTROOMS
WIBL
WOBL
烏野高校排球部
GEEZ, GUYS!! SLEEP OR EAT--PICK ONE!!
TWCH
KAW!
FWUF FWUF
ZIP
*JACKETS: KARASUNO HIGH SCHOOL VOLLEYBALL CLUB

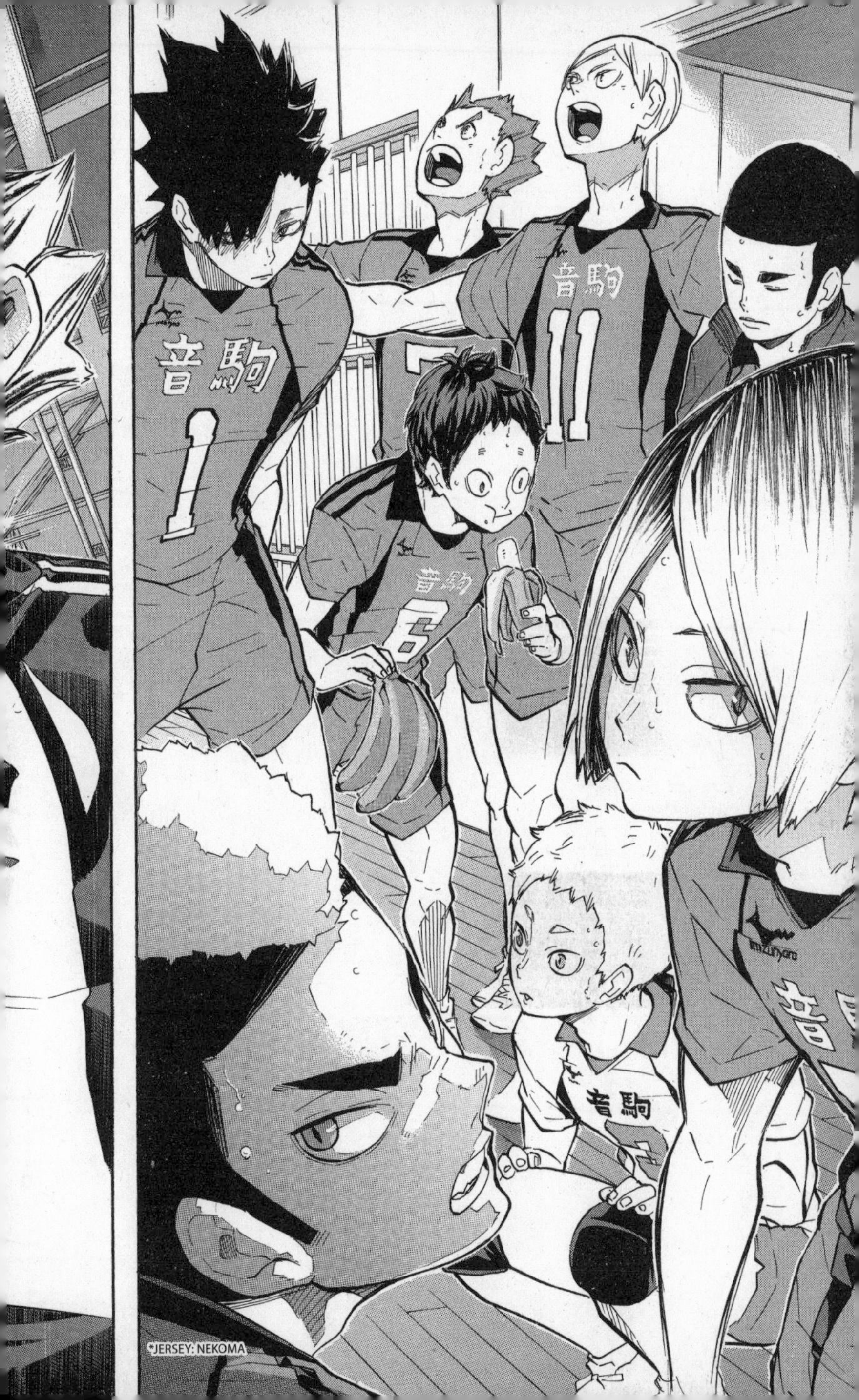
*JERSEY: NEKOMA

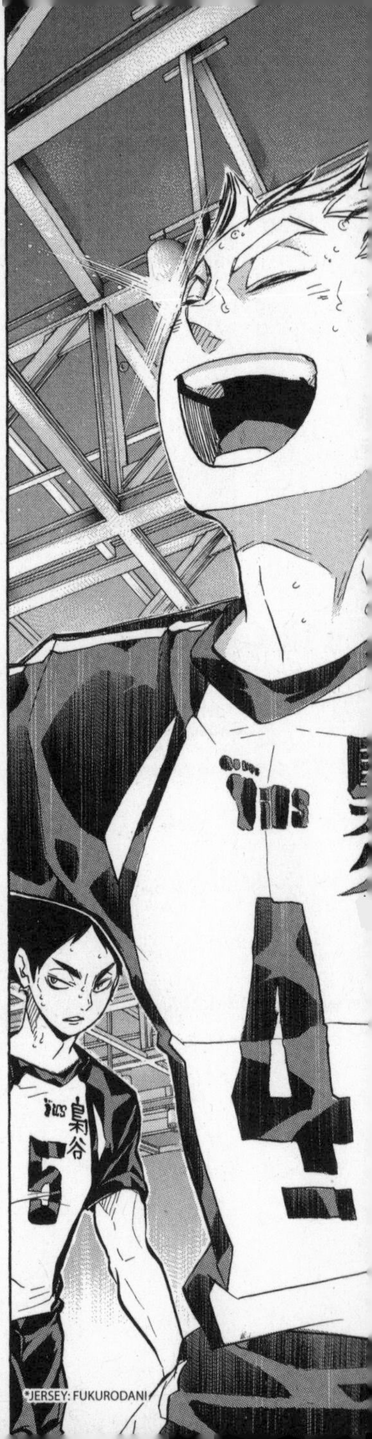
梟谷
*JERSEY: FUKURODANI

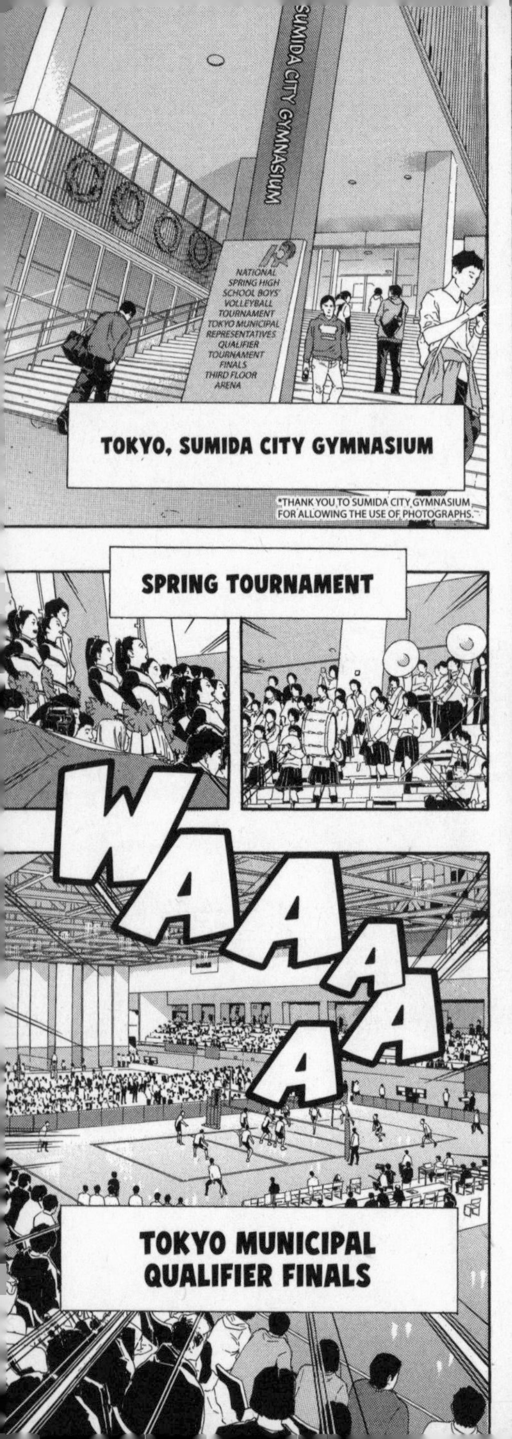
SUMIDA CITY GYMNASIUM
NATIONAL SPRING HIGH SCHOOL BOYS' VOLLEYBALL TOURNAMENT TOKYO MUNICIPAL REPRESENTATIVES QUALIFIER TOURNAMENT FINALS THIRD FLOOR ARENA
TOKYO, SUMIDA CITY GYMNASIUM
*THANK YOU TO SUMIDA CITY GYMNASIUM FOR ALLOWING THE USE OF PHOTOGRAPHS.
SPRING TOURNAMENT
WAAAAA
TOKYO MUNICIPAL QUALIFIER FINALS

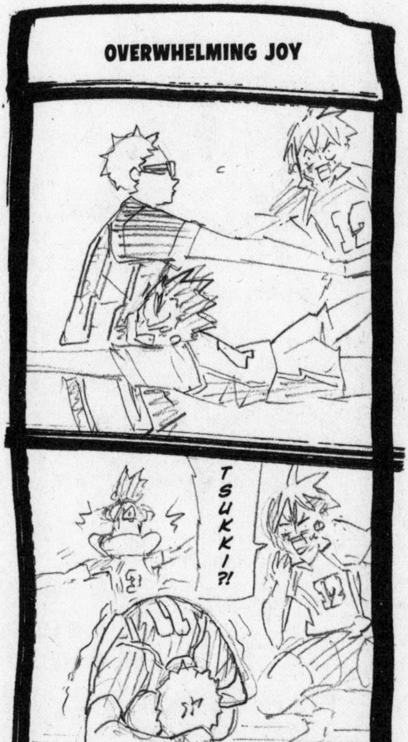
OVERWHELMING JOY
TSUKKI?!

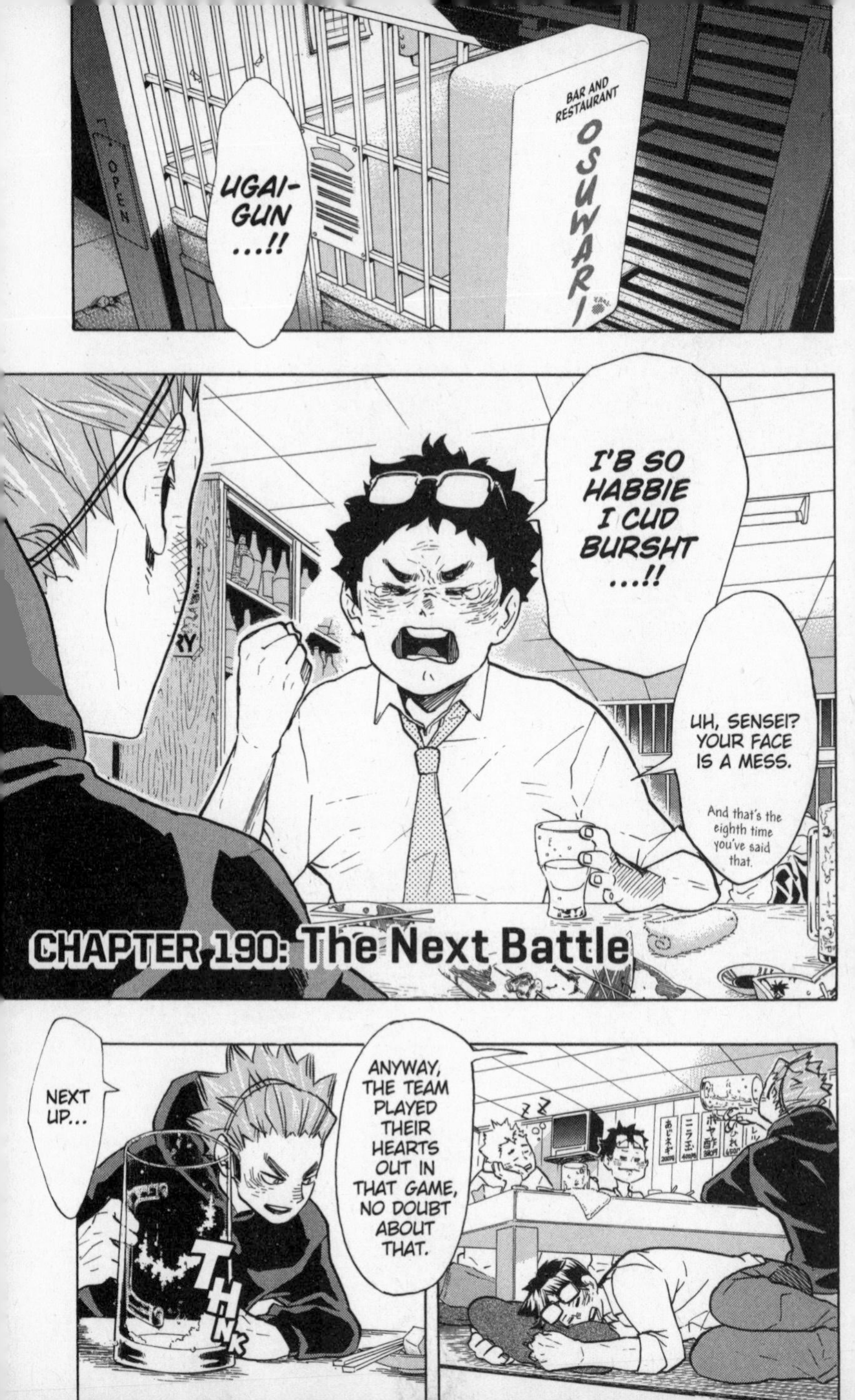
BAR AND RESTAURANT
OSUWARI
UGAI-GUN ...!!
OPEN
I'B SO HABBIE I CUD BURSHT ...!!
UH, SENSEI? YOUR FACE IS A MESS.
And that's the eighth time you've said that.
CHAPTER 190: The Next Battle
ANYWAY, THE TEAM PLAYED THEIR HEARTS OUT IN THAT GAME, NO DOUBT ABOUT THAT.
NEXT UP...
THNK

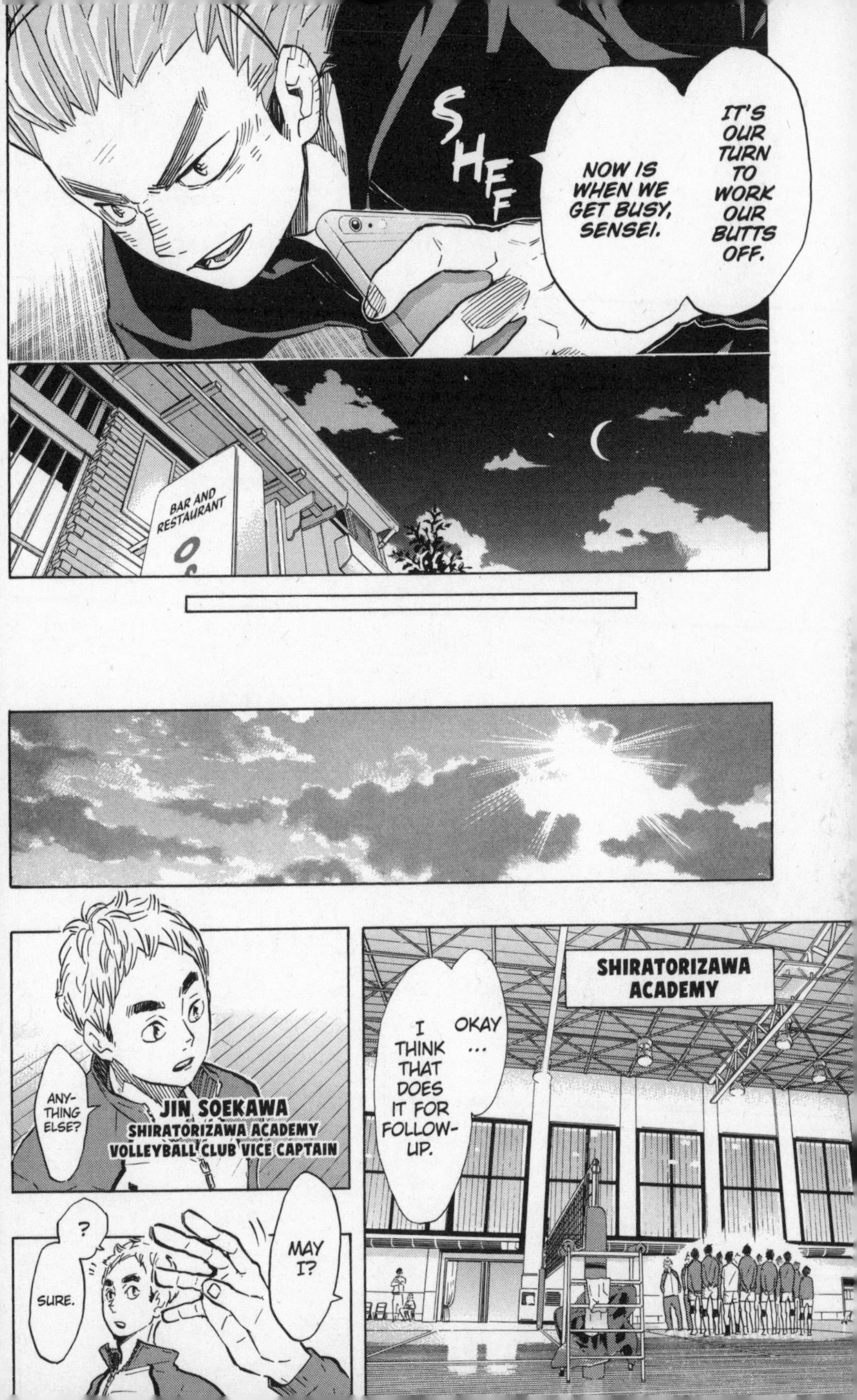
IT'S OUR TURN TO WORK OUR BUTTS OFF.
NOW IS WHEN WE GET BUSY, SENSEI.
SHFF
BAR AND RESTAURANT
SHIRATORIZAWA ACADEMY
OKAY ...
I THINK THAT DOES IT FOR FOLLOW-UP.
ANY-THING ELSE?
JIN SOEKAWA
SHIRATORIZAWA ACADEMY VOLLEYBALL CLUB VICE CAPTAIN
MAY I?
?
SURE.

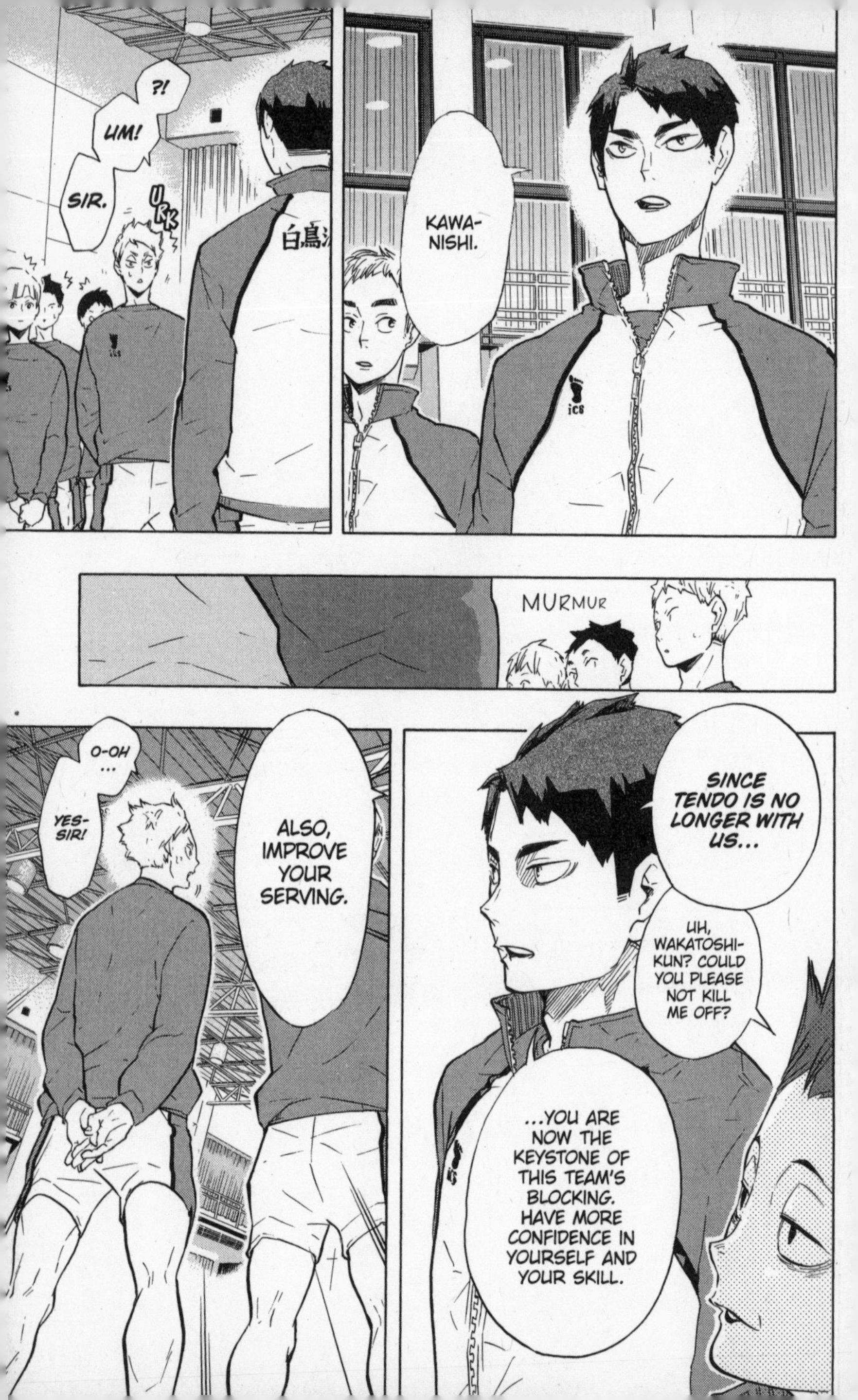
KAWA-NISHI.
?!
UM!
SIR.
URK
MURMUR
SINCE TENDO IS NO LONGER WITH US...
UH, WAKATOSHI-KUN? COULD YOU PLEASE NOT KILL ME OFF?
...YOU ARE NOW THE KEYSTONE OF THIS TEAM'S BLOCKING. HAVE MORE CONFIDENCE IN YOURSELF AND YOUR SKILL.
ALSO, IMPROVE YOUR SERVING.
O-OH...
YES-SIR!

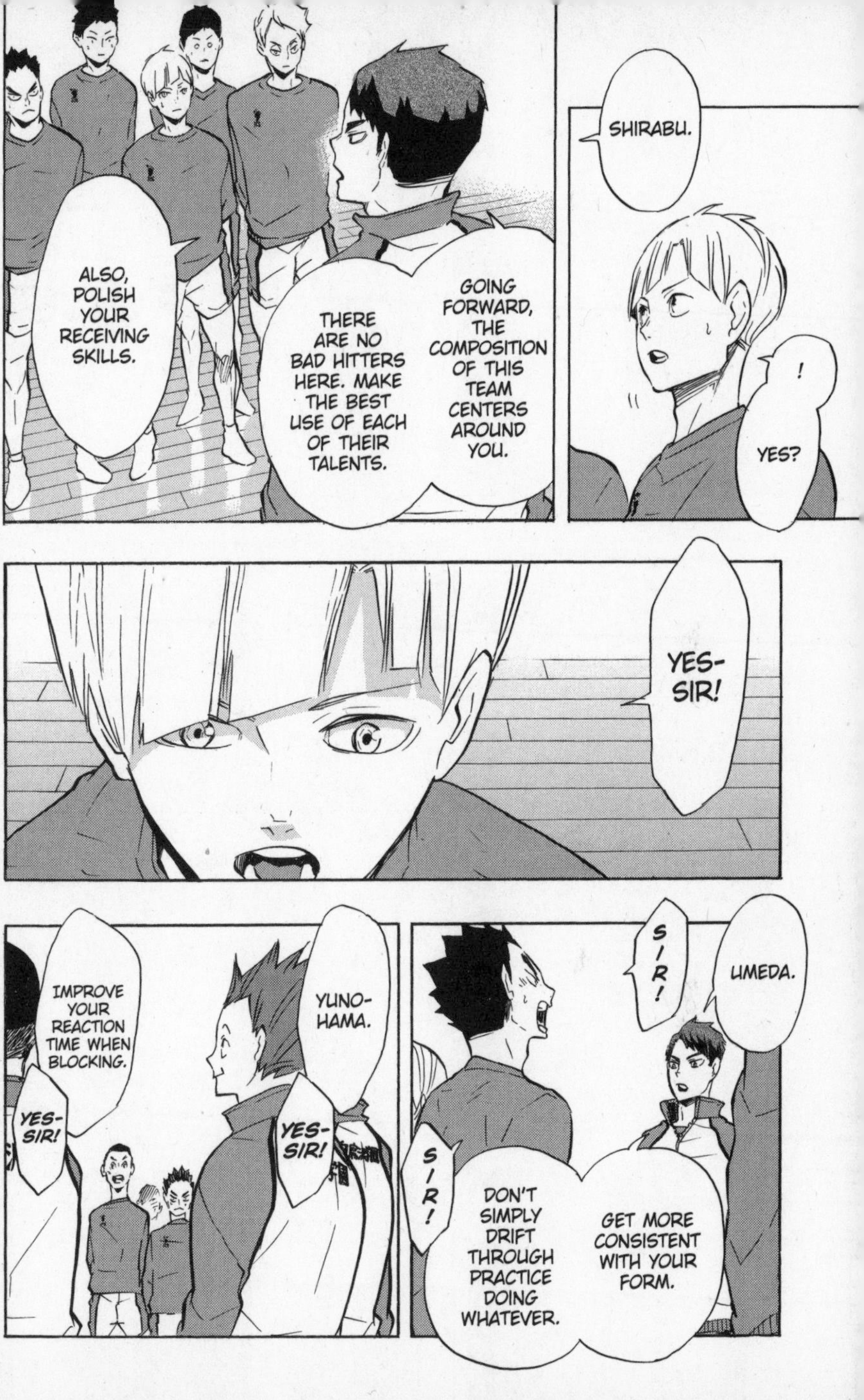
SHIRABU.
!
YES?
GOING FORWARD, THE COMPOSITION OF THIS TEAM CENTERS AROUND YOU.
THERE ARE NO BAD HITTERS HERE. MAKE THE BEST USE OF EACH OF THEIR TALENTS.
ALSO, POLISH YOUR RECEIVING SKILLS.
YES-SIR!
UMEDA.
SIR!
GET MORE CONSISTENT WITH YOUR FORM.
DON'T SIMPLY DRIFT THROUGH PRACTICE DOING WHATEVER.
SIR!
YUNO-HAMA.
YES-SIR!
IMPROVE YOUR REACTION TIME WHEN BLOCKING.
YES-SIR!

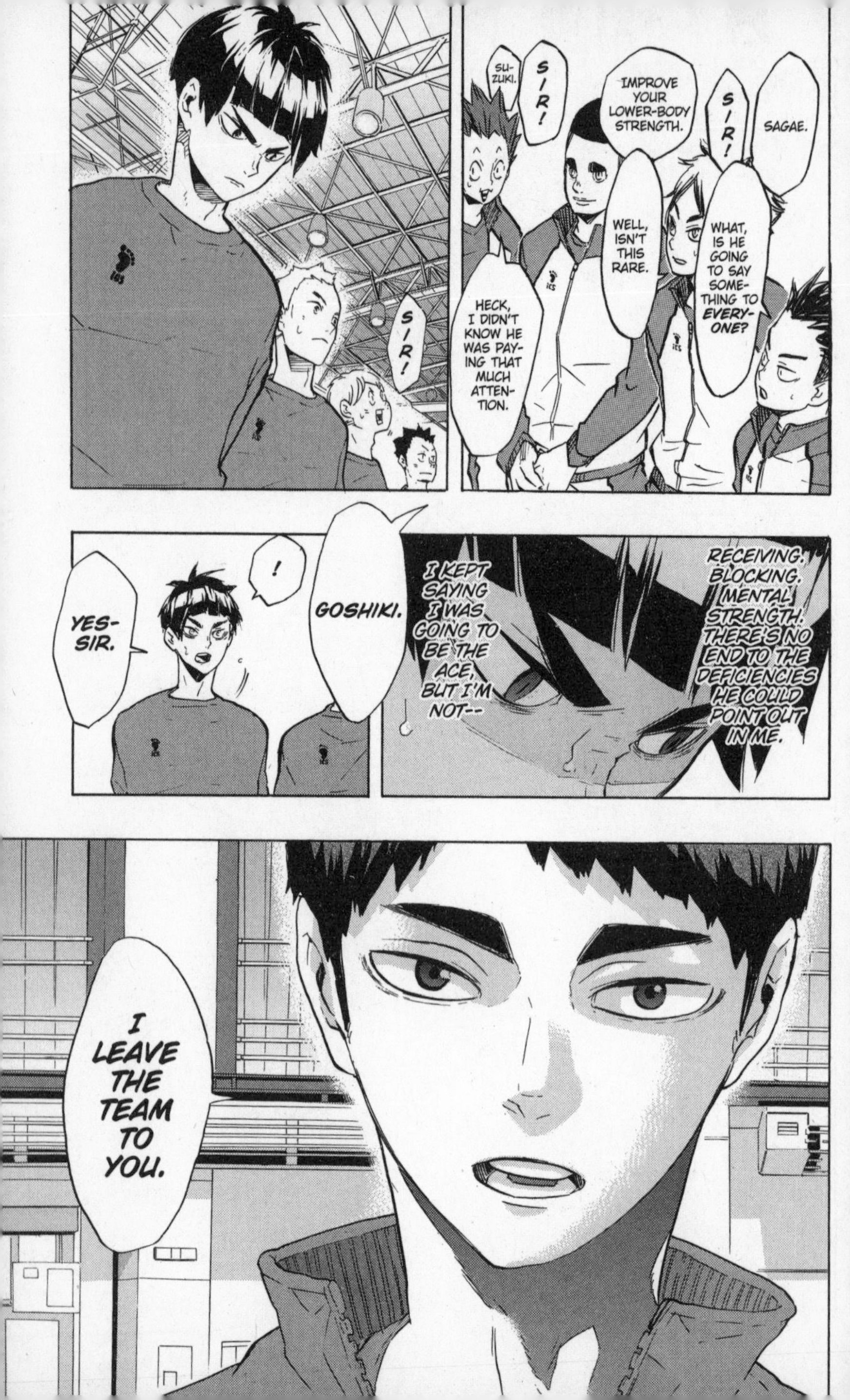
SAGAE.
SIR!
IMPROVE YOUR LOWER-BODY STRENGTH.
SIR!
SU-ZUKI.
WHAT, IS HE GOING TO SAY SOME-THING TO EVERY-ONE?
WELL, ISN'T THIS RARE.
HECK, I DIDN'T KNOW HE WAS PAY-ING THAT MUCH ATTEN-TION.
SIR!
RECEIVING. BLOCKING. MENTAL STRENGTH. THERE'S NO END TO THE DEFICIENCIES HE COULD POINT OUT IN ME.
I KEPT SAYING I WAS GOING TO BE THE ACE, BUT I'M NOT--
GOSHIKI.
!
YES-SIR.
I LEAVE THE TEAM TO YOU.

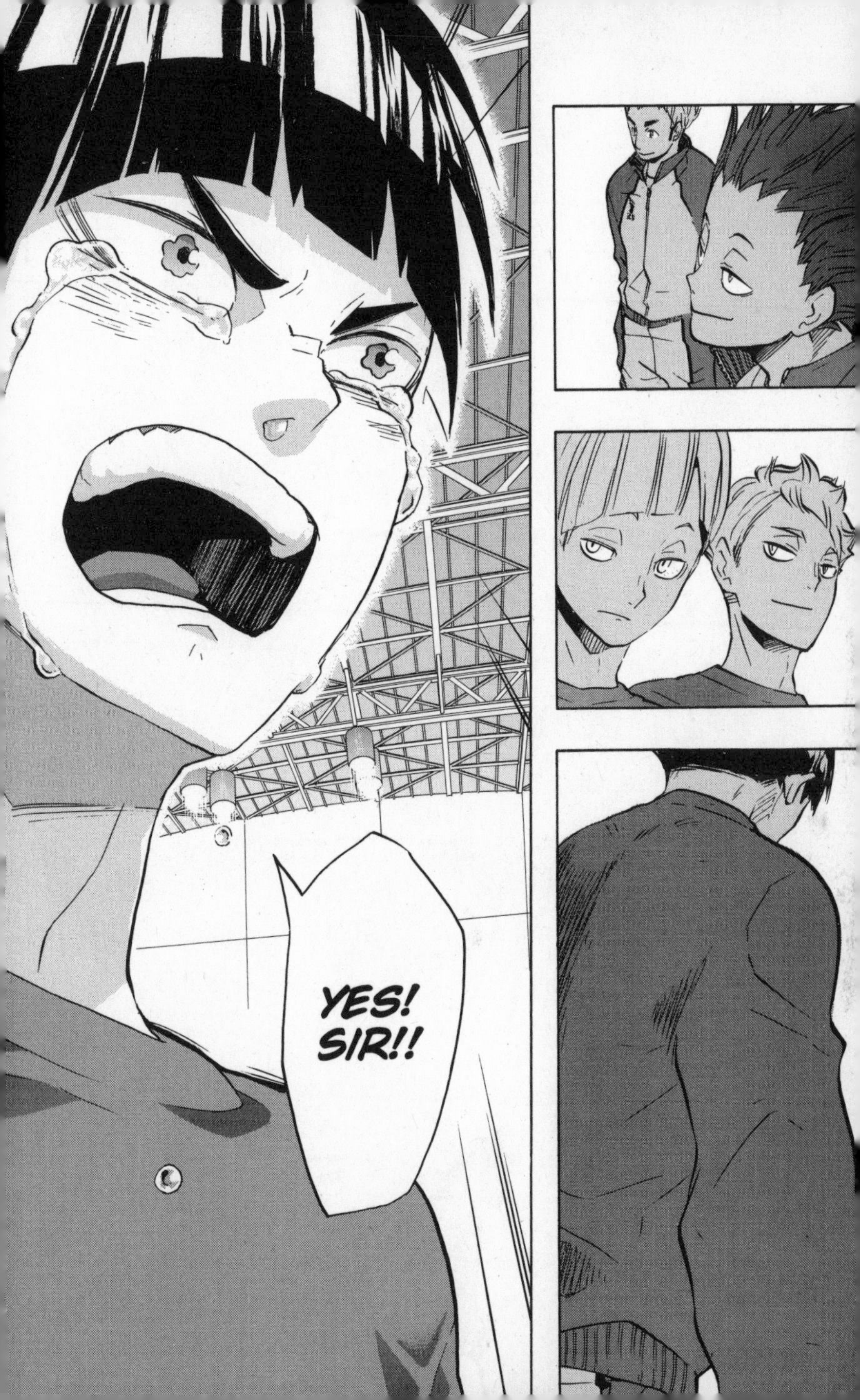
YES! SIR!!

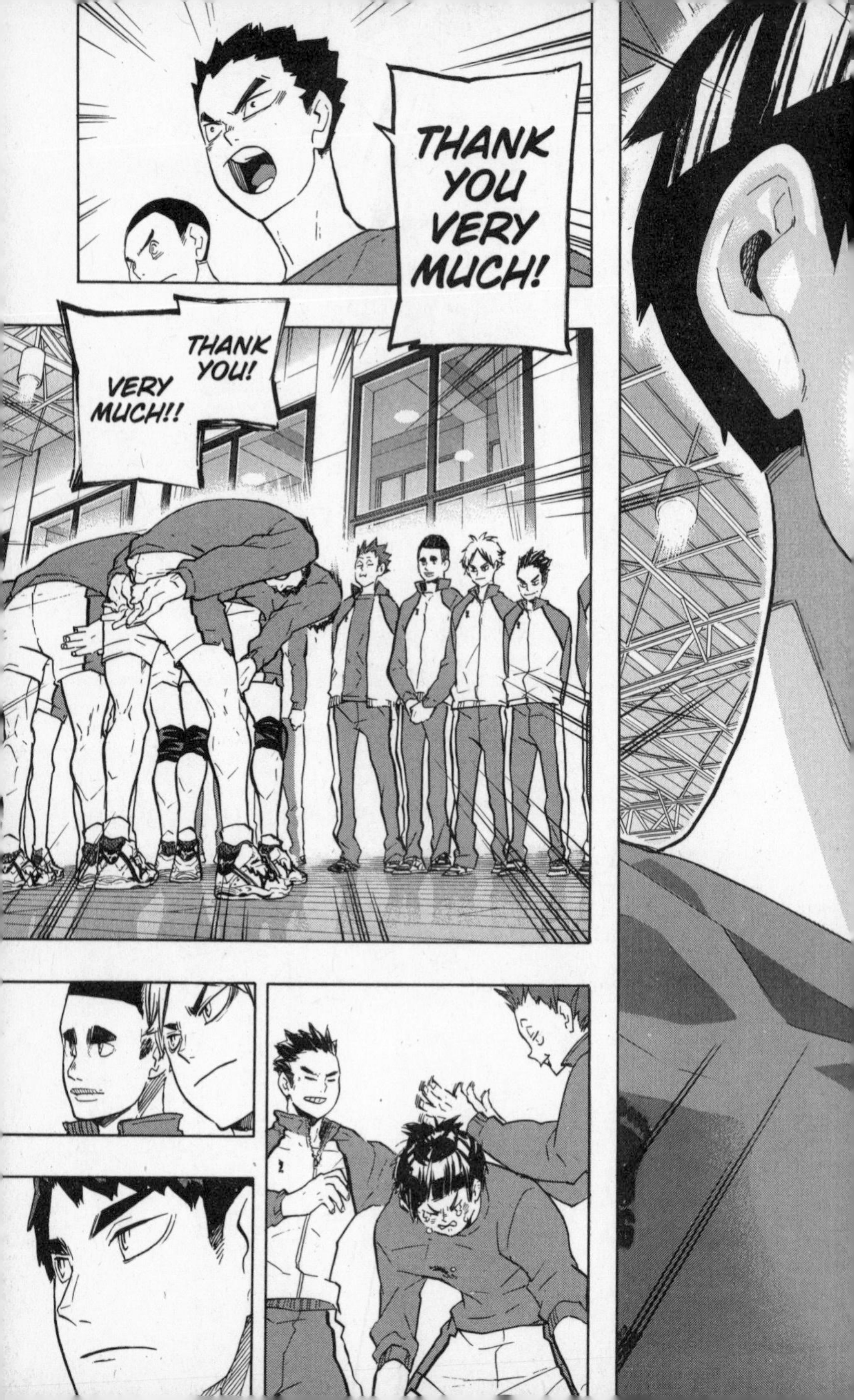
THANK YOU VERY MUCH!
THANK YOU!
VERY MUCH!!

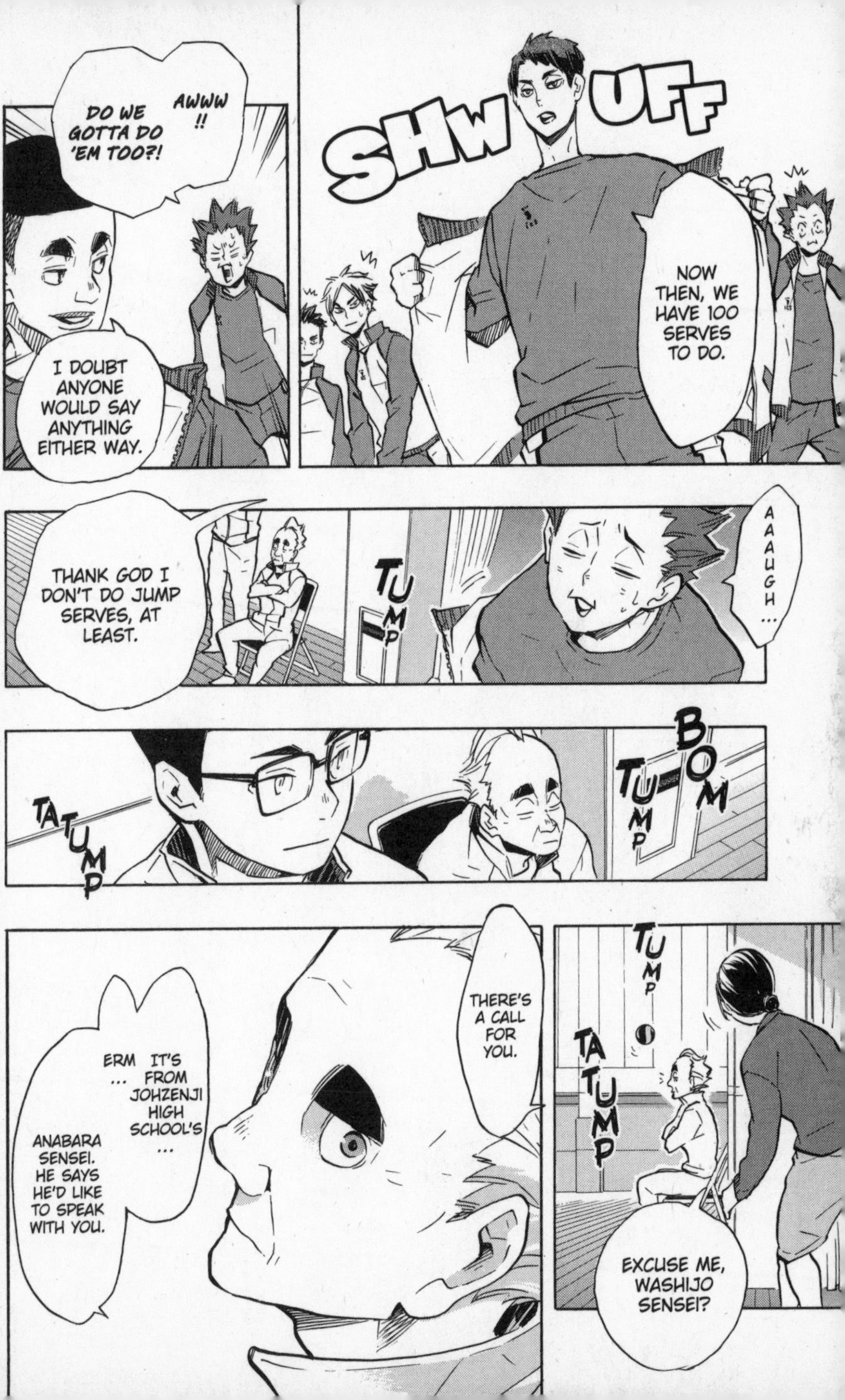
SHWUFF
NOW THEN, WE HAVE 100 SERVES TO DO.
AWWW !!
DO WE GOTTA DO 'EM TOO?!
I DOUBT ANYONE WOULD SAY ANYTHING EITHER WAY.
AAAUGH...
TUMP
THANK GOD I DON'T DO JUMP SERVES, AT LEAST.
BOM
TUMP
TATUMP
TUMP
TATUMP
EXCUSE ME, WASHIJO SENSEI?
THERE'S A CALL FOR YOU.
ERM... IT'S FROM JOHZENJI HIGH SCHOOL'S...
ANABARA SENSEI. HE SAYS HE'D LIKE TO SPEAK WITH YOU.

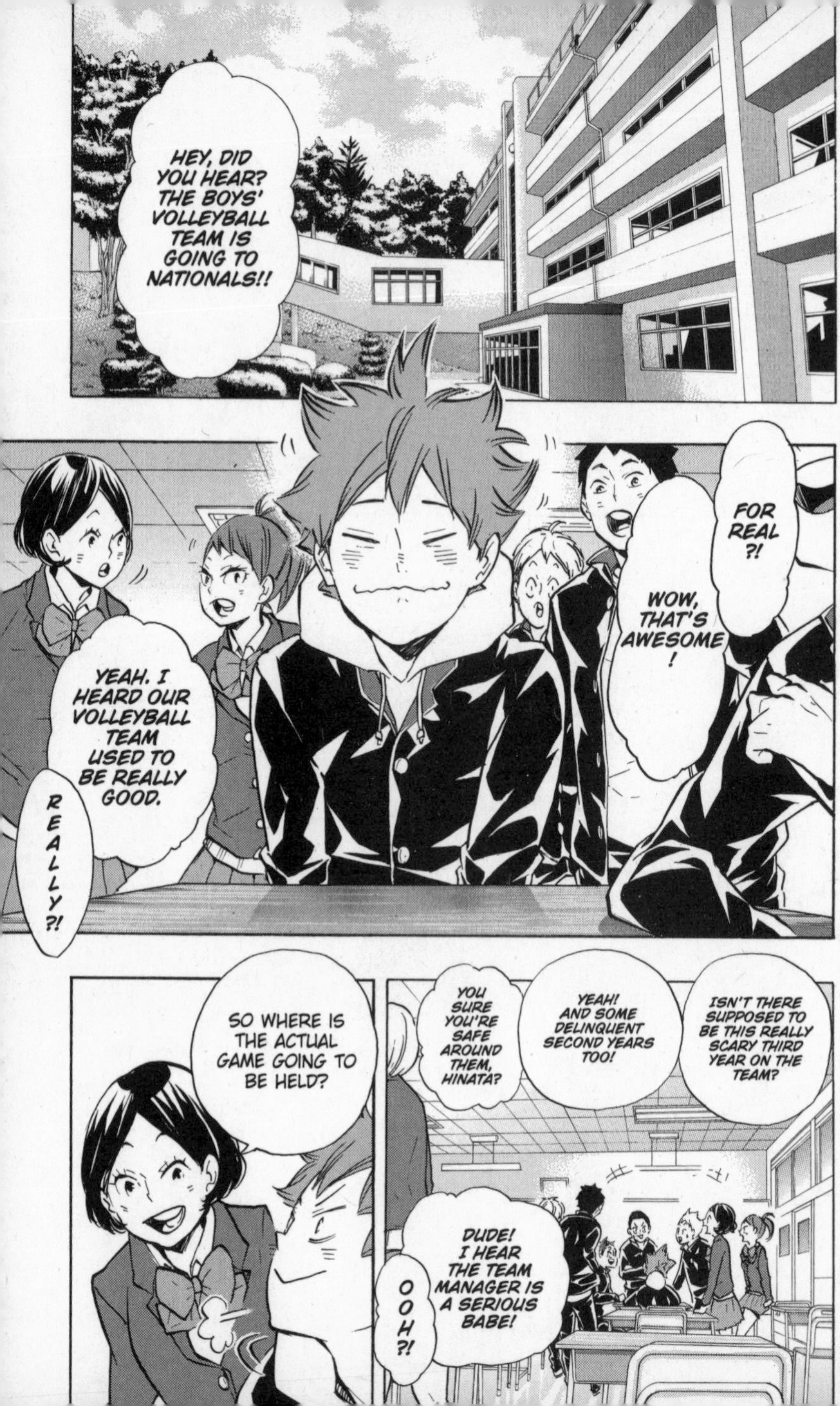
HEY, DID YOU HEAR? THE BOYS' VOLLEYBALL TEAM IS GOING TO NATIONALS!!
FOR REAL?!
WOW, THAT'S AWESOME!
YEAH. I HEARD OUR VOLLEYBALL TEAM USED TO BE REALLY GOOD.
REALLY?!
ISN'T THERE SUPPOSED TO BE THIS REALLY SCARY THIRD YEAR ON THE TEAM?
YEAH! AND SOME DELINQUENT SECOND YEARS TOO!
YOU SURE YOU'RE SAFE AROUND THEM, HINATA?
DUDE! I HEAR THE TEAM MANAGER IS A SERIOUS BABE!
OOH?!
SO WHERE IS THE ACTUAL GAME GOING TO BE HELD?

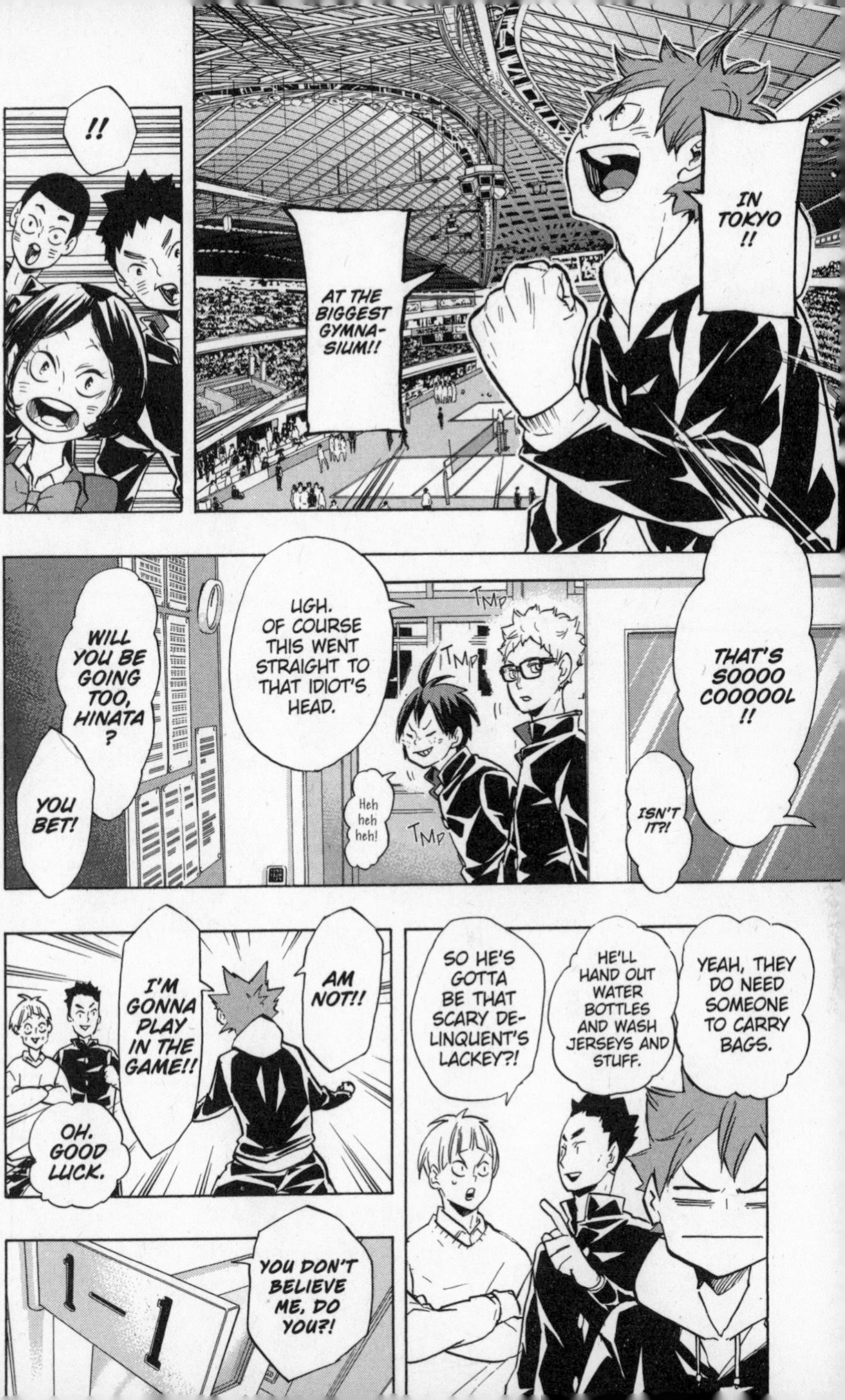
IN TOKYO!!
AT THE BIGGEST GYMNASIUM!!
!!
THAT'S SOOOO COOOOOL!!
ISN'T IT?!
TMP
TMP
UGH. OF COURSE THIS WENT STRAIGHT TO THAT IDIOT'S HEAD.
Heh heh heh!
TMP
WILL YOU BE GOING TOO, HINATA?
YOU BET!
YEAH, THEY DO NEED SOMEONE TO CARRY BAGS.
HE'LL HAND OUT WATER BOTTLES AND WASH JERSEYS AND STUFF.
SO HE'S GOTTA BE THAT SCARY DE-LINQUENT'S LACKEY?!
AM NOT!!
I'M GONNA PLAY IN THE GAME!!
OH. GOOD LUCK.
YOU DON'T BELIEVE ME, DO YOU?!
1-1

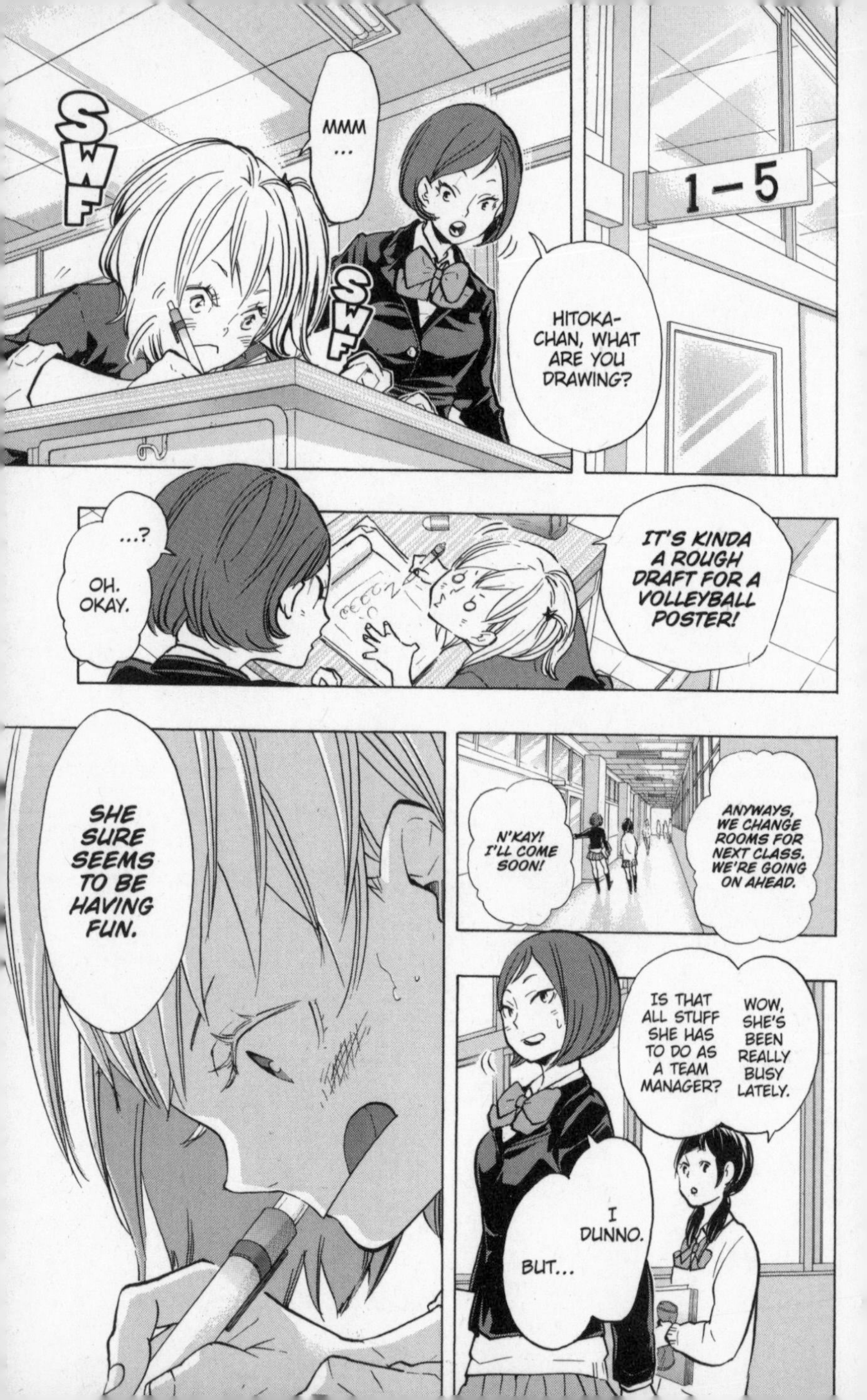
1-5
SWF
SWF
HITOKA-CHAN, WHAT ARE YOU DRAWING?
MMM...
IT'S KINDA A ROUGH DRAFT FOR A VOLLEYBALL POSTER!
...?
OH. OKAY.
ANYWAYS, WE CHANGE ROOMS FOR NEXT CLASS. WE'RE GOING ON AHEAD.
N'KAY! I'LL COME SOON!
WOW, SHE'S BEEN REALLY BUSY LATELY.
IS THAT ALL STUFF SHE HAS TO DO AS A TEAM MANAGER?
I DUNNO.
BUT...
SHE SURE SEEMS TO BE HAVING FUN.

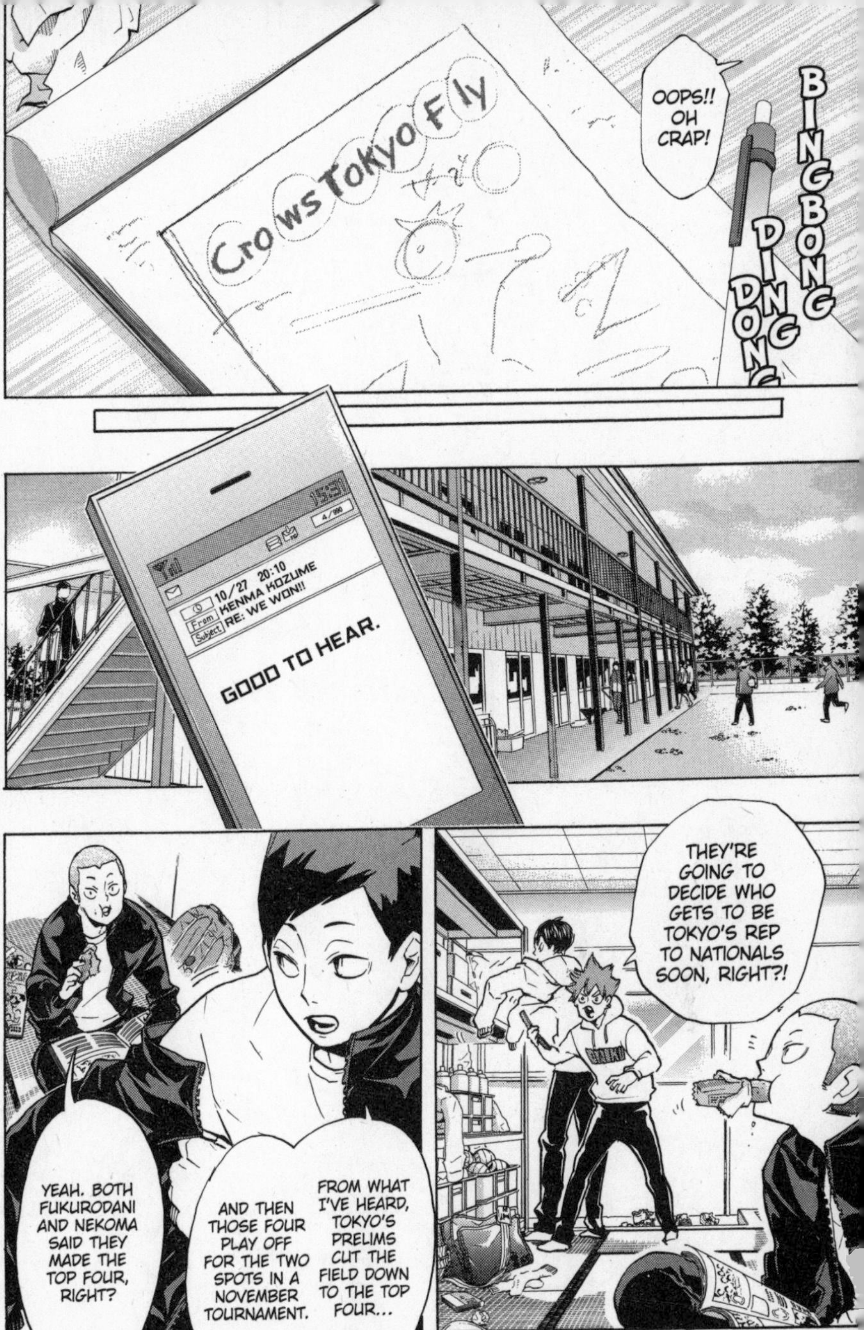
BING BONG
OOPS!! OH CRAP!
DING DONG
Crows Tokyo Fly
15:31
4/990
10/27 20:10
From KENMA KOZUME
Subject RE: WE WON!!
GOOD TO HEAR.
THEY'RE GOING TO DECIDE WHO GETS TO BE TOKYO'S REP TO NATIONALS SOON, RIGHT?!
FROM WHAT I'VE HEARD, TOKYO'S PRELIMS CUT THE FIELD DOWN TO THE TOP FOUR...
AND THEN THOSE FOUR PLAY OFF FOR THE TWO SPOTS IN A NOVEMBER TOURNAMENT.
YEAH. BOTH FUKURODANI AND NEKOMA SAID THEY MADE THE TOP FOUR, RIGHT?

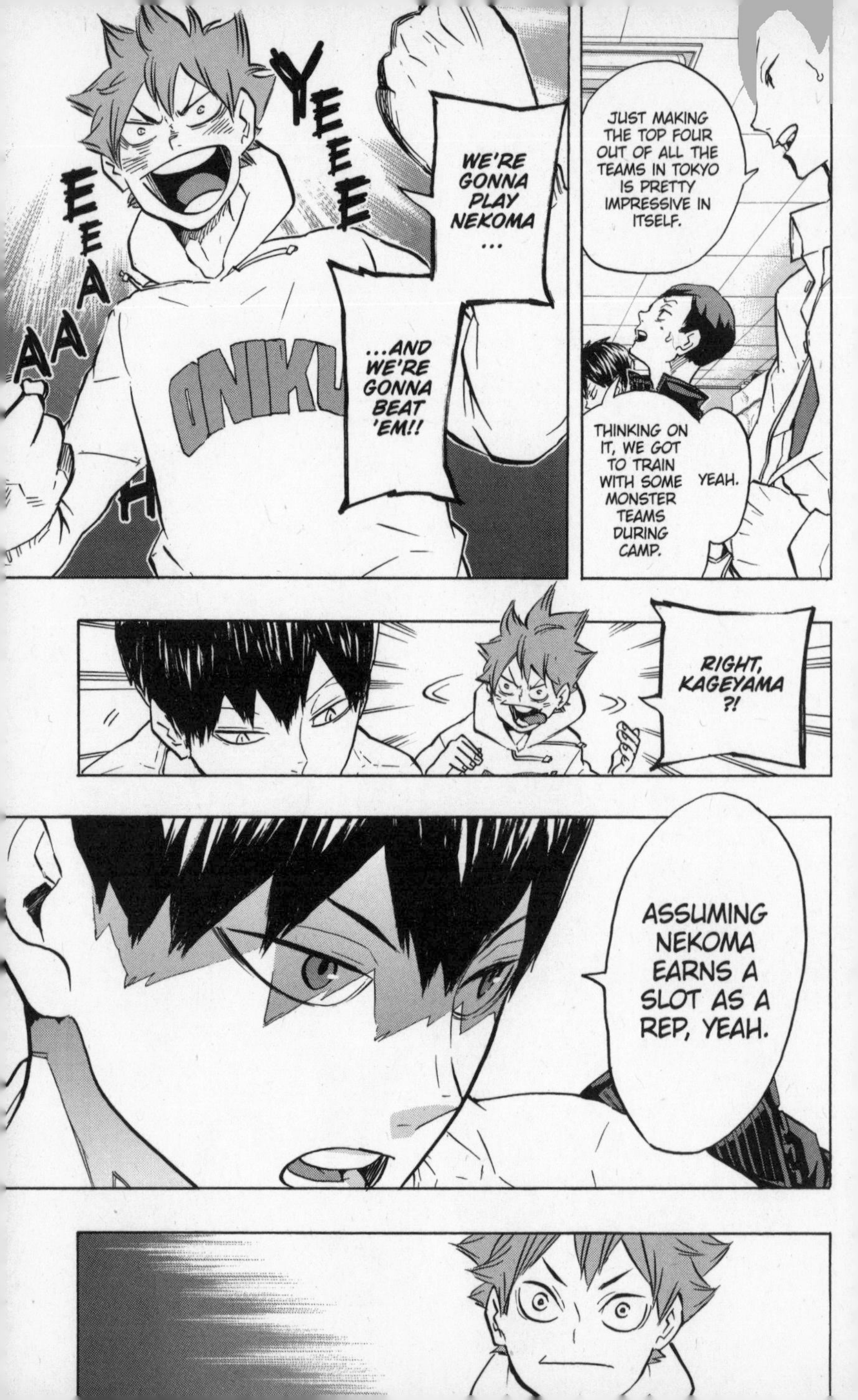
JUST MAKING THE TOP FOUR OUT OF ALL THE TEAMS IN TOKYO IS PRETTY IMPRESSIVE IN ITSELF.
YEAH.
THINKING ON IT, WE GOT TO TRAIN WITH SOME MONSTER TEAMS DURING CAMP.
WE'RE GONNA PLAY NEKOMA ...
...AND WE'RE GONNA BEAT 'EM!!
YEEEEEEAAAA
RIGHT, KAGEYAMA ?!
ASSUMING NEKOMA EARNS A SLOT AS A REP, YEAH.

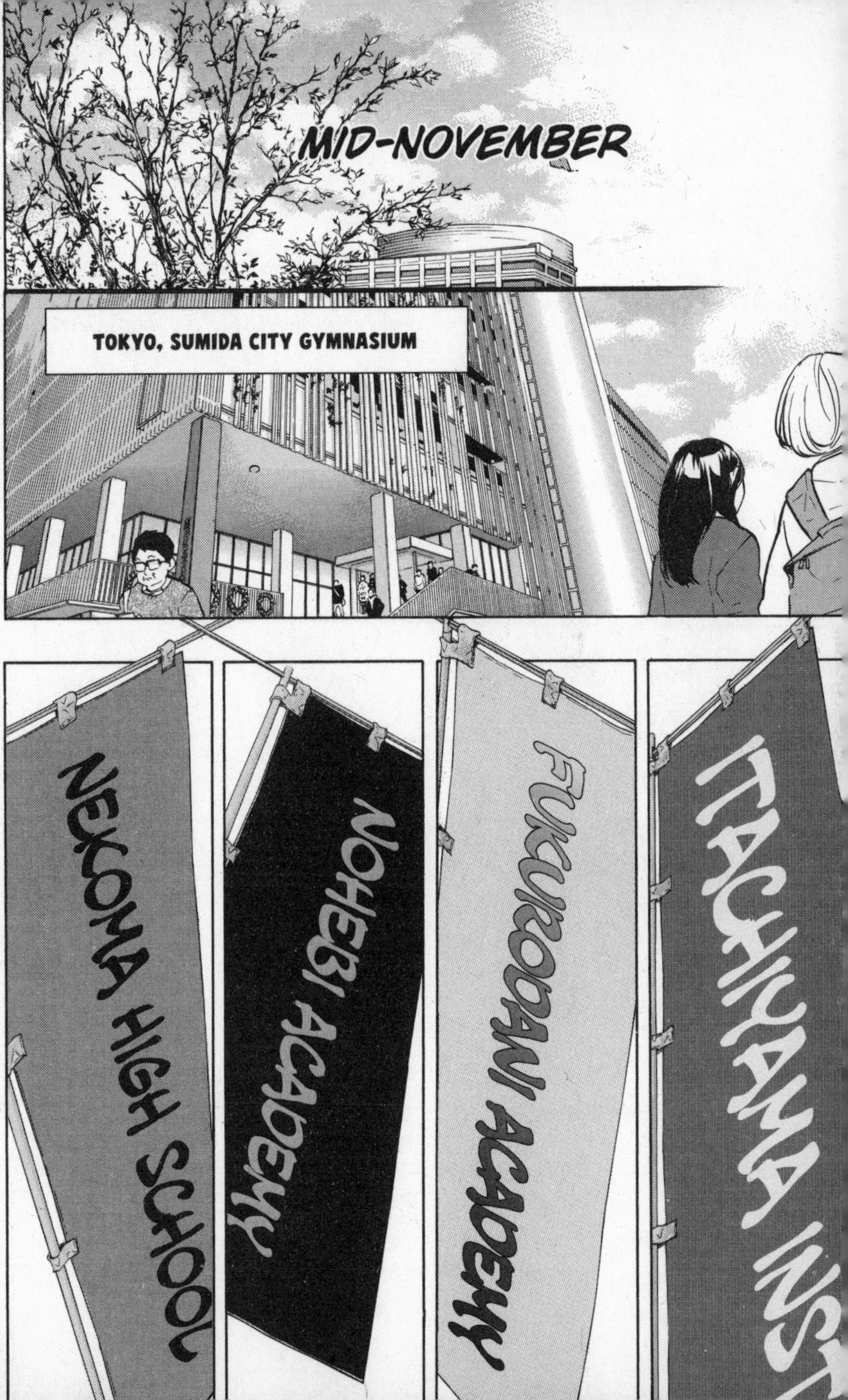
MID-NOVEMBER
TOKYO, SUMIDA CITY GYMNASIUM
ITACHIYAMA INST
FUKURODANI ACADEMY
NOHEBI ACADEMY
NEKOMA HIGH SCHOOL

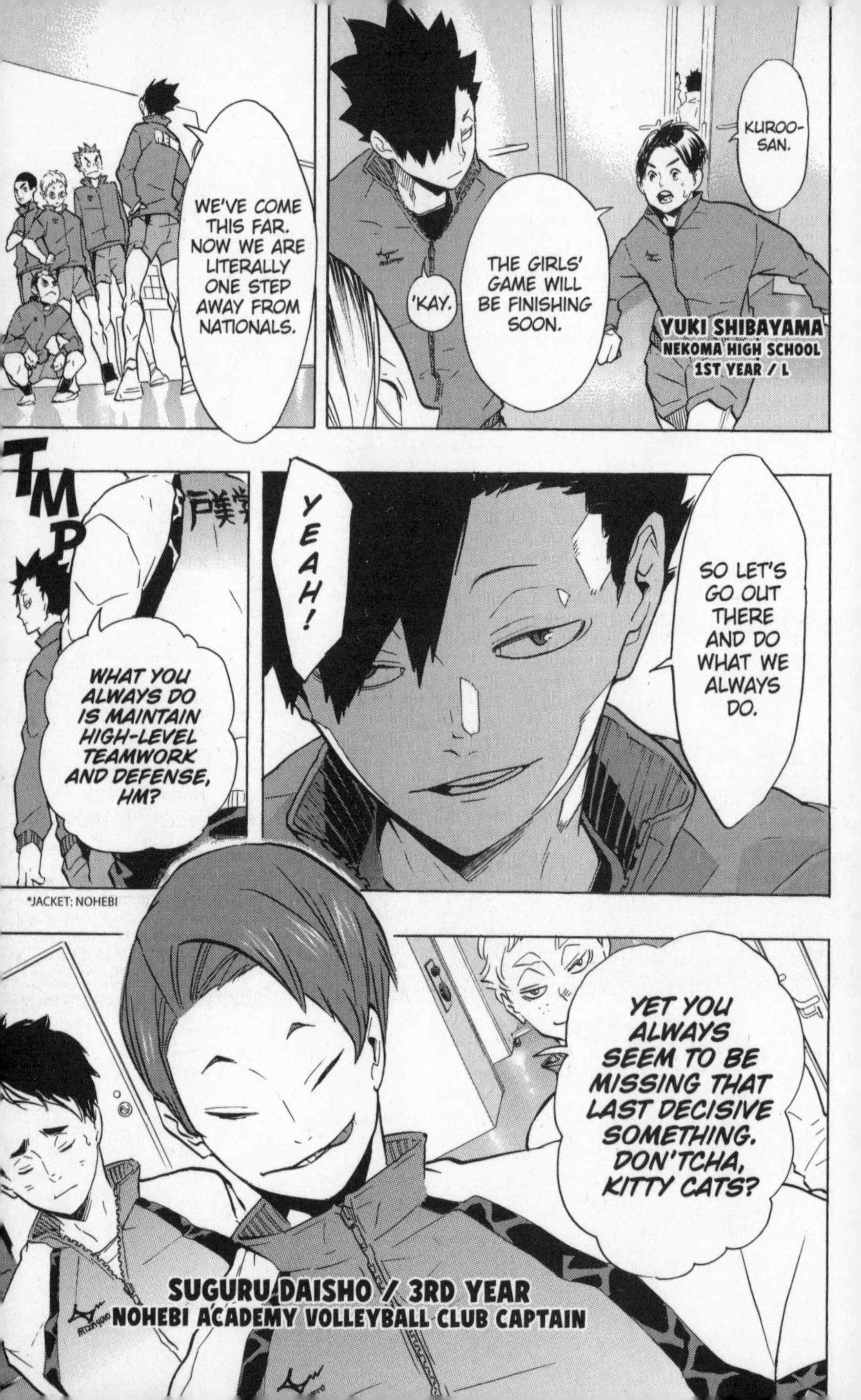
KUROO-SAN.
THE GIRLS' GAME WILL BE FINISHING SOON.
'KAY.
YUKI SHIBAYAMA
NEKOMA HIGH SCHOOL
1ST YEAR / L
WE'VE COME THIS FAR. NOW WE ARE LITERALLY ONE STEP AWAY FROM NATIONALS.
SO LET'S GO OUT THERE AND DO WHAT WE ALWAYS DO.
YEAH!
TMP
WHAT YOU ALWAYS DO IS MAINTAIN HIGH-LEVEL TEAMWORK AND DEFENSE, HM?
*JACKET: NOHEBI
YET YOU ALWAYS SEEM TO BE MISSING THAT LAST DECISIVE SOMETHING. DON'TCHA, KITTY CATS?
SUGURU DAISHO / 3RD YEAR
NOHEBI ACADEMY VOLLEYBALL CLUB CAPTAIN

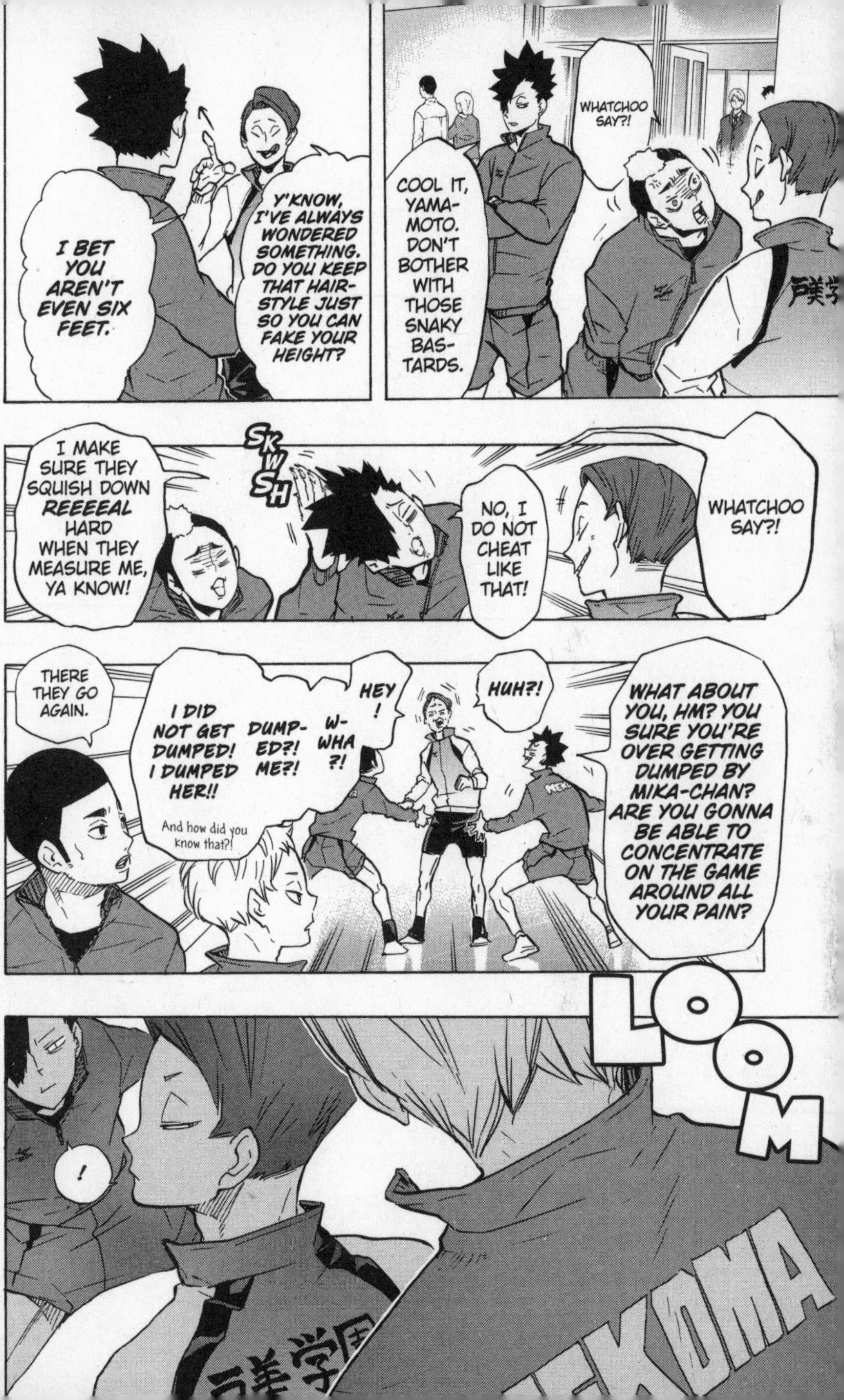
WHATCHOO SAY?!
COOL IT, YAMA-MOTO. DON'T BOTHER WITH THOSE SNAKY BAS-TARDS.
Y'KNOW, I'VE ALWAYS WONDERED SOMETHING. DO YOU KEEP THAT HAIR-STYLE JUST SO YOU CAN FAKE YOUR HEIGHT?
I BET YOU AREN'T EVEN SIX FEET.
WHATCHOO SAY?!
NO, I DO NOT CHEAT LIKE THAT!
SKWSH
I MAKE SURE THEY SQUISH DOWN REEEEAL HARD WHEN THEY MEASURE ME, YA KNOW!
WHAT ABOUT YOU, HM? YOU SURE YOU'RE OVER GETTING DUMPED BY MIKA-CHAN? ARE YOU GONNA BE ABLE TO CONCENTRATE ON THE GAME AROUND ALL YOUR PAIN?
HUH?!
HEY!
W-WHA?!
DUMP-ED?! ME?!
I DID NOT GET DUMPED! I DUMPED HER!!
And how did you know that?!
THERE THEY GO AGAIN.
LOOOM
!

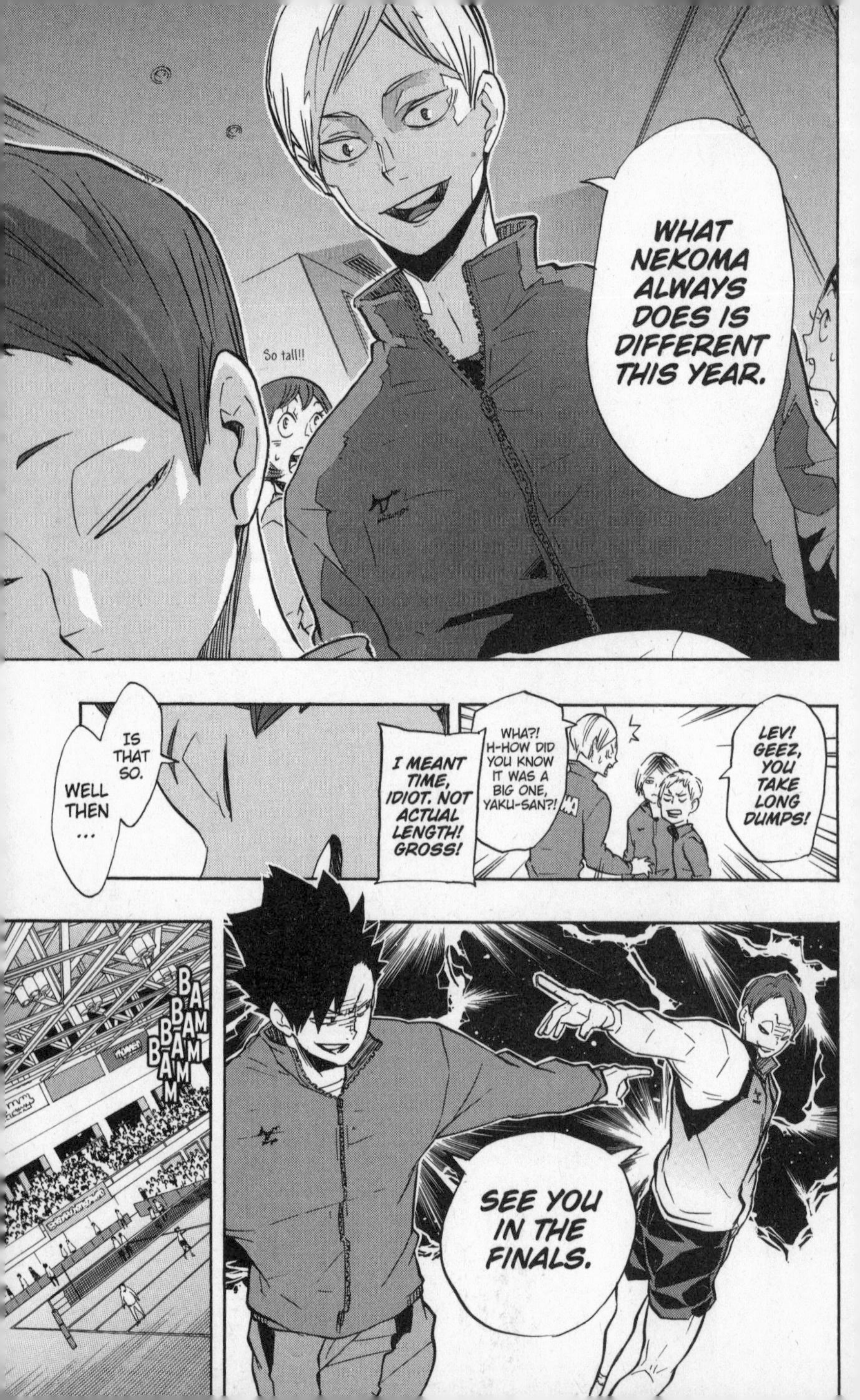
WHAT NEKOMA ALWAYS DOES IS DIFFERENT THIS YEAR.
So tall!!
LEV! GEEZ, YOU TAKE LONG DUMPS!
WHA?! H-HOW DID YOU KNOW IT WAS A BIG ONE, YAKU-SAN?!
I MEANT TIME, IDIOT. NOT ACTUAL LENGTH! GROSS!
IS THAT SO.
WELL THEN ...
SEE YOU IN THE FINALS.
BA BAM BAM BAM

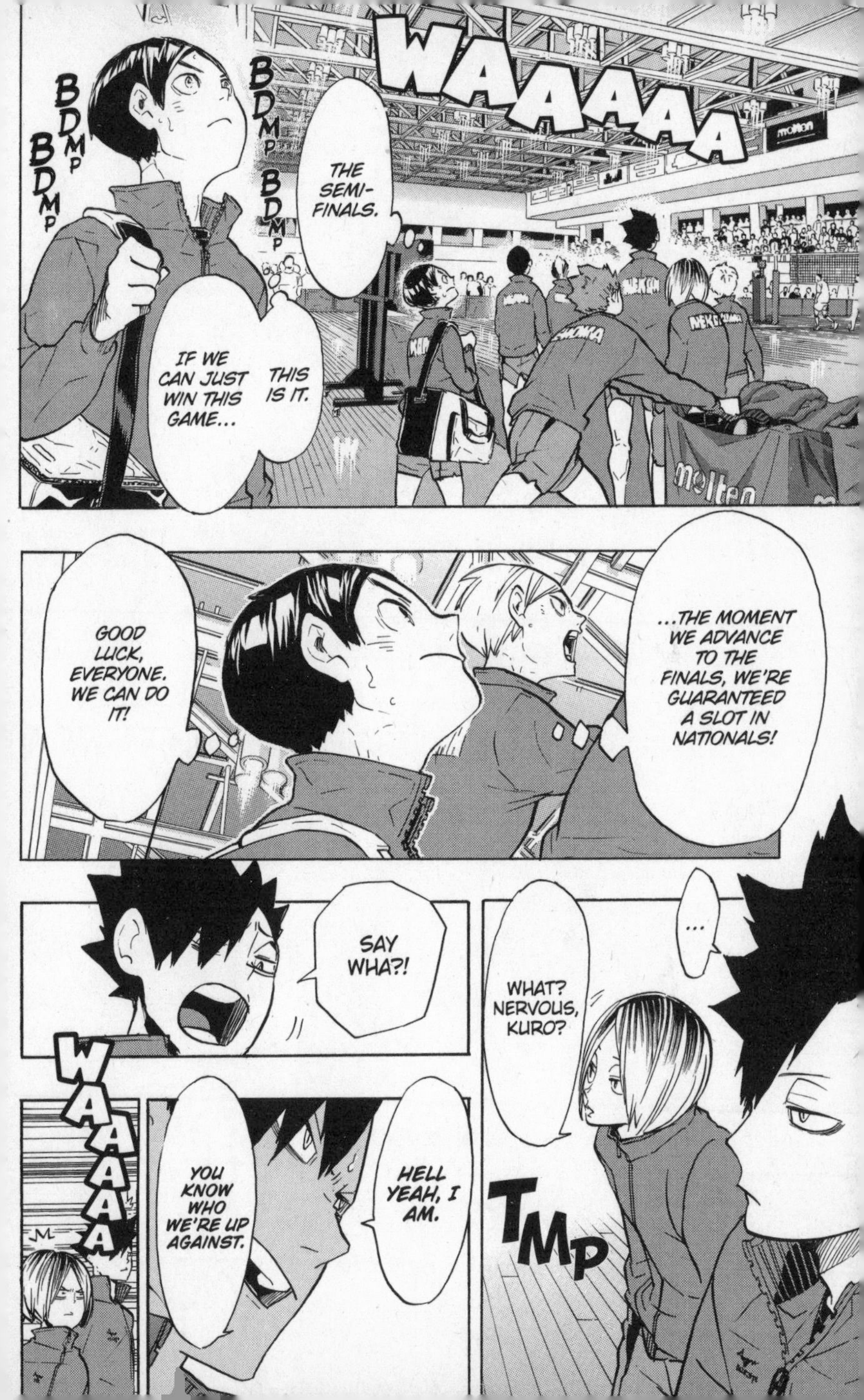
WAAAAAA
THE SEMI-FINALS.
BDMP BDMP
BDMP BDMP
THIS IS IT.
IF WE CAN JUST WIN THIS GAME...
...THE MOMENT WE ADVANCE TO THE FINALS, WE'RE GUARANTEED A SLOT IN NATIONALS!
GOOD LUCK, EVERYONE. WE CAN DO IT!
...
WHAT? NERVOUS, KURO?
TMP
SAY WHA?!
HELL YEAH, I AM.
YOU KNOW WHO WE'RE UP AGAINST.
WAAAAA

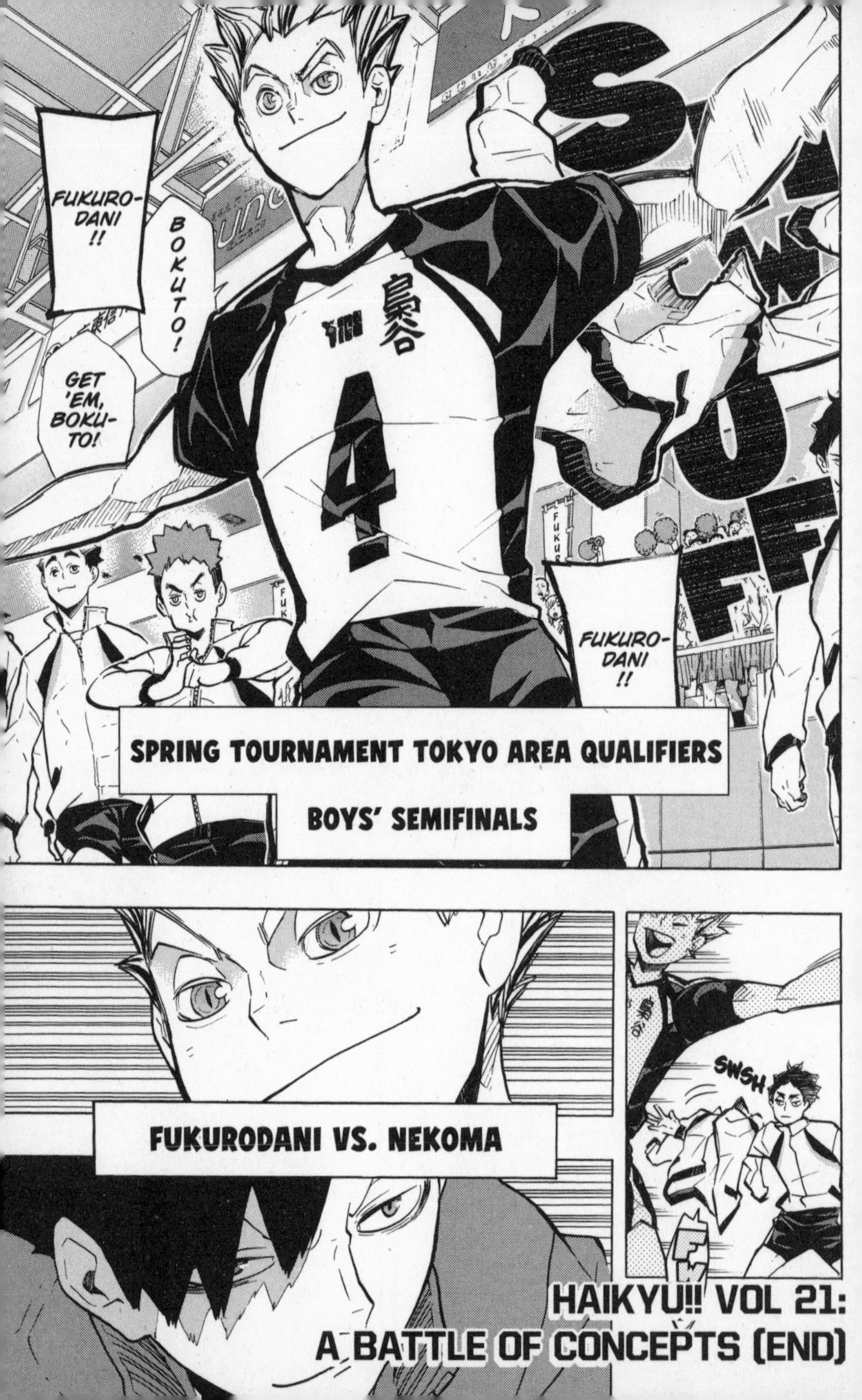
FUKURO-DANI !!
BOKUTO!
GET 'EM, BOKU-TO!
FUKURO-DANI !!
SPRING TOURNAMENT TOKYO AREA QUALIFIERS
BOYS' SEMIFINALS
SWSH
FUKURODANI VS. NEKOMA
HAIKYU!! VOL 21:
A BATTLE OF CONCEPTS (END)

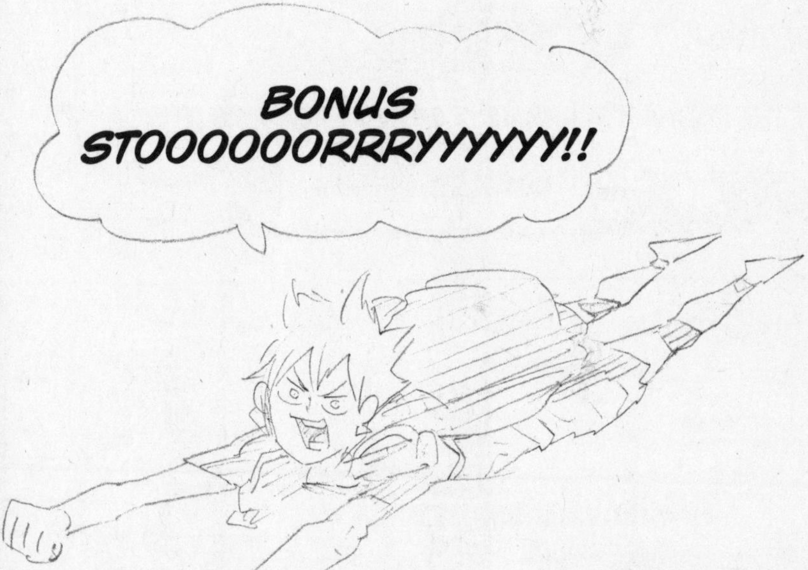
BONUS STOOOOOOORRRRYYYYYYY!!

— ON THE NEXT PAGE IS ANOTHER JOKE MOVIE POSTER THAT RAN IN *JUMP NEXT*!

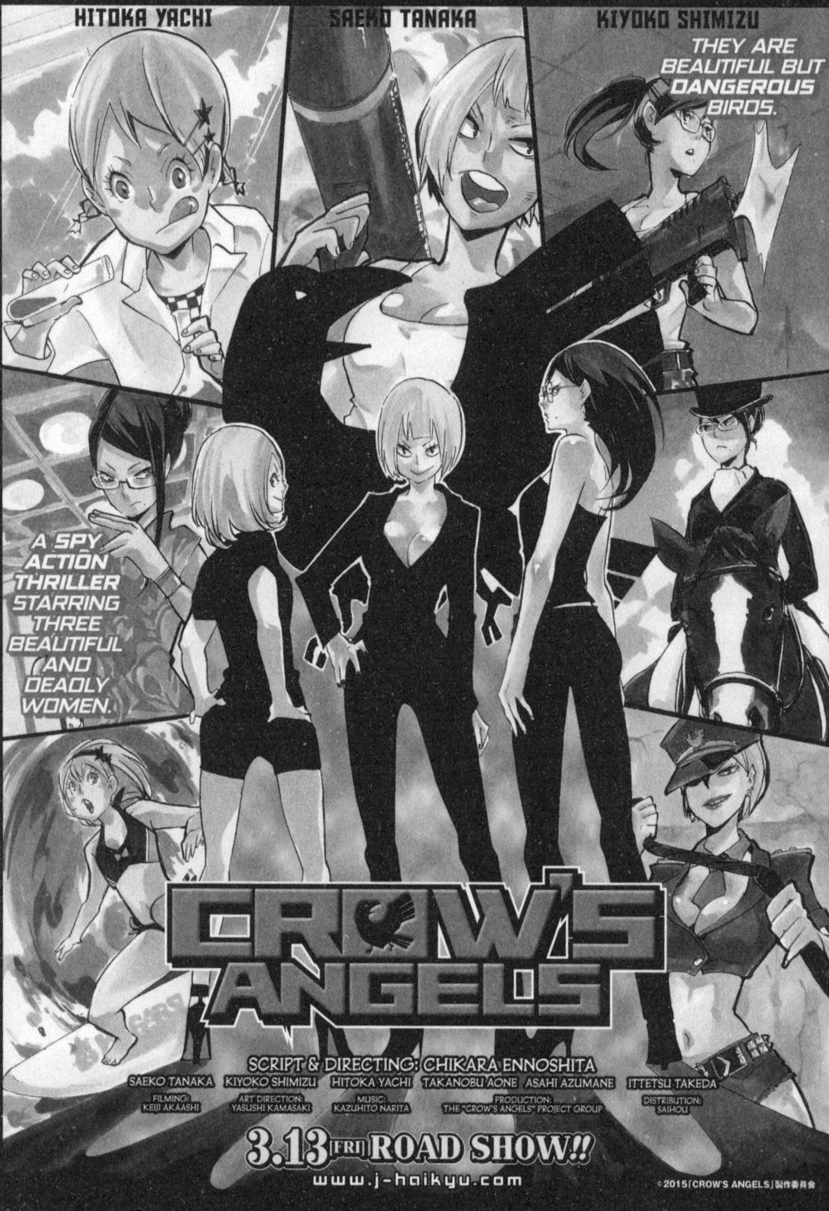
HITOKA YACHI
SAEKO TANAKA
KIYOKO SHIMIZU
THEY ARE BEAUTIFUL BUT DANGEROUS BIRDS.
A SPY ACTION THRILLER STARRING THREE BEAUTIFUL AND DEADLY WOMEN.
CROW'S ANGELS
SCRIPT & DIRECTING: CHIKARA ENNOSHITA
SAEKO TANAKA KIYOKO SHIMIZU HITOKA YACHI TAKANOBU AONE ASAHI AZUMANE ITTETSU TAKEDA
FILMING: KEIJI AKAASHI
ART DIRECTION: YASUSHI KAMASAKI
MUSIC: KAZUHITO NARITA
PRODUCTION: THE "CROW'S ANGELS" PROJECT GROUP
DISTRIBUTION: SAIHOU
3.13 [FRI] ROAD SHOW!!
www.j-haikyu.com
©2015「CROW'S ANGELS」製作委員会

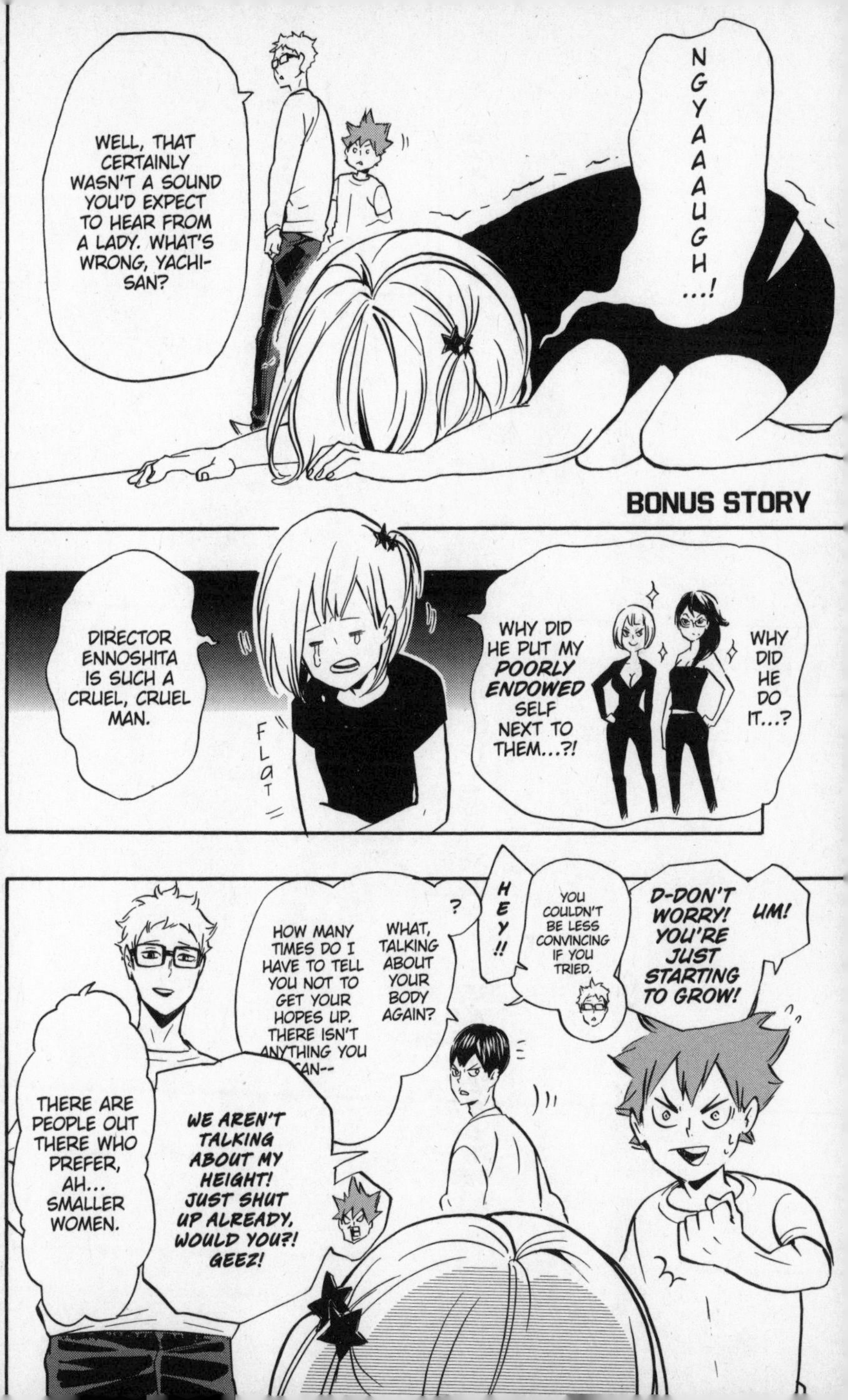

NGYAAAAUGH...!
WELL, THAT CERTAINLY WASN'T A SOUND YOU'D EXPECT TO HEAR FROM A LADY. WHAT'S WRONG, YACHI-SAN?
BONUS STORY
WHY DID HE PUT MY POORLY ENDOWED SELF NEXT TO THEM...?!
WHY DID HE DO IT...?
FLAT
DIRECTOR ENNOSHITA IS SUCH A CRUEL, CRUEL MAN.
UM!
D-DON'T WORRY! YOU'RE JUST STARTING TO GROW!
YOU COULDN'T BE LESS CONVINCING IF YOU TRIED.
HEY!!
?
WHAT, TALKING ABOUT YOUR BODY AGAIN?
HOW MANY TIMES DO I HAVE TO TELL YOU NOT TO GET YOUR HOPES UP. THERE ISN'T ANYTHING YOU CAN--
WE AREN'T TALKING ABOUT MY HEIGHT! JUST SHUT UP ALREADY, WOULD YOU?! GEEZ!
THERE ARE PEOPLE OUT THERE WHO PREFER, AH... SMALLER WOMEN.

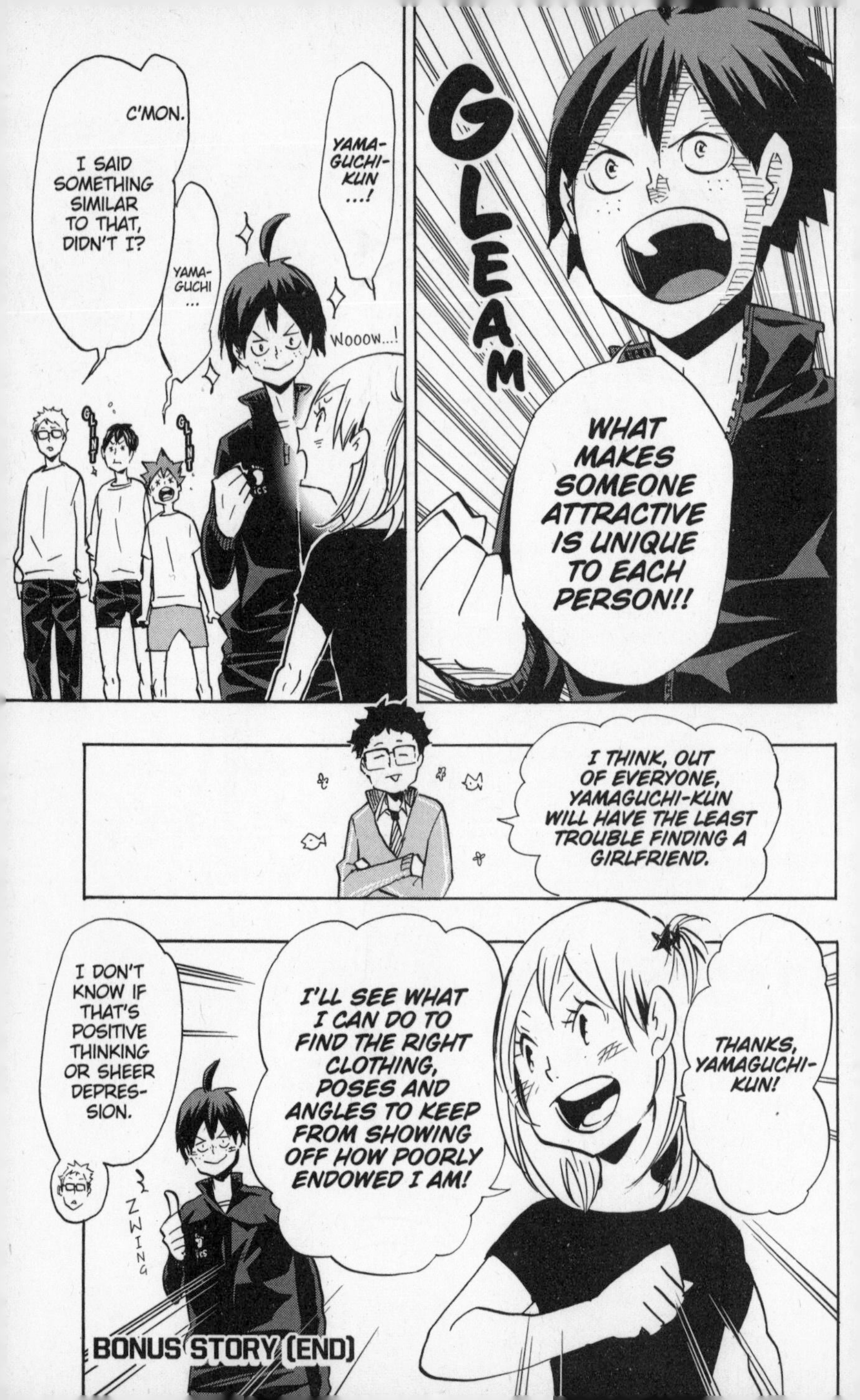
GLEAM
WHAT MAKES SOMEONE ATTRACTIVE IS UNIQUE TO EACH PERSON!!
YAMAGUCHI-KUN ...!
WOOOW...!
YAMAGUCHI ...
C'MON.
I SAID SOMETHING SIMILAR TO THAT, DIDN'T I?
GLINT
GLINT
I THINK, OUT OF EVERYONE, YAMAGUCHI-KUN WILL HAVE THE LEAST TROUBLE FINDING A GIRLFRIEND.
THANKS, YAMAGUCHI-KUN!
I'LL SEE WHAT I CAN DO TO FIND THE RIGHT CLOTHING, POSES AND ANGLES TO KEEP FROM SHOWING OFF HOW POORLY ENDOWED I AM!
I DON'T KNOW IF THAT'S POSITIVE THINKING OR SHEER DEPRES-SION.
ZWING
BONUS STORY (END)

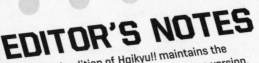

EDITOR'S NOTES

The English edition of Haikyu!! maintains the honorifics used in the original Japanese version. For those of you who are new to these terms, here's a brief explanation to help with your reading experience!

When saying someone's name in Japanese, a suffix is often attached to indicate how familiar the speaker is with the person. Some are more polite and respectful, while others are endearing.

1 **-kun** is often used for young men or boys, usually someone you are familiar with.

2 **-chan** is used for young children and can be used as a term of endearment.

3 **-san** is used for someone you respect or are not close to, or to be polite.

4 **Senpai** is used for someone who is older than you or in a higher position or grade in school.

5 **Kohai** is used for someone who is younger than you or in a lower position or grade in school.

6 **Sensei** means teacher.

Kuroko's BASKETBALL

TADATOSHI FUJIMAKI

When incoming first-year student Taiga Kagami joins the Seirin High basketball team, he meets Tetsuya Kuroko, a mysterious boy who's plain beyond words. But Kagami's in for the shock of his life when he learns that the practically invisible Kuroko was once a member of "the Miracle Generation"—the undefeated legendary team—and he wants Kagami's help taking down each of his old teammates!

THE HIT SPORTS MANGA

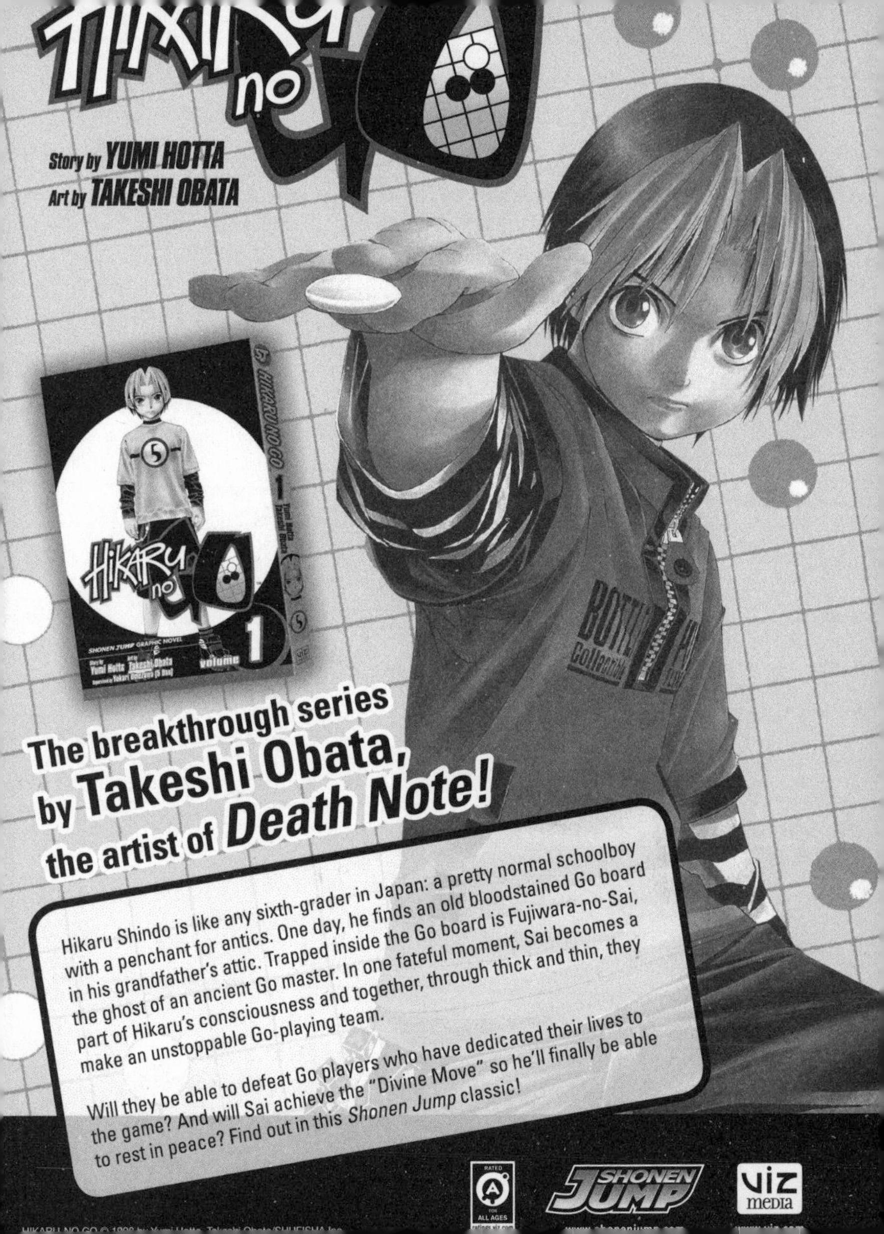

Hikaru no Go
Story by YUMI HOTTA
Art by TAKESHI OBATA
HIKARU NO GO
1
SHONEN JUMP GRAPHIC NOVEL
volume
The breakthrough series by Takeshi Obata, the artist of Death Note!
Hikaru Shindo is like any sixth-grader in Japan: a pretty normal schoolboy with a penchant for antics. One day, he finds an old bloodstained Go board in his grandfather's attic. Trapped inside the Go board is Fujiwara-no-Sai, the ghost of an ancient Go master. In one fateful moment, Sai becomes a part of Hikaru's consciousness and together, through thick and thin, they make an unstoppable Go-playing team.
Will they be able to defeat Go players who have dedicated their lives to the game? And will Sai achieve the "Divine Move" so he'll finally be able to rest in peace? Find out in this Shonen Jump classic!
RATED A FOR ALL AGES
SHONEN JUMP
VIZ media

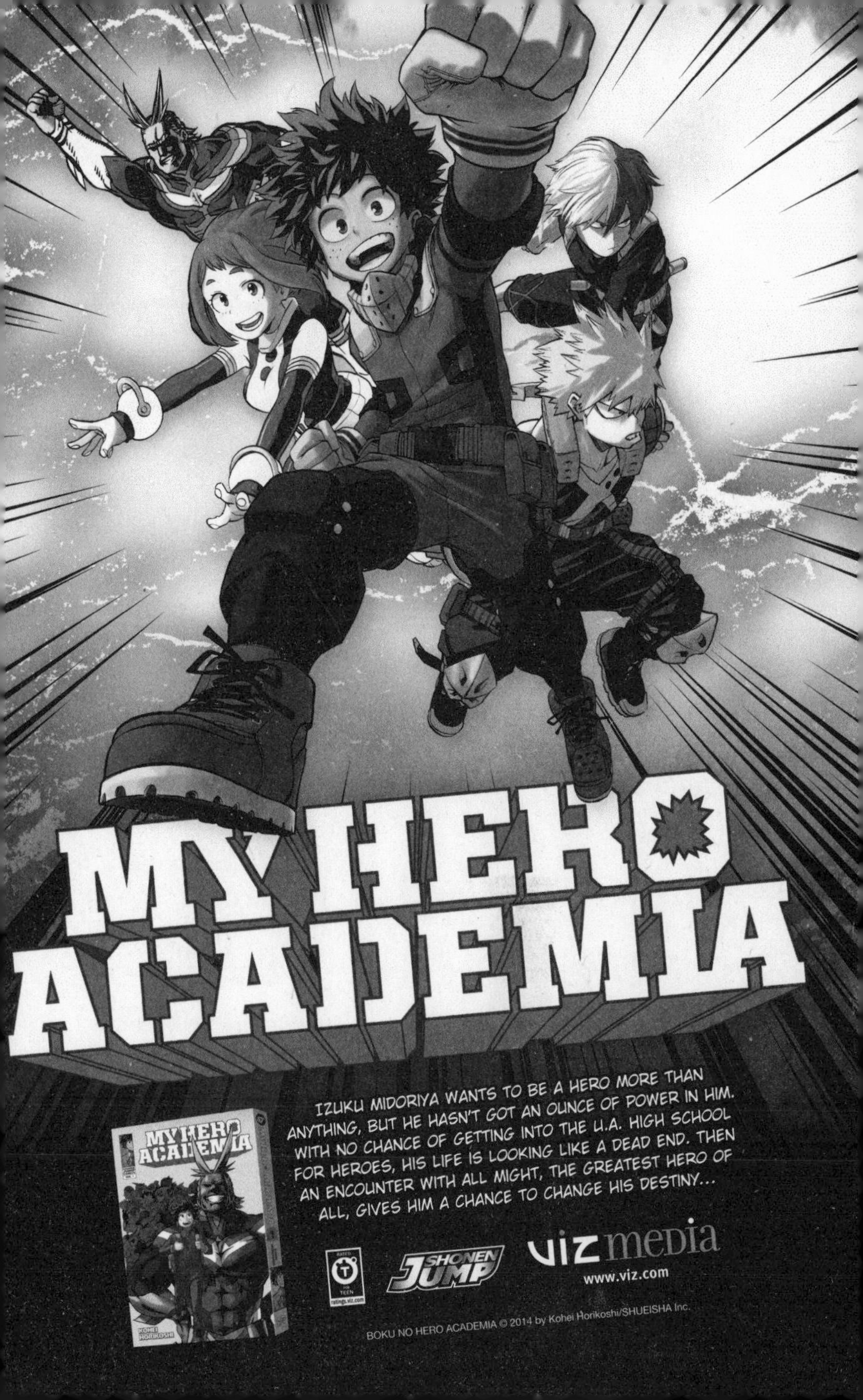
MY HERO ACADEMIA
IZUKU MIDORIYA WANTS TO BE A HERO MORE THAN ANYTHING, BUT HE HASN'T GOT AN OUNCE OF POWER IN HIM. WITH NO CHANCE OF GETTING INTO THE U.A. HIGH SCHOOL FOR HEROES, HIS LIFE IS LOOKING LIKE A DEAD END. THEN AN ENCOUNTER WITH ALL MIGHT, THE GREATEST HERO OF ALL, GIVES HIM A CHANCE TO CHANGE HIS DESTINY...
MY HERO ACADEMIA
KOHEI HORIKOSHI
RATED T TEEN
ratings.viz.com
SHONEN JUMP
viz media
www.viz.com
BOKU NO HERO ACADEMIA © 2014 by Kohei Horikoshi/SHUEISHA Inc.

A PREMIUM BOX SET OF THE FIRST TWO STORY ARCS OF ONE PIECE!

A PIRATE'S TREASURE FOR ANY MANGA FAN!

STORY AND ART BY EIICHIRO ODA

Comes with EXCLUSIVE POSTER and the ROMANCE DAWN mini-comic!

As a child, Monkey D. Luffy dreamed of becoming King of the Pirates. But his life changed when he accidentally gained the power to stretch like rubber...at the cost of never being able to swim again! Years later, Luffy sets off in search of the "One Piece," said to be the greatest treasure in the world...

This box set includes VOLUMES 1-23, which comprise the EAST BLUE and BAROQUE WORKS story arcs.

EXCLUSIVE PREMIUMS and GREAT SAVINGS over buying the individual volumes!

ONE PIECE © 1997 by Eiichiro Oda/SHUEISHA Inc.

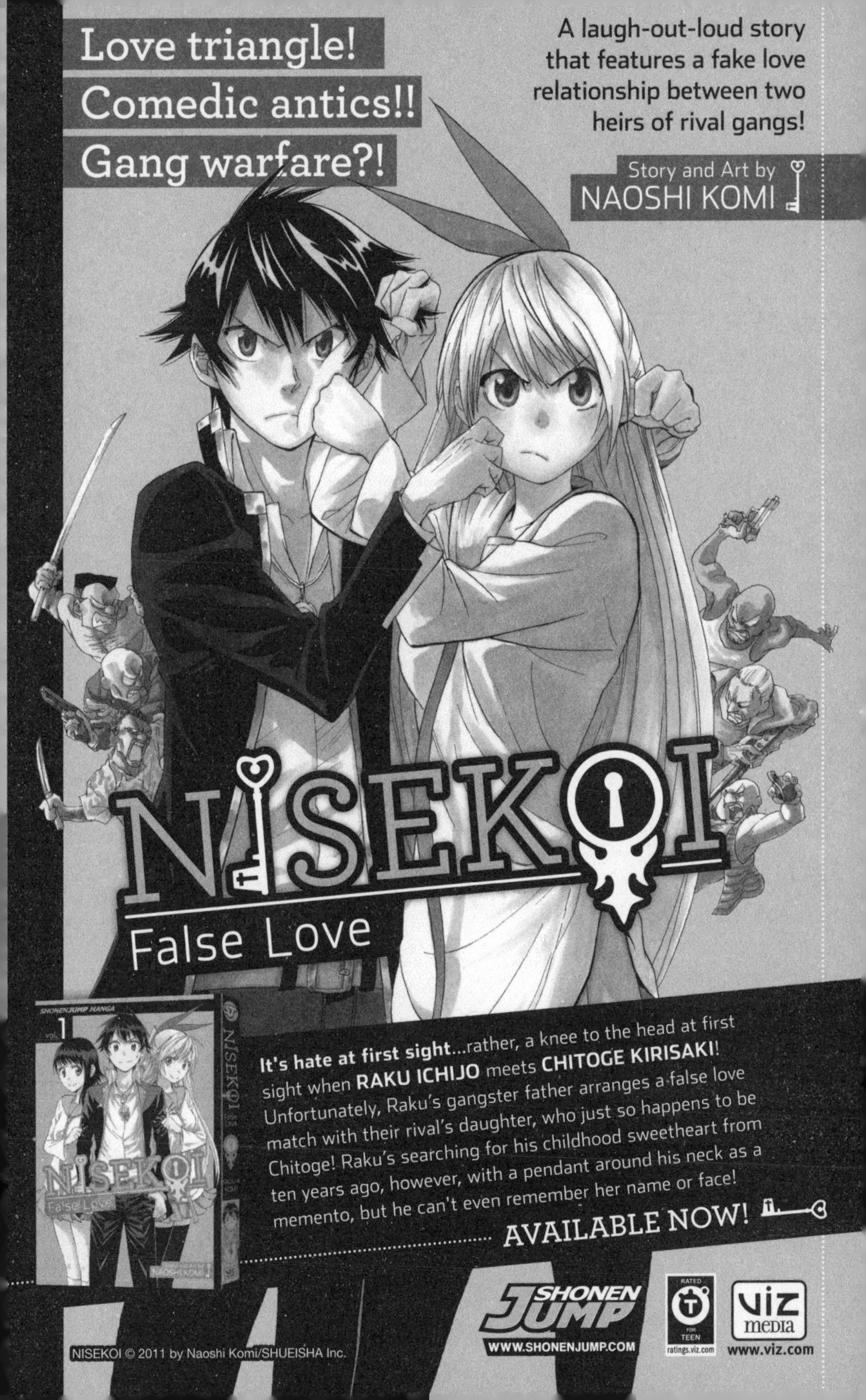
Love triangle!
Comedic antics!!
Gang warfare?!
A laugh-out-loud story that features a fake love relationship between two heirs of rival gangs!
Story and Art by
NAOSHI KOMI
NISEKOI
False Love
SHONENJUMP MANGA
vol. 1
NISEKOI
False Love
NAOSHI KOMI
It's hate at first sight...rather, a knee to the head at first sight when RAKU ICHIJO meets CHITOGE KIRISAKI! Unfortunately, Raku's gangster father arranges a false love match with their rival's daughter, who just so happens to be Chitoge! Raku's searching for his childhood sweetheart from ten years ago, however, with a pendant around his neck as a memento, but he can't even remember her name or face!
AVAILABLE NOW!
SHONEN JUMP
WWW.SHONENJUMP.COM
RATED T FOR TEEN
ratings.viz.com
viz media
www.viz.com
NISEKOI © 2011 by Naoshi Komi/SHUEISHA Inc.

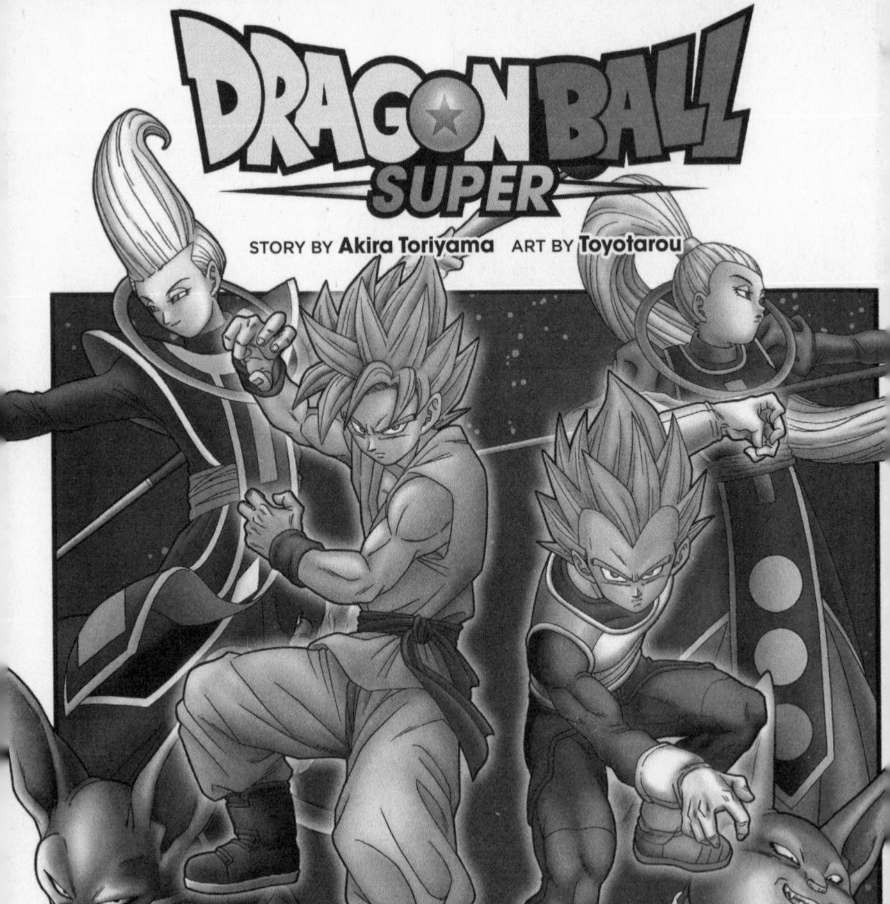
DRAGON BALL SUPER
STORY BY Akira Toriyama ART BY Toyotarou

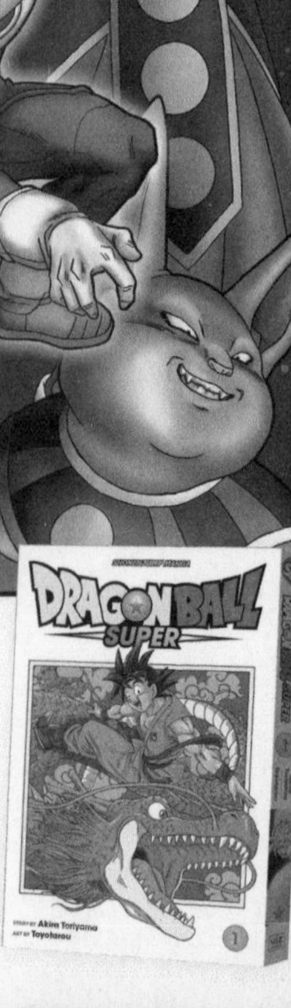
DRAGON BALL SUPER

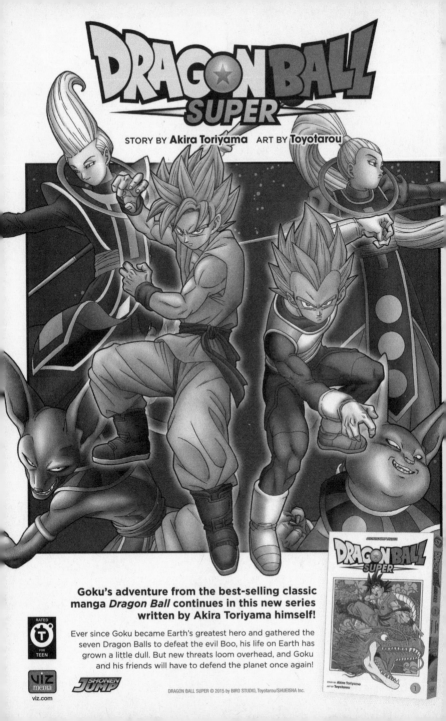

You're Reading the WRONG WAY!

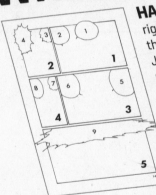

HAIKYU!! reads from right to left, starting in the upper-right corner. Japanese is read from right to left, meaning that action, sound effects and word-balloon order are completely reversed from English order.